Śrīla Prabhupāda-līlāmṛta, Volume 2

PLANTING THE SEED

"Lord Caitanya says that the living entities, bound up by fruitive activities, are wandering throughout the whole universe, and if by some chance or pious activities they get in touch with a bona fide spiritual master, by the grace of Kṛṣṇa, then they get the seed of devotional service. After getting this seed, if one sows it within his heart and pours water on it by hearing and chanting, the seed grows into a big plant, and there are fruits and flowers which the living entity can enjoy, even in this material world."

—*from the Bhaktivedanta purports to Śrīmad-Bhāgavatam*

Śrīla Prabhupāda-līlāmṛta, Volume 2

PLANTING THE SEED

New York City
1965–1966

A Biography by

Satsvarūpa dāsa Goswami

THE BHAKTIVEDANTA BOOK TRUST
Los Angeles • New York • London • Paris • Frankfurt • Bombay

Readers interested in the subject matter of this book are invited by the Bhaktivedanta Book Trust to correspond with its Secretary.

Bhaktivedanta Book Trust
3764 Watseka Avenue
Los Angeles, California 90034

First Printing, 1980: 50,000 copies

Printed in the United States of America

Library of Congress Cataloging in Publication Data

Gosvāmī, Satsvarūpa Dāsa, 1939–
Srila Prabhupada-lilamrta.

"Books by . . . A. C. Bhaktivedanta Swami Prabhupada"
v. 2, p.
Includes index.
CONTENTS —v. 2. New York City, 1965–1966: planting the seed.
1. Bhaktivedanta Swami, A. C., 1896–1977. 2. Gurus —Biography. 3. International Society for Krishna Consciousness—Biography. I. Title.
BL1175.B445G67 294.5'61'0924 [B] 80-5071
ISBN 0-89213-106-3 (v. 2)

Contents

Foreword	*vii*
Preface	*ix*
Introduction	*xiii*
1. The Journey to America	1
2. Butler, Pennsylvania: The First Testing Ground	9
3. Struggling Alone	21
4. "It Will Not Be Possible to Assist You"	37
5. Free to Preach	51
6. On the Bowery	67
7. Breaking Ground	105
8. Planting the Seed	145
9. "Stay High Forever"	191
10. Beyond the Lower East Side	237
Appendixes	
"Prayer to the Lotus Feet of Kṛṣṇa"	277
"Mārkine Bhāgavata-dharma"	281
Books by His Divine Grace A. C. Bhaktivedanta Swami Prabhupāda	285
ISKCON Centers	286
Acknowledgments	289
Sanskrit Pronunciation Guide	290
Glossary	291
Index	295
The Author	331

Foreword

The story you are about to read is, like many true stories, highly improbable. An elderly Indian swami comes to New York City in the mid-1960s on a vaguely defined mission. Charged by his teacher in India to bring his spiritual message to the West, he arrives in New York with no prior knowledge of America, no base of support, almost no money, and no clear plan of action. He moves about the city somewhat aimlessly, lives for a while in an artist's loft on the Bowery, and finally—with help from a few early followers—rents a storefront building in the area known as East Village, the heart of the 1960s' drug and counterculture movement. There he begins to preach an unlikely message of sexual restraint, abstention from drugs, and purity of mind and body—and in behalf of devotion to the Hindu God Kṛṣṇa.

What follows is a remarkable tale of faith, determination, and success beyond anyone's expectation. The present volume gives only the beginnings of the story, but it tells us in fascinating detail how the first seeds of success were planted in what seemed such unpromising ground. It is a very human story, with a very human A. C. Bhaktivedanta Swami at the center.

Religions are a composite of many factors, some of which are largely collective products such as social movements, institutions, and systems of belief and practice. The history of religions is often put in terms of these relatively objective factors, so that religious history becomes part of the more general history of various times and places. The story of Bhaktivedanta Swami reminds us forcefully that there are other factors, more personal and elusive, which also shape the history of world religion. Social and cultural factors make a difference, but so also do individuals: holy men, saints, religious leaders, and their often flawed but faithful followers. The value of this book is the way in which it brings together these two dimensions—social history and individuals—to describe the founding of a major religious movement.

The temporal setting of the story is important. The 1960s was a unique period in American history, a time when major changes were taking place in our society. The place is important also, since New York City in general and East Village in particular were on the leading edge of these changes. The author of this biography was very much a part of this time and place as one of Bhaktivedanta Swami's earliest disciples in New York. From his own recollections, from recordings and writings of the time, and from extensive interviews with other participants, he has put together a series of striking vignettes of the 1960s that have independent historical value. Threading through these scenes, however, and binding the individuals together in collective effort, is the dominant figure of A. C. Bhaktivedanta Swami. Bhaktivedanta Swami seems curiously out of place in this setting. Born in the late nineteenth century, he had spent his whole career in India and for many years had lived the life of a celibate Hindu monk. What relevance could he have in the center of American youth culture, where "do your own thing" was the die for action, and "don't trust anyone over thirty" was the watchword against authority? The answer to this can best be conveyed in the book which follows. Since spiritual power can never be precisely pinned down, this book will not give a complete answer—nor will all of the massive evidence on which it is based. It is to Bhaktivedanta's credit that he believed in keeping nothing secret, and it is to Satsvarūpa's credit that he has presented the events of this critical period as objectively as possible. Seldom before have we had such an intimate and detailed account of a spiritual master bringing forth a new religious movement, and probably never has there been such a wealth of contemporary data to back it up. Those of us who are historians of religion will be working this rich vein for years to come.

Some who read this book will simply enjoy an absorbing story. Others, perhaps more appropriately, will respond in faith or greater commitment to their own religious quest. Whatever your response, this first published volume of a great religious biography will be a rare treat.

Dr. Thomas J. Hopkins
Chairman
Department of Religious Studies
Franklin and Marshall College
Lancaster, Pennsylvania

Preface

After the disappearance of His Divine Grace A. C. Bhaktivedanta Swami Prabhupāda from this mortal world on November 14, 1977, many of his disciples saw a need for an authorized biography of Śrīla Prabhupāda. The responsibility of commissioning such a work rested with the Governing Body Commission of the International Society for Krishna Consciousness. At their annual meeting in 1978, the GBC resolved that a biography of Śrīla Prabhupāda should be written and that I would be the author.

According to the Vaiṣṇava tradition, if one aspires to write transcendental literature, he must first take permission from his spiritual master and Kṛṣṇa. A good example of this is Kṛṣṇadāsa Kavirāja Gosvāmī, the author of Lord Caitanya Mahāprabhu's authorized biography, *Śrī Caitanya-caritāmṛta.* As Kṛṣṇadāsa Kavirāja has explained:

> In Vṛndāvana there were also many other great devotees, all of whom desired to hear the last pastimes of Lord Caitanya.
>
> By their mercy, all these devotees ordered me to write of the last pastimes of Śrī Caitanya Mahāprabhu. Because of their order only, although I am shameless, I have attempted to write this *Caitanya-caritāmṛta.*
>
> Having received the order of the Vaiṣṇavas, but being anxious within my heart, I went back to the temple of Madana-mohana in Vṛndāvana to ask His permission also.

This transcendental process is further described by His Divine Grace Śrīla Prabhupāda in his commentary on the *Caitanya-caritāmṛta* as follows:

> To write about the transcendental pastimes of the Supreme Personality of Godhead is not an ordinary endeavor. Unless one is empowered by the higher authorities or advanced devotees, one cannot write transcendental

> literature, for all such literature must be above suspicion, or in other words, it must have none of the defects of conditioned souls, namely mistakes, illusions, cheating, and imperfect sense perception. The words of Kṛṣṇa and the disciplic succession that carries the orders of Kṛṣṇa are actually authoritative. . . . One must first become a pure devotee following the strict regulative principles and chanting sixteen rounds daily, and when one thinks he is actually on the Vaiṣṇava platform, he must then take permission from the spiritual master, and that permission must also be confirmed by Kṛṣṇa from within his heart.

So to say the *Śrīla Prabhupāda-līlāmṛta* is an authorized biography does not mean that it is a flattering portrait commissioned by an official body, but that it is an authorized literature presented by one who is serving the order of Kṛṣṇa and *guru* through the disciplic succession. As such, *Śrīla Prabhupāda-līlāmṛta* is not written from the mundane or speculative viewpoint, nor can ordinary biographers comprehend the significance and meaning of the life of a pure devotee of God. Were such persons to objectively study the life of Śrīla Prabhupāda, the esoteric meanings would evade them. Were they to charitably try to praise Śrīla Prabhupāda, they would not know how. But because *Śrīla Prabhupāda-līlāmṛta* is authorized through the transcendental process, it can transparently present the careful reader with a true picture of Śrīla Prabhupāda.

Another important aspect of the authenticity of *Śrīla Prabhupāda-līlāmṛta* is the vast amount of carefully researched information that I am able to focus into each volume. The leading devotees of the Kṛṣṇa consciousness movement, in addition to giving me permission to render this work, have also invited the world community of ISKCON devotees to help me in gathering detailed information about the life and person of Śrīla Prabhupāda. The Bhaktivedanta Book Trust, Prabhupāda's publishing house, has given me his collection of letters, totaling over seven thousand; and scores of Prabhupāda's disciples have granted interviews and submitted diaries and memoirs of their association with Śrīla Prabhupāda. Aside from his disciples, we have interviewed many persons in various walks of life who met Śrīla Prabhupāda over the years. The result is that we have a rich, composite view of Śrīla Prabhupāda, drawn from many persons who knew him in many different situations and stages of his life. An Acknowledgments section in the back of this book lists the persons who are cooperating to bring about *Śrīla Prabhupāda-līlāmṛta.*

Despite the authorized nature of this book and despite the support of my many well-wishers, I must confess that in attempting to describe the glories of our spiritual master, His Divine Grace A. C. Bhaktivedanta Swami Prabhupāda, I am like a small bird trying to empty the ocean by carrying drops of water to the land. The picture I have given of Śrīla Prabhupāda is only a glimpse into his unlimited mercy, and that glimpse has only been possible by the grace of *guru* and Kṛṣṇa.

Satsvarūpa dāsa Goswami
Gīta-nāgarī Farm Community
Port Royal, Pennsylvania
October, 1979

Introduction

As the present volume begins, A. C. Bhaktivedanta Swami, age sixty-nine, is traveling aboard a steamship from Calcutta to New York City. He carries with him the Indian equivalent of eight dollars. He has no institutional backing, and no support awaits him. He is coming, on the order of his spiritual master, to teach Kṛṣṇa consciousness to the English-speaking world. *Planting the Seed* is the story of Śrīla Prabhupāda's first year in America; it is the story of how an individual will, patiently persisting, overcame great obstacles; and it is the story of a time, the 1960s, when American youth underwent a revolution in consciousness. *Planting the Seed* tells how Śrīla Prabhupāda carried the all-but-forgotten spiritual culture of Vedic India to New York's Lower East Side and planted it there in the heart of America's cultural turmoil of 1966.

The story of the sixty-nine years of Śrīla Prabhupāda's life before he boarded the steamship for America is presented in the first volume of this series, *A Lifetime in Preparation.* The present volume, however, is complete in itself, and the reader meets His Divine Grace A. C. Bhaktivedanta Swami Prabhupāda exactly as did the first persons he confronted in America—where suddenly he appeared as an elderly, golden-skinned Bengali *sādhu,* very grave and philosophically inward, yet humorous and talkative, a stranger, wearing saffron robes and white, pointy shoes and carrying an umbrella. He was known simply as "the Swami," and he lived a spiritually dedicated life previously unheard of in the West—translating the Vedic scriptures in his room, chanting Kṛṣṇa's name, teaching the *Bhagavad-gītā.* When he walked in Manhattan, people would sometimes come up to him on the street and ask who he was and what he was doing; and he would tell them, from the Vedic scriptures, about Kṛṣṇa consciousness. At first he lived in a tiny rented room, later in a Bowery loft, and finally in a Second Avenue storefront on the Lower East Side, where he drew an affectionate following from the local youth.

Śrīla Prabhupāda did not regard his personal history as an important subject for study; his interest was to publish many volumes about Kṛṣṇa, the Supreme Personality of Godhead. But according to the spiritual science, a pure devotee of God is as important as God Himself, because he delivers the message of Godhead to a forgetful humanity. Śrīla Prabhupāda's life, therefore, is an important and absorbing subject, and it is a tangible proof of the existence of spiritual reality and love of God.

SDG

CHAPTER ONE

The Journey to America

Today the ship is plying very smoothly. I feel today better. But I am feeling separation from Sri Vrindaban and my Lords Sri Govinda, Gopinath, Radha Damodar. My only solace is Sri Chaitanya Charitamrita in which I am tasting the nectarine of Lord Chaitanya's lila. I have left Bharatabhumi just to execute the order of Sri Bhaktisiddhanta Saraswati, in pursuance of Lord Chaitanya's order. I have no qualification, but have taken up the risk just to carry out the order of His Divine Grace. I depend fully on Their mercy, so far away from Vrindaban.

—*Jaladuta* diary
September 10, 1965

The *Jaladuta* is a regular cargo carrier of the Scindia Steam Navigation Company, but there is a passenger cabin aboard. During the voyage from Calcutta to New York in August and September of 1965, the cabin was occupied by "Sri Abhoy Charanaravinda Bhaktivedanta Swami," whose age was listed as sixty-nine and who was taken on board bearing "a complimentary ticket with food."

The *Jaladuta*, under the command of Captain Arun Pandia, whose wife was also aboard, left at 9:00 A.M. on Friday, August 13. In his diary, Śrīla Prabhupāda noted: "The cabin is quite comfortable, thanks to Lord Sri Krishna for enlightening Sumati Morarji for all these arrangements. I am quite comfortable." But on the fourteenth he reported: "Seasickness, dizziness, vomiting—Bay of Bengal. Heavy rains. More sickness."

On the nineteenth, when the ship arrived at Colombo, Ceylon (now Sri Lanka), Prabhupāda was able to get relief from his seasickness. The captain took him ashore, and he traveled around Colombo by car. Then the ship went on toward Cochin, on the west coast of India. Janmāṣṭamī, the appearance day of Lord Kṛṣṇa, fell on the twentieth of August that year. Prabhupāda took the opportunity to speak to the crew about the philosophy of Lord Kṛṣṇa, and he distributed *prasādam* he had cooked himself. August 21 was his seventieth birthday, observed (without ceremony) at sea. That same day the ship arrived at Cochin, and Śrīla Prabhupāda's trunks of *Śrīmad-Bhāgavatam* volumes, which had been shipped from Bombay, were loaded on board.

By the twenty-third the ship had put out to the Red Sea, where Śrīla Prabhupāda encountered great difficulty. He noted in his diary: "Rain, seasickness, dizziness, headache, no appetite, vomiting." The symptoms persisted, but it was more than seasickness. The pains in his chest made him think he would die at any moment. In two days he suffered two heart attacks. He tolerated the difficulty, meditating on the purpose of his mission, but after two days of such violent attacks he thought that if another were to come he would certainly not survive.

On the night of the second day, Prabhupāda had a dream. Lord Kṛṣṇa, in His many forms, was rowing a boat, and He told Prabhupāda that he should not fear, but should come along. Prabhupāda felt assured of Lord Kṛṣṇa's protection, and the violent attacks did not recur.

The *Jaladuta* entered the Suez Canal on September 1 and stopped in Port Said on the second. Śrīla Prabhupāda visited the city with the captain and said that he liked it. By the sixth he had recovered a little from his illness and was eating regularly again for the first time in two weeks, having cooked his own *kicharī* and *purīs*. He reported in his diary that his strength renewed little by little.

> Thursday, September 9
> To 4:00 this afternoon, we have crossed over the Atlantic Ocean for twenty-four hours. The whole day was clear and almost smooth. I am taking my food regularly and have got some strength to struggle. There is also a slight tacking of the ship and I am feeling a slight headache also. But I am struggling and the nectarine of life is Sri Chaitanya Charitamrita, the source of all my vitality.

Friday, September 10
Today the ship is plying very smoothly. I feel today better. But I am feeling separation from Sri Vrindaban and my Lords Sri Govinda, Gopinath, Radha Damodar. The only solace is Sri Chaitanya Charitamrita in which I am tasting the nectarine of Lord Chaitanya's lila [pastimes]. I have left Bharatabhumi just to execute the order of Sri Bhaktisiddhanta Saraswati in pursuance of Lord Chaitanya's order. I have no qualification, but have taken up the risk just to carry out the order of His Divine Grace. I depend fully on Their mercy, so far away from Vrindaban.

During the voyage, Śrīla Prabhupāda sometimes stood on deck at the ship's rail, watching the ocean and the sky and thinking of *Caitanya-caritāmṛta*, Vṛndāvana-dhāma, and the order of his spiritual master to go preach in the West. Mrs. Pandia, the captain's wife, whom Śrīla Prabhupāda considered to be "an intelligent and learned lady," foretold Śrīla Prabhupāda's future. If he were to pass beyond this crisis in his health, she said, it would indicate the good will of Lord Kṛṣṇa.

The ocean voyage of 1965 was a calm one for the *Jaladuta*. The captain said that never in his entire career had he seen such a calm Atlantic crossing. Prabhupāda replied that the calmness was Lord Kṛṣṇa's mercy, and Mrs. Pandia asked Prabhupāda to come back with them so that they might have another such crossing. Śrīla Prabhupāda wrote in his diary, "If the Atlantic would have shown its usual face, perhaps I would have died. But Lord Krishna has taken charge of the ship."

On September 13, Prabhupāda noted in his diary: "Thirty-second day of journey. Cooked bati kichari. It appeared to be delicious, so I was able to take some food. Today I have disclosed my mind to my companion, Lord Sri Krishna. There is a Bengali poem made by me in this connection."

This poem was a prayer to Lord Kṛṣṇa, and it is filled with Prabhupāda's devotional confidence in the mission that he had undertaken on behalf of his spiritual master. An English translation of the opening stanzas follows:*

I emphatically say to you, O brothers, you will obtain your good fortune from the Supreme Lord Kṛṣṇa only when Śrīmatī Rādhārāṇī becomes pleased with you.

---

*See Appendix for the complete Bengali verses with English translation.

> Śrī Śrīmad Bhaktisiddhānta Sarasvatī Ṭhākura, who is very dear to Lord Gaurāṅga [Lord Caitanya], the son of mother Śacī, is unparalleled in his service to the Supreme Lord Śrī Kṛṣṇa. He is that great, saintly spiritual master who bestows intense devotion to Kṛṣṇa at different places throughout the world.
>
> By his strong desire, the holy name of Lord Gaurāṅga will spread throughout all the countries of the Western world. In all the cities, towns, and villages on the earth, from all the oceans, seas, rivers, and streams, everyone will chant the holy name of Kṛṣṇa.
>
> As the vast mercy of Śrī Caitanya Mahāprabhu conquers all directions, a flood of transcendental ecstasy will certainly cover the land. When all the sinful, miserable living entities become happy, the Vaiṣṇavas' desire is then fulfilled.
>
> Although my Guru Mahārāja ordered me to accomplish this mission, I am not worthy or fit to do it. I am very fallen and insignificant. Therefore, O Lord, now I am begging for Your mercy so that I may become worthy, for You are the wisest and most experienced of all. . . .

The poem ends:

> Today that remembrance of You came to me in a very nice way. Because I have a great longing I called to You. I am Your eternal servant, and therefore I desire Your association so much. O Lord Kṛṣṇa, except for You there is no means of success.

In the same straightforward, factual manner in which he had noted the date, the weather, and his state of health, he now described his helpless dependence on his "companion, Lord Krishna," and his absorption in the ecstasy of separation from Kṛṣṇa. He described the relationship between the spiritual master and the disciple, and he praised his own spiritual master, Śrī Śrīmad Bhaktisiddhānta Sarasvatī, "by whose strong desire the holy name of Lord Gaurāṅga will spread throughout all the countries of the Western world." He plainly stated that his spiritual master had ordered him to accomplish this mission of worldwide Kṛṣṇa consciousness, and feeling unworthy he prayed to Lord Kṛṣṇa for strength. The last verses give an unexpected, confidential glimpse into Śrīla Prabhupāda's direct relationship with Lord Kṛṣṇa. Prabhupāda called on Kṛṣṇa as his "dear friend" and longed for the joy of again wandering the fields of Vraja. This memory of Kṛṣṇa, he wrote, came because of a great desire to serve the Lord. Externally, Śrīla Prabhupāda was experiencing great inconvenience; he had been aboard ship for a month and had suffered heart attacks and repeated seasickness. Moreover, even if he were to recover from these difficulties, his arrival in America would undoubtedly bring many more difficulties. But remembering the desire of his spiritual master, taking strength from his reading of *Caitanya-caritāmṛta*, and revealing his mind in his prayer to Lord Kṛṣṇa, Prabhupāda remained confident.

After a thirty-five-day journey from Calcutta, the *Jaladuta* reached Boston's Commonwealth Pier at 5:30 A.M. on September 17, 1965. The ship was to stop briefly in Boston before proceeding to New York City. Among the first things Śrīla Prabhupāda saw in America were the letters "A & P" painted on a pierfront warehouse. The gray waterfront dawn revealed the ships in the harbor, a conglomeration of lobster stands and drab buildings, and, rising in the distance, the Boston skyline.

Prabhupāda had to pass through U.S. Immigration and Customs in Boston. His visa allowed him a three-month stay, and an official stamped it to indicate his expected date of departure. Captain Pandia invited Prabhupāda to take a walk into Boston, where the captain intended to do some shopping. They walked across a footbridge into a busy commercial area with old churches, warehouses, office buildings, bars, tawdry bookshops, nightclubs, and restaurants. Prabhupāda briefly observed the city, but the most significant thing about his short stay in Boston, aside from the fact that he had now set foot in America, was that at Commonwealth Pier he wrote another Bengali poem, entitled "Mārkine Bhāgavata-dharma" ("Teaching Kṛṣṇa Consciousness in America"). Some of the verses he wrote on board the ship that day are as follows:*

> My dear Lord Kṛṣṇa, You are so kind upon this useless soul, but I do not know why You have brought me here. Now You can do whatever You like with me.
>
> But I guess You have some business here, otherwise why would You bring me to this terrible place?

---

*See Appendix for the complete Bengali verses with English translation.

Most of the population here is covered by the material modes of ignorance and passion. Absorbed in material life they think themselves very happy and satisfied, and therefore they have no taste for the transcendental message of Vāsudeva [Kṛṣṇa]. I do not know how they will be able to understand it.

But I know that Your causeless mercy can make everything possible, because You are the most expert mystic.

How will they understand the mellows of devotional service? O Lord, I am simply praying for Your mercy so that I will be able to convince them about Your message.

All living entities have come under the control of the illusory energy by Your will, and therefore, if You like, by Your will they can also be released from the clutches of illusion.

I wish that You may deliver them. Therefore if You so desire their deliverance, then only will they be able to understand Your message. . . .

How will I make them understand this message of Kṛṣṇa consciousness? I am very unfortunate, unqualified, and the most fallen. Therefore I am seeking Your benediction so that I can convince them, for I am powerless to do so on my own.

Somehow or other, O Lord, You have brought me here to speak about You. Now, my Lord, it is up to You to make me a success or failure, as You like.

O spiritual master of all the worlds! I can simply repeat Your message. So if You like You can make my power of speaking suitable for their understanding.

Only by Your causeless mercy will my words become pure. I am sure that when this transcendental message penetrates their hearts, they will certainly feel gladdened and thus become liberated from all unhappy conditions of life.

O Lord, I am just like a puppet in Your hands. So if You have brought me here to dance, then make me dance, make me dance, O Lord, make me dance as You like.

I have no devotion, nor do I have any knowledge, but I have strong faith in the holy name of Kṛṣṇa. I have been designated as Bhaktivedanta, and now, if You like, You can fulfill the real purport of Bhaktivedanta.

Signed—the most unfortunate, insignificant beggar,
A. C. Bhaktivedanta Swami,
On board the ship *Jaladuta*, Commonwealth Pier,
Boston, Massachusetts, U.S.A.
Dated 18th September 1965.

He was now in America. He was in a major American city, rich with billions, populated with millions, and determined to stay the way it was. Prabhupāda saw Boston from the viewpoint of a pure devotee of Kṛṣṇa. He saw the hellish city life, people dedicated to the illusion of material happiness. All his dedication and training moved him to give these people the transcendental knowledge and saving grace of Kṛṣṇa consciousness, yet he was feeling weak, lowly, and unable to help them on his own. He was but "an insignificant beggar" with no money. He had barely survived the two heart attacks at sea, he spoke a different language, he dressed strangely—yet he had come to tell people to give up meat-eating, illicit sex, intoxication, and gambling, and to teach them to worship Lord Kṛṣṇa, who to them was a mythical Hindu god. What would he be able to accomplish?

Helplessly he spoke his heart directly to God: "I wish that You may deliver them. I am seeking Your benediction so that I can convince them." And for convincing them he would trust in the power of God's holy name and in the *Śrīmad-Bhāgavatam.* This transcendental sound would clean away desire for material enjoyment from their hearts and awaken loving service to Kṛṣṇa. On the streets of Boston, Prabhupāda was aware of the power of ignorance and passion that dominated the city; but he had faith in the transcendental process. He was tiny, but God was infinite, and God was Kṛṣṇa, his dear friend.

On the nineteenth of September the *Jaladuta* sailed into New York Harbor and docked at a Brooklyn pier, at Seventeenth Street. Śrīla Prabhupāda saw the awesome Manhattan skyline, the Empire State Building, and, like millions of visitors and immigrants in the past, the Statue of Liberty.

Śrīla Prabhupāda was dressed appropriately for a resident of Vṛndāvana. He wore *kanthi-mālā* (neck beads) and a simple cotton *dhotī,* and he carried *japa-mālā* (chanting beads) and an old *chādar,* or shawl. His complexion was golden, his head shaven, *śikhā* in the back, his forehead decorated with the whitish Vaiṣnava *tilaka.* He wore pointed white rubber slippers, not uncommon for *sādhus* in India. But who in New York had ever seen or dreamed of anyone appearing like this Vaiṣṇava? He was possibly the first Vaiṣṇava *sannyāsī* to arrive in New York with uncompromised appearance. Of course, New Yorkers have an expertise in not giving much attention to any kind of strange new arrival.

Śrīla Prabhupāda was on his own. He had a sponsor, Mr. Agarwal, somewhere in Pennsylvania. Surely someone would be here to greet him. Although he had little idea of what to do as he walked off the ship onto the pier—"I did not know whether to turn left or right"—he passed through the dockside formalities and was met by a representative from Traveler's Aid, sent by the Agarwals in Pennsylvania, who offered to take him to the Scindia ticket office in Manhattan to book his return passage to India.

At the Scindia office, Prabhupāda spoke with the ticket agent, Joseph Foerster, who was impressed by this unusual passenger's Vaiṣṇava appearance, his light luggage, and his apparent poverty. He regarded Prabhupāda as a priest. Most of Scindia's passengers were businessmen or families, so Mr. Foerster had never seen a passenger wearing the traditional Vaiṣṇava dress of India. He found Śrīla Prabhupāda to be "a pleasant gentleman" who spoke of "the nice accommodations and treatment he had received aboard the *Jaladuta.*" Prabhupāda asked Mr. Foerster to hold space for him on a return ship to India. His plans were to leave in about two months, and he told Mr. Foerster that he would keep in touch. Carrying only forty rupees cash, which he himself called "a few hours' spending in New York," and an additional twenty dollars he had collected from selling three volumes of the *Bhāgavatam* to Captain Pandia, Śrīla Prabhupāda, with umbrella and suitcase in hand, and still escorted by the Traveler's Aid representative, set out for the Port Authority Bus Terminal to arrange for his trip to Butler.

CHAPTER TWO

Butler, Pennsylvania: The First Testing Ground

By the grace of Lord Krishna, the Americans are prosperous in every respect. They are not poverty stricken like the Indians. The people in general are satisfied so far as their material needs are concerned, and they are spiritually inclined. When I was in Butler, Pennsylvania, about five hundred miles from New York City, I saw there many churches, and they were attending regularly. This shows that they are spiritually inclined. I was also invited by some churches and church governed schools and colleges, and I spoke there, and they appreciated it and presented me some token rewards. When I was speaking to the students, they were very eager to hear about the principles of Srimad Bhagwatam. But the clergymen were cautious about allowing students to hear me so patiently. They feared that the students might be converted to Hindu ideas—as is quite natural for any religious sect. But they do not know that devotional service of the Lord Sri Krishna is the common religion for everyone, including even the aborigines and cannibals in the jungle.

—from a letter to Sumati Morarji

The bus came swinging out of the terminal into the daylight of midtown Manhattan, riding along in the shadows of skyscrapers, through asphalt streets crowded with people, trucks, and automobiles and into the heavy traffic bound toward the Lincoln Tunnel. The bus entered the tunnel and emerged on the Jersey side of the Hudson River, continuing down the New Jersey Turnpike past fields of huge oil tanks and sprawling refineries. The Manhattan skyline was on the left, while three lanes of traffic sped sixty miles an hour in each direction. Newark Airport came up close by on the right, with jets visible on the ground. Electric power lines, spanning aloft between steel towers, stretched into the horizon.

Śrīla Prabhupāda had never before witnessed anything of such magnitude. He was now seeing for himself that American culture was based on passion for more and more sense gratification—and it was a scene of madness. For what important business were people rushing to and fro at breakneck speed? He could see their goals advertised on the billboards.

Of course, he had many times traveled the road from Delhi to Vṛndāvana, but it did not have many advertisements. A traveler would see mostly the land, roadside streams, temples, homes, farmers in their fields. Most people went on foot or traveled by oxcart or bicycle. And in Vṛndāvana even the ordinary passersby greeted each other by calling the names of God: "Jaya Rādhe!" "Hare Kṛṣṇa!" Now there were factories outside Delhi, but nothing like this. The cumulative effect did not pack nearly the materialistic punch of these fields of oil tanks, mammoth factories, and billboards alongside the crowded superhighway. Meat-eating, illicit sex, intoxication, and gambling—the very sins Śrīla Prabhupāda had come to preach against—were proudly glamorized on mile after mile of billboards. The signs promoted liquor and cigarettes, roadside restaurants offered slaughtered cows in the form of steaks and hamburgers, and no matter what the product, it was usually advertised by a lusty-looking woman. But Prabhupāda had come to teach the opposite: that happiness is not found in the passion for sense gratification, and that only when one becomes detached from the mode of passion, which leads to sinful acts, can one become eligible for the eternal happiness of Kṛṣṇa consciousness.

Prabhupāda felt compassion. The compassion of a Kṛṣṇa conscious saint had been explained in an age long ago by Prahlāda Mahārāja: "I see that there are many saintly persons indeed, but they are interested only in their own deliverance. Not caring for the big cities and towns, they go to the Himalayas or the forests to meditate with vows of silence. They are not interested in delivering others. As for me, however, I do not wish to be liberated alone, leaving aside all these poor fools and rascals. I know that without Kṛṣṇa consciousness, without taking shelter of Your lotus feet, one cannot be happy. Therefore I wish to bring them back to shelter at Your lotus feet."

The scenery gradually changed to the Pennsylvania countryside, and the bus sped through long tunnels in the mountains. Night came. And it was late—after eleven—when the bus entered the heavily industrialized Pittsburgh area on the shore of the Allegheny River. Śrīla Prabhupāda couldn't see the steel mills clearly, but he could see their lights and their industrial fires and smoking stacks. Millions of lights shone throughout the city's prevailing dinginess.

When the bus finally pulled into the terminal, it was past midnight. Gopal Agarwal was waiting with the family Volkswagen bus to drive Prabhupāda to Butler, about one hour north. He greeted Prabhupāda with folded palms and "Welcome, Swamiji," bowing from the waist several times.

This was not any of Gopal's doing. His father, a Mathurā businessman with a fondness for *sādhus* and religious causes, had requested him to host the Swamiji. This wasn't the first time his father had arranged for a *sādhu* acquaintance to come to America. Several times he had sent sponsorship papers for Gopal to sign, and Gopal had obediently done so—but nothing had ever come of them. So when the sponsorship letter for A. C. Bhaktivedanta Swami had come, Gopal had promptly signed and returned it, thinking that this would be the last they would hear of it. But then just a week ago a letter had come. Sally Agarwal had opened it and then, in alarm, called to her husband: "Honey, sit down. Listen to this: the Swami is coming." Śrīla Prabhupāda had enclosed his picture so that they would not mistake him. The Agarwals had looked curiously at the photograph. "There'll be no mistake *there*," Gopal had said.

The unsuspecting Agarwals were "simple American people," according to Sally Agarwal, who had met her Indian husband while he was working as an engineer in Pennsylvania. What would they do with an Indian swami in their house? Prabhupāda was a shock for them. But there was no question of *not* accepting him; they were bound by the request of Gopal's father. Dutifully, Gopal had purchased Śrīla Prabhupāda's ticket from New York to Pittsburgh and had arranged for the agent from Traveler's Aid to meet him. And dutifully he had driven tonight to meet him. So it was with a mixture of embarrassment, disbelief, and wonder that Gopal Agarwal helped his guest into the VW and drove back home to Butler.

* * *

September 20

"BUTLER, PENNSYLVANIA, HOME OF THE JEEP" read a granite plaque in the city park. Butler, famous as the town where the U.S. Army jeep was invented in 1940, was an industrial city of twenty thousand, settled amid the hills of an area rich in oil, coal, gas, and limestone. Its industry consisted mainly of factories for plate glass, railroad cars, refrigerators, oil equipment, and rubber goods. Ninety percent of the local laborers were native Americans. The nominal religion had always been Christian, mostly Protestant with some Catholic, and in later years a few synagogues had appeared. But there was no Hindu community at that time; Gopal Agarwal was the first Indian to move to Butler.

As the VW bus pulled into town, the predawn air was warm and humid. The morning edition of the *Butler Eagle* would soon be going to the newsstands—"Red Chinese Fire on India"; "Prime Minister Shastri Declares Chinese Communists Out to Dominate World"; "United Nations Council Demands Pakistan and India Cease-fire in 48 Hours."

Śrīla Prabhupāda arrived at the Agarwals' home—Sterling Apartments—at 4:00 A.M., and Gopal invited him to sleep on the couch. Their place, a townhouse apartment, consisted of a small living room, a dining room, a kitchenette, two upstairs bedrooms, and a bath. Here they lived with their two young children. The Agarwals had lived in Butler for a few years now and felt themselves established in a good social circle. Since their apartment had so little space, they decided that it would be better if the Swami took a room at the YMCA and came to visit them during the day. Of course, living space wasn't the real difficulty—it was *him.* How would he fit into the Butler atmosphere? He was their guest, so they would have to *explain* him to their friends and neighbors.

Śrīla Prabhupāda was immediately a curiosity for whoever saw him. In anxiety, Mrs. Agarwal decided that instead of having people speculate about the strange man in orange robes living at her house, it would be better to let them know about him from the newspapers. She explained her plan to Prabhupāda, who laughed, understanding that he didn't fit in.

Sally hurried Prabhupāda off to a Pittsburgh newspaper office, but the interviewer wasn't able to comprehend why this person should make an interesting story. Sally then took him to the local *Butler Eagle*, where his presence was accepted as indeed newsworthy.

September 22

A feature article appeared in the *Butler Eagle:* "In Fluent English, Devotee of Hindu Cult Explains Commission to Visit the West." A photographer had come to the Agarwals' apartment and had taken a picture of Śrīla Prabhupāda standing in the living room holding an open volume of *Śrīmad-Bhāgavatam.* The caption read, "Ambassador of Bhakti-yoga."

The article began:

> A slight brown man in faded orange drapes and wearing white bathing shoes stepped out of a compact car yesterday and into the Butler YMCA to attend a meeting. He is A. C. Bhaktivedanta Swamiji, a messenger from India to the peoples of the West.

The article referred to *Śrīmad-Bhāgavatam* as "Biblical literature" and to Śrīla Prabhupāda as "the learned teacher." It continued:

> "My mission is to revive a people's God consciousness," says the Swamiji. "God is the Father of all living beings, in thousands of different forms," he explains. "Human life is a stage of perfection in evolution; if we miss the message, back we go through the process again," he believes.... Bhaktivedanta lives as a monk, and permits no woman to touch his food. On a six-week ocean voyage and at the Agarwal apartment in Butler he prepares his meals in a brass pan with separate levels for steaming rice, vegetables, and making "bread" at the same time. He is a strict vegetarian, and is permitted to drink only milk, "the miracle food for babies and old men," he noted.... If Americans would give more attention to their spiritual life, they would be much happier, he says.

The Agarwals had their own opinion as to why Prabhupāda had come to America: "to finance his books," and nothing more. They were sure that he was hoping only to meet someone who could help him with the publication of his *Śrīmad-Bhāgavatam*, and that he did not want any followers. At least they hoped he wouldn't do anything to attract attention; and they felt that this was his mentality also. "He didn't create waves," Sally Agarwal says. "He didn't want any crowd. He didn't want anything. He only wanted to finance his books." Perhaps Prabhupāda, seeing their nervousness, agreed to keep a low profile, out of consideration for his hosts.

At Prabhupāda's request, however, Mr. Agarwal held a kind of open house in his apartment every night from six to nine.

Sally: *It was quite an intellectual group that we were in, and they were fascinated by him. They hardly knew what to ask him. They didn't know enough. This was just like a dream out of a book. Who would expect to meet a swami in someone's living room in Butler, Pennsylvania? It was just really tremendous. In the middle of middle-class America. My parents came from quite a distance to see him. We knew a lot of people in Pittsburgh, and they came up. This was a very unusual thing, having him here. But the real interest shown in him was only as a curiosity.*

He had a typewriter, which was one of his few possessions, and an umbrella. That was one of the things that caused a sensation, that he always carried an umbrella. And it was a little chilly and he was balding, so he always wore this hat that someone had made for him, like a swimming cap. It was a kind of sensation. And he was so brilliant that when he saw someone twice, he knew who they were—he remembered. He was a brilliant man. Or if he met them in our apartment and saw them in a car, he would remember their name, and he would wave and say their name. He was a brilliant man. All the people liked him. They were amazed at how intelligent he was. The thing that got them was the way he remembered their name. And his humorous way. He looked so serious all the time, but he was a very humorous person. He was forbidding in his looks, but he was very charming.

He was the easiest guest I have had in my life, because when I couldn't spend time with him he chanted, and I knew he was perfectly happy. When I couldn't talk to him, he chanted. He was so easy, though, because I knew he was never bored. I never felt any pressure or tension about having him. He was so easy that when I had to take care of the children he would just chant. It was so great. When I had to do things, he would just be happy chanting. He was a very good guest. When the people would come, they were always smoking cigarettes, but he would say, "Pay no attention. Think nothing of it." That's what he said. "Think nothing of it." Because he knew we were different. I didn't smoke in front of him. I knew I wasn't supposed to smoke in front of Gopal's father, so I sort of considered him the same. He didn't make any problems for anybody.

One evening a guest asked Prabhupāda, "What do you think of Jesus Christ?" And Prabhupāda replied, "He is the Son of God." Then he added that he—the guest—was also a son of God. Everyone was interested to hear that the Swami accepted Jesus Christ as the Son of God.

Gopal: *His intent was not to have you change your way of life. He wasn't telling anybody they should be vegetarian or anything. All he wanted you to do was to follow what you are, but be better. He didn't stress that we should give up many things.*

Śrīla Prabhupāda followed a regulated daily schedule. Every morning he would walk the six or seven blocks from the YMCA to Sterling Apartments, arriving there about seven. When he had first landed in New York, he had in his luggage a large bundle of dried cereal, similar to rolled oats. This supply was enough for several weeks, and every morning at breakfast he would take some with milk. At seven forty-five Gopal would leave for work, and around nine-thirty Prabhupāda would start preparing his lunch in the kitchen. He made his *capātīs* by hand, without even a rolling pin. He worked alone for two hours, while Mrs. Agarwal did housework and took care of her children. At eleven-thirty he took *prasādam*.

Sally: *When he cooked he used only one burner. The bottom-level pot created the steam. He had the* dāl *on the bottom, and it created the steam to cook many other vegetables. So for about a week he was cooking this great big lunch, which was ready about eleven-thirty, and Gopal always came home for lunch about twelve. I used to serve Gopal a sandwich, and then he would go back to work. But it didn't take me long to realize that the food the Swami was cooking we'd enjoy too, so he started cooking that noon meal for all of us. Oh, and we enjoyed it so much.*

Our fun was to show him what we knew of America. And he had never seen such things. It was such fun to take him to the supermarket. He loved opening the package of okra or frozen beans, and he didn't have to clean them and cut them and do all those things. He opened the freezer every day and just chose his items. It was fun to watch him. He sat on the couch while I swept with the vacuum cleaner, and he was so interested in that, and we talked for a long time about that. He was so interesting.

So every day he'd have this big feast, and everything was great fun. We really enjoyed it. I would help him cut the things. He would spice it, and we would laugh. He was the most enjoyable man, most enjoyable man. I really felt like a sort of daughter to him, even in such a short time. Like he was my father-in-law. He was a friend of my father-in-law, but I really felt very close to him. He enjoyed everything. I liked him. I thought he was tremendous.

After lunch, Prabhupāda would leave, about 1:00 P.M., and walk to the YMCA, where the Agarwals figured he must have worked at his writing until five. He would come back to their apartment about six in the evening, after they had taken their meal. They ate meat, so Mrs. Agarwal was careful to have it cleared away before he came. When one night he came early, she said, "Oh, Swamiji, we have just cooked meat, and the smell will be very disagreeable to you." But he said, "Oh, think nothing of it. Think nothing of it."

In the evening he would speak with guests. The guests would usually take coffee and other refreshments, but he would request a glass of warm milk at nine o'clock. He would stay, speaking until nine-thirty or ten, and then Mr. Agarwal would drive him back to the YMCA.

Prabhupāda would also do his own laundry every day. He washed his clothes in the Agarwals' bathroom and hung them to dry outside. He sometimes accompanied the Agarwals to the laundromat and was interested to see how Americans washed and dried their clothes. To Sally he seemed "very interested in the American ways and people."

Sally: *Our boy Brij was six or seven months old when the Swami came—and the Indians love boys. The Swami liked Brij. He was there when Brij first stood. The first time Brij made the attempt and actually succeeded, the Swami stood up and clapped. It was a celebration. Another time, our baby teethed on the Swami's shoes. I thought, "Oh, those shoes. They've been all over India, and my kid is chewing on them." You know how a mother would feel.*

Almost every night he used to sit in the next-door neighbor's backyard. We sat out there sometimes with him, or we stayed in the living room. One time something happened with our little girl, Pamela, who was only three years old. I used to take her to Sunday school, and she learned about Jesus in Sunday school. Then when she would see Swamiji with his robes on and everything, she called him Swami Jesus. And this one time when it first dawned on us what she was saying, she called him Swami Jesus, and Swami smiled and said, "And a little child shall lead them." It was so funny.

Prabhupāda spoke to various groups in the community. He spoke at the Lions Club in early October and received a formal document:

> Be it known that A. C. Bhaktivedanta Swami was a guest at the Lions Club of Butler, Pa., and as an expression of appreciation for services rendered, the Club tenders this acknowledgement.

He also gave a talk at the Y and at St. Fidelis Seminary College in Herman, Pennsylvania, and he spoke regularly to guests at the Agarwal home.

* * *

When Professor Larsen, the chairman of the philosophy department at Slippery Rock State College, read in the *Butler Eagle* of a visiting Indian swami and Vedic scholar, he phoned the Agarwals' home to invite Prabhupāda to lecture on campus.

Allen Larsen: *I called the number given in the newspaper article, but it turned out that the Swamiji was actually staying in a room at the YMCA. When I arrived, he was waiting on the street corner, and I picked him up. He seemed very much alone. When we were driving to Slippery Rock, I asked him to pronounce his name for me so I would have it right when I introduced him to my class. He said, "Swamiji Bhaktivedanta," and then he proceeded to tell me what that meant. Since I was not used to Indian names, he had to repeat it several times before I got it right. He showed no impatience with my slowness. Even at this early junction of our association, I was convinced that this man had an inner stability and strength that would be very difficult to shake, and this initial impression was further reinforced throughout the rather busy day.*

A hundred students from several classes had gathered to hear the lecture, as Prabhupāda, in his natural, unrehearsed manner, walked down the aisle, up the three wooden steps, and onto the plain wooden stage. He sat down, erect and cross-legged, and began softly singing Hare Kṛṣṇa, his eyes closed. Then he stood and spoke (without a lectern or microphone) and answered questions from the audience. The program lasted only fifty minutes and ended abruptly with a bell signaling the next class.

Allen Larsen: *After the first class, I had a short conversation with the Swamiji while sitting outside on a bench on the campus lawn. Most of the time when he was not directly engaged in conversation he would repeat a short prayer while moving prayer beads through his fingers. He was sitting up cross-legged, and we were speaking back and forth. He said that the trees around us were beautiful, and he asked, "What kind of trees are these?" I replied, "They're shade trees." Then he said that it was too bad they weren't fruit or nut trees to provide food and benefit people.*

At one o'clock Prabhupāda lectured again. Afterward, he accompanied Dr. Mohan Sharma, a member of the faculty who had attended the lecture, and his sixteen-year-old daughter, Mini, to Dr. Sharma's campus residence. Prabhupāda accepted warm milk and dried fruit, and at Dr. Sharma's request, blessed his home and touched the forehead of his daughter in a gesture of benediction. Around three o'clock, Professor Larsen drove him back to Butler.

Allen Larsen: *The Swamiji seemed to present himself as an Indian scholar who had come for a short time to do translation work. I never thought of him as a missionary. But during the course of the day there grew in me a warm affection for this man, because he was unmistakably a good man who had found his way to a stability and peace that is very rare.*

The lectures in Pennsylvania gave Prabhupāda his first readings of how his message would be received in America. At Commonwealth Pier in Boston he had stated in his poem: "I am sure that when this transcendental message penetrates their hearts, they will certainly feel gladdened and thus become liberated from all unhappy conditions of life." Now this

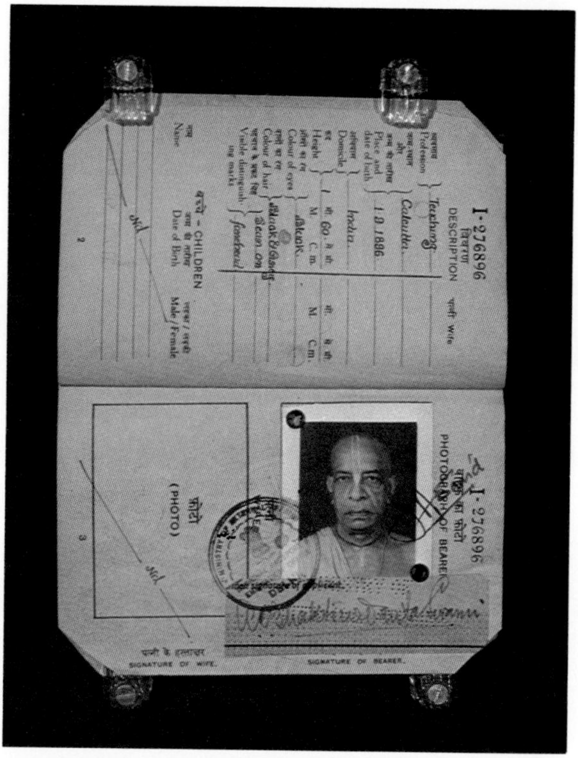

Śrīla Prabhupāda's passport.

The *Jaladuta: "If the Atlantic would have shown its usual face, perhaps I would have died. But Lord Kṛṣṇa has taken charge of the ship."*

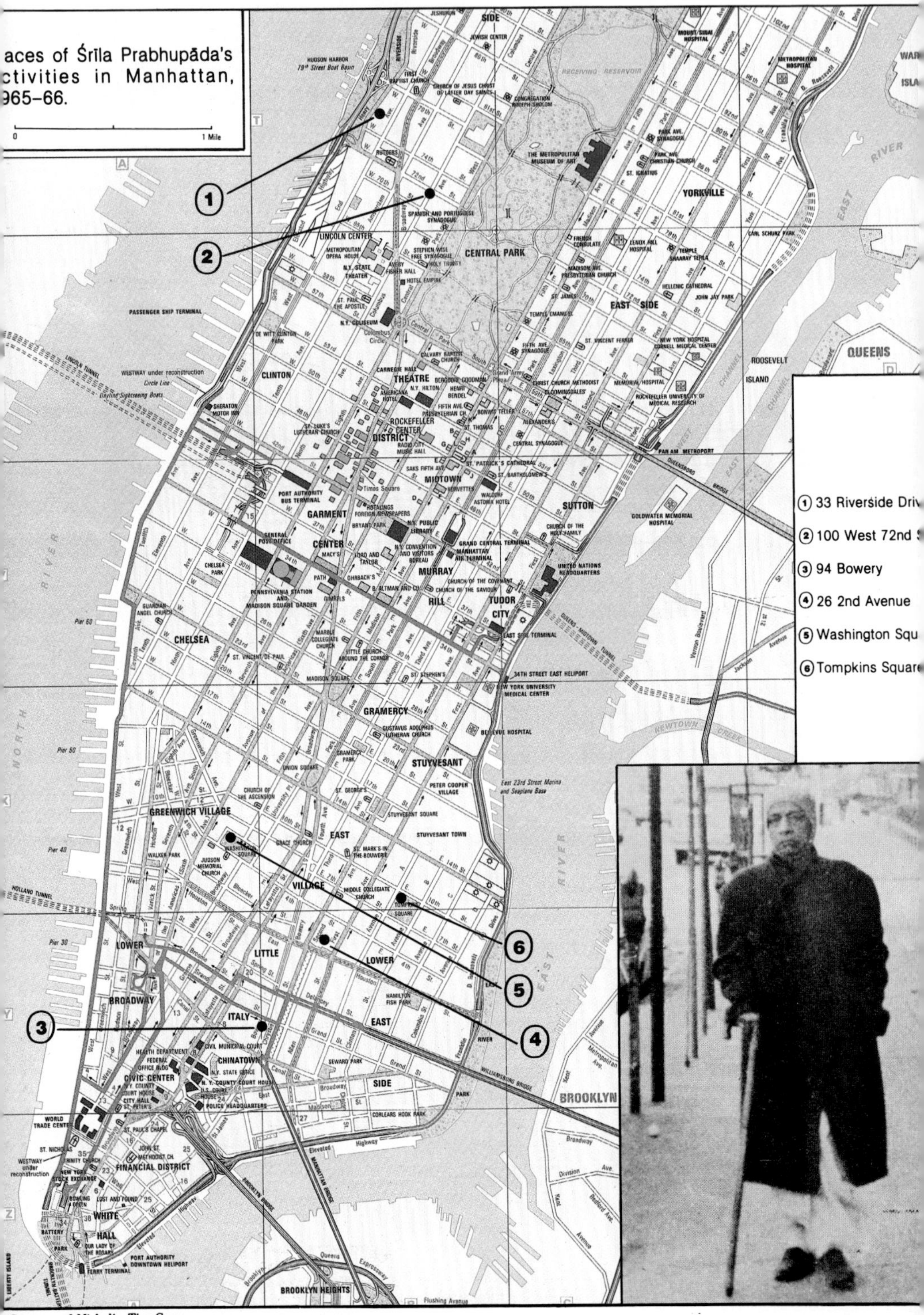

Courtesy of Michelin Tire Corp.

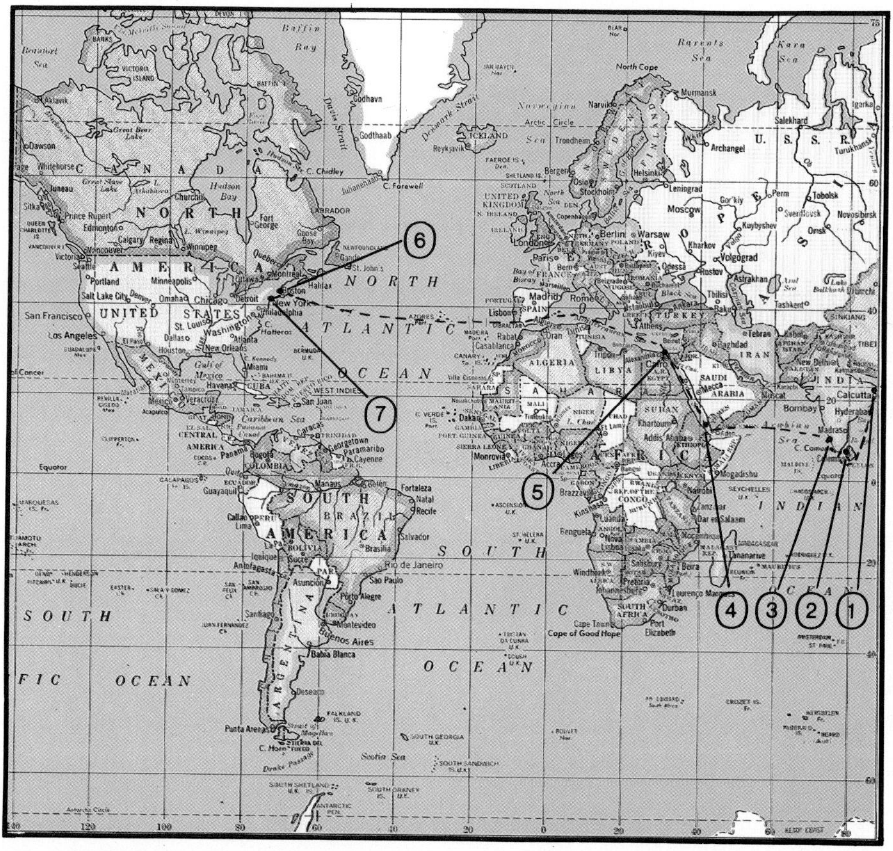

Śrīla Prabhupāda's journey to America, 1965.

① August 13 – Calcutta

② August 19 – Colombo

③ August 21 – Cochin

④ August 23 – Red Sea

⑤ September 1 – Port Said (Suez Canal)

⑥ September 17 – Boston

⑦ September 19 – New York

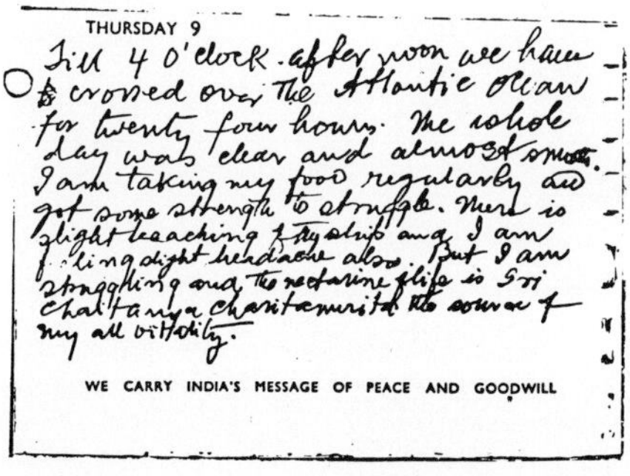

THURSDAY 9

Till 4 O'clock afternoon we have crossed over the Atlantic Ocean for twenty four hours. The whole day was clear and almost smooth. I am taking my food regularly and got some strength to struggle. There is slight reaching of the ship and I am feeling slight headache also. But I am struggling and the nectarine of life is Sri Chaitanya Charitamrita the source of my all vitality.

WE CARRY INDIA'S MESSAGE OF PEACE AND GOODWILL

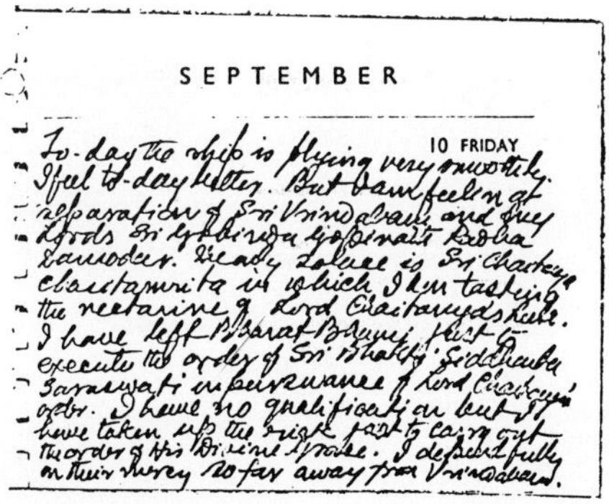

SEPTEMBER

10 FRIDAY

To-day the ship is plying very smoothly. I feel to-day better. But I am feeling separation of Sri Vrindaban and my Lords Sri Govinda, Gopinath, Radha Damodar. The only solace is Sri Chaitanya Charitamrita in which I am tasting the nectarine of Lord Chaitanya's lila. I have left Bharat Bhumi just to execute the order of Sri Bhaktisiddhanta Saraswati in pursuance of Lord Chaitanya's order. I have no qualification but I have taken up the risk just to carry out the order of His Divine Grace. I depend fully on their mercy so far away from Vrindaban.

Some pages from Śrīla Prabhupāda's diary.

Photo from the *Butler Eagle*, September 22, 1965. This was the first news coverage of Śrīla Prabhupāda in America.

Cooking lunch in Sally Agarwal's kitchen: *"He prepares his meals in a brass pan with separate levels for steaming rice, vegetables, and making 'bread' at the same time."*

"He was there when Brij first stood. . . . It was a celebration."

Butler YMCA.

"Who would expect to meet a swami in someone's living room in Butler, Pennsylvania?"

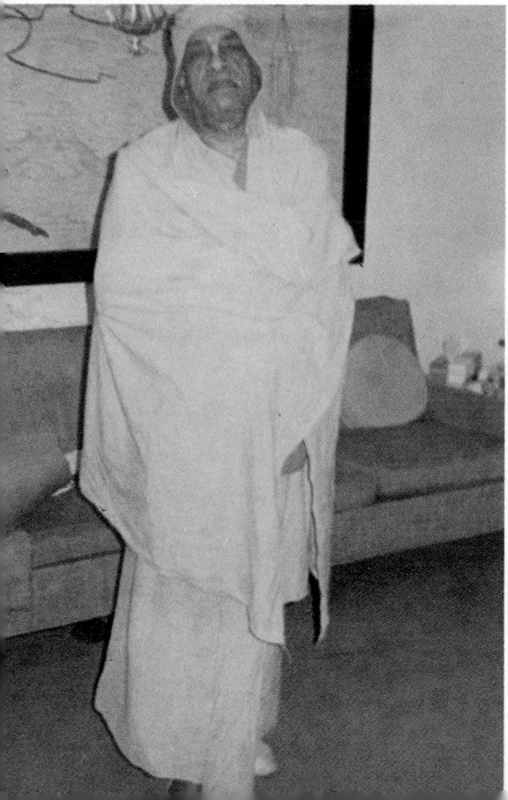

33 Riverside Drive. Dr. Mishra's apartment was on the fourteenth floor.

When it became inconvenient to maintain Śrīla Prabhupāda at the apartment, Dr. Mishra shifted him to his haṭha-yoga *studio on the fifth floor of 100 West 72nd Street, near Central Park.*

Śrīla Prabhupāda talking with Dr. Mishra at Ananda Ashram.

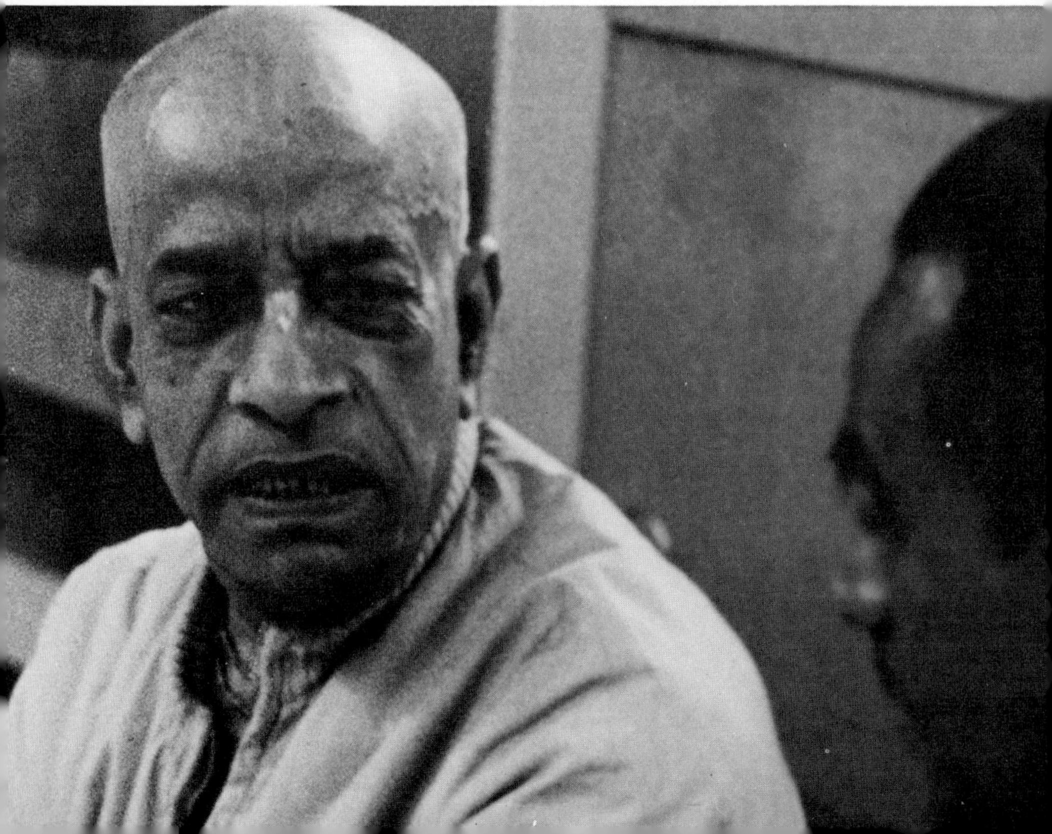

The block where Śrīla Prabhupāda lived on the Bowery consisted of two saloons, a flophouse, and two buildings with lofts.

143 West 72nd Street: *"The ground floor may be utilized for preparation of prasadam . . . After purchasing the house, we can build another story upon it with a temple dome, cakra, etc."*

75th Street, along Śrīla Prabhupāda's daily walk to Dr. Mishra's apartment.

The street entrance to 94 Bowery.

Śrīla Prabhupāda on the Bowery, photographed by Fred McDarrah of *The Village Voice*, June 1965.

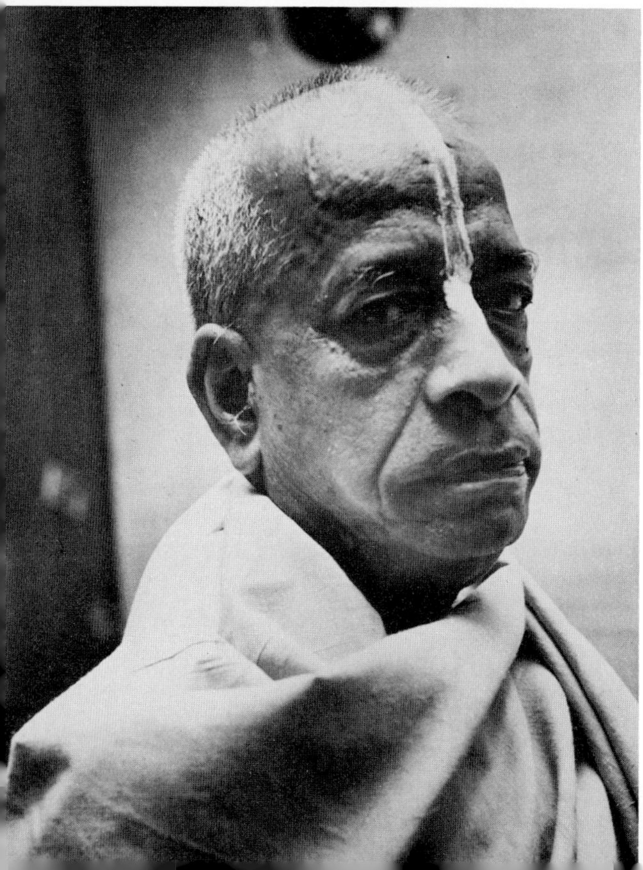

principle was actually being tested in the field. Would they be able to understand? Were they interested? Would they surrender?

* * *

October 15

Śrīla Prabhupāda received a letter from Sumati Morarji in Bombay:

> Poojya Swami,
>
> I am in due receipt of your letter dated the 24th ultimo, and glad to know that you have safely reached the U.S.A. after suffering from seasickness. I thank you for your greetings and blessings. I know by now you must have recovered fully from the sickness and must be keeping good health. I was delighted to read that you have started your activities in the States and have already delivered some lectures. I pray to Lord Bala Krishna to give you enough strength to enable you to carry the message of Sri Bhagwatam. I feel that you should stay there until you fully recover from your illness and return only after you have completed your mission.
>
> Here everything is normal. With respects,
>
> Yours sincerely,
> Sumati Morarji

Prabhupāda regarded the last line of this letter as especially significant: his well-wisher was urging him to stay in America until he had completed his mission. He had told the immigration officials in New York that he would be staying in America for two months. "I have one month's sponsorship in Butler," he thought, "and then I have no support. So perhaps I can stay another month." So he had said two months. Sumati Morarji, however, was urging him to stay on. He saw that the prospects for preaching to the Americans were good, but he felt he would need support from India.

At any rate, he had spent long enough in Butler, and he now had one month left in America. So he decided to go to New York City and try to preach there, before his time was up. But first he wanted to visit Philadelphia, where he had arranged a meeting with a Sanskrit professor, Dr. Norman Brown, at the University of Pennsylvania.

Mrs. Agarwal was sorry to see him go.

Sally: *After a month I really loved the Swami. I felt protective in a way, and he wanted to go to Philadelphia. But I couldn't imagine—I told him—I could not imagine him going to Philadelphia for two days. He was going to speak there, and then to New York. But he knew no one in New York. If the thing didn't pan out in Philadelphia, he was just going to New York, and then there was no one. I just couldn't imagine. It made me sick.*

I remember the night he was leaving, about two in the morning. I remember sitting there as long as he could wait before Gopal took him to Pittsburgh to get on that bus. Gopal got a handful of change, and I remember telling him how to put the money in the slot so that he could take a bath at the bus station—because he was supposed to take a bath a few times a day. And Gopal told him how to do that, and told him about the automats in New York. He told him what he could eat and what he couldn't eat, and he gave him these coins in a sock, and that's all he left us with.

As a *sannyāsī*, Śrīla Prabhupāda was used to picking up and leaving one place for another. As a mendicant preacher, he had no remorse about leaving behind the quiet life of the Butler YMCA. And he had no attachment for the domestic habitat where he would cook and talk with Sally Agarwal about vacuum cleaners, frozen foods, and American ways.

But why had he gone to Butler? And why was he going to New York? He saw it as Kṛṣṇa's grace. As a pure devotee of Kṛṣṇa, he wanted to be an instrument for distributing Kṛṣṇa consciousness.

His stay in Butler had been helpful. He had gotten first-hand experience of American life, and he gained confidence that his health was strong and his message communicable. He was glad to see that America had the necessary ingredients for his Indian vegetarian diet, and that the people could understand his English. He had learned that casual one-time lectures here and there were of limited value, and that although there would be opposition from the established religions, people individually were very much interested in what he had to say.

On October 18, he left Butler, via Philadelphia, for New York City.

CHAPTER THREE

Struggling Alone

I used to sit in the back and listen to his meetings silently. He was speaking all impersonal nonsense, and I kept my silence. Then one day he asked if I would like to speak, and I spoke about Kṛṣṇa consciousness. I challenged that he was speaking manufactured philosophy and all nonsense from Śaṅkarācārya. He tried to back out and said he *was not speaking, Śaṅkarācārya was speaking. I said, "You are representing him. That is the same thing." He then said to me, "Swamiji, I like you very much, but you cannot speak here." But although our philosophies differed and he would not let me speak, he was kind, and I was nice to him.*

—Śrīla Prabhupāda in conversation

Prabhupāda knew no one in New York City, but he had a contact: Dr. Ramamurti Mishra. He had written Dr. Mishra from Butler, enclosing the letter of introduction Paramananda Mehra had given him in Bombay. He had also phoned Dr. Mishra, who welcomed Prabhupāda to join him in New York.

At the Port Authority Bus Terminal, a student of Dr. Mishra's met him as he arrived from Philadelphia and escorted him directly to an Indian festival in the city. There Prabhupāda met Dr. Mishra as well as Ravi Shankar and his brother, the dancer Udai Shankar. Prabhupāda then accompanied Dr. Mishra to his apartment at 33 Riverside Drive, beside the Hudson River. The apartment was on the fourteenth floor and had large windows overlooking the river. Dr. Mishra gave Prabhupāda a room to himself.

Dr. Mishra was a dramatic, showy personality, given to flashing glances and making expressive gestures with his hands. He regularly used words like "lovely" and "beautiful." Presenting an artfully polished image of what a *guru* should be, he was what some New Yorkers referred to as "an uptown swami." Before coming to America, Dr. Mishra had been a Sanskrit scholar and a *guru*, as well as a doctor. He had written a number of books, such as *The Textbook of Yoga Psychology* and *Self-Analysis and Self-Knowledge*, a work based on the teachings of the monistic philosopher Śaṅkara. After he came to the United States, he continued with his medical profession, but as he began taking disciples he gradually dropped his practice. Although a *sannyāsī*, he did not wear the traditional saffron *dhotī* and *kurtā*, but instead wore tailored Nehru jackets and white slacks. His complexion was dark, whereas Prabhupāda's was golden, and he had thick, black hair. At forty-four, he was young enough to be Prabhupāda's son. Dr. Mishra had been suffering from bad health when Śrīla Prabhupāda came into his life, and Prabhupāda's arrival seemed the perfect medicine.

Ramamurti Mishra: *His Holiness Prabhupāda Bhaktivedanta Gosvāmījī really knocked me down with love. He was really an incarnation of love. My body had become a skeleton, and he really brought me back to life—his cooking, and especially his love and his devotion to Lord Kṛṣṇa. I was very lazy in the matter of cooking, but he would get up and have ready.*

Dr. Mishra appreciated that Prabhupāda, cooking with the precision of a chemist, would prepare many dishes, and that he had a gusto for eating.

Ramamurti Mishra: *It was not bread he gave me—he gave me* prasādam. *This was life, and he saved my life. At that time I was not sure I would live, but his habit to eat on time, whether I was hungry or not—that I very much liked. He'd get up and say, "All right, this is* bhagavat-prasādam," *and I would say, "All right."*

Joan Suval, an old student of Dr. Mishra's, often saw Śrīla Prabhupāda and her teacher together at the Riverside Drive apartment.

Joan Suval: *I have a memory of Swamiji as a child, in the sense of his being very innocent, a very simple person, very pure. The impression I have from Dr. Mishra is that he regarded Swamiji as a father figure who was kindly and good. But basically the words most often used referring to*

Swamiji were "like a child," meaning that he was simple in a classical, beautiful sense. Dr. Mishra mentioned to me when I was first introduced to Swamiji that he was a very holy man, very religious, rapt in God consciousness.

Swamiji was very sweet. I myself remember him as a very, very good man, even in the practical details of living in New York, which seemed to involve him very much, because he was a practical man and was looking for the best place to begin his work. I remember very well that he was always careful about washing his clothes out every night. I would come in and find a group of students in the living area of Dr. Mishra's apartment, and in the bathroom would be hung Swamiji's orange robes.

Śrīla Prabhupāda would sometimes discuss with Dr. Mishra the aim of his visit to America, expressing his spiritual master's vision of establishing Kṛṣṇa consciousness in the West. He requested Dr. Mishra to help him, but Dr. Mishra would always refer to his own teaching work, which kept him very busy, and to his plans for leaving the country soon. After a few weeks, when it became inconvenient to maintain Prabhupāda at the apartment, Dr. Mishra shifted him to his *haṭha-yoga* studio on the fifth floor of 100 West Seventy-second Street, near Central Park. The large studio was located in the center of the building and included an office and an adjoining private room, where Prabhupāda stayed. It had no windows.

Philosophically at complete odds with Prabhupāda, Dr. Mishra accepted the Absolute Truth in the impersonal feature (or Brahman) to be supreme. Prabhupāda stressed the supremacy of the personal feature (or Bhagavān), following the Vedic theistic philosophy that the most complete understanding of the Absolute Truth is personal. The *Bhagavad-gītā* says that the impersonal Brahman is subordinate to Bhagavān and is an emanation from Him, just as the sunshine is an emanation from the sun planet. This conclusion had been taught by the leading traditional *ācāryas* of ancient India, such as Rāmānuja and Madhva, and Śrīla Prabhupāda was in disciplic succession from Madhva. Dr. Mishra, on the other hand, followed Śaṅkara, who taught that the impersonal presence of the Absolute Truth is all in all and that the Personality of Godhead is ultimately an illusion. Whereas Prabhupāda's theistic philosophy accepted the individual spiritual self (*ātmā*) as an eternal servant of the supreme spiritual being (Bhagavān), Dr. Mishra's view accepted the spiritual self as not an individual. Rather, his idea was that since each person is identical with God, the Supreme Brahman, there is no need to worship God outside oneself. As Dr. Mishra would put it, "Everything is one."

Prabhupāda challenged: If each of us is actually the Supreme, then why is this "Supreme" suffering and struggling in the material world? Dr. Mishra would counter that the Supreme is only temporarily covered by illusion and that through *haṭha-yoga* and meditation one would become enlightened, understanding, "It is all the Supreme." Prabhupāda would again challenge: But if the Supreme could be covered by illusion, then illusion would be greater than God, greater than the Supreme.

Prabhupāda considered Dr. Mishra a "Māyāvādī" because of his inadvertent acceptance that *māyā*, illusion, is greater than the Absolute Truth. For Śrīla Prabhupāda, not only was the impersonal philosophy unpalatable, it was an insult to the Personality of Godhead. According to Kṛṣṇa in the *Bhagavad-gītā* (7.24, 9.11), "Unintelligent men, who know Me not, think that I have assumed this form and personality. Due to their small knowledge, they do not know My higher nature, which is changeless and supreme.... Fools deride Me when I appear in this human form. They do not know My transcendental nature and My supreme dominion over all that be." Lord Caitanya had also strongly refuted the Māyāvāda philosophy: "Everything about the Supreme Personality of Godhead is spiritual, including His body, opulence, and paraphernalia. Māyāvāda philosophy, however, covers His spiritual opulence and advocates the theory of impersonalism."

Before coming to America, Śrīla Prabhupāda had written in his *Bhāgavatam* purports, "The ambitious Māyāvādī philosophers desire to merge into the existence of the Lord. This form of *mukti* (liberation) means denying one's individual existence. In other words, it is a kind of spiritual suicide. It is absolutely opposed to the philosophy of *bhakti-yoga*. *Bhakti-yoga* offers immortality to the individual conditioned soul. If one follows the Māyāvāda philosophy, he misses his opportunity to become immortal after giving up the material body." In the words of Lord Caitanya, *māyāvādī kṛṣṇa-aparādhī:* "Māyāvādī impersonalists are great offenders unto Lord Kṛṣṇa." Thus Lord Caitanya had concluded that if one even *hears* the commentary of Śaṅkara, one's entire spiritual life is spoiled. Dr. Mishra was content to align himself with the philosophy of Śaṅkara and allow Prabhupāda to stay with Lord Kṛṣṇa and the

Bhagavad-gītā. But Śrīla Prabhupāda pointed out that even Śaṅkara accepted that the Personality of Godhead, Kṛṣṇa, or Nārāyaṇa, exists eternally beyond the material world. Therefore, He is a transcendental person—*nārāyaṇaḥ paro 'vyaktāt.*

A mendicant, Prabhupāda was temporarily dependent on the good will of his Māyāvādī acquaintance, with whom he regularly ate and conversed and from whom he accepted shelter. But what a great inconvenience it was! He had come to America to speak purely and boldly about Kṛṣṇa, but he was being restricted. In Butler he had been confined by his hosts' middle-class sensibilities; now he was silenced in a different way. He was treated with kindness, but he was considered a threat. Dr. Mishra could not allow his students to hear the exclusive praise of Lord Kṛṣṇa as the Supreme Personality of Godhead.

Spending most of his time in his new room, Śrīla Prabhupāda kept at his typing and translating. But when Dr. Mishra held his *yoga* classes, Prabhupāda would sometimes come out and lead a *kīrtana* or lecture.

Robert Nelson (one of Prabhupāda's first young sympathizers in New York): *I went to Dr. Mishra's service, and Dr. Mishra talked. Swamiji was sitting on a bench, and then all of a sudden Dr. Mishra stops the service and he gets a big smile and says, "Swamiji will sing us a song." I think Dr. Mishra wouldn't let him speak. Somebody told me Dr. Mishra didn't want him to preach.*

Every morning, several hours before dawn, Prabhupāda would rise, take his bath, chant Hare Kṛṣṇa on his beads, and work at his translating, while outside his closed-in, windowless chamber, dawn came and the city awoke. He had no stove, so daily he had to walk the seven blocks to the Riverside Drive apartment to cook. It would be late morning when he would come out onto the busy street. He would walk north on Columbus Avenue amid the steady flow of pedestrians, pausing at each intersection in the sweeping breeze from the river. Instead of the small-town scenery of Butler, he passed through the rows of thirty-story office buildings on Columbus Avenue. At street level were shoe repair shops, candy stores, laundries, and continental restaurants. The upper stories held the professional suites of doctors, dentists, and lawyers. At Seventy-fifth Street, he would turn west and walk through a neighborhood of brownstone apartments and then across Amsterdam to Broadway, with its center-island park. The greenery here could more accurately be described as "blackery," since it was covered with soot and city grime.

Broadway displayed its produce shops and butcher shops, with their stands extending onto the sidewalk, and old men sat on benches in the thin strip of park between the northbound and southbound traffic. The last block on Seventy-fifth before Riverside Drive held high-rise apartment buildings with doormen standing. Thirty-three Riverside Drive also had a doorman.

Sometimes Prabhupāda would walk in Riverside Park. Still careful for the condition of his heart, he liked the long stretches of flat walking area. Sometimes he would walk from Dr. Mishra's studio down Seventy-second Street to Amsterdam Avenue, to the West End Superette, where he would buy produce and spices for his cooking. Sometimes he would wander through Manhattan, without any fixed direction, and sometimes he would take buses to different areas of the city.

On weekends, Prabhupāda would accompany Dr. Mishra to his Ananda Ashram, one hour north of the city, in Monroe, New York. Joan Suval, who used to drive them, would overhear their animated conversations in the back seat of her car. Although they spoke in Hindi, she could hear their discussions turn into loud, shouting arguments; and afterward they would again become friends.

At Ananda Ashram Prabhupāda would usually hold *kīrtana*, with Dr. Mishra's students joining him in the chanting, and even in dancing. Dr. Mishra was particularly fond of Prabhupāda's chanting.

Ramamurti Mishra: *I have never seen or met any devotee who sang so much. And his* kīrtana *was just ambrosial. If you pay attention and become relaxed, that voice has very electrical vibrations on your heart. You cannot avoid it. Ninety-nine percent of the students, whether they liked it or not, got up and danced and chanted. And I felt very blessed to meet such a great soul.*

Harvey Cohen (a visitor to Ananda Ashram): *Everyone got up early and went to morning meditation. Dr. Mishra was dressed in a golden Indian-style jacket, and his students were already deeply into it when I entered the room. All the cushions were taken, so I picked a spot in the back of the room where I could lean against the wall to facilitate my meditation. Seated at one side was an older Indian man in saffron cloth and wrapped in a pinkish wool blanket. He seemed to be muttering to himself, and I later discovered that he was praying. It was Swami*

Bhaktivedanta. His forehead was painted with a white V-shaped sign, and his eyes were half shut. He seemed very serene.

Harvey tried, but he couldn't do the *rāja-yoga.* He was new to Ananda Ashram and had only come up for a weekend retreat. During his morning meditation, he found himself more attracted to the green mists above the lake outside the window than to the circle on the wall he was supposed to be meditating on.

Harvey: *I went to my room. The rain was increasing and beating against the windows. It was peaceful, and I was glad to be alone. I read for a while. Suddenly I sensed someone standing in the doorway. Looking up, I saw it was the Swami. He was wrapped in his pink blanket, like a shawl. "Can I come in?" he asked. I nodded yes, and he asked if he could sit in the chair in the corner. "What are you reading?" He smiled. "Kafka's* Diaries,*" I replied, feeling a little embarrassed. "Uh," he said, and I put the book down. He asked what I was doing at the* āśrama *and if I was interested in* yoga. *"What kind of* yoga *are you studying?" "I don't know much about it," I answered, "but I think I'd like to study* haṭha-yoga.*" This didn't impress him. "There are better things than this," he explained. "There are higher, more direct forms of* yoga. Bhakti-yoga *is the highest—it is the science of devotion to God."*

As he spoke, I got the overpowering realization that he was right. He was speaking the truth. A creepy ecstatic sensation came over me that this man was my teacher. His words were so simple. And I kept looking at him all weekend. He would sit so calm and dignified with warmth. And he asked me to visit him when we got back to the city.

Dr. Mishra would give lectures carrying the impersonal interpretation of *Bhagavad-gītā* according to Śaṅkara, and Prabhupāda, when allowed to speak, would counter them. Once Prabhupāda asked Dr. Mishra to help him in spreading Lord Caitanya's movement, but Dr. Mishra sidestepped Prabhupāda by saying that he considered Prabhupāda an incarnation of Caitanya Mahāprabhu and therefore not in need of help. Prabhupāda replied that since "Mishra" was also the name of Lord Caitanya's father, Dr. Mishra should help spread Lord Caitanya's movement. Śrīla Prabhupāda offered to engage him in checking the Sanskrit to his translations of *Śrīmad-Bhāgavatam,* but Dr. Mishra declined—a decision he later regretted.

Hurta Lurch (a student at Ananda Ashram): *My direct encounter with him was in the kitchen. He was very particular and very definite that he would only eat what he cooked himself. He would come and say, "Get me a pot." So when I brought him a pot, he'd say, "No, bigger." So I brought a bigger pot, and he'd say, "No, smaller." Then he would say, "Get me potato," so I'd bring him a potato. He prepared food very, very quietly. He never spoke very much. He prepared potatoes and then some vegetables and then* capātīs. *After cooking, he would eat outside. He would usually cook enough to go around for Dr. Mishra and about five or six other people. Every day he would cook that much when he was there. I learned to make* capātīs *from him. He usually stayed only for the weekends and then went back to the city. I think he felt that was where his main work was to be done.*

* * *

That was certainly true, but what could he do there with no money or support? He was thinking of staying for only a few weeks and then going back to India. In the meantime, he was working on his *Śrīmad-Bhāgavatam* manuscripts, walking in Manhattan, and writing letters. He was studying a new culture, calculating practically and imagining hopefully how to introduce Kṛṣṇa consciousness to the Western world. He expressed his thoughts to Sumati Morarji:

October 27

> So far as I have studied, the American people are very much eager to learn about the Indian way of spiritual realization, and there are so many so-called yoga ashrams in America. Unfortunately, they are not very much adored by the government, and it is learned that such yoga ashrams have exploited the innocent people, as has been the case in India also. The only hope is that they are spiritually inclined, and immense benefit can be done to them if the cult of Srimad Bhagwatam is preached here....

Śrīla Prabhupāda noted that the Americans were also giving a good reception to Indian art and music. "Just to see the mode of reception," he attended the performance of a Madrasi dancer, Bala Saraswati.

> I went to see the dance with a friend, although for the last forty years I have never attended such dance ceremonies. The dancer was successful in her demonstration. The music was in Indian classical tune, mostly in Sanskrit language, and the American public appreciated them. So I was encouraged to see the favorable circumstances about my future preaching work.

He said the *Bhāgavatam* could also be preached through music and dance, but he had no means to introduce it. The Christian missions, backed by huge resources, were preaching all over the world, so why couldn't the devotees of Kṛṣṇa combine to preach the *Bhāgavatam* all over the world? He also noted that the Christian missions had not been effective in checking the spread of Communism, whereas a *Bhāgavatam* movement could be, because of its philosophical, scientific approach.

He was deliberately planting a seed of inspiration in the mind of the devoted, wealthy Sumati Morarji.

November 8

Prabhupāda wrote to his Godbrother Tīrtha Mahārāja, who had become president of the Gaudiya Math, to remind him that their spiritual master, Śrīla Bhaktisiddhānta Sarasvatī, had a strong desire to open preaching centers in the Western countries. Śrīla Bhaktisiddhānta had several times attempted to do this by sending *sannyāsīs* to England and other European countries, but, Prabhupāda noted, "without any tangible results."

> I have come to this country with the same purpose in view, and as far as I can see, here in America there is very good scope for preaching the cult of Lord Chaitanya. . . .

Prabhupāda pointed out that there were certain Māyāvādī groups who had buildings but were not attracting many followers. But he had talked with Swami Nikhilananda of the Ramakrishna Mission, who had given the opinion that the Americans were suitable for *bhakti-yoga.*

> I am here and see a good field for work, but I am alone, without men and money. To start a center here, we must have our own buildings. . . .

If the leaders of the Gaudiya Math would consider opening their own branch in New York, Śrīla Prabhupāda would be willing to manage it. But without their own house, he reported, they could not conduct a mission in the city. Śrīla Prabhupāda wrote that they could open centers in many cities throughout the country if his Godbrothers would cooperate. He repeatedly made the point that although other groups did not have the genuine spiritual philosophy of India, they were buying many buildings. The Gaudiya Math, however, had nothing.

> If you agree to cooperate with me as I have suggested above, then I shall extend my visa period. My present visa period ends by the end of this November. But if I receive your confirmation immediately, then I shall extend my visa period. Otherwise, I shall return to India.

* * *

November 9
(6:00 P.M.)

While Prabhupāda sat alone in his fifth-floor room in Dr. Mishra's *yoga* studio, the lights suddenly went out. This was his experience of the first moments of the New York City blackout of 1965. In India, power failure occurred commonly, so Prabhupāda, while surprised to find the same thing in America, remained undisturbed. He began chanting the Hare Kṛṣṇa *mantra* on his beads. Meanwhile, outside his room, the entire New York metropolitan area had been plunged into darkness. The massive power failure had suddenly left the entire city without electricity, trapping 800,000 people in the subways and affecting more than 30,000,000 people in nine states and three Canadian provinces.

Two hours later, a man from Dr. Mishra's apartment arrived at the door with candles and some fruit. He found Prabhupāda in a pleasant mood, sitting there in the darkness chanting Hare Kṛṣṇa. The man informed him of the serious nature of such a blackout in New York City; Prabhupāda thanked him and returned again to his chanting. The blackout lasted until 7:00 the next morning.

Śrīla Prabhupāda received a reply to his letter of November 8 to Tīrtha Mahārāja in Calcutta. Prabhupāda had explained his hopes and plans for staying in America, but he had stressed that his Godbrothers would have to give him their vote of confidence as well as some tangible support. His Godbrothers had not been working cooperatively. Each leader was interested more in maintaining his own building than in working with the others to spread the teachings of Lord Caitanya around the world. So how would it be possible for them to share Śrīla Prabhupāda's vision of establishing a branch in New York City? They would see it as his separate attempt. Yet despite the unlikely odds, he appealed to their missionary spirit and reminded them of the desires of their spiritual master, Śrīla Bhaktisiddhānta Sarasvatī Ṭhākura. Their Guru Mahārāja wanted Kṛṣṇa consciousness to be spread in the West. But when Prabhupāda finally got Tīrtha Mahārāja's reply, he found it unfavorable. His Godbrother did not argue against his attempting something in New York, but he politely said that the Gaudiya Math funds could not be used for such a proposal.

Prabhupāda replied, "It is not very encouraging, still I'm not a man to be disappointed." In fact, he found a little hope in Tīrtha Mahārāja's reply, so he described to his Godbrother the property he had recently found for sale at 143 West Seventy-second Street. The building, only eighteen-and-a-half feet wide and one hundred feet deep, consisted of the first-floor store, a basement, and a mezzanine. Prabhupāda presented Tīrtha Mahārāja the price—$100,000 with a $20,000 cash down payment—and remarked that this building was twice the size of their Research Institute in Calcutta. Prabhupāda conceived of the basement as a kitchen and dining area, the first floor as a lecture hall, and the mezzanine as personal apartments, with a separate area for the Deity of Lord Kṛṣṇa.

Appropriately, Prabhupāda had described himself as "a man not to be disappointed." He was convinced that if there were a center where people could come hear from a pure devotee, the genuine God conscious culture of India could begin in America. Yet because he had made his plans dependent on obtaining an expensive building in Manhattan, his goal seemed unreachable. Still, he was persistently writing to prominent devotees in India, though they were not interested in his plans.

"Why should they not help?" he thought. After all, they were devotees of Kṛṣṇa. Shouldn't the devotees come forward to establish the first Kṛṣṇa temple in America? Certainly he was qualified and authorized to spread the message of Kṛṣṇa. As for the place, New York was perhaps the most cosmopolitan city in the world. He had found a building—not very expensive, a good location—and there was a great need for a Kṛṣṇa temple here to offset the propaganda of the Indian Māyāvādīs. The *kṛṣṇa-bhaktas* to whom he was writing understood Lord Kṛṣṇa to be not simply a Hindu Deity but the Supreme Lord, worshipable for the whole world. So they should be pleased to see Kṛṣṇa worshiped in New York. Kṛṣṇa Himself said in the *Bhagavad-gītā*, "Give up all other duties and surrender to Me." So if they were Kṛṣṇa's devotees, why would they not help? What kind of devotee was it who did not want to glorify the Lord?

But Śrīla Prabhupāda did not judge beforehand who would serve Kṛṣṇa's mission and who would not. He was fully surrendered and fully dependent on Kṛṣṇa, and in obedience to his spiritual master he would approach everyone, without discrimination, to ask for help.

There was Sumati Morarji. She had helped him in publishing the *Bhāgavatam*, and she had sent him to America. In a recent letter to her he had only given hints:

> I am just giving you the idea, and if you kindly think over the matter seriously and consult your beloved Lord Bala Krishna, surely you will be further enlightened in the matter. There is scope and there is certainly necessity also, and it is the duty of every Indian, especially the devotees of Lord Krishna, to take up the matter.

But he had received no reply. He had not heard from her since Butler, though her words to him had seemed prophetic. And they had stuck with him: "I feel that you should stay there until you fully recover from your illness and return only after you have completed your mission."

Now Sumati Morarji must do something big. He told her point-blank:

> I think therefore that <u>a temple of Bala Krishna in New York</u> may immediately be started for this purpose. And as a devotee of Lord Bala Krishna, you should execute this great and noble work. Till now there is no worshipable temple of the Hindus in New York, although in India there are

> so many American missionary establishments and churches. So I shall request you to do this noble act, and it will be recorded in the history of the world that the first Hindu temple is started by a pious Hindu lady SRIMATI SUMATI MORARJI who is not only a big business magnate in India, but a pious Hindu lady and great devotee of Lord Krishna. This task is for you, and glorious at the same time....

He assured her that he had no ambition to become the proprietor of a house or temple in America; but for preaching, a building would be absolutely required:

> They should have association of bona fide devotees of the Lord, they should join the kirtan glorifying the Lord, they should hear the teachings of Srimad Bhagwatam, they should have intimate touch with the temple or place of the Lord, and they should be given ample chance to worship the Lord in the temple. Under the guidance of the bona fide devotee, they can be given such facilities, and the way of the Srimad Bhagwatam is open for everyone....

He informed her that he had located a building "just suitable for this great missionary work." It was ideal, "as if it was built for this purpose only."

> ...and your simple willingness to do the act will complete everything smoothly.
>
> The house is practically three stories. Ground floor, basement, and two stories up, with all the suitable arrangements for gas, heat, etc. The ground floor may be utilized for preparation of prasadam of Bala Krishna, because the preaching center will not be for dry speculation but for actual gain—for delicious prasadam. I have already tested how the people here like the vegetable prasadam prepared by me. They will forget meat-eating and pay for the expenses. American people are not poor men like the Indians, and if they appreciate a thing, they are prepared to spend any amount on such hobby. They are being exploited simply by jugglery of words and bodily gymnastics, and still they are spending for that. But when they will have the actual commodity and feel pleasure by eating very delicious prasadam of Bala Krishna, I am sure a unique thing will be introduced in America.

Now, according to his plans, he had a week left in America.

> My term to stay in America will be finished by the 17th of November, 1965. But I am believing in your foretelling, "You should stay there until you fully recover your health, and return after you have completed your mission."

* * *

TAGORE SOCIETY OF NEW YORK Inc.
CORDIALLY INVITES YOU
to a lecture:
"GOD CONSCIOUSNESS"
by A. C. Bhaktivedanta Swami

Date: Sunday, November 28, 1965
Time: Lecture, 3:30 P.M. Tea, 4:30 P.M.
Place: New India House, 3 East 64th Street

A widely respected scholar and religious leader in India, Swami Bhaktivedanta is briefly visiting New York. He has been engaged in a monumental endeavor of translating the sixty-volume Srimad Bhagwatam from Sanskrit into English.

November 28

Daoud Haroon had never met Śrīla Prabhupāda. He was a musician living downtown, and he used to attend the meetings of the Tagore Society up on Sixty-fourth Street.

Daoud Haroon: *I went uptown and walked into the auditorium, and I noticed that the stage was empty and a few people were sitting toward the rear of the auditorium. I walked forward down the center aisle, because I usually like to sit up front. Then I saw an old gentleman sitting over to the right, and he sort of drew me over to him. So I went over and sat beside him, and then I noticed that he was saying his beads. Even though he had his beads in a bag, I could hear them, and I could see his body moving. And I felt very comfortable, because this was something I was used to.*

As I was sitting there looking around the auditorium, he just turned around and smiled at me very nicely. He nodded his head, and I nodded my head, and he smiled and turned around. Then he turned back to me again and softly asked me if I was from India. I said, "No, sir, I'm not from India. I am from here, the United States." He turned back, and he kept chanting with his beads. Then he turned around the next time and asked if I was a Hindu. I said, "No, sir, I'm not a Hindu. I'm a Muslim." And he said, "Oh, very good, very good. Yes, many times I hear the children in India reciting the Koran." And then he turned back around and his body was moving, rocking, and he was working with his beads.

Then there were a few more exchanges of pleasantries, sort of intermittent. And then a lady came up on the stage and announced that the lecture was to begin and if the folks could give the speaker a round of applause they would welcome him to the stage. At that point, the man I was sitting next to put his hand on my shoulder and said, "Excuse me, sir, could you do me a favor?" And I said, "Yes, anything." He said, "Would you watch over my books?" I looked down on the floor, and he had several boxes of books and an umbrella and several other articles. I said yes I would watch over these. And he said, "Excuse me." He walked up the aisle, and surprisingly, he walked up on the stage. And it was the man I had come to hear—Swami Bhaktivedanta!

He walked up on the stage and introduced himself to the people and tried to get them to come forward. He said, "Come forward, come forward." A few of them came up to the front. There were mixed couples, many Indians, male and female, mostly middle-aged and some college-aged, a lot of professor-types and ladies were there.

Then he began his speech. He dove right into it. He just started exclaiming, proclaiming, the greatness of the Creator and that the most important thing is to remember the Creator and remember God. He began to expand on God consciousness, what God consciousness is and how God is everywhere and how it behooves us all to remember God—no matter what we call Him, what names we call Him by, but that we should call Him. He gave a demonstration which was very moving. He chanted Hare Kṛṣṇa, Hare Rāma and spoke about the power and saving grace in the mantra. *He took a little break about halfway through and had some water.*

The last thing he said as he was coming down from the podium was that he had copies of the Śrīmad-Bhāgavatam. *He explained that he had been working on them and that they came in three volumes and were sixteen dollars. Then he concluded and came down.*

A lot of people went over to him. Some were timid, some were enthusiastic. Some people shook his hand and were asking for books. At first there were about fifteen people gathered around him talking to him and asking questions. With so many people around, he came over to me and said, "Sir, would you do me one more favor? Will you kindly take over the selling of the books? People will be coming to you for the books, so you sell the books and put the money in this little box, and I will be with you in a minute." I said, "Fine."

So while he talked to the people, others came up to me. They must have thought I was somehow his secretary or his traveling companion, and people were coming over to me and asking me personal questions about him, which I couldn't really answer because I didn't know. Some people were buying the books or looking through them. So this went on, and I was trying to listen to him carry on his conversations with people and carry on the book-selling at the same time.

Some of the people were looking for a guru *and trying to find out what he was supposed to be. Some of them were really interrogating him. But he just smiled and answered all their questions simply. I remember he told them, "You will know. There's no pressure. You will know if I am your* guru.*" He suggested that people go over and read the books.*

And then the group dwindled down to about half a dozen, and the few remaining were just looking at him, and some were too timid to approach him. He walked over to them and spoke to them, putting them at ease. Later he came over, and we counted the collection, and I helped him pack up his box and carry downstairs the boxes of books that were left. As we parted he thanked me very much, and I gave him my name and address and phone number and purchased a set of the Śrīmad-Bhāgavatams.

CHAPTER FOUR

"It Will Not Be Possible to Assist You"

I have come here in this old age neither for sightseeing nor for any personal interest. It is for the interest of the entire humanity that I am trying to implement the science of Krishna which will actually make them happy. So it is the duty of every devotee of Lord Krishna to help me by all means.

—from a letter to Sumati Morarji

November passed and December came, and Prabhupāda, having obtained an extension on his visa, stayed on. America seemed so opulent, yet many things were difficult to tolerate. The sirens and bells from fire engines and police cars seemed like they would crack his heart. Sometimes at night he would hear a person being attacked and crying for help. From his first days in the city, he had noted that the smell of dog stool was everywhere. And although it was such a rich city, he could rarely find a mango to purchase, and if he did, it was very expensive and usually had no taste. From his room he would sometimes hear the horns of ocean liners, and he would dream that some day he would sail around the world with a *saṅkīrtana* party, preaching in all the major cities of the world. The weather went below freezing, colder than he had ever experienced in India. Daily he had to walk toward the Hudson against a west wind that even on an ordinary winter's day would take your breath away and make your eyes water and your face grow numb. On a stormy day, the driving wind and sudden gusts could even knock a man down. Sometimes a cold rain would turn the streets slick with ice. The cold would become especially severe as one approached the shelterless, windswept area of West Side Drive, where occasional whirlwinds carried brown leaves and paper trash mysteriously high into the air.

Śrīla Prabhupāda wore a coat Dr. Mishra had given him, but he never gave up wearing his *dhotī,* despite the cold, windy walks. Swami Nikhilananda of the Ramakrishna Mission had advised Prabhupāda that if he wanted to stay in the West he should abandon his traditional Indian dress and strict vegetarianism. Meat-eating and liquor, as well as pants and coat, were almost a necessity in this climate, he had said. Before Prabhupāda had left India, one of his Godbrothers had demonstrated to him how he should eat in the West with a knife and fork. But Prabhupāda never considered taking on Western ways. His advisors cautioned him not to remain an alien but to get into the spirit of American life, even if it meant breaking vows he had held in India; almost all Indian immigrants compromised their old ways. But Prabhupāda's idea was different, and he could not be budged. The others may have had to compromise, he thought, but they had come to beg technological knowledge from the West. "I have not come to beg something," he said, "but to *give* something."

In his solitary wanderings, Śrīla Prabhupāda made acquaintances with a number of local people. There was Mr. Ruben, a Turkish Jew, who worked as a New York City subway conductor. Mr. Ruben met Prabhupāda on a park bench and, being a sociable fellow and a world traveler, sat and talked with the Indian holy man.

Mr. Ruben: *He seemed to know that he would have temples filled up with devotees. He would look out and say, "I am not a poor man, I am rich. There are temples and books, they are existing, they are there, but the time is separating us from them." He always mentioned "we" and spoke about the one who sent him, his spiritual master. He didn't know people at that time, but he said, "I am never alone." He always looked like a lonely man to me. That's what made me think of him like a holy man, Elijah, who always went out alone. I don't believe he had any followers.*

When the weather was not rainy or icy, Prabhupāda would catch the bus to Grand Central Station and visit the central library on Forty-second

Street. His *Śrīmad-Bhāgavatams* were there—some of the same volumes he had sold to the U.S. embassy in New Delhi—and he took pleasure in seeing them listed in the card catalog and learning that they were being regularly checked out and read. He would sometimes walk through U.N. Plaza or walk up to New India House on Sixty-fourth Street, where he had met Mr. Malhotra, a consulate officer. It was through Mr. Malhotra that he had contacted the Tagore Society and had secured an invitation to lecture before one of their meetings back in November.

Riding the bus down Fifth Avenue, he would look out at the buildings and imagine that some day they could be used in Kṛṣṇa consciousness. He would take a special interest in certain buildings: one on Twenty-third Street and one with a dome on Fourteenth Street attracted his attention. He would think of how the materialists had constructed such elaborate buildings and had yet made no provisions for spiritual life. Despite all the great achievements of technology, the people felt empty and useless. They had built these great buildings, but the children were going to LSD.

December 2

New York Times headlines: "New York City Hospitals Report Marked Rise in LSD Cases Admitted for Care." "Protest Against U.S. Participation in Vietnam War Mounts."

The weather grew cold, but there was no snow in December. On Columbus Avenue shops were selling Christmas trees, and the continental restaurants were bright with holiday lighting. On Seventy-second the Retailers' Association erected tall red poles topped with green tinsel Christmas trees. The tops of the trees on both sides of the street sprouted tinsel garlands that spanned the street and joined in red tinsel stars surrounded by colored lights.

Although Śrīla Prabhupāda did no Christmas shopping, he visited many bookstores—Orientalia, Sam Weiser's, Doubleday, the Paragon, and others—trying to sell his *Śrīmad-Bhāgavatams.* Mrs. Ferber, the wife of the Paragon Book Gallery proprietor, considered Prabhupāda "a pleasant and extremely polite small gentleman." The first time he called she wasn't interested in his books, but he tried again, and she took several volumes. Prabhupāda used to stop by about once a week, and since his books were selling regularly, he would collect. Sometimes when he needed copies to sell personally, he would come by and pick them up from Mrs. Ferber, and sometimes he would phone to ask her how his books were selling.

Mrs. Ferber: *Every time he came he would ask for a glass of water. If a customer would make such a request, I would ordinarily say,* "There *is the water cooler.*" *But because he was an old man, I couldn't tell him that, of course. He was very polite always, very modest, and a great scholar. So whenever he would ask, I would fetch him a cup of water personally.*

Once Prabhupāda was talking with Mrs. Ferber about Indian cuisine, and she mentioned that she especially liked *samosās*. The next time he paid her a visit, he brought a tray of *samosās*, which she enjoyed.

* * *

Harvey Cohen came often to room 501 to visit the swami who had so impressed him at Ananda Ashram.

Harvey: *The room he occupied was a tiny office in the back of the Yoga Society in uptown Manhattan. I began to go there regularly, and we sat facing each other on the floor in this little office with his typewriter and a new tape recorder on top of two suitcases. And there was a box of books he had brought from India and a color reproduction of dancing figures which he looked at often. I told Swami Bhaktivedanta that I was an artist, and he asked me to please paint the picture of the dancers, which he explained was of Lord Caitanya and His disciples. The painting was called* "*Saṅkīrtana.*" *Whenever I came to visit him, Swami would always be happy to see me. I told him about myself, and we chanted Hare Kṛṣṇa together in his room many nights that winter. I would get the train uptown from my apartment to go see him.*

* * *

January 11, 1966

Prime Minister Lal Bahadur Shastri died of a heart attack while visiting Russia. The prime minister had been a personal acquaintance of Śrīla Prabhupāda's in India and an admirer of his *Śrīmad-Bhāgavatam* translation. He had been scheduled to visit America, and Prabhupāda had expected to obtain a personal sanction from him for the release of funds from India. His untimely death was a great upset in Śrīla Prabhupāda's plans to purchase the building at 143 West Seventy-second Street. The realtors had shown him the building, and he had already mentally designed the interior for Deity worship and distribution of *prasādam*. The money was to come from India, and Prime Minister Shastri was to give personal sanction for release of the funds. But suddenly that was all changed.

January 14

Prabhupāda decided to write to the owner of the building, Mr. A. M. Hartman. He explained how his plans had been upset, and he posed a new plan.

> Now the Prime Minister, Mr. Lal Bahadur Shastri, is suddenly dead, and I am greatly perplexed. . . . As there is now great difficulty for getting money from India, I am requesting you to allow me to use the place for the International Institution for God Consciousness, at least for some time. The house is lying vacant for so many days without any use, and I learn it that you are paying the taxes, insurance, and other charges for the house, although you have no income from there. If you, however, allow this place for this public institution, you shall at least save the taxes and other charges which you are paying now for nothing.
>
> If I can start the institution immediately, certainly I shall be able to get sympathy locally, and in that case I may not be required to get money from India. I am also requesting that your honor become one of the Directors of this public institution, because you will give a place to start the institution.

A. M. Hartman wasn't interested.

On the same day he wrote Mr. Hartman, Prabhupāda received a letter from Sir Padampat Singhania, the director of the very large JK Organization in India. Prabhupāda had written Sir Padampatji for financial support, and his reply gave him hope. Not only was the Singhania family fabulously wealthy, but its members were devotees of Lord Kṛṣṇa.

> My dear Swamiji,
>
> I have gone through your letter. I am very glad to note your idea of erecting a Shri Radha Krishna temple in New York. I think the proposal is a

good one, but the following are the difficulties:

1. We have got to send foreign exchange for building the temple, for which Government sanction is required. Without the Government sanction, no money can be sent abroad. If the Government of India agrees, then one can think of erecting the temple in New York.
2. I doubt whether with this small amount of Rs. 7 lakhs [$110,000.00] a temple can be built in New York. I mean to carry out a nice construction with Indian type of architecture. To get a temple completed in Indian type of architecture, we have to send a man from India.

These are the two main difficulties, otherwise, your idea is very good.

Śrīla Prabhupāda and Mr. Singhania had a basic disagreement. A magnificent Indian temple in New York would cost many millions of dollars to construct. Prabhupāda knew, of course, that if Padampat Singhania wanted, he could provide millions of dollars. But then how would they get so much money out of India? Prabhupāda therefore again suggested that they spend only seven lakhs. "After purchasing the house," he wrote, "we can build another story upon it with a temple dome, *cakra*, etc." Prabhupāda had his own line of reasoning:

> Lord Dwarkadish exhibited His opulence at Dwarka with 16,000 queens, and it is understood that He built a palace for each and every queen. And the palaces were made with jewels and stones so that there was no necessity for artificial light in the palaces. So your conception of building a temple of Lord Krishna is in opulence. But we are residents of Vrindaban, and Vrindaban has no palaces like your Dwarka. Vrindaban is full of forests and cows on the bank of the Jamuna, and Lord Krishna in His childhood played the part of a cowherd boy without any royal opulence as you people, the inhabitants of Dwarka, are accustomed. So when the Dwarka walas meet the Vrindaban walas, there may be a via media.

With Sir Padampat's Dvārakā-like wealth and Śrīla Prabhupāda's Vṛndāvana-like devotion, Lord Kṛṣṇa, the Lord of both Vṛndāvana and Dvārakā, could be properly worshiped.

January 21

He received Bon Mahārāja's reply. Two weeks before, Prabhupāda had written to his Godbrother, the director of the Institute of Oriental Philosophy in Vṛndāvana, that he had found a place for a temple in New York and that he wanted to install Deities of Rādhā and Kṛṣṇa. In his reply, Bon Mahārāja quoted price estimates for fourteen-inch brass Deities of Rādhā-Kṛṣṇa, but he also warned that to begin Deity worship would be a heavy responsibility. Śrīla Prabhupāda responded:

> I think that after the temple has started, some men, even from America, may be available, as I see they have at the Ramakrishna Mission as well as in so many yoga societies. So I am trying to open a temple here because Srila Prabhupad [Bhaktisiddhānta Sarasvatī] wanted it.

Prabhupāda also requested Bon Mahārāja's assistance in getting the government to sanction release of the money he felt Padampat Singhania would donate. He mentioned that he had carried on an extensive personal correspondence with the vice-president of India, Dr. Radhakrishnan, who was also known to Bon Mahārāja.

> Tell him that it is not an ordinary temple of worship but an international institution for God consciousness based on the Srimad Bhagwatam.

January 22

While Śrīla Prabhupāda prayed to receive Rādhā-Kṛṣṇa in New York, a snowstorm hit the city. That morning, Śrīla Prabhupāda, who had perhaps never before seen snow, woke and thought that someone had whitewashed the side of the building next door. Not until he went outside did he discover that it was snow. The temperature was ten degrees.

The city went into a state of emergency, but Prabhupāda continued his daily walks. Now he had to walk through heavy snow, only a thin *dhotī* beneath his overcoat, his head covered with his "swami hat." The main roads were cleared, but many sidewalks were covered with snow. Along the strip of park dividing Broadway, the gusting winds piled snowbanks to shoulder height and buried the benches. The Broadway kiosks, plastered with layers of posters and notices, were now plastered with additional layers of snow and ice. But despite the weather, New Yorkers still walked their dogs, the pets now wearing raincoats and mackinaws. Such pampering by American dog owners left Prabhupāda with a feeling of surprised amusement. As he approached West End Avenue, he found the doormen blowing whistles to signal taxis as usual, but also scattering salt to melt the ice and create safe sidewalks in front of the buildings. In Riverside Park the benches, pathways, and trees were glazed with ice and gave off a shimmering reflection from the sky.

In the news, Selective Service officials announced the first substantial increase in the draft since the Korean war; a month-long peace ended with the U.S. Air Force bombing North Vietnam; the New York transit strike ended after three weeks, and the transit labor leader died in jail of a heart attack.

January 30

The East Coast was hit by severe blizzards. Seven inches of snow fell on the city, with winds up to fifty miles an hour. The City of New York offered warm rooms and meals for people living in tenements without heat. JFK Airport was closed, as were train lines and roadways into the city. For the second time within eight days, a state of emergency was declared because of snow.

As a lone individual, Śrīla Prabhupāda could not do anything about the snow emergency or the international warfare—he saw these as mere symptoms of the Age of Kali. Always there would be misery in the material world. But if he could bring Rādhā and Kṛṣṇa to a building in New York . . . Nothing was impossible for the Supreme Lord. Even in the midst of Kali-yuga a golden age could appear, and people could get relief. If Americans could take to Kṛṣṇa consciousness, the whole world would follow. Seeing through the eyes of the scriptures, Śrīla Prabhupāda pushed on through the blizzard and pursued the thin trail for support of his Kṛṣṇa consciousness mission.

February 4

He wrote again to Tīrtha Mahārāja, who had agreed to try for the government sanction if he first received written confirmation from a responsible donor pledging the funds for a temple. Prabhupāda informed him that the donor would be Sir Padampat Singhania, and he enclosed Mr. Singhania's favorable letter of the fourteenth. Prabhupāda reminded his Godbrother:

> Srila Prabhupad Bhaktisiddhanta wanted such temples in foreign cities like New York, London, Tokyo, etc., and I had personal talks with him when I first met him at Ulta Danga in 1922. Now here is a chance for me to carry out his transcendental order. I am just seeking your favor and mercy in making this attempt successful.

February 5

Discouragement came to the plans Śrīla Prabhupāda had formed around the promise of support by Padampat Singhania. The Dvārakāvālā wrote to express his dissatisfaction with the Seventy-second Street building.

> I am afraid that I cannot agree with your suggestion that you should buy a small house and erect something on top of it. Unfortunately, such a kind of proposal will not suit me. The temple must be a small one, but it must be constructed properly. I quite agree that you cannot spend a lot of money at present, but within the amount the government may sanction, you should build something according to the architecture of Indian temples. Then only will we be able to create some impression on the American people. This is all I can write to you in this connection. I am very grateful for your taking the trouble of writing me.

Prabhupāda did not take this letter as final. He maintained hope that Sir Padampat Singhania would still give money for the temple, if only the transfer of money could be arranged. He continued writing his Godbrothers and other devotees, asking them to try to secure the government's sanction. He maintained his same aspirations, even though his sole prospective donor had rejected his scheme of a *cakra* and dome atop a conventional two-story building.

* * *

February 15

He moved from room 501 downstairs two floors to a room all his own.

> I have changed my room to Room 307, in the same building as above mentioned, for better air and light. It is on the roadside junction of two roads, the Columbus Avenue and 72nd Street.

According to Dr. Mishra, Prabhupāda moved in order to have his own place, independent of the Mishra Yoga Society.

* * *

February 16

Prabhupāda wrote to the proprietors of the Universal Book House of Bombay, giving some hints for selling his *Śrīmad-Bhāgavatam* in the Bombay area. He explained that he was trying to establish a Rādhā-Kṛṣṇa temple and that "a big industrialist of India has promised to pay for the cost." Since it seemed that he might stay in the United States "for many more days," he wanted the Book House to take increased charge of selling his books throughout India. They were his agent for selling his books in Maharashtra, but now he recommended they take the responsibility in *all* provinces and introduce his books in colleges and universities throughout India. He also requested that they credit his bank account there for the books sold so far.

February 26

Mr. A. P. Dharwadkar of the Universal Book House replied:

> I cannot give you very happy news on the progress of the sale of Srimad Bhagwatam, because the subject is religious and only a small section of society may personally be interested in the books. . . . We tried to push them through some book sellers to Nagpur, Ahmedabad, Poona, etc., but regret to inform you that after some time these book sellers return the books for want of response. As such, we are not only unenthusiastic to agree to your proposal of taking up sales for all India, but we were just thinking of requesting you to nominate some other people in our place to represent your sale program in Maharashtra.

So far, they had sold only six sets of his books, for which they were about to transfer Rs. 172 to his account. This was hardly encouraging to the author. Again, India was not interested. Even in "the land of religion," religious subjects were only for "a small section of society."

March 4

Another reverse. On February 8, Śrīla Prabhupāda had written to India's new prime minister, Indira Gandhi, requesting her to sanction the release of money from India. A reply, dated February 25, New Delhi, came from the prime minister's official secretary, Mr. L. K. Gha.

> Dear Swamiji,
>
> The Prime Minister has seen your letter of February 8, 1966. She appreciates the spirit which prompted you to carry the spiritual message of Srimad Bhagwat Geeta and Srimad Bhagwatam to other countries. Owing to the critical foreign exchange situation which the country is facing, it is greatly regretted that it will not be possible to assist you from here in your plan to set up a Radha Krishna temple.

But Prabhupāda had other hopes. After writing to the prime minister, he had written again to Tīrtha Mahārāja, asking him to request Dr. Radhakrishnan to persuade the government to sanction the release of funds. He waited for one month. No answer.

Apparently his Godbrothers felt little obligation toward preaching in America; he had written that he needed encouragement from them to continue in America, because it was so expensive. He had explained that he was spending the equivalent of one thousand rupees a month. "As such, I am counting every day to receive your favorable replies." But there was no reply.

March 18

He wrote again to Sir Padampat Singhania, requesting him to send a man from India to supervise work on the temple in New York, as Mr. Singhania had previously suggested.

There is no record of any reply to this request.

Prabhupāda wrote again to Sumati Morarji, requesting her to please send him a *mṛdaṅga* to accompany his chanting of the Hare Kṛṣṇa *mantra.* He also requested her that in the future, when he would send many men from India, she oblige by giving them free passage on Scindia Steamship Lines.

No reply.

As his financial situation became more urgent and his hopes more strained, his support from India withdrew in silence. His unanswered correspondence was itself a kind of message, loud and clear: "We cannot help you."

Although no one encouraged him, Śrīla Prabhupāda trusted in the order of his spiritual master and the will of Kṛṣṇa. The word from the prime minister regarding government sanction had been a definite no. But he had received another extension of his visa. Now his last hope was Sir Padampat Singhania. Prabhupāda knew that he was so influential a man in India that if he wanted he could send the money. He was Prabhupāda's final hope.

April 2

Mr. Singhania did not reply personally. He had his secretary, Mr. Easwara Iyer, write to Prabhupāda, thoroughly discouraging his last hopes for purchasing a building in New York.

> I regret to write that Sir Padampatji is not interested in the scheme of building a Radha Krishna temple in New York at present. In regard to the inquiry contained in the last paragraph of your letter, Sir Padampatji duly received your books of Srimad Bhagwatam from your Delhi office. Yours faithfully.

* * *

Seeing him from a distance—a tiny figure walking Manhattan's streets and avenues among many other tiny figures, a foreigner whose visa had almost run out—we come upon only the external appearance of Śrīla Prabhupāda. These days of struggle were real enough and very difficult, but his transcendental consciousness was always predominant. He was not living in Manhattan consciousness, but was absorbed in dependence upon Kṛṣṇa, just as when on the *Jaladuta* he had suffered his heart attacks, his reading of *Caitanya-caritāmṛta* had supplied him "the nectarine of life."

He had already succeeded. Certainly he wanted to provide Rādhā and Kṛṣṇa a temple in New York, but his success was that he was remembering Kṛṣṇa, even in New York City in the winter of 1965–66, whether the world recognized him or not. Not a day went by when he did not work on Kṛṣṇa's book, *Śrīmad-Bhāgavatam.* And not a day went by when he did not offer food to Kṛṣṇa and speak on Kṛṣṇa's philosophy of *Bhagavad-gītā.*

Lord Kṛṣṇa says in *Bhagavad-gītā*, "For one who sees Me everywhere and sees everything in Me, I am never lost to him, and he is never lost to Me." And Kṛṣṇa assures His pure devotees that, "My devotee will never be vanquished." There was never any doubt about this for Prabhupāda. The only question was whether Americans would take notice of the pure devotee in their midst. At this point it seemed that no one was going to take him seriously.

CHAPTER FIVE

Free to Preach

Here I am now sitting in New York, the world's greatest city, such a magnificent city, but my heart is always hankering after that Vṛndāvana. I shall be very happy to return to my Vṛndāvana, that sacred place. But then, "Why are you here?" Now, because it is my duty. I have brought some message for you people. Because I have been ordered by my superior, my spiritual master: "Whatever you have learned, you should go to the Western countries, and you must distribute this knowledge." So in spite of all my difficulties, all my inconveniences, I am here. Because I am obligated by duty.

—from a lecture by Śrīla Prabhupāda

Room 307 was never meant for use as a residence or *āśrama* or lecture hall. It was only a small, narrow office without furniture or a telephone. It's door held a large pane of frosted glass, the kind common in old offices; above the door was a glass-paned transom. Prabhupāda placed his blankets on the floor before his metal footlocker, which now became a makeshift desk where he wrote. He slept on the floor. There were no facilities here for cooking or even for bathing, so daily he had to walk to Dr. Mishra's apartment.

When he had lived in room 501 at Dr. Mishra's *yoga āśrama*, Dr. Mishra had financed his needs. But now Prabhupāda was on his own, and whatever he could raise by selling his books, he would have to use for his daily maintenance and for the monthly rent of seventy-two dollars. He noted that for a little powdered chili the West End Superette charged twenty-five cents, ten times what he would have paid in India. He had no guaranteed income, his expenses had increased, and his physical comforts had reduced. But at least he had his own place. Now he was free to preach as he liked.

He had come to America to speak about Kṛṣṇa, and even from the beginning he had found the opportunity to do so, whether at an informal get-together in the Agarwals' living room or before a formal gathering at the Butler Lions Club, Dr. Norman Brown's Sanskrit class, Dr. Mishra's Yoga Society, or the Tagore Society. But he did not attach much importance to lecturing where the people who gathered would hear him only once. This was the main reason he wanted his own building in New York: so that people could come *regularly*, chant Hare Kṛṣṇa, take *prasādam* in his company, and hear him speak from *Bhagavad-gītā* and *Śrīmad-Bhāgavatam.*

Moving out of the *yoga* studio into the small office downstairs gave Prabhupāda what he was looking for—his own place—but not even euphemistically could that place be called a temple. His name was on the door; anyone seeking him there could find him. But who would come there? By its opulence and beauty, a temple was supposed to attract people to Kṛṣṇa. But room 307 was just the opposite: it was bare poverty. Even a person interested in spiritual topics would find it uncomfortable to sit on the rugless floor of a room shaped like a narrow railroad car.

One of Dr. Mishra's students had donated a reel-to-reel tape recorder, and Prabhupāda recorded some of his solitary *bhajanas*, which he sang to his own accompaniment of hand cymbals. He also recorded a long philosophical essay, *Introduction to Gītopaniṣad.* "Even if no one attends," Śrīla Bhaktisiddhānta Sarasvatī had told him, "you can go on chanting to the four walls." But since he was now free to speak his message in the new situation God had provided, he decided to lecture three evenings a week (Monday, Wednesday, and Friday) to whoever would come.

His first audiences consisted mainly of people who had heard about him or met him at Dr. Mishra's *yoga* studio. And despite the poverty of his room, the meetings became a source of new life for him.

March 18

He expressed his optimism in a letter to Sumati Morarji:

> I was very much encouraged when you wrote to say, "I feel that you should stay there until you fully recover from your illness, and return only after you have completed your mission." I think these lines dictated by you are the words of Lord Bala Krishna expressed through your goodness.
>
> You will be pleased to know that I have improved my health back to normal, and my missionary work is nicely progressing. I hope my project to start a temple of Sri Sri Radha Krishna will also be realized by the grace of the Lord.
>
> Since I came to New York from Butler, Pennsylvania, I have rented the above room at seventy dollars per month, and am delivering lectures on the Bhagwat Geeta and Srimad Bhagwatam, accompanied by sankirtan, and the American ladies and gentlemen come to hear me. You will be surprised to know that they do not understand the language of sankirtan, yet they hear with attention. The movement which I have started here is completely new to them, because the Americans are generally acquainted with the Indian yoga gymnastics as performed by some Indian yogis here. They have never heard of the bhakti cult of the science of Krishna before, and still they are hearing me. This is a great success for me.

* * *

Outside the closed windows of room 307, the late winter night has fallen. Prabhupāda's words are punctuated with the muted sounds of car horns and occasional sirens from the street, and sometimes by the startling chords of a lonely foghorn on the Hudson. Although bare, the room is warm. Prabhupāda is speaking on the Second Chapter of *Bhagavad-gītā.*

Now Arjuna is perplexed. He is perplexed about whether to fight or not to fight. After seeing in front of him his relatives with whom he was to fight, he was perplexed. And there was some argument with Kṛṣṇa.

Now here is a point: Kṛṣṇa is the Supreme Personality of Godhead. . . .

Prabhupāda's voice is earnest, persuading. Sometimes his speech becomes high-pitched and breaks with urgency. His cultured British diction bears a heavy Bengali accent.

Suddenly he pauses in his lecture and addresses someone in the room.

Prabhupāda: *What is that?*

Man: *What?*

Prabhupāda: *What is this book?*

Man: *Well, this is a translation of the* Bhagavad-gītā.

Prabhupāda is obviously displeased that while he is speaking someone is looking through a book. This is hardly like the respect offered to learned speakers described in the *Śrīmad-Bhāgavatam.*

Prabhupāda: *Well, no, you can hear me.*

Man: *I* am *hearing.*

Prabhupāda: *Yes, don't turn your attention. Just hear me.*

He is taking the role of a teacher correcting his student. Of course, there is no compelling reason why any of his casual guests should feel obliged to obey him. He simply begs for their attention, and yet demands it—"Just hear me"—as he attempts to convince them of Kṛṣṇa consciousness.

You have heard that one must accept the spiritual master after careful examination, just as one selects a bride or a bridegroom after careful examination. In India they are very careful. Because the marriage of boys and girls takes place under the guidance of the parents, so the parents very carefully see to it. Similarly, one has to accept the spiritual master. It is necessary. According to Vedic injunctions, everyone should have a spiritual master. Perhaps you have seen a sacred thread. We have got sacred thread. Mr. Cohen? You have seen? Sacred thread.

Prabhupāda pauses. His audience has not noted the thin, white cords he wears beneath his shirt across the upper part of his body. For thousands of years, *brāhmaṇas* in India have worn such threads, placed diagonally across the torso, looped over the left shoulder and down to the right waist. A *brāhmaṇa* holds his thread in his right hand while chanting the sacred Gāyatrī *mantra* three times a day. But this is all strange indeed to Americans. Prabhupāda himself is exotic to them. His gray *chādar* wrapped around his shoulders, he sits cross-legged and erect on a thin pillow, and they sit facing him on the other side of his trunk, which now serves as a desk and lectern. They are close together in the narrowness of the room. He is frail and small and foreign to them, yet somehow he is completely assured, in a way that has nothing to do with being a foreigner in New York. Visitors sense his strong presence. Two white lines of clay run neatly vertical on his forehead. His pale peach clothes are gathered in loose folds around his body. He pauses only a few seconds to inquire whether they have seen a sacred thread.

That sacred thread is a sign that a person has a spiritual master. Here, of course, there is no such distinction, but according to the Hindu system a married girl also has some sign so that people can understand that this girl is married. She wears a red mark so that others may know that she is married. And according to the division in the hair... what is this line called?

Man: *Part.*

Prabhupāda: *Hmm?*

Man: *Part.*

Prabhupāda: *What is the spelling?*

Man: *Part.*

Prabhupāda: *Part. This parting also has some meaning.* (They know English, and he knows the *Gītā*. But he knows a good deal of English, whereas they know practically nothing of the *Gītā*, which he has to spoon-feed to them. But occasionally he asks their help in English vocabulary.) *When the part is in the middle, then the girl has her husband, and she is coming from a respectable family. And if the part is here, then she is a prostitute.* (With a slight gesture he raises his hand toward, but never really reaching, his head. Yet somehow the half-gesture clearly indicates a part on the side of the head.) *And then again when a girl is well dressed, it should be understood that she has her husband at home. And when she is not well dressed, it is to be understood that her husband is away from home. You see? And a widow's dress... There are so many symptoms. So, similarly, the sacred thread is a sign that a person has accepted a spiritual master, just as the red mark symbolizes that a girl has a husband.*

Although his audience may be momentarily enamored by what appears to be a description of Indian social customs, a careful listener can grasp the greater context of Prabhupāda's speech: Everyone must accept a spiritual master. It's a heavy topic for a casual audience. What is the need of taking a spiritual master? Isn't this just for India? But he says, "Everyone should have a spiritual master." What is a spiritual master anyway? Maybe he means that accepting a spiritual master is just another cultural item from Hinduism, like the thread, or the part in a woman's hair, or the widow's dress. The audience can easily regard his discussion as a kind of cultural exposition, just as one comfortably watches a film about the living habits of people in a foreign land although one has no intention of adopting these habits as one's own. The Swami is wearing one of those threads on his body, but that's for Hindus, and it doesn't mean that Americans should wear them. But these Hindu beliefs are interesting.

Actually, Prabhupāda has no motive but to present the Absolute Truth as he has heard it in disciplic succession. But if anyone in that railroad-car-shaped room were to ask himself, "Should I surrender to a spiritual master?" he would be confronted by the existential presence of a genuine *guru.* One is free to regard his talk as one likes.

*In every step of one's life, the spiritual master guides. Now, to give such guidance a spiritual master should also be a very perfect man. Otherwise how can he guide? Now, here Arjuna knows that Śrī Kṛṣṇa is the perfect person. So therefore he is accepting Him—*śiṣyas te 'haṁ śādhi māṁ tvāṁ prapannam.

Sanskrit! No one knows a word of it! But there is never any question for Śrīla Prabhupāda—even if they don't understand it, the transcendental sound of *śāstra* will purify them. It is his authority, and he cannot omit it. And even at first impression, it presents an air of scholarly authority—the original, though foreign, words of the sages.

"I am just surrendering unto You, and You accept me as Your disciple," Arjuna says. Friendly talks cannot make a solution to perplexity. Friendly talks may be going on for years together, but no solution. So here, Arjuna accepts Kṛṣṇa as the spiritual master. This means that whatever Kṛṣṇa will decide, he has to accept. One cannot deny the order of the spiritual master. Therefore, one has to select a spiritual master by whose orders one will not commit a mistake.

Suppose you accept the wrong person as spiritual master and he guides you wrongly. Then your whole life is spoiled. So one has to accept a spiritual master whose guidance will make one's life perfect. That is the relationship between spiritual master and disciple. It is not a formality. It is a great responsibility, both for the disciple and for the spiritual master.

And . . . Yes?

Student: *But if the disciple is in ignorance before . . .*

Prabhupāda: *Yes.* (Prabhupāda acknowledges a serious question. It is for answering questions like this—from "disciples in ignorance"—that he has left retirement in India and come to America.)

Student: . . . *how does he know which master to choose?—because he doesn't have the knowledge to make a wise decision.*

Prabhupāda: *Yes. So the first thing is that one should be searching after a spiritual master, just as you search after some school. You must at least have some preliminary knowledge of what a school is. You can't search for a school and go to a cloth shop. If you are so ignorant that you do not know what is a school and what is a cloth shop, then it is very difficult for you. You must know at least what a school is. So that knowledge is like this:*

> tad-vijñānārthaṁ sa gurum evābhigacchet
> samit-pāṇiḥ śrotriyaṁ brahma-niṣṭham

According to this verse, the spiritual master is required for a person who is inquisitive about transcendental knowledge. There's another verse in the Śrīmad-Bhāgavatam: tasmād guruṁ prapadyeta jijñāsuḥ śreya uttamam. *"One should search after a spiritual master if one is inquisitive about transcendental subject matters." Unless one is at least conversant with preliminary knowledge of transcendental matters, how can he inquire from the spiritual master?*

His questioner seems satisfied. The lecture is not a prepared speech on a specific subject. Though grave and thorough in scholarship, it ranges over several philosophical points. Yet he never pauses, groping for words. He knows exactly what he wants to say, and it is only a question of how much his audience can take.

But sometimes his mood is light, and he commiserates with his fellow New Yorkers, chuckling about the difficulties they share: "Suppose there is a heavy snowfall, the whole New York City is flooded with snow, and you are all put into inconvenience. That is a sort of suffering, but you have no control over it." Sometimes he praises Dr. Mishra's students for having learned so nicely from their teacher: "Now, what Dr. Mishra is teaching is very nice. He is teaching that first of all you must know, 'Who am I?' That is very good, but that 'Who am I?' can be known from *Bhagavad-gītā* also—'I am not this body.' " And sometimes a guest suddenly speaks out with an irrelevant question, and the Swami patiently tries to consider it.

Yet behind his tolerance, Prabhupāda's mood is always one of urgency. Sometimes he talks quickly, and one senses his desire to establish Kṛṣṇa consciousness in the West as soon as possible. He has no followers, only a few books, no temples, and he openly states that he is racing against time: "I am an old man. I could leave at any time." So behind the formal delivery of Kṛṣṇa conscious philosophy is an anxiety, an almost desperate desire to convince at least one soul to take up Kṛṣṇa consciousness. Immediately.

Now the constrained situations of Butler and the Ananda Ashram and Dr. Mishra are behind him. He is free to speak about the Absolute Truth in full. Throughout his life he has prepared for this, yet he is still discovering the best ways to present Kṛṣṇa, exploring his Western audience, testing their reactions.

We should always remember that He is God. He is all-powerful. In strength, no one could conquer Him. In beauty—as far as beauty is concerned, when He was on the battlefield . . . Have any of you seen a picture of Kṛṣṇa? Have you seen? Have any of you ever seen Kṛṣṇa? Oh. . . . No?

Prabhupāda's voice fades as he pauses, looking out at his audience. No one has ever seen Kṛṣṇa. None of them have the slightest previous knowledge of Lord Kṛṣṇa. In India, hundreds of millions worship Lord Kṛṣṇa daily as the eternal form of all beauty and truth and view His graceful form in sculpture, painting, and dance. His philosophical teachings in *Bhagavad-gītā* are all-famous, and Prabhupāda is His intimate emissary. Yet the ladies and gentlemen in room 307 look back at the Swami blankly.

Prabhupāda is discussing the real meaning of going to a sacred place in India.

One should go to a sacred place in order to find some intelligent scholar in spiritual knowledge living there and make association with him. Just like I . . . my residence is at Vṛndāvana. So at Vṛndāvana there are many big scholars and saintly persons living. So one should go to such holy places, not simply to take bath in the water. One must be intelligent enough to find some spiritually advanced man living there and take instruction from him and be benefited by that. If a man has attachment for going to a place of pilgrimage to take a bath but has no attraction for hearing from learned people there, he is considered to be an ass. (He laughs.) Sa eva go-kharaḥ. Go *means "cow," and* khara *means "ass." So the whole civilization is moving like a civilization of cows and asses. Everyone is identifying with the body. . . . Yes, you want to speak?*

Woman: *In the places known as secret places—*

Prabhupāda: *Sacred. Yes.*

Woman: *Is it "sacred" places?*

Prabhupāda: *Yes.*

Woman: *Isn't it also a fact that there is more magnetism because of the meeting of saints and more advanced people?*

Prabhupāda: *Oh, yes, certainly. Certainly. Therefore the place itself has got some magnetism.*

Woman: *Yes, and when—*

Prabhupāda: *Just like at Vṛndāvana—that is practical. Here I am now sitting in New York, the world's greatest city, such a magnificent city, but my heart is always hankering after that Vṛndāvana.*

Woman: *Yes.* (Laughs.)

Prabhupāda: *Yes. I am not happy here.*

Woman: *Yes, I know.*

Prabhupāda: *I shall be very happy to return to my Vṛndāvana, that sacred place. But then, "Why are you here?" Now, because it is my duty. I have brought some message for you people. Because I have been ordered by my superior, my spiritual master: "Whatever you have learned you should go to the Western countries, and you must distribute this knowledge." So in spite of all my difficulties, all my inconveniences, I am here. Because I am obligated by duty. If I go and sit down in Vṛndāvana, that will be good for my personal conveniences—I shall be very comfortable there, and I will have no anxiety, nothing of the sort. But I have taken all the risk in this old age because I am duty-bound. I am duty-bound. So I have to execute my duty, despite all my inconveniences.*

An outsider opens the door and hesitantly glances inside.

Prabhupāda (stopping his lecture): *Yes, yes, come in. You can come here.*

* * *

Robert Nelson was like a slow, simple country boy with a homespun manner, even though he had grown up in New York City. He was twenty years old. He wasn't part of the growing hippie movement, he didn't take marijuana or other drugs, and he didn't socialize much. He was a loner. He had gotten some technical education at Staten Island Community College and had tried his hand at the record manufacturing business, but without much success. He was interested in God and would attend various spiritual meetings around the city. So one night he wandered into the Yoga Society to hear Dr. Mishra's lecture, and there he saw Prabhupāda for the first time.

Robert: *Swami was sitting cross-legged on a bench. There was a meeting, and Dr. Mishra was standing up before a group of people—there were about fifty people coming there—and he talked on "I Am Consciousness." Dr. Mishra talked and then gave Swami a grand introduction with a big smile. "Swamiji is here," he said. And he swings around and waves his hand for a big introduction. It was beautiful. This was after Dr. Mishra spoke for about an hour. The Swami didn't speak. He sang a song.*

Afterward, I went up to him. He had a big smile, and he said that he likes young people to take to Kṛṣṇa consciousness. He was very serious about it. He wanted all young people. So I thought that was very nice. It made sense. So I wanted to help.

We stood there talking for about an hour. Mishra had a library in the back, and we looked at certain books—Arjuna, Kṛṣṇa, chariots, and things. And then we walked around. We looked at some of the pictures of swamis on the wall. By that time it was getting very late, and Prabhupāda said come back the next day at ten to his office downstairs.

The next day, when Robert Nelson went to room 307, Prabhupāda invited him in. The room was clearly not intended to serve as a living quarters—there was no toilet, shower, chair, bed, or telephone. The walls were painted "a dark, dismal color." Prabhupāda showed Robert the three-volume set of *Śrīmad-Bhāgavatam*, which Robert purchased for $16.50. Then Prabhupāda handed him a small piece of paper with the Hare Kṛṣṇa *mantra* printed on it.

Robert: *While Swamiji was handing it to me, he had this big smile on his face like he was handing me the world.*

We spent the whole day together. At one point he said, "We are going to take a sleep." So he lay down there by his little desk, and so I said, "I am tired too." So I lay down at the other end of the room, and we rested. I just lay on the floor. It was the only place to do it. But he didn't rest that long—an hour and a half, I think—and we spent the rest of the day together. He was talking about Lord Caitanya and the Lord's pastimes, and he showed me a small picture of Lord Caitanya. Then he started talking about the devotees of Lord Caitanya—Nityānanda and Advaita. He had a picture of the five of them and a picture of his spiritual master. He said some things in Sanskrit, and then he translated. It wasn't much of a room, though. You'd really be disappointed if you saw it.

Robert Nelson couldn't give Prabhupāda the kind of assistance he needed. Lord Caitanya states that a person has at his command four assets—his life, money, intelligence, and words—at least one of which he should give to the service of God. Robert Nelson did not seem able to give his whole life to Kṛṣṇa consciousness, and as for money, he had very little. His intelligence was also limited, and he spoke unimpressively, nor did he have a wide range of friends or contacts among whom to speak. But he was affectionate toward the Swami, and out of the eight million people in the city, he was practically the only one who showed personal interest in him and offered to help.

From his experience in the record business, Mr. Robert, as Swamiji called him, developed a scheme to produce a record of Swamiji's singing. People were always putting out albums with almost anything on them, he explained, and they would always make money, or at least break even. So it would be almost impossible to lose money. It was a way he thought he could help make the Swami known, and he tried to convince Prabhupāda of the idea. And Prabhupāda didn't discourage Mr. Robert, who seemed eager to render this service.

Robert: *Me and the Swami went around to this record company on Forty-sixth Street. We went there, and I started talking, and the man was all business. He was all business and mean—they go together. So we went in there with a tape, and we tried talking to the man. Swami was talking, but the man said he couldn't put the tape out. I think he listened to the tape, but he wouldn't put it out. So we felt discouraged. But he didn't say much about it.*

Prabhupāda had been in business in India, and he wasn't about to think that he could suddenly take up business in a foreign country on the advice of a young boy in New York City. Besides, he had come not to do business but to preach. Robert, however, was enthusiastically offering service. Perhaps he wouldn't become a regular *brahmacārī* student, but he had a desire to serve Kṛṣṇa. For Prabhupāda to refuse him would be perhaps to turn away an interested Western young person. Prabhupāda had come to speak about Kṛṣṇa, to present the chanting, and if Mr. Robert wanted to help by arranging for an American record album, then that was welcome.

Mr. Robert and the Swami made an odd combination. Prabhupāda was elderly and dignified, a deep scholar of the *Bhāgavatam* and the Sanskrit language, whereas Robert Nelson was artless, even in Western culture, and inept in worldly ways. Together they would walk—the Swami wearing his winter coat (with its imitation fur collar), his Indian *dhotī*, and white, pointed shoes; Mr. Robert wearing old khaki pants and an old coat. Prabhupāda walked with rapid, determined strides, outpacing the lumbering, rambling, heavyset boy who had befriended him.

Mr. Robert was supposed to help Prabhupāda in making presentations to businessmen and real estate men, yet he himself was hardly a slick fellow. He was innocent.

Robert: *Once we went over to this big office building on Forty-second Street, and we went in there. The rent was thousands of dollars for a whole floor. So I was standing there talking to the man, but I didn't understand how all this money would come. The Swami wanted a big place, and I didn't know what to tell the man.*

Prabhupāda wanted a big place, and a big place meant a big price. He had no money, and Robert Nelson had only his unemployment checks. Still, Prabhupāda was interested. If he were to find a building, that would be a great step in his mission. And this was also another way of engaging Mr. Robert. Besides, Kṛṣṇa might do anything, give anything, or work in any way—ordinary or miraculous. So Prabhupāda had his reasoning, and Mr. Robert had his.

Robert: *The building was between Sixth and Broadway on Forty-second Street. Some place to open Kṛṣṇa's temple! We went in and up to the second floor and saw the renting agent, and then we left. I think it was five thousand a month or ten thousand a month. We got to a certain point, and the money was too much. And then we left. When he brought up the prices, I figured we had better not. We had to stop.*

On another occasion, Robert Nelson took Prabhupāda by bus to the Hotel Columbia, at 70 West Forty-sixth Street. The hotel had a suite that Prabhupāda looked at for possible use as a temple, but again it was very expensive. And there was no money.

Sometimes Robert would make purchases for Prabhupāda with the money from his unemployment checks. Once he bought orange-colored T-shirts. Once he went to Woolworth's and bought kitchen pots and pans and some picture frames for Prabhupāda's pictures of Lord Caitanya and his spiritual master.

Robert: *One time I wanted to know how to make* capātī *cakes, so Swami says, "A hundred dollars please, for the recipe. A hundred dollars please." So I went and got some money, but I couldn't get a hundred dollars. But he showed me anyway. He taught me to cook and would always repeat, "Wash hands, wash hands," and, "You should only eat with your right hand."*

And whoever met the Swami was almost always impressed. They would start smiling back to him, and sometimes they would say funny things to each other that were nice. The Swami's English was very technical always. I mean, he had a big vocabulary. But sometimes people had a little trouble understanding him, and you had to help sometimes.

* * *

The Paradox, at 64 East Seventh Street on the Lower East Side, was a restaurant dedicated to the philosophy of Georges Ohsawa and the macrobiotic diet. It was a storefront below street level with small dining tables placed around the candlelit room. The food was inexpensive and well reputed. Tea was served free, as much as you liked. More than just a restaurant, the Paradox was a center for spiritual and cultural interests, a meeting place reminiscent of the cafes of Greenwich Village or Paris in the 1920s. A person could spend the whole day at the Paradox without buying anything, and no one would complain. The crowd at the Paradox was a mystical congregation, interested in teachings from the East. When news of the new swami uptown at Dr. Mishra's reached the Paradox, the word spread quickly.

Harvey Cohen and Bill Epstein were friends. Harvey was a free-lance artist, and Bill worked at the Paradox. After Harvey had been to Prabhupāda's place at Dr. Mishra's *yoga* studio a few times, he came by the Paradox and began to describe all about the new swami to Bill and other friends.

Bill: *I was working at the Paradox one night, when Harvey came to me and said, "I went to visit Mishra, and there's a new swami there, and he's really fantastic!" Well, I was involved in macrobiotics and Buddhism, so at first I couldn't care less. But Harvey was a winning and warm personality, and he seemed interested in this. He said, "Why don't you come uptown? I would like you to see this."*

So I went to one of the lectures on Seventy-second Street. I walked in there, and I could feel a certain presence from the Swami. He had a certain very concentrated, intense appearance. He looked pale and kind of weak. I guess he had just come here and he had been through a lot of things. He was sitting there chanting on his beads, which he carried in a little bead bag. One of Dr. Mishra's students was talking, and he finally got around to introducing the Swami. He said, "We are the moons to the Swami's sun." He introduced him in that way. The Swami got up and talked. I didn't know what to think about it. At that time, the only steps I had taken in regard to Indian teaching were through Ramakrishna, but this was the first time, to my knowledge, that bhakti *religion had come to America.*

Bill Epstein, quite in contrast to Robert Nelson, was a dashing, romantic person, with long, wavy dark hair and a beard. He was good-looking and effervescent and took upon himself a role of informing people at the restaurant of the city's spiritual news. Once he became interested in the new swami, he made the Swami an ongoing topic of conversation at the restaurant.

Bill: *I went in the back, and I asked Richard, the manager, "I'm going to take some food to the Swami. You don't mind, do you?" He said, "No. Take anything you want." So I took some brown rice and other stuff, and I brought it up there.*

I went upstairs, and I knocked on the door, and there was no answer. I knocked again, and I saw that the light was on—because it had a glass panel—and finally he answered. I was really scared, because I had never really accepted any teacher. He said, "Come in! Come in! Sit down." We started talking, and he said to me, "The first thing that people do when they meet is to show each other love. They exchange names, they exchange something to eat." So he gave me a slice of apple, and he showed me the tape recorder he had, probably for recording his chants. Then he said, "Have you ever chanted?" I said, "No, I haven't chanted before." So he played a chant, and then he spoke to me some more. He said, "You must come back." I said, "Well, if I come back I'll bring you some more food."

James Greene, a thirty-year-old carpentry teacher at Cooper Union, was delving into Eastern philosophy. He lived on the same block as the Paradox and began hearing about the Swami from Harvey Cohen and Bill Epstein while regularly taking his evening meal at the restaurant.

James: *It was really Harvey and Bill who got things going. I remember one evening at Mishra's in which Swamiji was only a presence but did not speak. Mishra's students seemed more into the bodily aspect of* yoga. *This seemed to be one of Swamiji's complaints.*

His room on Seventy-second Street was quite small. He was living in a fairly narrow room with a door on the one end. Swamiji would set himself up along one side, and we were rather closely packed. It may have been no more than eight feet wide, and it was rather dim. He sat on his thin mattress, and then we sat on the floor.

We wouldn't chant. We would just come, and he would lecture. There was no direction other than the lecture on the Bhagavad-gītā. *I had read a lot of literature, and in my own shy way I was looking for a master, I think. I have no aggression in me or go-getting quality. I was really just a listener, and this seemed right—hearing the* Bhagavad-gītā*—so I kept coming. It just seemed as if things would grow from there. More and more people began coming. Then it got crowded, and he had to find another place.*

The new group from the Paradox was young and hip, in contrast to the older, more conservative uptown people who had been attending Prabhupāda's classes. In those days, it was still unusual to see a person with long hair and a beard, and when such people started coming to the

Swami's meetings on the West Side, some of the older people were alarmed. As one of them noted: "Swami Bhaktivedanta began to pick up another kind of people. He picked them up at the Bowery or some attics. And they came with funny hats and gray blankets wrapped around themselves, and they startled me."

David Allen, a twenty-one-year-old seeker who came up from the Paradox, had just moved to the city, optimistically attracted by what he had read about experimentation with drugs. He saw the old group as "a kind of fussbudgety group of older women on the West Side" listening to the Swami's lectures.

David: *We weren't known as hippies then. But it was strange for the people who had originally been attracted to him. It was different for them to relate to this new group. I think most of the teachers from India up to that time had older followers, and sometimes wealthy widows would provide a source of income. But Swamiji changed right away to the younger, poorer group of people. The next thing that happened was that Bill Epstein and others began talking about how it would be better for the Swami to come downtown to the Lower East Side. Things were really happening down there, and somehow they weren't happening uptown. People downtown really needed him. Downtown was right, and it was ripe. There was life down there. There was a lot of energy going around.*

CHAPTER SIX

On the Bowery

I couldn't understand the difference between friends and enemies. My friend was shocked to hear that I was moving to the Bowery, but although I passed through many dangers, I never thought that, "This is danger." Everywhere I thought, "This is my home."

—Śrīla Prabhupāda in conversation

April, 1966

Someone broke into room 307 while Śrīla Prabhupāda was out and stole his typewriter and tape recorder. When Prabhupāda returned to the building, the janitor informed him of the theft: an unknown burglar had broken the transom glass, climbed through, taken the valuables, and escaped. As Prabhupāda listened, he became convinced that the janitor himself was the culprit. Of course, he couldn't prove it, so he accepted the loss with disappointment. Some friends offered replacements for his old typewriter and tape recorder.

In a letter to India, he described the theft as a loss of more than one thousand rupees ($157.00).

It is understood that such crime as has been committed in my room is very common in New York. This is the way of material nature. American people have everything in ample, and the worker gets about Rs. 100 as daily wages. And still there are thieves for want of character. The social condition is not very good.

Prabhupāda had told Joseph Foerster, the Scindia ticket agent, that he would be returning to India in a couple of months. That was seven months ago. Now, for the first time since his arrival, Prabhupāda had returned to the Scindia ticket office in Brooklyn. He talked about the theft to Mr. Foerster, who responded with, "Welcome to the club," and told Prabhupāda about the recent theft of his own automobile. Such things, he explained, were not unusual for New York City. He told Prabhupāda of the dangers of the city and how to avoid thefts and muggings. Prabhupāda listened, shaking his head. He told Mr. Foerster that American young people were misguided and confused. He discussed his plans for returning to India and showed Mr. Foerster one of his *Bhāgavatams.*

Prabhupāda had lost his spirit for living in room 307. What would prevent the janitor from stealing again? Harvey Cohen and Bill Epstein had advised him to relocate downtown and had assured him of a more interested following among the young people there. It had been an attractive proposal, and he began to reconsider it. Then Harvey offered Prabhupāda his studio on the Bowery.

Harvey had been working as a commercial artist for a Madison Avenue advertising firm when a recently acquired inheritance had spurred him to move into a loft on the Bowery to pursue his own career as a painter. But he was becoming disillusioned with New York. A group of acquaintances addicted to heroin had been coming around and taking advantage of his generosity, and his loft had recently been burglarized. He decided to leave the city and go to California, but before leaving he offered his loft for Prabhupāda to share with David Allen.

David Allen had heard that Harvey Cohen was moving to San Francisco if he could sublet his A.I.R. loft. Harvey hadn't known David very long, but on the night before Harvey was supposed to leave, he coincidentally met David three different times in three different places on the Lower East Side. Harvey took this as a sign that he should rent the loft to David, but he specifically stipulated that the Swami should move in too.

As Prabhupāda was preparing to leave his Seventy-second Street address, an acquaintance, an electrician who worked in the building, came to warn him. The Bowery was no place for a gentleman, he protested. It was the most corrupt place in the world. Prabhupāda's things had been stolen from room 307, but moving to the Bowery was not the answer.

* * *

Śrīla Prabhupāda's new home, the Bowery, had a long history. In the early 1600s, when Manhattan was known as New Amsterdam and was controlled by the Dutch West India Company, Peter Minuit, the governor of New Netherland, staked out a north-south road that was called "the Bowery" because a number of *bouweries*, or farms, lay on either side. It was a dusty country road, lined with quaint Dutch cottages and bordered by the peach orchards growing in the estate of Peter Stuyvesant. It became part of the high road to Boston and was of strategic importance during the American Revolution as the only land entrance to New York City.

In the early 1800s the Bowery was predominated by German immigrants, later in the century it became predominantly Jewish, and gradually it became the city's center of theatrical life. However, as a history of Lower Manhattan describes, "After 1870 came the period of the Bowery's celebrated degeneration. Fake auction rooms, saloons specializing in five-cent whiskey and knock-out drops, sensational dime museums, filthy and rat-ridden stale beer dives, together with Charles M. Hoyte's song, 'The Bowery! The Bowery!—I'll Never Go There Any More!' fixed it forever in the nation's consciousness as a place of unspeakable corruption."

The reaction of Prabhupāda's electrician friend was not unusual. The Bowery is still known all over the world as Skid Row, a place of ruined and homeless alcoholics. Perhaps the uptown electrician had done business in the Bowery and had seen the derelicts sitting around passing a bottle or lying unconscious in the gutter, or staggering up to passersby and drunkenly bumping into them to ask for money.

Most of the Bowery's seven or eight thousand homeless men slept in lodging houses that required them to vacate their rooms during the day. Having nowhere else to go and nothing else to do, they would loiter on the street—standing silently on the sidewalks, leaning against a wall, or shuffling slowly along, alone or in groups. In cold weather they would wear two coats and several suits of clothes at once and would sometimes warm themselves around a fire they would keep going in a city garbage can. At night, those without lodging slept on the sidewalks, doorsteps, and street corners, crawled into discarded boxes, or sprawled side by side next to the bars. Thefts were commonplace; a man's pockets might be searched ten or twenty times while he slept. The rates of hospitalization and death in the Bowery were five times higher than the national average, and many of the homeless men bore marks of recent injuries or violence.

Prabhupāda's loft, 94 Bowery, was six blocks south of Houston Street. At Houston and Bowery, derelicts converged in the heavy crosstown traffic. When cars stopped for the light, bums would come up and wash the windshields and ask for money. South of Houston, the first blocks held mostly restaurant supply stores, lamp stores, taverns, and luncheonettes. The buildings were of three and four stories—old, narrow, crowded tenements, their faces covered with heavy fire escapes. Traffic on the Bowery ran uptown and downtown. Cars parked on both sides of the street, and the constant traffic passed tightly. During the business day, working people passed briskly among the slow-moving derelicts. Many of the store windows were covered with protective iron gates, but behind the gates the store-owners lit their varieties of lamps to attract prospective wholesale and retail customers.

Ninety-four Bowery was just two doors north of Hester Street. The corner was occupied by the spacious Half Moon Tavern, which was frequented mostly by neighborhood alcoholics. Above the tavern sat a four-story Bowery flophouse, marked by a neon sign—Palma House—which was covered by a protective metal cage and hung from the second floor on large chains. The hotel's entrance at 92 Bowery (which had no lobby, but only a desolate hallway covered with dirty white tiles) was no more than six feet from the entrance to 94.

Ninety-four Bowery was a narrow four-story building. It had long ago been painted gray and bore the usual facing of a massive, black fire escape. A well-worn, black double door, its glass panels reinforced with chicken wire, opened onto the street. The sign above the door read, "A.I.R. 3rd & 4th," indicating that artists-in-residence occupied those floors.

The first floor of the next building north, 96 Bowery, was used for storage, and its front entrance was covered with a rusty iron gate. At 98 Bowery was another tavern—Harold's—smaller and dingier than the

Half Moon. Thus the block consisted of two saloons, a flophouse, and two buildings with lofts.

In the 1960s, loft-living was just beginning in that area of New York City. The City had given permission for painters, musicians, sculptors, and other artists (who required more space than available in most apartments) to live in buildings that had been constructed as factories in the nineteenth century. After these abandoned factories had been fitted with fireproof doors, bathtubs, shower stalls, and heating, an artist could inexpensively use a large space. These were the A.I.R. lofts.

Harvey Cohen's loft, on the top floor of 94 Bowery, was an open space almost a hundred feet long (from east to west) and twenty-five feet wide. It received a good amount of sunlight on the east, the Bowery side, and it also had windows at the west end, as well as a skylight. The exposed rafters of the ceiling were twelve feet above the floor.

Harvey Cohen had used the loft as an art studio, and racks for paintings still lined the walls. A kitchen and shower were partitioned off in the northwest corner, and a room divider stood about fifteen feet from the Bowery-side windows. This divider did not run from wall to wall, but was open at both ends, and it was several feet short of the ceiling.

It was behind this partition that Prabhupāda had his personal living area. A bed and a few chairs stood near the window, and Prabhupāda's typewriter sat on his metal trunk next to the small table that held his stacks of *Bhāgavatam* manuscripts. His *dhotīs* hung drying on a clothesline.

On the other side of the partition was a dais, about ten feet wide and five feet deep, on which Prabhupāda sat during his *kīrtanas* and lectures. The dais faced west, toward the loft's large open space—open, that is, except for a couple of rugs and an old-fashioned solid wood table and, on an easel, Harvey's painting of Lord Caitanya dancing with His associates.

The loft was a four-flight walk up, and the only entrance, usually heavily bolted, was a door in the rear, at the west end. From the outside, this door opened into a hallway, lit only by a red EXIT light over the door. The hallway led to the right a few steps and into the open area. If a guest entered during a *kīrtana* or a lecture, he would see the Swami about thirty feet from the entrance, seated on his dais. On other evenings the whole loft would be dark but for the glow of the red EXIT light in the little hallway and a soft illumination radiating from the other side of the partition, where Prabhupāda was working.

Prabhupāda lived on the Bowery, sitting under a small light, while hundreds of derelicts also sat under hundreds of naked lights on the same city block. He had no more fixed income than the derelicts, nor any greater security of a fixed residence, yet his consciousness was different. He was translating *Śrīmad-Bhāgavatam* into English, speaking to the world through his Bhaktivedanta purports. His duty, whether on the fourteenth floor of a Riverside Drive apartment building or in a corner of a Bowery loft, was to establish Kṛṣṇa consciousness as the prime necessity for all humanity. He went on with his translating and with his constant vision of a Kṛṣṇa temple in New York City. Because his consciousness was absorbed in Kṛṣṇa's universal mission, he did not depend on his surroundings for shelter. Home for him was not a matter of bricks and wood, but of taking shelter of Kṛṣṇa in every circumstance. As Prabhupāda had said to his friends uptown, "Everywhere is my home," whereas without Kṛṣṇa's shelter the whole world would be a desolate place.

Often he would refer to a scriptural statement that people live in three different modes: goodness, passion, and ignorance. Life in the forest is in the mode of goodness, life in the city is in passion, and life in a degraded place like a liquor shop, a brothel, or the Bowery is in the mode of ignorance. But to live in a temple of Viṣṇu is to live in the spiritual world, Vaikuṇṭha, which is transcendental to all three material modes.

And this Bowery loft where Prabhupāda was holding his meetings and performing *kīrtana* was also transcendental. When he was behind the partition, working in his corner before the open pages of *Śrīmad-Bhāgavatam*, that room was as good as his room back at the Rādhā-Dāmodara temple in Vṛndāvana.

News of the Swami's move to the Bowery loft spread, mostly by word of mouth at the Paradox restaurant, and people began to come by in the evening to chant with him. The musical *kīrtanas* were especially popular on the Bowery, since the Swami's new congregation consisted mostly of local musicians and artists, who responded more to the transcendental music than to the philosophy. Every morning he would hold a class on *Śrīmad-Bhāgavatam*, attended by David Allen, Robert Nelson, and another boy, and occasionally he would teach cooking to whoever was interested. He was usually available for personal talks with any inquiring visitors or with his new roommate.

Although Prabhupāda and David each had a designated living area in the large loft, the entire place soon became dominated by Prabhupāda's preaching activities. Prabhupāda and David got on well together, and at first Prabhupāda considered David an aspiring disciple.

April 27

He wrote to his friends in India, describing his relationship with David Allen.

> He was attending my class at Seventy-second Street along with others, and when I experienced this theft case in my room, he invited me to his residence. So I am with him and training him. He has good prospect because already he has given up all bad habits. In this country, illicit connection with women, smoking, drinking, and eating of meats are common affairs. Besides that, there are other bad habits, like using [only] toilet paper [and not bathing] after evacuating, etc. But by my request he has given up ninety percent of his old habits, and he is chanting maha mantra regularly. So I am giving him the chance, and I think he is improving. Tomorrow I have arranged for some prasadam distribution, and he has gone to purchase some things from the market.

When David first came to the Bowery, he appeared like a clean-cut college student. He was twenty-one, six feet tall, blue-eyed, handsome, and intelligent-looking. Most of his new friends in New York were older and considered him a kid. David's family lived in East Lansing, Michigan, and his mother was paying one hundred dollars monthly to sublease the loft. Although he did not have much experience, he had read that a new realm of mind expansion was available through psychedelic drugs, and he was heading fast into the hazardous world of LSD. His meeting with the Swami came at a time of radical change and profoundly affected his life.

David: *It was a really good relationship I had with the Swami, but I was overwhelmed by the tremendous energy of being that close to him. It spurred my consciousness very fast. Even my dreams at night would be so vivid of Kṛṣṇa consciousness. I was often sleeping when the Swami was up, because he was up late in the night working on his translations.*

That's possibly where a lot of the consciousness and dreams just flowed in, because of that deep relationship. It also had to do with studying Sanskrit. There was a lot of immediate impact with the language. The language seemed to have such a strong mystical quality, the way he translated it word for word.

Prabhupāda's old friend from uptown, Robert Nelson, continued to visit him on the Bowery. He was impressed by Prabhupāda's friendly relationship with David, who he saw was learning many things from the Swami. Mr. Robert bought a small American-made hand organ, similar to an Indian harmonium, and donated it to David for chanting with Prabhupāda. At seven in the morning Mr. Robert would come by, and after *Bhāgavatam* class he would talk informally with Prabhupāda, telling his ideas for making records and selling books. He wanted to continue helping the Swami. They would sit in chairs near the front window, and Mr. Robert would listen while Prabhupāda talked for hours about Kṛṣṇa and Lord Caitanya.

New people began coming to see Prabhupāda on the Bowery. Carl Yeargens, a thirty-year-old black man from the Bronx, had attended Cornell University and was now independently studying Indian religion and Zen Buddhism. He had experimented with drugs as "psychedelic tools," and he had an interest in the music and poetry of India. He was influential among his friends and tried to interest them in meditation. He had even been dabbling in Sanskrit.

Carl: *I had just finished reading a book called* The Wonder That Was India. *I had gotten the definition of a* sannyāsī *and a* brahmacārī *and so forth. There was a vivid description in that particular book of how you could see a* sannyāsī *coming down the road with his saffron robe. It must have made more than just a superficial impression on me, because it came to me this one chilly evening. I was going to visit Michael Grant—probably going to smoke some marijuana and sit around, maybe play some music—and I was coming down Hester Street. If you make a left on Bowery, you can go up to Mike's place on Grand Street. But it's funny that I chose to go that way, because the shorter way would have been to go down Grand Street. But if I had gone that way, I would probably have missed Swamiji.*

So I decided to go down Hester and then make a left. All of a sudden I saw in this dingy alcove a brilliant saffron robe. As I passed, I saw it was

Swamiji knocking on the door, trying to gain entrance. There were two bums hunched up against the door. It was like a two-part door—one of them was sealed, and the other was locked. The two bums were lying on either side of Swamiji. One of these men had actually expired—which often happened, and you had to call the police or health department to get them.

I don't think I saw the men lying in the doorway until I walked up to Swamiji and asked him, "Are you a sannyāsī*?" And he answered, "Yes." We started this conversation about how he was starting a temple, and he mentioned Lord Caitanya and the whole thing. He just came out with this flow of strange things to me, right there in the street. But I knew what he was talking about somehow. I had the familiarity of having just read this book and delved into Indian religion. So I knew that this was a momentous occasion for me, and I wanted to help him. We banged on the door, and eventually we got into the loft. He invited me to come to a* kīrtana, *and I came back later that night for my first* kīrtana. *From that point on, it was a fairly regular thing—three times a week. At one point Swamiji asked me to stay with him, and I stayed for about two weeks.*

It was perhaps because of Carl's interest in Sanskrit that Prabhupāda began holding Sanskrit classes. Carl and David and a few others would spend hours learning Sanskrit under Prabhupāda's guidance. Using a chalkboard he found in the loft, Prabhupāda taught the alphabet, and his students wrote their exercises in notebooks. Prabhupāda would look over their shoulders to see if they were writing correctly and would review their pronunciation. His students were learning not simply Sanskrit but the instructions of *Bhagavad-gītā*. Each day he would give them a verse to copy in the Sanskrit alphabet (*devanāgarī*), transliterate into the roman alphabet, and then translate word for word into English. But their interest in Sanskrit waned, and Prabhupāda gradually gave up the daily classes to spend time working on his own translations of the *Śrīmad-Bhāgavatam*.

His new friends may have regarded these lessons as Sanskrit classes, but actually they were *bhakti* classes. He had not come to America as the ambassador of Sanskrit; his Guru Mahārāja had ordered him to teach Kṛṣṇa consciousness. But since he had found in Carl and some of his friends a desire to investigate Sanskrit, he encouraged it. As a youth, Lord Caitanya had also started a Sanskrit school, with the real purpose of teaching love of Kṛṣṇa. He would teach in such a way that every word meant Kṛṣṇa, and when His students objected He closed the school. Similarly, when Prabhupāda found that his students' interest in Sanskrit was transitory—and since he himself had no mission on behalf of Sanskrit linguistics—he gave it up.

By the standard of classical Vedic scholars, it takes ten years for a boy to master Sanskrit grammar. And if one does not start until his late twenties or thirties, it is usually too late. Certainly none of Swamiji's students were thinking of entering a ten-year concentration in Sanskrit grammar, and even if they were, they would not realize spiritual truth simply by becoming grammarians.

Prabhupāda thought it better to utilize his own Sanskrit scholarship in translating the verses of *Śrīmad-Bhāgavatam* into English, following the Sanskrit commentaries of the previous authorities. Otherwise, the secrets of Kṛṣṇa consciousness would remain locked away in the Sanskrit. Teaching Carl Yeargens *devanāgarī, sandhi,* verb conjugations, and noun declensions was not going to give the people of America transcendental Vedic knowledge. Better that he utilize his proficiency in Sanskrit for translating many volumes of the *Bhāgavatam* into English for millions of potential readers.

Carol Bekar came from an immigrant Catholic background, and she immediately associated with Catholicism the Swami's presence as a spiritual authority and his devotional practices of chanting on beads and reciting from Sanskrit scriptures. Sometimes she would accompany Prabhupāda to nearby Chinatown, where he would purchase ingredients for his cooking. He would cook daily, and sometimes Carol and others would come by to learn the secrets of cooking for Lord Kṛṣṇa.

Carol: *He used to cook with us in the kitchen, and he was always aware of everyone else's activities in addition to his own cooking. He knew exactly how things should be. He washed everything and made sure everyone did everything correctly. He was a teacher. We used to make* capātīs *by hand, but then one day he asked me to get him a rolling pin. I brought my rolling pin, and he appropriated it. He put some men on rolling* capātīs *and supervised them very carefully.*

I made a chutney for him at home. He always accepted our gifts graciously, although I don't think he ever ate them. Perhaps he was worried we might put in something that wasn't allowed in his diet. He used to take things from me and put them in the cupboard. I don't know what he finally did with them, but I am sure he didn't throw them away. I never saw him eat anything that I had prepared, although he accepted everything.

Prabhupāda held his evening meetings on Mondays, Wednesdays, and Fridays, just as he had uptown. The loft was out of the way for most of his acquaintances, and it was on the Bowery. A cluster of sleeping derelicts regularly blocked the street-level entrance, and visitors would find as many as half a dozen bums to step over before climbing the four flights of stairs. But it was something new; you could go and sit with a group of hip people and watch the Swami lead *kīrtana*. The room was dimly lit, and Prabhupāda would burn incense. Many casual visitors came and went. One of them—Gunther—had vivid impressions.

Gunther: *You walked right off the Bowery into a room filled with incense. It was quiet. Everyone was talking in hushed tones, not really talking at all. Swamiji was sitting in the front of the room, and in meditation. There was a tremendous feeling of peace which I have never had before. I'd happened to have studied for two years to become a minister and was into meditation, study, and prayer. But this was my first time to do anything Eastern or Hindu. There were lots of pillows around and mats on the floor for people to sit on. I don't think there were any pictures or statues. It was just Swamiji, incense, and mats, and obviously the respect of the people in the room for him.*

Before we went up, Carl was laughing and saying how Swami wanted everyone to use the hand cymbals just correctly. I had never played the cymbals before, but when it began I just tried to follow Swamiji, who was doing it in a certain way. Things were building up, the sound was building up, but then someone was doing it wrong. And Swamiji just very, very calmly shook a finger at someone and they looked, and then everything stopped. He instructed this person from a distance, and this fellow got the right idea, and they started up again. After a few minutes . . . the sound of the cymbals and the incense . . . we weren't in the Bowery any longer. We started chanting Hare Kṛṣṇa. That was my first experience in chanting—I'd never chanted before. There's nothing in Protestant religion that comes even close to that. Maybe Catholics with their Hail Marys, but it's not quite the same thing. It was relaxing and very interesting to be able to chant, and I found Swamiji very fascinating.

The loft was more open than Prabhupāda's previous place uptown, so there was less privacy. And here some of the visitors were skeptical and even challenging, but everyone found him confident and joyful. He seemed to have far-reaching plans, and he had dedication. He knew what he wanted to do and was single-handedly carrying it out. "It is not one man's job," he had said. But he went on doing all he could, depending on Kṛṣṇa for the results. David was beginning to help, and more people were coming by to visit him.

Almost all of Prabhupāda's Bowery friends were musicians or friends of musicians. They were into music—music, drugs, women, and spiritual meditation. Because Prabhupāda's presentation of the Hare Kṛṣṇa *mantra* was both musical and meditative, they were automatically interested. Prabhupāda stressed that all the Vedic *mantras* (or hymns) were *sung*—in fact, the words *Bhagavad-gītā* meant "The Song of God." But the words of the Vedic hymns were incarnations of God in the form of transcendental sound. The musical accompaniment of hand cymbals, drum, and harmonium was just that—an accompaniment—and had no spiritual purpose independent of the chanting of the name of God. Prabhupāda allowed any instrument to be used, as long as it did not detract from the chanting.

Carol: *It was a very interracial, music-oriented scene. There were a few professional musicians, and a lot of people who enjoyed playing or just listening. Some people were painting in some of the lofts, and that's basically what was going on. We had memorable* kīrtanas. *One time there was a beautiful ceremony. Some of us went over early to prepare for it. There must have been a hundred people who came that day.*

For the Bowery crowd, sound was spirit and spirit was sound, in a merging of music and meditation. But for Prabhupāda, music without the name of God wasn't meditation; it was sense gratification, or at most a kind of stylized impersonal meditation. But he was glad to see the musicians coming to play along in his *kīrtanas*, to hear him, and to chant responsively. Some, having stayed up all night playing somewhere on their instruments, would come by in the morning and sing with the Swami. He did not dissuade them from their focus on sound; rather, he gave them sound. In the *Vedas*, sound is said to be the first element of material creation; the source of sound is God, and God is eternally a person. Prabhupāda's emphasis was on getting people to chant God's personal, transcendental name. Whether they took it as jazz, folk music, rock, or Indian meditation made no difference, as long as they began to chant Hare Kṛṣṇa.

Carol: *Whenever he had the chanting, the people were fairly in awe of the Swami. On the Bowery, a kind of transcendence came out of the ringing of the cymbals. He used the harmonium, and many people played hand cymbals. Sometimes he played the drum. In the very beginning, he stressed the importance of sound and the realization of Godhead through sound. That was, I suppose, the attraction that these musicians found in him—the emphasis on sound as a means to attaining transcendence and the Godhead. But he wanted a serious thing. He was interested in discipleship.*

One serious newcomer was Michael Grant. Mike was twenty-four. His father, who was Jewish, owned a record shop in Portland, Oregon, where Mike grew up. After studying music at Portland's Reed College and at San Francisco State, Mike, who played the piano and many other instruments, moved to New York City, along with his girl friend, hoping to get into music professionally. But he quickly became disenchanted with the commercial music scene. Playing in nightclubs and pandering to commercial demands seemed particularly unappealing. In New York he joined the musicians' union and worked as a musical arranger and as an agent for several local groups.

Mike lived on the Bowery in an A.I.R. loft on Grand Street. It was a large loft where musicians often congregated for jam sessions. But as he turned more and more to serious composing, he found himself retiring from the social side of the music scene. His interests ran more to the spiritual, quasi-spiritual, and mystical books he had been reading. He had encountered several swamis, *yogīs*, and self-styled spiritualists in the city and had taken up *haṭha-yoga*. From his first meeting with the Swami, Mike was interested and quite open, as he was with all religious persons. He thought all genuinely religious people were good, although he did not care to identify with any particular group.

Mike: *There was a little bit of familiarity because I had seen other swamis. The way he was dressed, the way he looked—older and swarthy—weren't new to me. But at the same time there was an element of novelty. I was very curious. I didn't hear him talk when I first came in—he was just chanting—but mainly I was waiting to hear what he was going to say. I had already heard people chant before. I thought, why else would he put himself in such a place, without any comforts, unless the message he's trying to get across is more important than his own comfort? I think the thing that struck me the most was the poverty that was all around him. This was curious, because the places that I had been before had been just the opposite—very opulent. There was a Vedānta center in upper Manhattan, and others. They were filled with staid, older men with their leather chairs and pipe tobacco—that kind of environment. But this was real poverty. The whole thing was curious.*

The Swami looked very refined, which was also curious—that he was in this place. When he talked, I immediately saw that he was a scholar and that he spoke with great conviction. Some statements he made were very daring. He was talking about God, and this was all new—to hear someone talk about God. I always wanted to hear someone I could respect talk about God. I always liked to hear religious speakers, but I measured them very carefully. When he spoke, I began to think, "Well, here is someone talking about God who may really have some realization of God." He was the first one I had come across who might be a person of God, who could feel really deeply.

* * *

Prabhupāda is lecturing.

Śrī Kṛṣṇa is just trying to place Arjuna on the platform of working in pure consciousness. We have already discussed for so many days that we are not this dull body but we are consciousness. Somehow or other we are in contact with matter. Therefore our freedom is checked.

Attendance is better now than it had been uptown. The loft offers a larger space; in fact, the platform where Prabhupāda sits nearly equals the area of his entire office cubicle on Seventy-second Street. The dingy loft with its unpainted rafters is more like an old warehouse than a temple. The members of his audience, most of them musicians, have come to meditate on the mystical sounds of the Swami's *kīrtana.*

Carl, Carol, Gunther, Mike, David, the crowd from the Paradox, and others join him on Monday, Wednesday, and Friday night, when he holds classes beginning punctually at eight o'clock. The program consists of half an hour of chanting Hare Kṛṣṇa, followed by a lecture from *Bhagavad-gītā* (usually forty-five minutes long), then a question-and-answer period, and finally another half hour of chanting, everything ending by ten o'clock.

The *kīrtana* has just ended, and Swamiji is speaking.

As spiritual beings we are free to act, free to have anything. Pure, no contamination—no disease, no birth, no death, no old age. And besides that, we have got many, many other qualifications in our spiritual life.

When he speaks he is pure spiritual form. The Vedic scriptures say that a *sādhu*, a saint, is not seen but heard. If the people in the audience want to know Swamiji, they will have to hear him. He is no longer simply the old Indian immigrant who lives on the other side of the partition of this loft, hanging his clothes to dry, barely getting his meals.

But now he is speaking as the emissary of Lord Kṛṣṇa, beyond time and space, and hundreds of spiritual masters in the chain of disciplic succession are speaking through him. He has entered amid New York's Bohemians in 1966 saying that 1966 is temporary and illusory, that he is eternal and they are eternal. This was the meaning of the *kīrtana*, and now he is explaining it philosophically, advocating a total change in consciousness. Yet, knowing that they can't take it all, he urges them to take whatever they can.

You will be glad to hear that this process of spiritual realization, once begun, guarantees one to have his next life as a human being. Once karma-yoga *is begun it will continue. It doesn't matter—even if one fails to complete the course, still he is not loser, he is not loser. Now, if someone begins this* yoga *of self-realization but unfortunately cannot prosecute this task in a nice way—if he falls down from the path—still there is encouragement that you are not a loser. You will be given a chance next life, and the next life is not ordinary next life. And for one who is successful—oh, what to speak of him! The successful goes back to Godhead. So we are holding this class, and although you have multifarious duties, you come here thrice a week and try to understand. And this will not go in vain. Even if you stop coming here, that impression will never go. I tell you, the impression will never go. If you do some practical work, that is very, very nice. But even if you do not do any practical work, simply if you give your submissive aural reception and understand what is the nature of God—if you simply hear and have an idea even—then you will be free from this material bondage.*

He is talking to a crowd who are deeply set in their hip life. He knows that they can't immediately give up taking drugs, and there they sit, with their common-law wives. Their path is to play music, live with a woman, and meditate sometimes. And be free. After hearing his lecture they'll stay up all night with their instruments, their women, their drugs, their interracial Bohemian scene. Yet somehow they are drawn to Swamiji. He's got the good vibrations of the *kīrtana*, and they want to help him out. They're glad to help, because he has no one else. So Prabhupāda is saying to them, "That's all right. Even if you can only do a little, it will be good for you. We are all pure spirit souls. But you have forgotten. You have fallen into the cycle of birth and death. Whatever you can do toward reviving your original consciousness is good for you. There is no loss."

The Swami's main stress is on what he calls "dovetailing your consciousness with the Supreme Consciousness." . . . *Kṛṣṇa is the Supreme Consciousness. And Arjuna, as the representative individual consciousness, is asked to act intelligently in collaboration with the Supreme Consciousness. Then he will be free from the bondage of birth, death, old age, and disease.*

Consciousness is a popular word in America. There's consciousness expansion, cosmic consciousness, altered states of consciousness, and now—dovetailing the individual consciousness with the Supreme Consciousness. This is the perfection of consciousness, Prabhupāda explains. This is the love and peace that everyone is really after. And yet Prabhupāda talks of it in terms of war.

They are talking on the battlefield, and Arjuna says, "I will not fight. I will not fight with my relatives and brothers for the sake of achieving some kingdom. No, no." Now, to the ordinary man it appears that, "Oh, Arjuna is a very nice man, nonviolent. He has given up everything for the sake of his relatives. Oh, what a nice man he is." This is the ordinary calculation.

But what does Kṛṣṇa say? He says, "You are damned fool number one." Now just see. The things which are estimated in the public eye as very nice, very good, that is here condemned by God. So you have to see whether the Supreme Consciousness is pleased with your actions. And Arjuna's action was not approved by Lord Kṛṣṇa. It was for his own whim, sense gratification, that at first he would not fight—but in the end, for Kṛṣṇa's satisfaction, he did fight. And that is our perfection—when we act for the satisfaction of the Supreme Consciousness.

At this point, some in the audience are filled with reservations. They are all opposed to the role of the United States in Vietnam, and this idea is very difficult for them. Like Arjuna, they want peace. So why is a swami sanctioning war?

He explains: Yes, Arjuna's idea not to fight is good, but then Kṛṣṇa, the Supreme Consciousness, instructs him to fight anyway. Therefore, Arjuna's fighting is above mundane ethics. It is absolute. If we follow Arjuna, give up good and bad, and act for Kṛṣṇa, not for our sense gratification, then that is perfect—because Kṛṣṇa is the Supreme Consciousness.

To some in his audience, although his answer seems philosophically sound, it's not quite what they want to hear. Still, they want to know his political views. Does he support America's involvement in Vietnam? Is he antiwar? But Prabhupāda is neither hawk nor dove. He has no political motive behind his example of Kṛṣṇa and Arjuna. His theme is simple and pure: beyond the good and the bad is the Absolute, and to act in accord with the Absolute is also beyond good and bad.

But what about Vietnam—does Kṛṣṇa say to fight there? No, Swamiji answers. The Vietnam war is different from the Kurukṣetra war. In the battle of Kurukṣetra, Kṛṣṇa was personally present asking Arjuna to fight. Vietnam is different.

But his audience has yet another objection: If he is not addressing the Vietnamese war, then why not? After all, this is 1966. If he isn't talking about the war, then what is his relevancy? The Swami replies that his message is actually the most urgent and relevant. The Vietnamese war was an inevitable karmic reaction; it was one symptom, not the whole problem. And only *this* philosophy—surrender to the Supreme Consciousness—addresses the real problem.

But for many the reference to fighting is so emotionally charged that they can't go beyond the immediate politics of Vietnam to Prabhupāda's real message of surrender to the Supreme Consciousness. They respect the Swami—they realize he's referring to a deeper philosophy—yet the story of Arjuna and the war makes things difficult. The Swami nonetheless continues to refer to Arjuna's fighting as the classic example of *Bhagavad-gītā's* basic teaching.

It's not the basic teaching his audience is having difficulty with. It's the example. Prabhupāda has deliberately handed his audience a volatile analogy. He hasn't come to join their peace movement, and he doesn't accept their shortsighted concept of peace. He confronts them: It is better to fight in Kṛṣṇa consciousness than to live in a so-called peace devoid of God realization. Yes, the example is hard for them to accept. It makes them think. And if they do accept, then they might come near to understanding the Absolute.

Is it very difficult, dovetailing our consciousness with the Supreme Consciousness? Not at all. Not at all! No sane man will say, "Oh, it is not possible."

He isn't suggesting that to dovetail with the Supreme Consciousness *they* will have to go fight in Vietnam or perform some other horrible act on behalf of God. He knows that spiritual life will have to be more attractive than material life, or his audience will never take to it. He wants to bring the theme of dovetailing with the Supreme Consciousness down to something practical, something all-attractive and beautiful, something anyone could do and would want to do. He wants to encourage them by saying that they can do their own thing—but for Kṛṣṇa. Arjuna, after all, was a lifetime warrior. Kṛṣṇa didn't ask him to give up his work, but to do it for the Supreme. So Prabhupāda is asking the same of his audience. And they can begin with something as simple as offering their food to God.

Because everyone has to eat. So God wants to eat something. Why don't you first offer your food to God? Then you eat. But you may say, "But if God takes it away, then how shall I eat?" No, no. God will not take it. Daily, after preparing our foodstuffs, we are offering to Kṛṣṇa. There is a witness. Mr. David has seen. (Prabhupāda laughs.) *God eats! But His spiritual eating is such that, even after His eating, the whole thing is still there.*

So we shall not suffer a pinch if we dovetail our desires with the Supreme Lord. We simply have to learn the art—how to dovetail. Nothing has to be changed. The fighting man did not change into an artist or a musician. If you are a fighting man, you remain a fighting man. If you are a musician, you remain a musician. If you are a medical man, you remain a medical man. Whatever you are, you remain. But dovetail it. If by my eating the Lord is satisfied, then that is my perfection. If by my fighting the Lord is satisfied, then that is my perfection. So in every sphere of life we have to know whether the Lord is satisfied. That technique we have to learn. Then it is as easy as anything. We have to stop creating our own plans and thoughts and take the perfect plans from the Supreme Lord and execute them. That will become the perfection of our life.

*And Lord Caitanya has made acting on the platform of consciousness very easy. Just as there are some note-makers of school books—*Easy Study*—so Lord Caitanya has recommended that you be engaged in whatever occupation, but just hear about Kṛṣṇa. Continue to hear the* Bhagavad-gītā *and chant Hare Kṛṣṇa. It is for this that we are trying to organize this institution. So you have come, and whatever work you do, it doesn't matter. Everything will be adjusted by and by, as our mind becomes clear simply by hearing. If you continue this process, chanting the Kṛṣṇa name, you will practically see how much your heart is becoming clear and how much you are making progress toward spiritual realization, the real identity of pure consciousness.*

Prabhupāda is speaking on behalf of the Supreme Consciousness, and he offers his day-to-day activities as an example of dovetailing with the Supreme.

I am here always working at something, reading or writing—something, reading or writing—twenty-four hours. Simply when I feel hungry, I take some food. And simply when I feel sleepy, I go to bed. Otherwise, I don't feel fatigued. You can ask Mr. David whether I am not doing this.

Of course, the Swami's daily routine doesn't require certification from David Allen, and any of his regular visitors can see that he is transcendental. His personal life is a perfect example of dovetailing with the Supreme Consciousness. Prabhupāda has always kept himself dovetailed with the Supreme. He had been perfectly dovetailed in Vṛndāvana also and had no personal need or motive to come to America and live on the Bowery. It was for others' sake that he came to the Bowery, and it is for others' benefit that he is speaking tonight. His spiritual master and Lord Kṛṣṇa want the conditioned souls to come out of their illusion before it is too late.

Speaking vigorously, even until he becomes physically exhausted—sometimes shouting, sometimes pleading, sometimes laughing—he gives his audience as much as he feels they can take. As the emissary of Kṛṣṇa and the disciplic succession, he can boldly shout that everyone should dovetail with the Supreme. He can speak as strongly as he likes for as long as they're willing to listen. He is a *sādhu.* (The Sanskrit word means "saint" and "one who cuts.") And he repeats the same message that for thousands of years *sādhus* of the original Vedic culture have spoken. He is reviving the eternal spirit of the Vedic wisdom—to cut the knots of ignorance and illusion.

So everything is illusion. From the beginning of our birth. And that illusion is so strong it is very difficult to get out of. The whole thing is illusion. Birth is illusion. The body is illusion. The bodily relationship and the country are illusion. The father is illusion. The mother is illusion. The wife is illusion. The children are illusion. Everything is illusion. And we are contacting that illusion, thinking we are very learned, advanced. We are imagining so many things. But as soon as death comes—the actual fact—then we forget everything. We forget our country. We forget our relatives. We forget our wife, children, father, mother. Everything is gone.

* * *

Mike Grant: *I went up to him afterward. I had the same feeling I'd had on other occasions when I'd been to hear famous people in concerts. I was always interested in going by after concerts to see musicians and singers just to meet them and see what they were like. I had a similar feeling after Swamiji spoke, so I went up and started talking. But the experience was different from the others in that he wasn't in a hurry. He could talk to me, whereas with others all you could do was get in a few words. They were always more interested in something else. But he was a person who was actually showing some interest in me as a person, and I was so overwhelmed that I ran out of things to say very quickly. I was surprised. Our meeting broke off on the basis of my not having anything further to say. It was just the opposite of so many other experiences, where some performer would be hurrying off to do something else. This time, I was the one who couldn't continue.*

* * *

Prabhupāda liked to take walks. From his doorstep at 94 Bowery, he would see directly across the street the Fulton Hotel, a five-story flophouse. Surrounding him were other lower-Manhattan lodging houses, whose tenants wandered the sidewalks from early morning till dark. An occasional flock of pigeons would stir and fly from one rooftop to the next or descend to the street. Traffic was heavy. The Bowery was part of a truck route to and from Brooklyn by way of the Brooklyn and Manhattan bridges.

The Bowery sloped gently downhill toward the north, and Prabhupāda could see signboards, a few scraggly Manhattan trees, and the street lights and traffic signals as far up as Fourth Street. He could see Con Edison, with its prominent clock tower, and (if there were no clouds) the top of the Empire State Building on Thirty-fourth Street.

He would walk alone in the morning through the Bowery neighborhood. The month of May that year saw more frequent rains than was normal, and Prabhupāda carried an umbrella. Sometimes he walked in the rain. He was not always alone; sometimes he walked with one of his new friends and talked. Sometimes he shopped. Bitter melon, *dāl, hiṅg*, chick-pea flour, and other specialty foods common in Indian vegetarian cuisine were available in Chinatown's nearby markets. On leaving the loft, he would walk south a few steps to the corner of Bowery and Hester Street. Turning right on Hester, he would immediately be in Chinatown, where the shops, markets, and even the Manhattan Savings Bank were identified by signs lettered in Chinese. Sometimes he would walk one block further south to Canal Street, with its Central Asian Food Market and many other streetside fruit and vegetable markets. In the early morning the sidewalks were almost deserted, but as the shops began to open for business, the streets became crowded with local workers, shopkeepers, tourists, and aimless derelicts. The winding side streets of Chinatown were lined with hundreds of small stores, and parked cars lined both sides of the street.

His walks on Hester would sometimes take him into Little Italy, which overlaps Chinatown at Mulberry Street. In this neighborhood, places like Chinese Pork Products and the Mee Jung Mee Supermarket stood alongside Umberto's Clam House and the Puglia Restaurant, advertising *capuccino a la puglia*, coffee from Puglia.

His walks west of Bowery into Chinatown and Little Italy were mainly for shopping. But he also noted prospective sites for a temple; Chatham Tower on Chatham Square particularly drew his attention. Sometimes he would walk in the opposite direction as far as the East River and Brooklyn Bridge. But when a friend warned him that a sniper had been firing at strollers along the river, he stopped going there.

Despite the bad neighborhood where Prabhupāda lived and walked, he was rarely disturbed. Often he would find several Bowery bums asleep or unconscious at his door, and he would have to step over them. Sometimes a drunk, simply out of his inability to maneuver, would bump into him, or a derelict would mutter something unintelligible or laugh at him. The more sober ones would stand and gesture courteously, ushering the Swami into or out of his door at 94 Bowery. He would pass among them, acknowledging their good manners as they cleared his path.

Certainly few of the Bowery men and others who saw him on his walks knew much about the small, elderly Indian *sādhu*, dressed in saffron and carrying an umbrella and a brown grocery sack.

Sometimes Prabhupāda would meet one of his new friends on the street. Jan, Michael Grant's girl friend, met him on several occasions as he was out walking.

Jan: *I would see him in the midst of this potpourri of people down there, walking down the street. He always had an umbrella, and he would always have such a serene look on his face. He would just be taking his afternoon jaunts, walking along, sometimes stepping over the drunks. And I would always get sort of nervous when I would meet him on the sidewalk. He would say, "Are you chanting?" and I would say, "Sometimes." And then he would say, "That's a good girl."*

* * *

Sitting cross-legged, his back to the shelf with its assortment of potted plants, a whitish *chādar* wrapped in wide, loose folds across his body, Prabhupāda looked grave, almost sorrowful. The picture and an accompanying article appeared in a June issue of *The Village Voice.* The article read:

> The meeting of the mystical West and practical East comes alive in the curious contrast between A. C. Bhaktivedanta Swami and his American disciples. The swami, a cultivated man of seventy with a distinguished education, is here for a year to preach his gospel of peace, good will, nearness to God, and, more practically, to raise money for his American church.... Like his teachings, the swami is sensible and direct. His main teaching is that mankind may come closer to God by reciting His holy name.
>
> Despite the fact that the swami came to America to seek out the root of godless materialism—a disease, he said, that has already enveloped India—he is a realistic man. "If there is any place on earth with money to build a temple, it is here." The swami wishes to found in America an International Society for Krishna Consciousness, which will be open for anyone—including women.

The article had been written by Howard Smith. He had first heard of the Swami by a phone call from a contact who had told him of an interesting holy man from India living in a loft in the Bowery. "Go there any time," Howard's contact had told him. "He's always there. I think you will find it fascinating. I believe he's about to start a major religious movement."

Howard Smith: *So I went down there and went upstairs into this very funky artists' loft. There were carpets all over the place, old and worn out, and a lot of people sitting around in various kinds of hippie garb, plus what I think they must have thought was Indian garb. Most of them were sitting alone around the room facing the wall, like they had nothing to do with each other. They were sitting cross-legged, and each one seemed to be doing something different. Nobody paid any attention to me when I walked in.*

I saw shoes lined up, and I thought, "Maybe I am supposed to take off my shoes," but nobody said anything to me. So I walked around the edge of the carpet, looking for somebody to pay attention to me. I wondered what was going on, and I didn't want to interrupt anybody, because they all seemed deep into whatever kind of prayers they were doing.

In the back of the loft I noticed a little curtain—an Indian madras type of curtain—and so I decided I'd peer into that area. I looked in, and there was Swami Bhaktivedanta sitting there cross-legged in saffron garments, with the markings on his forehead and nose and his hand in the bead bag. Even though he looked like the real thing, he seemed more approachable, and I said, "Hello," and he looked up. I said, "Swami Bhaktivedanta?" and he said, "Yes." I said, "I am Howard Smith." I was expecting to sit down, so I said, "Excuse me, I have to take off my shoes," and he said, "Why do you want to take off your shoes?" I said, "I don't know—I saw all the shoes out there." And he said, "I didn't ask you to take your shoes off." I said, "What are all those people out there doing?" and he said, "I don't know. And they don't know what they're doing. I am trying to teach them, and they seem to be misunderstanding me. They are very confused people."

Then we sat and talked, and I liked him a lot right away. I mean, I'd met a lot of other swamis, and I didn't like them too much. And I don't think it's fair to lump them all together and say, "Those swamis in India." Because he was very, very basic, and that's what I seemed to like about him. He not only made me feel at ease, but he seemed very open and honest—like he asked my advice on things. He was very new in the country.

I thought his ideas stood a good chance of taking hold, because he seemed so practical. His head didn't seem in the clouds. He wasn't talking mysticism every third word. I guess that is where his soul was at, but that isn't where his normal conversational consciousness was at.

Then he said several people had told him that the Voice *would be a very good place to be written up and that basically it would reach the kind of people who already perhaps had a leaning or interest in what he was preaching. And I said that I thought he was correct. He asked me if I had read any books or knew anything about Indian culture, and I said no, I didn't really. We talked a little, and he explained to me that he had these books in English that he had already translated in India. And he handed those to me and said, "If you want more background, you can read these."*

It was obvious to me that I was not talking to some fellow who had just decided that he had seen God and was going to tell people about it. He seemed to be an educated man, much more than myself, actually. And I liked his humbleness. I just plain liked the guy.

He explained everything I wanted to know—the significance of what he was wearing, the mark on his forehead, the bead bag. And I liked all his explanations. Everything was very practical. Then he talked about temples all over the world, and he said, "Well, we have got a long way to go. But I am very patient."

* * *

Prabhupāda had hope for what the *Voice* article had referred to as "his American church." There was life in his lectures and *kīrtanas*, and at least he was acquiring a small, regular following. But from India there was no hope. He had continued corresponding with Sumati Morarji, his Godbrothers, and the Indian Central Government, but their replies had not been encouraging.

In the faith that Padampat Singhania would agree to his plans for a Kṛṣṇa temple in Manhattan and finance its construction, Prabhupāda had petitioned New Delhi to sanction the release of foreign exchange. He had written to the Reserve Bank of India, New Delhi.

> I want to establish this cultural center, and for this I wish to get some exchange from India. I think there are good prospects all over the world for propagating the culture of how to love God in these days of forgetfulness.

A month later the Indian bank had advised him to resubmit his request, through the Indian Embassy in Washington, to the finance minister of the Indian Central Government. Prabhupāda had complied. And another month had passed, with no word from the government.

One of his Godbrothers had written that Swamiji should come back to India and work personally to get the government's sanction. But Prabhupāda didn't want to leave America now. He wrote to Sumati Morarji:

> I am trying to avoid the journey to India and again coming back. Especially for the reason that I am holding at the above address classes thrice a week and training some American youth in the matter of sankirtan and devotional service to the Lord. Some of them are taking the lessons very sincerely and in the future they may be very good Vaisnavas according to the rigid standards.

One day a curious, unsolicited correspondent wrote to Prabhupāda from India. His name was Mukti Brahmacārī. Introducing himself as a disciple of one of Prabhupāda's Godbrothers, and reminding Prabhupāda of their past slight acquaintance, Mukti wrote of his eagerness to join Prabhupāda in America. Certainly Prabhupāda still had hopes for getting assistance from his Godbrothers in India—"This mission is not simply one man's work." Therefore, he invited Mukti to come to America and asked him to request his *guru* to cooperate by working personally to secure government sanction for the release of foreign exchange. Mukti wrote back, reaffirming his eagerness but expressing doubt that his spiritual master would give him permission. Mukti thought he should first come to the United States and *then* request his spiritual master's help. Prabhupāda was annoyed, and he sent an immediate reply:

> Is preaching in America my private business? Srila Prabhupad Bhaktisiddhanta Saraswati wanted to construct some temples in foreign countries as preaching centers of the message of Srila Rupa Raghunath,* and I am trying to do this in this part of the world. The money is ready and the opportunity is open. If by seeing the Finance Minister this work can be facilitated, why should we wait because you cannot talk with your Guru Maharaj about cooperation because you are afraid your journey will be cancelled? Please do not think in that way. Take everything as Srila [Bhaktisiddhānta Sarasvatī] Prabhupad's work and try to do the needful. Do not think for a moment that my interest is different from that of your Guru Maharaj. We are executing the will of Srila Prabhupad according to our own capacity. A combined effort would have been far better.

Mukti submitted the entire proposal before his spiritual master, who, as Mukti predicted, canceled the trip. Although Mukti's *guru* was Śrīla Prabhupāda's Godbrother, he did not want to be involved, and he doubted that Prabhupāda would actually get a donation from Padampat Singhania.

---

*Śrīla Rūpa Gosvāmī and Śrīla Raghunātha dāsa Gosvāmī were two leading disciples of Lord Caitanya in the sixteenth century.

And now Mukti Brahmacārī also doubted: "If your program is not bona fide, the approach to a big personality will be a ludicrous one no doubt."

On the same day that Prabhupāda received the "ludicrous" letter, he also received the final blow of noncooperation from the Indian government. Second Secretary Prakash Shah of the Indian Embassy in Washington, D.C., wrote:

> Due to existing conditions of foreign exchange stringency, it is not possible for the government of India to accede to your request for release of foreign exchange. You may perhaps like to raise funds from residents in America.

It was confirmed: Prabhupāda would have to work without outside help. He would continue alone in New York City. His last letter to Mukti Brahmacārī reveals his deep faith and determination.

> So the controversy is now closed, and there is no need of help from anyone else. We are not always successful in our attempts at preaching work, but such failures are certainly not ludicrous. In the absolute field both success and failure are glorious. Even Lord Nityananda pretended to be a failure at converting Jagai and Madhai in the first attempt. Rather, He was personally injured in such an attempt. But that was certainly not ludicrous. The whole thing was transcendental, and it was glorious for all parties concerned.

If Kṛṣṇa consciousness were ever to take hold in America, it would have to be without assistance from the Indian government or Indian financiers. Not even a lone Indian *brahmacārī* would join him. Kṛṣṇa was revealing His plan to Prabhupāda in a different way. With the Singhania-sanction schemes finished and behind him, Prabhupāda would turn all his energy toward the young men and women coming to him in his Bowery loft. He wrote to Sumati Morarji:

> I am now trying to incorporate one corporation of the local friends and admirers under the name International Society for Krishna Consciousness, incorporated.

* * *

Of all his friends and admirers, Prabhupāda gave his roommate, David Allen, the most personal attention and training. He felt he was giving David a special chance to become America's first genuine Vaiṣṇava. Prabhupāda would eventually return to India, and he wanted to take David to Vṛndāvana. He would show him temple worship and train him for future preaching in the West. He had requested Sumati Morarji to provide free passage for David as well as for himself.

> You will be pleased to see this American boy. He is coming of a good family and is a sincere soul to this line of culture. There are others also in the class I am holding here, but I wish to take with me only one of them.

I am very glad to say (Prabhupāda said one evening in his lecture) *that our Mr. David says sometimes, "Swamiji, I want to increase my spiritual life* immediately." (Prabhupāda laughed as he imitated David's urgency.) *"Take patience, take patience," I tell him. "It will be done, of course. When you have got such desire, God will help you. He is within you. He is simply trying to see how sincere you are. Then He will give you all opportunities to increase your spiritual life."*

At first David and the Swami lived together peacefully in the large hall, the Swami working concentratedly on his side of the partition, David ranging throughout the large open space. David, however, continued taking marijuana, LSD, and amphetamines, and Prabhupāda had no choice but to tolerate it. Several times he told David that drugs and hallucinations would not help his spiritual life, but David would look distracted. He was becoming estranged from the Swami.

But Prabhupāda had a plan to use the loft as a temple—to transform it into New York's first temple of Rādhā-Kṛṣṇa—and he wanted David's cooperation. Although the neighborhood was one of the most miserable in the world, Prabhupāda talked of bringing Deities from Jaipur or Vṛndāvana and starting temple worship, even on the Bowery. He thought David might help. After all, they were roommates, so there could be no question of David's not cooperating; but he would have to give up his bad habits.

Prabhupāda was trying to help David, but David was too disturbed. He was headed for disaster, and so were Prabhupāda's plans for the loft. Sometimes, even not under the influence of a drug, he would pace around the loft. Other times he appeared to be deep in thought. One day, on a dose of LSD, he went completely crazy. As Carl Yeargens put it, "He just flipped out, and the Swami had to deal with a crazy man." Things had been leading to this—"he was a crazy kid who always took too much"—but the real madness happened suddenly.

Swamiji was working peacefully at his typewriter when David "freaked out." David started moaning and pacing around the large open area of the loft. Then he began yelling, howling, and running all around. He went back to where the Swami was. Suddenly Prabhupāda found himself face to face not with David—nice David, whom he was going to take to India to show the *brāhmaṇas* in Vṛndāvana—but a drugged, wild-eyed stranger, a madman.

Prabhupāda tried to speak to him—"What is the matter?"—but David had nothing to say. There was no particular disagreement. Just madness. . . .

Prabhupāda moved quickly down the four flights of stairs. He had not stopped to gather up any of his belongings or even to decide where he would go or whether he would return. There had been no time to consider anything. He had taken quite a shock, and now he was leaving the arena of David's madness. The usual group of bums were sitting in the doorway, and with their customary flourish of courtesy they allowed him to pass. They were used to the elderly swami's coming in and out, going shopping and returning, and they didn't bother him. But he was not going shopping today. Where was he going? He didn't know. He had come onto the street without knowing where he would go.

He wasn't going back to the loft—that was for sure. But where could he go? The pigeons flew from roof to roof. Traffic rumbled by, and the ever-present bums loitered about, getting drunker on cheap, poisonous alcohol. Although Prabhupāda's home had suddenly become an insane terror, the street at its door was also a hellish, dangerous place. He was shaken. He could call Dr. Mishra's, and they might take him in. But that chapter of his life was over, and he had gone on to something better. He had his own classes, young people chanting and hearing. Was it all over now? After nine months in America, he had finally gotten a good response to his preaching and *kīrtana*. He couldn't just quit now.

A. C. Bhaktivedanta Swami Mahārāja, whom everyone knew and respected in Vṛndāvana as a distinguished scholar and devotee, who had an open invitation to see the vice president of India and many other notables, now had to face starkly that he had not one friend of stature in the United States. Suddenly he was as homeless as any derelict on the street. In fact many of them, with their long-time berths in flophouses, were more secure than he. They were ruined, but settled. The Bowery could be a chaotic hell if you weren't on a very purposeful errand—going directly to the store, or back to your place. It was no place to stand wondering where will you live or is there a friend you can turn to. He wasn't on his way to Chinatown to shop, nor was he taking a little stroll, soon to return to the shelter of the loft. If he couldn't go to the loft, he had no place.

How difficult it was becoming to preach in America amid these crazy people! He had written prophetically in his poem the day he had arrived in Boston Harbor, "My dear Lord, I do not know why You have brought me here. Now You can do with me whatever You like. But I guess You have some business here, otherwise why would You bring me to this terrible place?" What about his scheduled classes? What about David—should he go back and try to talk with the boy? This had been David's first fit of violence, but there had been other tense moments. David had a habit of leaving the soap on the floor of the shower stall, and Prabhupāda had asked him not to, because it was a hazard. But David wouldn't listen. Prabhupāda had continued to remind him, and one day David had gotten angry and shouted at him. But there was no real enmity. Even today's incident had not been a matter of personal differences—the boy was a victim.

Prabhupāda walked quickly. He had free passage on the Scindia Line. He could go home to Vṛndāvana. But his spiritual master had ordered him to come here. "By the strong desire of Śrī Śrīmad Bhaktisiddhānta Sarasvatī Ṭhākura," he had written while crossing the Atlantic, "the holy name of Lord Gaurāṅga will spread throughout all the countries of the Western world." Before nightfall he would have to find some place to stay, a way to keep up the momentum of his preaching. This is what it meant to be working without government sponsorship, without the support of any religious organization, without a patron. It meant being vulnerable and insecure. Prabhupāda faced the crisis as a test from

Kṛṣṇa. The instruction of *Bhagavad-gītā* was to depend on Kṛṣṇa for protection: "In all activities just depend upon Me and work always under My protection. In such devotional service be fully conscious of Me. . . . You will pass over all the obstacles of conditional life by My grace."

He decided to phone Carl Yeargens and ask him to help. Hearing the Swami's voice on the phone—it was an emergency!—Carl at once agreed that Prabhupāda could move in with him and his wife, Eva. Their place was close by, on Centre Street, five blocks west of Bowery near Chinatown. Carl would be right over.

After Carl found Prabhupāda, they went straight to Carl's place, an A.I.R. loft, smaller than the one Prabhupāda had been living in. It had a main living area, large and open, with areas for the kitchen and bedroom partitioned off. There were decorative indoor plants and a profusion of throw pillows placed all around. Carl's loft was much brighter than the dingy, factorylike space in the loft on the Bowery. The floor was painted bright orange—Carl used to say it looked like the deck of a ship. The walls and ceiling were white, and light from seven skylights filled the room. Carl and Eva settled the Swami in one corner.

Prabhupāda had left his belongings at David's loft and didn't want to go back, so Carl went over to pick up a few essential items. Prabhupāda asked him to leave most of his things, including his books, suitcases, and reel-to-reel tape recorder, where they were.

Although by this time David had come down from the intense effects of the LSD, he remained crazy. When Carl arrived at the loft, the door was locked and David was inside, afraid to let anyone in, although finally he relented. He had shut and locked all the windows, making the loft oppressively hot and stuffy. Bill Epstein, who also came by that day, analyzed David as having had "a drug-induced nervous breakdown, a narcopsychosis." And although David was sorry he had exploded at the Swami, neither Bill nor Carl thought Prabhupāda should live with David again. Apparently Prabhupāda's chances of making the loft into a Rādhā-Kṛṣṇa temple were finished. Carl and Bill gathered up a few of the Swami's belongings, and David stayed behind in the loft. He wanted to be alone.

Carl Yeargens knew Prabhupāda's living habits and wanted to accommodate him with a suitable place to live and work. In a small alcove at one end of his loft, Carl had a small study, which he allocated for the Swami. Carl also set up a cushioned dais and arranged the living room around it so that guests could sit on the floor in a semicircle. Carl's wife, who didn't really like the idea of a swami moving in, agreed to cover a few cushions with Indian madras material for him anyway.

Things went smoothly for a while. Prabhupāda continued his morning and evening classes, and many of the Bowery hip crowd came by. Three of his regular callers lived right in the same building, and a few others, including Carl's brother, were just around the block. Michael Grant, James Greene—even David Allen came once.

Don Nathanson (an artist): *I was at Carl's loft, and the Swami comes strolling in one day. So I already knew he was on the scene, from David's. Mostly musicians were coming. They were enjoying that private morning session with him. And that's really strange in itself, because these people were up almost all night, and he used to do it at six in the morning, for one hour. He would lead them in chanting with his hand cymbals—dot-dot-dah, dot-dot-dah. It was strange, because that crowd was heavy into drugs and they were well read. But for a short period they used to go every morning, nine or ten of them, and they felt very good about it. They felt very good that they did that in the morning.*

Carl felt that the creative group who came to see the Swami in his studio were all quick to enter into the mood of the *kīrtana*, but they were "using it in their own ways, to supplement their own private visions and ecstasies," with no real intention of adopting the disciplines or the undivided worship of Lord Kṛṣṇa. Prabhupāda was their first real contact with a spiritual person, and yet even without trying to understand, they became absorbed in his *kīrtanas* and in what he had to say. Carl would invite them: "Hey, come on. This is genuine. This is real. You'll like it. It's music. It's dance. It's celebration." Carl saw that "people just felt good being in the Swami's presence and meditating on the chanting and eating the Swami's cooking. It was unlike anything they had experienced before, except maybe for their moments of creative insight."

Yet for Carl and Eva, Prabhupāda's simple presence created difficulty. Never before during his whole stay in America had he been a more inconvenient or unwanted guest. Carl's studio was arranged for him and his wife to live in alone, using the bedroom, kitchen, and living room any way they liked. If they wanted to smoke marijuana or eat meat or whatever, that was their prerogative. This was Carl's home; he lived here with his wife Eva and their dogs and cats. But now they had to share it with the Swami.

Almost at once, the situation became intolerable for Eva. She resented the Swami's presence in her home. She was a feminist, a liberated white woman with a black husband and a good job. She didn't like the Swami's views on women. She hadn't read his books or attended his classes, but she had heard that he was opposed to sexual intercourse except for conceiving children, and that in his view a woman was supposed to be shy and chaste and help her husband in spiritual life. She knew about the Swami's four rules—no meat-eating, illicit sex, intoxication, or gambling—and she definitely did not want Carl's Swami trying to change *their* ways to suit *his.* And he had better not expect her to wait on him as his servant. She sensed the Swami objecting to almost everything she did. If she were to seek his advice, he would probably ask her to stop taking drugs, get rid of the cats and dogs, stop drinking, and stop contraceptive sex. If the Swami had his way, they would probably eat only at certain times and only certain foods. Eva was a heavy smoker, so he probably wouldn't like being around her. She was ready for a confrontation.

But Prabhupāda was not one to make intolerant demands while living in another's home. He kept to his allotted corner of the loft, and he made no demands or criticisms. Hadn't he seen his hosts in Butler eating meat and only remarked, "Think nothing of it"? Nevertheless, his imposing spiritual presence made Eva sorry Carl had ever met him. To Eva the Swami was an inimical force—and she, being candid and independent, let him know. As soon as he asked whether she could bring him something, she replied, "Get it yourself."

Carol Bekar saw the situation as being extremely uncomfortable and tense—"Eva was quite resentful." Eva complained to Carol: here she was paying rent for the loft, working hard, and this man was trying to change their way of life.

Carol: *Eva couldn't handle his teachings, and she couldn't handle his influence over Carl. She didn't feel so constrained, but she felt that Swamiji was making Carl feel constrained.*

This was Eva's main objection—the Swami was influencing Carl. Her relationship with Carl had only recently begun, and Carl was aware that she needed much of his time. He agreed with his wife, yet he couldn't refuse the Swami. He was interested in Indian music, poetry, and religions, and here was a living authority, vastly knowledgeable in all facets of Indian culture, right in his home. Prabhupāda would cook his meals in their kitchen, and right away Carl would be there, eager to learn the art of Indian cuisine. Carl also wanted the Swami to show him how to play the drum. They would have long talks together.

Carol: *Carl was trying to be something he really wasn't, but he would never have suggested that the Swami had to leave. Swami, I am sure, was astute enough to pick up on this tension. As soon as he could, he tried to move to another place.*

Gradually, Carl reached an impasse in his relationship with Prabhupāda. He couldn't share his life with both his wife and the Swami, and ultimately he was more inclined toward his wife.

Carl: *I couldn't see my loft becoming a temple. I was raising cats and dogs, and he wanted them removed. He used to call me a meat-eater. But then he changed our diet. Of course, he was hitting the American culture, which doesn't know what all this business is. I have to put it on myself as much as anyone. I could understand and absorb India through an impersonal agency like a book or a record, but here was the living representative of Godhead, and to me it was as difficult as anything I've ever had to do before or since.*

Prabhupāda was not insensitive to the distress his presence was causing. He didn't want to inconvenience anyone, and of course he could have avoided all inconvenience, both for himself and for people like Eva, if he had never come to America. But he wasn't concerned with convenience or inconvenience, pleasing Eva or displeasing her. He wanted to teach Kṛṣṇa consciousness.

Prabhupāda had a mission, and Carl's loft didn't seem to be the right base for it. Prabhupāda's friends all agreed: he should move more into the center of things. The Bowery and Chinatown were too far out of the way. They would find him a new place.

Forced by conditions he accepted as Kṛṣṇa's mercy, Prabhupāda sat patiently, trying not to disturb anyone, yet speaking about Kṛṣṇa consciousness day and night. Carl assured him that with half a dozen people searching, it wouldn't take long to find a new place, and they would all chip in together and help him with the rent.

* * *

A week passed, and no one had found a suitable place for the Swami. One day Prabhupāda suggested that he and Carl take a walk up to Michael Grant's place and ask him to help.

Mike: *I was awakened one morning very early, and Carl was on the phone saying, "Swamiji and I were just taking a walk, and we thought we'd come up and see you." I said, "But it's too early in the morning." And he said, "Well, Swamiji wants to see you." They were very near by, just down the street, so I had to quickly get dressed, and by the time I got to the door they were there.*

I was totally unprepared, but invited them up. The television had been on from the previous night, and there were some cartoons on. The Swami sat between Carl and me on the couch. I was keeping a pet cat, and the cat jumped up on Swamiji's lap, and he abruptly knocked it off onto the floor. We began to talk, but Swamiji glanced over at the cartoons on the television set and said, "This is nonsense." Suddenly I realized that the television was on and that it was *nonsense, and I got up very quickly saying, "Why, yes, it* is *nonsense," and turned it off.*

As Prabhupāda talked, he tried to impress on Mike how difficult it was for him to live with Carl and Eva, and Mike listened. But was the Swami so sure he couldn't go back to the Bowery loft and live with David Allen? Except for that one incident, it had been a nice setup, hadn't it? Prabhupāda explained that David had become a madman from too much LSD. He was dangerous. Mike gave the Swami a half-incredulous look—David Allen, dangerous? Prabhupāda then told a story: "There's an old saying in India that you get yourself a spiritual master, you sit opposite him, you learn everything from him that you can, then you kill him, you move his body to one side, and then you sit in his place, and you become the *guru*." As Prabhupāda spoke, Mike began to feel that David *was* dangerous, so he didn't ask for any more details.

Mike could see that Swamiji was appealing to him for help, and as they all sat together on the couch, Mike and Carl quietly nodded in agreement.

The Swami was looking at Mike, and Mike was trying to think.

"So how can we help Swamiji?" Carl interjected.

Mike explained that he was a pianist and he had to practice every day. He had two pianos, two sets of drums, a vibraphone, and other instruments right there in his apartment. Musicians were always coming over to practice, and they all played their instruments for hours. Also, he was living with a girl, and there was a cat in the apartment. But Mike promised that he would help find the Swami a new place. Prabhupāda thanked him and, along with Carl, stood to leave.

Mike felt obligated. He was good at getting things done, and he wanted to do this for the Swami. So the next day he went to *The Village Voice*, got the first newspaper off the press, looked through the classified ads until he found a suitable prospect, and phoned the landlord. It was a storefront on Second Avenue, and an agent, a Mr. Gardiner, agreed to meet Mike there. Carl and the Swami also agreed to come.

Mr. Gardiner and Mike were the first to arrive. Mike noted the unusual hand-painted sign—Matchless Gifts—above the front window. It was a holdover, Mr. Gardiner explained, from when the place had been a nostalgic-gift shop. Mike proceeded to describe the Swami as a spiritual leader from India, an important author, and a Sanskrit scholar. The rental agent seemed receptive. As soon as Prabhupāda and Carl arrived and everyone had been congenially introduced, Mr. Gardiner showed them the small storefront. Prabhupāda, Carl, and Mike carefully considered its possibilities. It was empty, plain, and dark—the electricity had not been turned on—and it needed repainting. It would be good for meetings, but not for the Swami's residence. But at $125 a month it seemed promising. Then Mr. Gardiner revealed a small, second-floor apartment just across the rear courtyard, directly behind the storefront. Another $71 a month and the Swami could live there, although first Mr. Gardiner would have to repaint it. The total rent would come to $196, and Carl, Mike, and the others would pitch in.

Prabhupāda had the idea of making Mr. Gardiner the first official trustee of his fledgling Kṛṣṇa consciousness society. During their conversation he presented Mr. Gardiner with a three-volume set of his *Śrīmad-Bhāgavatam*, and inside the front cover he wrote a personal dedication and then signed it, "A. C. Bhaktivedanta Swami." Mr. Gardiner felt flattered and honored to receive these books from their author himself. He agreed to become a trustee of the new society for Kṛṣṇa consciousness, and so pay the Society twenty dollars a month.

Mr. Gardiner took a week to paint the apartment. Meanwhile, Mike arranged for the electricity and water to be turned on and had a phone installed, and he and Carl raised the first month's rent among their friends. When everything was ready, Mike gave Prabhupāda a call at Carl's.

Now it was time to move the Swami into his new place. A few friends who were on hand accompanied the Swami over to the Bowery loft. Maybe they weren't prepared to become his surrendered disciples, but contributing toward the first month's rent and volunteering a few hours of work to help set up his place were exactly the kinds of things they could do very willingly.

At the loft, they all gathered up portions of the Swami's belongings, and then they started out on foot up Bowery. It was like a safari, a caravan of half a dozen men loaded with Prabhupāda's things. Michael carried the heavy Roberts reel-to-reel, and even the Swami carried two suitcases. They did everything so quickly that it wasn't until they were well on their way and Mike's arm began to ache that he realized, "Why didn't we bring a car?"

It was the end of June, and a hazy summer sun poured its heat down into the Bowery jungle. Starting and stopping, the strange safari, stretching for over a block, slowly trekked along. Prabhupāda struggled with his suitcases, past the seemingly unending row of restaurant supply shops and lamp stores between Grand, Broome, and Spring streets. Sometimes he paused and rested, setting his suitcases down. He was finally moving from the Bowery. His electrician friend on Seventy-second Street would have been relieved, although perhaps he would have disapproved of the Second Avenue address also. At least he was finished residing on Skid Row. He walked on, past the homeless men outside the Salvation Army shelter, past the open-door taverns, stopping at street-lights, standing alongside total strangers, keeping an eye on the progress of his procession of friends who struggled along behind him.

The Bowery artists and musicians saw him as "highly evolved." They felt that the spirit was moving him and were eager to help him set up his own place so that he could do his valuable spiritual thing and spread it to others. He was depending on them for help, yet they knew he was "on a higher level"; he was his own protector, or, as he said, God protected him.

The Swami and his young friends reached the corner of Bowery and Houston, turned right, and proceeded east. Gazing steadily ahead as he walked, Prabhupāda saw the southern end of Second Avenue, one block away. At Second Avenue he would turn left, walk just one block north across First Street, and arrive at his new home. As he passed the IND subway entrance, the storefront came into view—"Matchless Gifts." He gripped his suitcases and moved ahead. At Second Avenue and Houston he hurried through a break in the rapid traffic. He could see green trees holding their heads above the high courtyard wall, reaching up like overgrown weeds in the space between the front and rear buildings of his new address.

The streetside building housed his meeting hall, the rear building the apartment where he would live and translate. Adjoining the storefront building on its north side was a massive nine-story warehouse. The storefront structure was only six stories and seemed appended to the larger building like its diminutive child. On its southern side, Prabhupāda's new temple showed a surface of plain cement and was free of any adjoining structure; there was only the spacious lot of the busy Mobil service station that bordered on First Street. As Prabhupāda approached the storefront, he could see two small lanterns decorating the narrow doorway.

There was no certainty of what awaited him here. But already there had been good signs that these American young people, mad though they sometimes were, could actually take part in Lord Caitanya's *saṅkīrtana* movement. Perhaps this new address would be the place where he could actually get a footing with his International Society for Krishna Consciousness.

CHAPTER SEVEN

Breaking Ground

Swami Bhaktivedanta came to USA and went swiftly to the Archetype Spiritual Neighborhood, the New York Lower East Side, and installed intact an ancient perfectly preserved piece of street India. He adorned a storefront as his Ashram and adored Krishna therein and by patience and good humor singing chanting and expounding Sanskrit terminology day by day established Krishna Consciousness in the psychedelic (mind-manifesting) center of America East. . . . To choose to attend to the Lower East Side, what kindness and humility and intelligence!

—Allen Ginsberg
from his introduction to
the Macmillan *Bhagavad Gita As It Is*

Prabhupāda's new neighborhood was not as run-down as the nearby Bowery, though it certainly was less than quaint. Right across from his storefront, a row of tombstones looked out from the somber, dimly lit display windows of Weitzner Brothers and Papper Memorials. North of Weitzner Brothers was Sam's Luncheonette. Next to Sam's stood an ancient four-story building marked A.I.R., then Ben J. Horowitz Monuments (more gravestones), and finally Schwartz's Funeral Home. On the next block at number 43 a worn canvas awning jutted out onto the sidewalk: Provenzano Lanza Funeral Home. Then there was Cosmos Parcels (importers) and a few blocks further uptown the prominent black-and-white signboard of the Village East Theater.

Up a block, but on the same side of the avenue as the storefront, was the Church of the Nativity, an old three-story building with new blue paint and a gold-colored cross on top. The six-story 26 Second Avenue, its face covered by a greenish fire escape, crouched against the massive nine-story Knickerbocker Fireproof Warehouse.

Second Avenue was a main traffic artery for east Manhattan, and the stoplight at the intersection of Houston and Second pumped a stream of delivery trucks, taxis, and private autos past Prabhupāda's door. From early morning until night there would be cars zooming by, followed by the sound of brakes, the competitive tension of waiting bumper to bumper, the impetuous honking, then gears grinding, engines rumbling and revving, and again the zooming by. The traffic was distractingly heavy.

At 26 Second Avenue there were actually two storefronts. The one to the north was a coin laundry, and the one to the south had been a gift shop but was now vacant. Both had narrow entrances, large display windows, and dull paint. Beneath the Matchless Gifts sign was a window, six feet square, that a few weeks before had displayed matchboxes decorated with photos of movie stars of the thirties and forties. The sign—Matchless Gifts—was the only remaining memento of the nostalgic-gift shop that had recently moved out. Below the shop's window, a pair of iron doors in the sidewalk hid stone steps to the cellar and boiler room. The wide sidewalk had been laid down in sections of various shapes and sizes at different times, years past. Certain sections had cracked or caved in, and a fine dust with tiny sparkling shards of glass had collected in the cracks and depressions. A dull black fire hydrant stood on the curb. Midway between the entrances to the two storefronts was the main entrance to number 26. (This door opened into a foyer lined with mailboxes and intercoms, and then a locked inner door opened into a hallway leading to the stairs or back to the courtyard.)

To the left of the gift shop's window was its front door, a dark wooden frame holding a full-length pane of glass. The door opened into the long, narrow storefront, which was now completely bare. Just inside, to the right of the door, a platform extending beneath the display window was just the proper height for a seat. At the far end of the bare, dingy room, two grimy-paned windows covered with bars opened into the courtyard. To the left of the left-hand window was a small sink, fixed to the outside of a very small toilet closet, whose door faced the front of the store. A door on the store's left wall connected to a hallway that led into the courtyard.

The courtyard was paved with concrete geometric sections and encircled with shrub gardens and tall trees. There was a picnic table, a cement birdbath, and a birdhouse on a pole, and near the center of the courtyard were two shrub gardens. The courtyard was bordered north and south by high walls, and front and back by the two tenements. The patch of sky above gave relief.

Overlooking the courtyard from the rear building of 26 Second Avenue was Prabhupāda's second-floor apartment, where he would now live, work, and worship. With help from his Bowery friends, he had cleaned and settled into his new home. In the back room—his office—he had placed against one wall a thin cushion with an elephant-print cover and in front of the cushion his unpainted metal suitcase, which served as a desk. He had set his typewriter on the desk and his papers and books on either side. This became his work area. His manuscripts bundled in saffron cloth, his stock of *Śrīmad-Bhāgavatams*, and his few personal effects he kept in the closet opposite his desk. On the wall above his sitting place he hung an Indian calendar print of Lord Kṛṣṇa. (Kṛṣṇa, as a youth, was playing on His flute with a cow close behind Him. Lord Kṛṣṇa was standing on the planet earth, which curved like the top of a small hill beneath His feet.) There were two windows on the east wall, and the dappled morning sunlight, filtering in through the fire escape, fell across the floor.

The next room was bare except for a fancy coffee table, which became Prabhupāda's altar. Here he placed a framed picture of Lord Caitanya and His associates. On the wall he hung an Indian calendar print of four-armed Lord Viṣṇu and Ananta Śeṣa, the celestial snake. And, as in the Bowery loft, he put up a clothesline.

Both rooms were freshly painted, and the floors were clean hardwood parquet. The bathroom was clean and serviceable, as was the narrow, furnished kitchen. Prabhupāda would sometimes stand by the kitchen window, gazing beyond the courtyard wall. He had moved here without any prospects of paying the next month's rent.

Although Carl, Mike, Carol, James, Bill, and others had encouraged him to move here, some of them now found it a little inconvenient to visit him regularly, but they all wished him well and hoped new people would come here to help him. They felt that this location was the best yet. And he seemed more comfortable here. At the Paradox, Bill would spread the word of Swamiji's new address.

* * *

The Lower East Side has a history of change and human suffering as old as New York. Three hundred years before Prabhupāda's arrival, it had been part of Peter Stuyvesant's estate. Today's landmark of Tompkins Square Park had then been a salt marsh known as Stuyvesant's Swamp.

The Lower East Side first became a slum in the 1840s, when thousands of Irish immigrants, driven by the Irish potato famine, came and settled. Two decades later, the Irish became the image of the American to the next immigrants, the Germans, who gradually grew in numbers to become the largest immigrant group in New York City. Next came East European Jews (Poles and Ukranians), and by 1900 the Lower East Side had become the most densely populated Jewish ghetto in the world. But in the next generation the ghetto began to break up as Jews moved to the suburbs and economic advancement.

Next the Puerto Ricans thronged in—hundreds of thousands in the 1950s—immigrating from their island poverty or moving in from East Harlem. They, and the Negroes from Harlem and Bedford Stuyvesant who arrived next, were the new groups who along with the Poles and Ukranians populated the two square miles of tenements and crowded streets that formed the Lower East Side slums in the 1960s.

Then, only a few years before Prabhupāda's arrival, a different kind of slum-dweller had appeared on the Lower East Side. Although there have been many sociological and cultural analyses of this phenomenon, it remains ultimately inexplicable why they suddenly came, like a vast flock of birds swooping down or like animals in a great instinctual migration, and why after a few years they vanished.

At first the newcomers were mostly young artists, musicians, and intellectuals, similar to the hip crowd of Prabhupāda's Bowery days. Then came the young middle-class dropouts. Because living space was more available and rents were lower than in nearby Greenwich Village, they concentrated here on the Lower East Side, which in the parlance of the renting agents became known as the East Village. Many even came without finding a place to live and camped in the hallways of tenements. Drawn by cheap rent and the promise of Bohemian freedom, these young middle-class dropouts, the avant-garde of a nationwide youth movement soon to be known in the media as "hippies," wandered to the Lower East Side slums in living protest against America's good life of materialism.

As if responding to an instinctual call, younger teenage runaways joined the older hippies, and following the runaways came the police, counselors, social and welfare workers, youth hostels, and drug counseling centers. On St. Mark's Place a new hip commercialism sprang up, with head shops, poster shops, record shops, art galleries, and bookstores that carried everything from cigarette papers to hip clothes and psychedelic lighting.

The hippies journeyed to the Lower East Side in full conviction that this was the place to be, just as their immigrant predecessors had done. For the European immigrants of another age, New York Harbor had been the gateway to a land of riches and opportunity, as they at long last set their eyes on Manhattan's skyline and the Statue of Liberty. Now, in 1966, American youth thronged to New York City with hopes of their own and feasted on the vision of their newfound mystical land—the Lower East Side slums.

It was an uneasy coexistence, with hippies on one side and Puerto Ricans, Poles, and Ukranians on the other. The established ethnic groups resented the newcomers, who didn't really *have* to live in the slums, whereas they themselves did. In fact, many of the young newcomers were from immigrant families that had struggled for generations to establish themselves as middle-class Americans. Nevertheless, the youth migration to the Lower East Side was just as real as the immigration of Puerto Ricans or Poles or Ukranians had been, although the motives of course were quite different.

The hippies had turned from the suburban materialism of their parents, the inane happiness of TV and advertising—the ephemeral goals of middle-class America. They were disillusioned by parents, teachers, clergy, public leaders, and the media, dissatisfied with American policy in Vietnam, and allured by radical political ideologies that exposed America as a cruel, selfish, exploitative giant who must now reform or die. And they were searching for real love, real peace, real existence, and real spiritual consciousness.

By the summer of Śrīla Prabhupāda's arrival at 26 Second Avenue, the first front in the great youth rebellion of the sixties had already entered the Lower East Side. Here they were free—free to live in simple poverty and express themselves through art, music, drugs, and sex. The talk was of spiritual searching. LSD and marijuana were the keys, opening new realms of awareness. Notions about Eastern cultures and Eastern religions were in vogue. Through drugs, *yoga*, brotherhood, or just by being free—somehow they would attain enlightenment. Everyone was supposed to keep an open mind and develop his own cosmic philosophy by direct experience and drug-expanded consciousness, blended with his own eclectic readings. And if their lives appeared aimless, at least they had dropped out of a pointless game where the player sells his soul for material goods and in this way supports a system that is already rotten.

So it was that in 1966, thousands of young people were walking the streets of the Lower East Side, not simply intoxicated or crazy (though they often were), but in search of life's ultimate answers, in complete disregard of "the establishment" and the day-to-day life pursued by millions of "straight" Americans.

That the prosperous land of America could breed so many discontented youths surprised Prabhupāda. Of course, it also further proved that material well-being, the hallmark of American life, couldn't make people happy. Prabhupāda did not see the unhappiness around him in terms of the immediate social, political, economic, and cultural causes. Neither slum conditions nor youth rebellions were the all-important realities. These were mere symptoms of a universal unhappiness to which the only cure was Kṛṣṇa consciousness. He sympathized with the miseries of everyone, but he saw the universal solution.

Prabhupāda had not made a study of the youth movement in America before moving to the Lower East Side. He had never even made specific plans to come here amid so many young people. But in the ten months since Calcutta, he had been moved by force of circumstances, or, as he understood it, "by Kṛṣṇa's will," from one place to another. On the order of his spiritual master he had come to America, and by Kṛṣṇa's will he had come to the Lower East Side. His mission here was the same as it had been on the Bowery or uptown or even in India. He was fixed in the order of his spiritual master and the Vedic view, a view that wasn't going to be influenced by the radical changes of the 1960s. Now if it so happened that these young people, because of some change in the American cultural climate, were to prove more receptive to him, then that would be welcome. And that would also be by Kṛṣṇa's will.

Actually, because of the ominous influence of the Kali millennium, this was historically the worst of times for spiritual cultivation—hippie revolution or not. And Śrīla Prabhupāda was trying to transplant Vedic culture into a more alien ground than had any previous spiritual master. So he expected to find his work extremely difficult. Yet in this generally bad age, just prior to Prabhupāda's arrival on the Lower East Side, tremors of dissatisfaction and revolt against the Kali-yuga culture itself began vibrating through American society, sending waves of young people to wander the streets of New York's Lower East Side in search of something beyond the ordinary life, looking for alternatives, seeking spiritual fulfillment. These young people, broken from their stereotyped materialistic backgrounds and drawn together now on New York's Lower East Side, were the ones who were by chance or choice or destiny to become the congregation for the Swami's storefront offerings of *kīrtana* and spiritual guidance.

The Swami's arrival went unnoticed. The neighbors said someone new had taken the gift shop next to the laundry. There was a strange picture in the window now, but no one knew what to make of it. Some passersby noticed a piece of paper, announcing classes in *Bhagavad-gīta*, taped to the window. A few stopped to read it, but no one knew what to make of it. They didn't know what *Bhagavad-gītā* was, and the few who did thought, "Maybe a *yoga* bookstore or something." The Puerto Ricans in the neighborhood would look in the window at Harvey Cohen's painting and then blankly walk away. The manager of the Mobil gas station next door couldn't care less who had moved in—it just didn't make any difference. The tombstone-sellers and undertakers across the street didn't care. And for the drivers of the countless cars and trucks that passed by, Swamiji's place didn't even exist. But there were young people around who had been intrigued with the painting, who went up to the window to read the little piece of paper. Some of them even knew about the

Bhagavad-gītā, although the painting of Lord Caitanya and the dancers didn't seem to fit. A few thought maybe they would attend Swami Bhaktivedanta's classes and check out the scene.

* * *

July 1966

Howard Wheeler was hurrying from his apartment on Mott Street to a friend's apartment on Fifth Street, a quiet place where he hoped to find some peace. He walked up Mott Street to Houston, turned left and began to walk east, across Bowery, past the rushing traffic and stumbling derelicts, and toward Second Avenue.

Howard: *After crossing Bowery, just before Second Avenue, I saw Swamiji jauntily strolling down the sidewalk, his head held high in the air, his hand in the bead bag. He struck me like a famous actor in a very familiar movie. He seemed ageless. He was wearing the traditional saffron-colored robes of a* sannyāsī *and quaint white shoes with points. Coming down Houston, he looked like the genie that popped out of Aladdin's lamp.*

Howard, age twenty-six, was a tall, large-bodied man with long, dark hair, a profuse beard, and black-framed eyeglasses. He was an instructor in English at Ohio State University and was fresh from a trip to India, where he had been looking for a true *guru*.

Prabhupāda noticed Howard, and they both stopped simultaneously. Howard asked the first question that popped into his mind: "Are you from India?"

Prabhupāda smiled. "Oh, yes, and you?"

Howard: *I told him no, but that I had just returned from India and was very interested in his country and the Hindu philosophy. He told me he had come from Calcutta and had been in New York almost ten months. His eyes were as fresh and cordial as a child's, and even standing before the trucks that roared and rumbled their way down Houston Street, he emanated a cool tranquility that was unshakably established in something far beyond the great metropolis that roared around us.*

Howard never made it to his friend's place that day. He went back to his own apartment on Mott Street, to Keith and Wally, his roommates, to tell them and everyone he knew about the *guru* who had inexplicably appeared within their midst.

Keith and Howard had been to India. Now they were involved in various spiritual philosophies, and their friends used to come over and talk about enlightenment. Eighteen-year-old Chuck Barnett was a regular visitor.

Chuck: *You would open the door of the apartment, and thousands of cockroaches would disappear into the woodwork. And the smell was enough to knock you over. So Keith was trying to clean the place up and kick some people out. They were sharing the rent—Wally, Keith, Howard, and several others. Due to a lack of any other process, they were using LSD to try and increase their spiritual life. Actually we were all trying to use drugs to help in meditation. Anyway, Wally, Howard, and Keith were trying to find the perfect spiritual master, as we all were.*

Howard remembers his own spiritual seeking as "reading books on Eastern philosophy and religion, burning lots of candles and incense, and taking *gañjā* and peyote and LSD as aids to meditation. Actually, it was more intoxication than meditation. 'Meditation' was a euphemism that somehow connected our highs with our readings."

Keith, twenty-nine, the son of a Southern Baptist minister, was a Ph.D. candidate in history at Columbia University. He was preparing his thesis on "The Rise of Revivalism in the Southern United States." Dressed in old denim cutoffs, sandals, and T-shirt, he was something of a *guru* among the Mott Street coterie.

Wally was in his thirties, shabbily dressed, bearded, intellectual, and well read in Buddhist literature. He had been a radio engineer in the army and, like his roommates, was unemployed. He was reading Alan Watts, Hermann Hesse, and others, talking about spiritual enlightenment, and taking LSD.

In India, Howard and Keith had visited Hardwar, Rishikesh, Benares, and other holy cities, experiencing Indian temples, hashish, and dysentery. One evening in Calcutta they had come upon a group of *sādhus* chanting the Hare Kṛṣṇa *mantra* and playing hand cymbals. For Howard and Keith, as for many Westerners, the essence of Indian philosophy was Śaṅkara's doctrine of impersonal oneness: everything is false except the one impersonal spirit. They had bought books that told them, "Whatever way you express your faith, that way is a valid spiritual path."

Now the three roommates—Howard, Keith, and Wally—began to mix various philosophies into a hodgepodge of their own. Howard would mix in a little Whitman, Emerson, Thoreau, or Blake; Keith would cite Biblical references; and Wally would add a bit of Buddhist wisdom. And they all kept up on Timothy Leary, Thomas à Kempis, and many others, the whole mixture being subject to a total reevaluation whenever one of the group experienced a new cosmic insight through LSD.

This was the group that Howard returned to that day in July. Excitedly, he told them about the Swami—how he looked and what he had said. Howard told how after they had stood and talked together the Swami had mentioned his place nearby on Second Avenue, where he was planning to hold some classes.

Howard: *I walked around the corner with him. He pointed out a small storefront building between First and Second streets next door to a Mobil filling station. It had been a curiosity shop, and someone had painted the words Matchless Gifts over the window. At that time, I didn't realize how prophetic those words were. "This is a good area?" he asked me. I told him that I thought it was. I had no idea what he was going to offer at his "classes," but I knew that all my friends would be glad that an Indian swami was moving into the neighborhood.*

The word spread. Although it wasn't so easy now for Carl Yeargens and certain others to come up from the Bowery and Chinatown—they had other things to do—Roy Dubois, a twenty-five-year-old writer for comic books, had visited Prabhupāda on the Bowery, and when he heard about the Swami's new place, he wanted to drop by. James Greene and Bill Epstein had not forgotten the Swami, and they wanted to come. The Paradox restaurant was still a live connection and brought new interested people. And others, like Stephen Guarino, saw the Swami's sign in the window. Steve, age twenty-six, was a caseworker for the city's welfare department, and one day on his lunch break, as he was walking home from the welfare office at Fifth Street and Second Avenue, he saw the Swami's sign taped to the window. He had been reading a paperback *Gītā*, and he promised himself he would attend the Swami's class.

That day as he stood with the Swami before the storefront, Howard had also noticed the little sign in the window:

LECTURES IN BHAGAVAD GITA
A. C. BHAKTIVEDANTA SWAMI
MONDAY, WEDNESDAY, AND FRIDAY
7:00 to 9:00 P.M.

"Will you bring your friends?" Prabhupāda had asked.
"Yes," Howard promised. "Monday evening."

* * *

The summer evening was warm, and in the storefront the back windows and front door were opened wide. Young men, several of them dressed in black denims and button-down sport shirts with broad, dull stripes, had left their worn sneakers by the front door and were now sitting on the floor. Most of them were from the Lower East Side; no one had had to go to great trouble to come here. The little room was barren. No pictures, no furniture, no rug, not even a chair. Only a few plain straw mats. A single bulb hung from the ceiling into the center of the room. It was seven o'clock, and about a dozen people had gathered, when the Swami suddenly opened the side door and entered the room.

He wasn't wearing a shirt, and the saffron cloth that draped his torso left his arms and some of his chest bare. His complexion was smooth golden brown, and as they watched him, his head shaven, his ears long-lobed, and his aspect grave, he seemed like pictures they'd seen of the Buddha in meditation. He was old, yet erect in his posture, fresh and radiant. His forehead was decorated with the yellowish clay markings of the Vaiṣṇavas. Prabhupāda recognized big, bearded Howard and smiled. "You have brought your friends?"

"Yes," Howard answered in his loud, resonant voice.

"Ah, very good."

Prabhupāda stepped out of his white shoes, sat down on a thin mat, faced his congregation, and indicated they could all be seated. He distributed several pairs of brass hand cymbals and briefly demonstrated the rhythm: one . . . two . . . *three.* He began playing—a startling, ringing sound. He began singing: Hare Kṛṣṇa, Hare Kṛṣṇa, Kṛṣṇa Kṛṣṇa, Hare Hare/ Hare Rāma, Hare Rāma, Rāma Rāma, Hare Hare. Now it was the audience's turn. "Chant," he told them. Some already knew, gradually the others caught on, and after a few rounds, all were chanting together.

Most of these young men and the few young women present had at one time or another embarked on the psychedelic voyage in search of a new world of expanded consciousness. Boldly and recklessly, they had entered the turbulent, forbidden waters of LSD, peyote, and magic mushrooms. Heedless of warnings, they had risked everything and done it. Yet there was merit in their valor, their eagerness to find the extra dimensions of the self, to get beyond ordinary existence—even if they didn't know what the beyond was or whether they would ever return to the comfort of the ordinary. Nonetheless, whatever truth they had found, they remained unfulfilled, and whatever worlds they had reached, these young psychedelic voyagers had always returned to the Lower East Side. Now they were sampling the Hare Kṛṣṇa *mantra.*

When the *kīrtana* suddenly sprang up from the Swami's cymbals and sonorous voice, they immediately felt that it was going to be something far out. Here was another chance to "trip out," and willingly they began to flow with it. They would surrender their minds and explore the limits of the chanting for all it was worth. Most of them had already associated the *mantra* with the mystical *Upaniṣads* and *Gītā,* which had called out to them in words of mystery: "Eternal spirit . . . Negating illusion." But whatever it is, this Indian *mantra,* let it come, they thought. Let its waves carry us far and high. Let's take it, and let the effects come. Whatever the price, let it come. The chanting seemed simple and natural enough. It was sweet and wasn't going to harm anyone. It was, in its own way, far out.

As Prabhupāda chanted in his own inner ecstasy, he observed his motley congregation. He was breaking ground in a new land now. As the hand cymbals rang, the lead-and-response of the Hare Kṛṣṇa *mantra* swelled, filling the evening. Some neighbors were annoyed. Puerto Rican children, enchanted, appeared at the door and window, looking. Twilight came.

Exotic it was, yet anyone could see that a swami was raising an ancient prayer in praise of God. This wasn't rock or jazz. He was a holy man, a swami, making a public religious demonstration. But the combination was strange: an old Indian swami chanting an ancient *mantra* with a storefront full of young American hippies singing along.

Prabhupāda sang on, his shaven head held high and tilted, his body trembling slightly with emotion. Confidently, he led the *mantra,* absorbed in pure devotion, and they responded. More passersby were drawn to the front window and open door. Some jeered, but the chanting was too strong. Within the sound of the *kīrtana,* even the car horns were a faint staccato. The vibration of auto engines and the rumble of trucks continued, but in the distance now, unnoticed.

Gathered under the dim electric light in the bare room, the group chanted after their leader, growing gradually from a feeble, hesitant chorus to an approximate harmony of voices. They continued clapping and chanting, putting into it whatever they could, in hopes of discovering its secrets. This swami was not simply giving some five-minute sample demonstration. For the moment he was their leader, their guide in an unknown realm. Howard and Keith's little encounter with a *kīrtana* in Calcutta had left them outsiders. The chanting had never before come like this, right in the middle of the Lower East Side with a genuine swami leading them.

In their minds were psychedelic ambitions to see the face of God, fantasies and visions of Hindu teachings, and the presumption that "IT" was all impersonal light. Prabhupāda had encountered a similar group on the Bowery, and he knew this group wasn't experiencing the *mantra* in the proper disciplined reverence and knowledge. But he let them chant in their own way. In time their submission to the spiritual sound, their purification, and their enlightenment and ecstasy in chanting and hearing Hare Kṛṣṇa would come.

He stopped the *kīrtana*. The chanting had swept back the world, but now the Lower East Side rushed in again. The children at the door began to chatter and laugh. Cars and trucks made their rumblings heard once more. And a voice shouted from a nearby apartment, demanding quiet. It was now past 7:30. Half an hour had elapsed.

* * *

Now today, we shall begin the Fourth Chapter—what Lord Kṛṣṇa says to Arjuna.

His lecture is very basic and yet (for restless youth) heavily philosophical. Some can't take it, and they rise rudely upon hearing the Swami's first words, put on their shoes at the front door, and return to the street. Others have left as soon as they saw the singing was over. Still, this is his best group yet. A few of the Bowery congregation are present. The boys from Mott Street are here, and they're specifically looking for a *guru*. Many in the group have already read *Bhagavad-gītā*—and they're not too proud to hear and admit that they didn't understand it.

It's another hot and noisy July evening outside his door. Children are on summer vacation, and they stay out on the street until dark. Nearby, a big dog is barking—"*Row! Row! Row!*"—the traffic creates constant rumbling, just outside the window little girls are shrieking, and all this makes lecturing difficult. Yet despite the distraction of children, traffic, and dogs, he wants the door open. If it is closed, he says, "Why is it closed? People may come in." He continues, undaunted, quoting Sanskrit, holding his audience, and developing his urgent message, while the relentless cacophony rivals his every word. . . .

"*Row! Row! Row!*"

"*Eeeeeeeeek! Yaaaaaaaaa!*" Shrieking like little Spanish witches, the girls disturb the whole block. In the distance, a man shouts from his window: "Get outta here! Get outta here!"

Prabhupāda: *Ask them not to make noise.*

Roy (one of the boys in the temple): *The man is chasing the kids now.*

Prabhupāda: *Yes, yes, these children are making a disturbance. Ask them . . .*

Roy: *Yes, that's what . . . the man's chasing them right now.*

Prabhupāda: *They are making noises.*

Roy: *Yes, he's chasing them now.*

The man chases the children away, but they'll be back. You can't chase the children off the street—they live there. And the big dog never stops barking. And who can stop the cars? The cars are always there. Prabhupāda uses the cars to give an example: When a car momentarily comes into our vision on Second Avenue, we certainly don't think that it had no existence before we saw it or that it ceases to exist once it has passed from view; similarly, when Kṛṣṇa goes from this planet to another, it doesn't mean He no longer exists, although it may appear that way. Actually, He has only left our sight. Kṛṣṇa and His incarnations constantly appear and disappear on innumerable planets throughout the innumerable universes of the material creation.

The cars are always passing, roaring and rumbling through every word Prabhupāda speaks. The door is open, and he is poised at the edge of a river of carbon monoxide, asphalt, rumbling tires, and constant waves of traffic. He has come a long way from the banks of his Yamunā in Vṛndāvana, where great saints and sages have gathered through the ages to discuss Kṛṣṇa consciousness. But his audience lives *here* amid *this* scene, so he has come here, beside Second Avenue's rushing river of traffic, to speak loudly the ageless message.

He is still stressing the same point: whatever you do in Kṛṣṇa consciousness, however little it may be, is eternally good for you. Yet now, more than uptown or on the Bowery, he is calling his hearers to take to Kṛṣṇa consciousness *fully* and become devotees. He assures them. . . .

Anyone can become a devotee and friend of Kṛṣṇa like Arjuna. You will be surprised that Lord Caitanya's principal disciples were all so-called fallen in society. He appointed Haridāsa Ṭhākura to the highest position in His spiritual mission, although he happened to take birth in a Muhammadan family. So there is no bar for anyone. Everyone can become spiritual master, provided he knows the science of Kṛṣṇa. This is the science of Kṛṣṇa, this Bhagavad-gītā. *And if anyone knows it perfectly, then he becomes a spiritual master.*

And this transcendental vibration, Hare Kṛṣṇa, will help us by cleaning the dust from the mirror of our mind. On the mind we have accumulated material dust. Just like on the Second Avenue, due to the constant traffic of motorcars, there's always a creation of dust over everything. Similarly, by our manipulation of materialistic activities, there are some material dusts which are accumulated on the mind, and therefore we are unable to see things in true perspective. So this process, the vibration of the transcendental sound—Hare Kṛṣṇa, Hare Kṛṣṇa, Kṛṣṇa Kṛṣṇa, Hare Hare/ Hare Rāma, Hare Rāma, Rāma Rāma, Hare Hare—will cleanse the dust. And as soon as the dust is cleared, then, as you see your nice face in the mirror, similarly you can see your real constitutional position as spirit soul. In Sanskrit language it is said, bhava-mahā-dāvāgni. *Lord Caitanya said that. Lord Caitanya's picture you have seen in the front window. He is dancing and chanting Hare Kṛṣṇa. So, it doesn't matter what a person was doing before, what sinful activities. A person may not be perfect at first, but if he is engaged in service, then he will be purified.*

Suddenly a Bowery derelict enters, whistling and drunkenly shouting. The audience remains seated, not knowing what to make of it.

Drunk: *How are ya? I'll be right back. I brought another thing.*

Prabhupāda: *Don't disturb. Sit down. We are talking seriously.*

Drunk: *I'll put it up there. In a church? All right. I'll be right back.*

The man is white-haired, with a short, grizzly beard and frowsy clothing. His odor reeks through the temple. But then he suddenly careens out the door and is gone. Prabhupāda chuckles softly and returns immediately to his lecture.

So it doesn't matter what a person was doing before, if he engages in Kṛṣṇa consciousness—chanting Hare Kṛṣṇa and Bhagavad-gītā*—it should be concluded that he is a saint. He is a saintly person.* Api cet sudurācāro. *Never mind if he may have some external immoral habit due to his past association. It doesn't matter. Some way or other, one should become Kṛṣṇa conscious, and then gradually he will become a saintly person as he goes on executing this process of Kṛṣṇa consciousness.*

There is a story about how habit is second nature. There was a thief, and he went on pilgrimage with some friends. So at night when the others were sleeping, because his habit was to steal at night, he got up and was taking someone's baggage. But then he was thinking, "Oh, I have come to this holy place of pilgrimage, but still I am committing theft by habit. No, I shall not do it."

So then he took someone's bag and put it in another's place, and for the whole night the poor fellow moved the bags of the pilgrims from here to there. But due to his conscience, because he was on a holy pilgrimage, he did not actually take anything. So in the morning when everyone got up, they looked around and said, "Where is my bag? I don't see it." And another man says, "I don't see my bag." And then someone says, "Oh, there is your bag." So there was some row, so they thought, "What is the matter? How has it so happened?"

Then the thief rose up and told all of the friends, "My dear gentlemen, I am a thief by occupation, and because I have that habit to steal at night, I couldn't stop myself. But I thought, 'I have come to this holy place, so I won't do it.' Therefore I placed one person's bag in another man's place. Please excuse me."

So this is habit. He doesn't want to, but he has a habit of doing it. He has decided not to commit theft any more, but sometimes he does, habitually. So Kṛṣṇa says that in such conditions, when one who has decided to stop all immoral habits and just take to this process of Kṛṣṇa consciousness, if by chance he does something which is immoral in the face of society, that should not be taken account of. In the next verse Kṛṣṇa says, kṣipraṁ bhavati dharmātmā: *because he has dovetailed himself in Kṛṣṇa consciousness, it is sure that he will be saintly very soon.*

Suddenly the old derelict returns, announcing his entrance: "How are ya?" He is carrying something. He maneuvers his way through the group, straight to the back of the temple, where the Swami is sitting. He opens the toilet room door, puts two rolls of bathroom tissue inside, closes the door, and then turns to the sink, sits some paper towels on top of it and puts two more rolls of bathroom tissue and some more paper towels under the sink. He then stands and turns around toward the Swami and the audience. The Swami is looking at him and asks, "What is this?" The bum is silent now; he has done his work. Prabhupāda begins to laugh, thanking his visitor, who is now moving toward the door: "Thank you. Thank you very much." The bum exits. "Just see," Prabhupāda now addresses his congregation. "It is a natural tendency to give some service. Just see, he is not in order, but he thought that, 'Here is something. Let me give some service.' Just see how automatically it comes. This is natural."

The young men in the audience look at one another. This is really far out—first the chanting with the brass cymbals, the Swami looking like Buddha and talking about Kṛṣṇa and chanting, and now this crazy stuff with the bum. But the Swami stays cool, he's really cool, just sitting on the floor like he's not afraid of anything, just talking his philosophy about the soul and us becoming saints and even the old drunk becoming a saint!

After almost an hour, the dog still barks, and the kids still squeal.

Prabhupāda is asking his hearers, who are only beginners in spiritual life, to become totally dedicated preachers of Kṛṣṇa consciousness: "In the *Bhagavad-gītā*, you will find that anyone who preaches the gospel of *Bhagavad-gītā* to the people of the world is the most dear, the dearest person to Kṛṣṇa. Therefore it is our duty to preach the principles of this *Bhagavad-gītā* to make people Kṛṣṇa conscious." Prabhupāda can't wait to tell them—even if they aren't ready. It's too urgent. The world needs Kṛṣṇa conscious preachers.

People are suffering for want of Kṛṣṇa consciousness. Therefore, each and every one of us should be engaged in the preaching work of Kṛṣṇa consciousness for the benefit of the whole world. Lord Caitanya, whose picture is in the front of our store, has very nicely preached the philosophy of Kṛṣṇa consciousness. The Lord says, "Just take my orders, all of you, and become a spiritual master." Lord Caitanya gives the order that in every country you go and preach Kṛṣṇa consciousness. So if we take up this missionary work to preach Bhagavad-gītā *as it is, without interpretation and without any material motives behind it—as it is—then Kṛṣṇa says it shall be done. We should not have any attraction for worldly activities, otherwise we can't have Kṛṣṇa. But it doesn't mean that we should be inimical to the people of the world. No, it is our duty to give them the highest instruction, that you become Kṛṣṇa conscious and—*

A young man in the audience seems unable to contain himself and begins making his own incoherent speech.

Prabhupāda: *No. You cannot disturb just now.*

Man (standing up): *Now wait a minute, man.* (A quarrel begins as others try to quiet him.)

Prabhupāda: *No, no, no. No, no, no, no. Not just now. No, no, you cannot ask just now.*

Man: *Well, I am trying to talk.*

Prabhupāda: *No, just now you cannot ask.*

Man: *But wait a minute, man. Wait.*

Prabhupāda: *Why do you interfere just now? We have a regular question time.*

Others in the audience: *Let the man finish. Yeah, let him talk.* (The man's supporters defend his right to speak, while others try to silence him.)

Second man: *I have just one question, please. How long is an individual allowed or expected to go on without any type of thought? How long?*

Prabhupāda: *I am not finished. We'll give question time after finishing the talk.* (The parties go on quarreling.) *All right, I am very glad you are curious, but please wait. Have some patience, because we have not finished. As soon as we finish, after five minutes, ten minutes, I will tend to your question. Don't be impatient. Sit down.* (The audience quiets down, and the Swami goes on with his talk.)

After five minutes. . . .

Prabhupāda: *All right. This gentleman is impatient. We shall stop here. Now what is your question, sir?*

Man: *Practically we tend to place emphasis on those we identify with the fact itself. Many people are meant to explain the whyfores and wherefores of the metaphysical truth, that I think, therefore I am.*

Prabhupāda: *What is your particular question?*

Man: *I have no answer to that question. Rather, but that I attempt, I live, I breathe.*

Prabhupāda: *Yes.*

Man: *So ability—tell me why I have nothing to do with it. May I understand the whyfores and wheres?*

Prabhupāda: *That's all right.*

Man: *I have difficulty in you. I have difficulty in saying.*

Prabhupāda: *So long as we are in this material world there are so many problems.*

Man: *Not many problems. It is not many problems. This is the greatest fact. I have . . . I know . . .*

Prabhupāda: *Yes.*

Man: *I also know that the whys and wherefores of my particular . . .*

Prabhupāda: *Yes.*

Man: *I didn't come here . . . But let me explain my position. This isn't necessarily . . . I feel I must . . . I think the difference is to learn . . . You'll find it innumerable times by the same token . . . Maybe we are able to reconcile the fact of individual being for a long time to find out why . . .*

Prabhupāda (turning to one of the boys): *Roy, can you answer his question? It is a general question. You can answer, yes?*

Roy turns sympathetically to the rambling questioner, and Prabhupāda addresses his audience: "Enough questions." His voice now seems tired and resigned: "Let us have *kīrtana.*" And the Lower East Side once again abates. The chanting begins: the brass cymbals, Prabhupāda's voice carrying the melody, and the audience responding. It goes for half an hour and then stops.

It is now 9:00. The audience sits before Swamiji while a boy brings him an apple, a small wooden bowl, and a knife. As most of the audience still sits and watches, gauging the aftereffects of the chanting as though it had been some new drug, the Swami cuts the apple in half, then in fourths, then in eighths, until there are many pieces. He takes one himself and asks one of the boys to pass the bowl around. Swamiji holds back his head and deftly pops a slice of apple into his mouth, without touching his fingers to his lips. He chews a bit, ruminating, his lips closed.

The members of the congregation munch silently on little pieces of apple. Prabhupāda stands, slips into his shoes, and exits through the side door.

* * *

As Prabhupāda retired to his apartment and his guests disappeared through the front door, back into the city, Don and Raphael would turn out the lights, lock the front door, and go to sleep on the floor in their blankets. Don and Raphael had needed a place to stay when they heard about the Swami's place. Prabhupāda had a policy that any boy who expressed even a little interest in becoming his student could stay in the storefront and make it his home. Of course, Prabhupāda would ask them to contribute toward the rent and meals, but if, like Don and Raphael, they had no money, then it was still all right, provided they helped in other ways. Don and Raphael were the first two boys to take advantage of Prabhupāda's offer. The were attracted to Swamiji and the chanting, but they weren't serious about his philosophy or the disciplines of devotional life. They had no jobs and no money, their hair was long and unkempt, and they lived and slept in the same clothes day after day. Prabhupāda stipulated that at least while they were on the premises they could not break his rules—no intoxication, illicit sex, meat-eating, or gambling. He knew these two boarders weren't serious students, but he allowed them to stay, in hopes that gradually they would become serious.

Often, some wayfaring stranger would stop by, looking for a place to stay the night, and Don and Raphael would welcome him. An old white-bearded Indian-turned-Christian who was on a walking mission proclaiming the end of the world, and whose feet were covered with bandages, once slept for a few nights on a wooden bench in the storefront. Some nights, as many as ten drifters would seek shelter at the storefront, and Don and Raphael would admit them, explaining that the Swami didn't object, as long as they got up early. Even drifters whose only interest was a free meal could stay, and after the morning class and breakfast they would usually drift off again into *māyā.*

Don and Raphael were the Swami's steady boarders, although during the day they also went out, returning only for meals, sleep, and evening chanting. Occasionally they would bathe, and then they would use the Swami's bathroom up in his apartment. Sometimes they would hang out in the storefront during the day, and if someone stopped by, asking about the Swami's classes, they would tell the person all they knew (which wasn't much). They admitted that they weren't really into the Swami's philosophy, and they didn't claim to be his followers. If someone persisted in inquiring about the Swami's teachings, Don and Raphael would suggest, "Why don't you go up and talk to him? The Swami lives in the apartment building out back. Why don't you go up and see him?"

Prabhupāda usually stayed in his apartment. Occasionally he might look out his window and see, through the back windows of the storefront, that the light in the closet-sized bathroom had needlessly been left burning. Coming down to ask the boys to turn it off and not waste electricity, he might find a few boys lying on the floor talking or reading. Prabhupāda would stand gravely, asking them not to leave the light on, stressing the seriousness of wasting Kṛṣṇa's energy and money. He would stand dressed in *khādī*, that coarse handloomed cotton woven from handspun threads, a cloth that to Americans appears somehow exotic. Even the saffron color of Prabhupāda's *dhotī* and *chādar* was exotic; produced from the traditional Indian dye, it was a dull, uneven color, different from anything Western. After Prabhupāda turned off the light, the boys seemed to have nothing to say and nothing more appropriate to do than look with interest at him for a long, awkward moment, and the Swami would leave without saying anything more.

Money was scarce. From his evening meetings he would usually collect about five or six dollars in change and bills. Don talked of going up to New England to pick apples and bring back money for the Swami. Raphael said something about some money coming. Prabhupāda waited, and depended on Kṛṣṇa. Sometimes he would walk back and forth in the courtyard between the buildings. Seeming mysterious to the neighbors, he would chant on his beads, his hand deep in his bead bag.

Mostly he kept to his room, working. As he had said during a lecture when living on the Bowery, "I am here always working at something, reading or writing—something, reading or writing—twenty-four hours." His mission of translating *Śrīmad-Bhāgavatam*, of presenting the complete work in sixty volumes of four hundred pages each, could alone occupy all his days and nights. He worked at it whenever possible, sitting at his portable typewriter or translating the Sanskrit into English.

He especially worked in the very early hours of the morning, when he would not be interrupted. He would comb through the Sanskrit and Bengali commentaries of the great *ācāryas*, following their explanations, selecting passages from them, adding his own knowledge and realization, and then laboriously weaving it all together and typing out his Bhaktivedanta purports. He had no means or immediate plans for financing the publishing of further volumes, but he continued in the faith that somehow they would be published.

He had a broad mission, broader even than translating *Śrīmad-Bhāgavatam*, and so he gave much of his time and energy to meeting visitors. Had his only aim been to write, then there would have been no need to have taken the risk and trouble of coming to America. Now many people were coming, and an important part of his mission was to talk to them and convince them of Kṛṣṇa consciousness. His visitors were usually young men who had recently come to live on the Lower East Side. He had no secretary to screen his visitors, nor did he have scheduled visiting hours. Whenever anyone happened by, at any time, from early morning to ten at night, Prabhupāda would stop his typing or translating and speak with them. It was an open neighborhood, and many visitors would come by right off the street. Some were serious, but many were not; some even came intoxicated. Often they came not to inquire submissively but to challenge.

Once a young hippie on an LSD trip found his way upstairs and sat opposite the Swami: "Right now I am higher than you are," he announced. "*I am God.*" Prabhupāda bowed his head slightly, his palms folded: "Please accept my obeisances," he said. Then he asked "God" to please leave. Others admitted frankly that they were crazy or haunted by ghosts and sought relief from their mental suffering.

Lon Solomon: *I was looking for spiritual centers—places where one can go, not like stores where they ask you to leave, but where you can actually talk to people and try to understand the ultimate truth. I would come to the Swami's, knowing it was definitely a spiritual center. There was definitely something there. I was on drugs and disturbed with the notion that I must be God, or some very important personality way out of proportion to my actual situation. I was actually in trouble, mentally deranged because of so much suffering, and I would kind of blow in to see him whenever I felt the whim to do so. I didn't make a point of going to his meetings, but a lot of times I would just come. One time I came and spent the night there. I was always welcome at any time to sleep in the storefront. I wanted to show the Swami what a sad case I was so he should definitely do something for me. He told me to join him and he could solve my problems. But I wasn't ready.*

I was really into sex, and I wanted to know what he meant by illicit sex—what was his definition. He said to me, "This means sex outside of marriage." But I wasn't satisfied with the answer, and I asked him for more details. He told me to first consider the answer he had given me and then come back the next day and he would tell me more.

Then I showed up with a girl. The Swami came to the door and said, "I am very busy. I have my work, I have my translating. I cannot talk with you now." Well, that was the only time he didn't offer me full hospitality and full attention and talk with me as many questions as I had. So I left immediately with the girl. He was correct in his perception that I was simply going to see him just to try to impress the girl. He saw through it right away, and he rejected that type of association. But every time I came I was in trouble, and he always helped me.

Sometimes young men would come with scholarly pretentions to test the Swami's knowledge of *Bhagavad-gītā.* "You have read the *Gītā,*" Prabhupāda would say, "so what is your conclusion? If you claim to know the *Gītā,* then you should know the conclusion that Kṛṣṇa is presenting." But most people didn't think that there was supposed to be a definite conclusion to the *Gītā.* And even if there were such a conclusion, that didn't mean they were supposed to arrange their life around it. The *Gītā* was a *spiritual* book, and you didn't have to follow it.

One young man approached the Swami asking, "What book will you lecture from next week? Will you be teaching the *Tibetan Book of the Dead?*" as if Prabhupāda would teach spirituality like a college survey course in world religions. "Everything is there in *Bhagavad-gītā,*" Prabhupāda replied. "We could study one verse for three months."

And there were other questions: "What about Camus?"

"What is his philosophy?" Prabhupāda would ask.

"He says everything is absurd and the only philosophical question is whether to commit suicide."

"That means everything is absurd for *him.* The material world is absurd, but there is a spiritual world beyond this one. That means he does not know the soul. The soul cannot be killed."

Adherents of various thinkers approached him: "What about Nietzsche? Kafka? Timothy Leary? Bob Dylan?" Prabhupāda would ask what their philosophy was, and the particular follower would have to explain and defend his favorite intellectual hero.

"They are all mental speculators," Prabhupāda would say. "Here in this material world we are all conditioned souls. Your knowledge is imperfect. Your senses are blunt. What good is your *opinion*? We have to hear from the perfect authority, Kṛṣṇa."

"Do you mean to say that none of the great thinkers are God conscious?" a boy asked.

"Their sincerity is their God consciousness. But if we want perfect knowledge of God, then we have to consult *śāstra*."

Often there were challenges, but under the Swami's stare and hard logic, the challenger would usually trail off into thoughtful silence.

"Is the spiritual knowledge of China advanced?"

Prabhupāda would sometimes answer simply by making a sour face.

"Well, I am a follower of Vedānta myself."

"Do you know what *Vedānta* means? What is the first aphorism of the *Vedānta-sūtra*? Do you know?"

"No, I . . ."

"Then how can you speak of Vedānta? *Vedaiś ca sarvair aham eva vedyaḥ:* Kṛṣṇa says that He is the goal of Vedānta. So if you are a Vedāntist, then you must become Kṛṣṇa conscious."

"What about the Buddha?"

"Do you follow him?"

"No."

"No, you just talk. Why don't you follow? Follow Kṛṣṇa, follow Christ, follow Buddha. But don't just talk."

"This sounds the same as Christianity. How is it any different?"

"It is the same: love of God. But who is a Christian? Who follows? The Bible teaches, 'Thou shalt not kill,' but all over the world, Christians are expert in killing. Do you know that? I believe the Christians say that Jesus Christ died for our sins—so why are you still sinning?"

Although Prabhupāda was a stranger to America, they were strangers to absolute knowledge. Whenever anyone would come to see him, he wouldn't waste time—he talked philosophy, reason, and argument. He constantly argued against atheism and impersonalism. He spoke strongly, to prove the existence of God and the universality of Kṛṣṇa consciousness. He talked often and vigorously, day and night, meeting all kinds of questions and philosophies.

He would listen also, and he heard a wide range of local testimonies. He heard the dissatisfaction of young Americans with the war and with American society. One boy told him he didn't want to get married because he couldn't find a chaste girl; it was better to go with prostitutes. Another confided that his mother had planned to abort him, but at the last moment his grandmother had convinced her not to. He heard from homosexuals. Someone told him that a set of New Yorkers considered it chic to eat the flesh of aborted babies. And in every case, he told them the truth.

He talked with Marxists and explained that although Marx says that everything is the property of the State, the fact is that everything is the property of God. Only "spiritual communism," which puts God in the center, can actually be successful. He discounted LSD visions as hallucinations and explained how God can be seen factually and what God looks like.

Although these one-time visitors came and went away, a few new friends began to stay on, watching the Swami deal with different guests. They began to appreciate the Swami's arguments, his concern for people, and his devotion to Kṛṣṇa. He seemed actually to know how to help people, and he invariably offered them Kṛṣṇa consciousness—as much as they could take—as the solution to their problems. A few began to take the Swami's message to heart.

* * *

"We shall call our society ISKCON." Prabhupāda had laughed playfully when he first coined the acronym.

He had initiated the legal work of incorporation that spring, while still living on the Bowery. But even before its legal beginning, he had been talking about his "International Society for Krishna Consciousness," and so it had appeared in letters to India and in *The Village Voice*. A friend had suggested a title that would sound more familiar to Westerners, "International Society for *God* Consciousness," but Prabhupāda had insisted: "*Krishna* Consciousness." "God" was a vague term, whereas "Krishna" was exact and scientific; "God consciousness" was spiritually weaker, less personal. And if Westerners didn't know that Kṛṣṇa was God, then the International Society for *Krishna* Consciousness would tell them, by spreading His glories "in every town and village."

"Kṛṣṇa consciousness" was Prabhupāda's own rendering of a phrase from Śrīla Rūpa Gosvāmī's *Padyāvali*, written in the sixteenth century. *Kṛṣṇa-bhakti-rasa-bhāvita:* "to be absorbed in the mellow taste of executing devotional service to Kṛṣṇa."

But to register ISKCON legally as a nonprofit, tax-exempt religion required money and a lawyer. Carl Yeargens had already gained some experience in forming religious, political, and social welfare groups, and when he had met Prabhupāda on the Bowery he had agreed to help. He had contacted his lawyer, Stephen Goldsmith.

Stephen Goldsmith, a young Jewish lawyer with a wife and two children and an office on Park Avenue, was interested in spiritual movements. When Carl told him about Prabhupāda's plans, he was immediately fascinated by the idea of setting up a religious corporation for an Indian swami. He visited Prabhupāda at 26 Second Avenue, and they discussed incorporation, tax exemption, Prabhupāda's immigration status, and Kṛṣṇa consciousness. Mr. Goldsmith visited Prabhupāda several times. Once he brought his children, who liked the "soup" the Swami cooked. He began attending the evening lectures, where he was often the only nonhippie member of the congregation. One evening, having completed all the legal groundwork and being ready to complete the procedures for incorporation, Mr. Goldsmith came to Prabhupāda's lecture and *kīrtana* to get signatures from the trustees for the new society.

July 11

Prabhupāda is lecturing.

Mr. Goldsmith, wearing slacks and a shirt and tie, sits on the floor near the door, listening earnestly to the lecture, despite the distracting noises from the neighborhood. Prabhupāda has been explaining how scholars mislead innocent people with nondevotional interpretations of the *Bhagavad-gītā*, and now, in recognition of the attorney's respectable presence, and as if to catch Mr. Goldsmith's attention better, he introduces him into the subject of the talk.

I will give you a practical example of how things are misinterpreted.

Just like our president, Mr. Goldsmith, he knows that expert lawyers, by interpretation, can do so many things. When I was in Calcutta, there was a rent tax passed by the government, and some expert lawyer changed the whole thing by his interpretation. The government had to reenact a whole law because their purpose was foiled by the interpretation of this lawyer. So we are not out for foiling the purpose of Kṛṣṇa, for which the Bhagavad-gītā *was spoken. But unauthorized persons are trying to foil the purpose of Kṛṣṇa. Therefore, that is unauthorized.*

All right, Mr. Goldsmith, you can ask anything.

Mr. Goldsmith stands, and to the surprise of the people gathered, he makes a short announcement asking for signers on an incorporation document for the Swami's new religious movement.

Prabhupāda: *They are present here. You can take the addresses now.*

Mr. Goldsmith: *I can take them now, yes.*

Prabhupāda: *Yes, you can. Bill, you can give your address. And Raphael, you can give yours. And Don . . . Roy . . . Mr. Greene.*

As the meeting breaks up, those called on to sign as trustees come forward, standing around in the little storefront, waiting to leaf cursorily through the pages the lawyer has produced from his thin attaché, and to sign as he directs. Yet not a soul among them is committed to Kṛṣṇa consciousness.

Mr. Goldsmith meets his quota of signers—a handful of sympathizers with enough reverence toward the Swami to want to help him. The first trustees, who will hold office for a year, "until the first annual meeting of the corporation," are Michael Grant (who puts down his name and address without ever reading the document), Mike's girl friend Jan, and James Greene. No one seriously intends to undertake any formal duties as trustee of the religious society, but they are happy to help the Swami by signing his fledgling society into legal existence.

According to law, a second group of trustees will assume office for the second year. They are Paul Gardiner, Roy, and Don. The trustees for the third year are Carl Yeargens, Bill Epstein, and Raphael.

None of them know exactly what the half a dozen, legal-sized typed pages mean, except that "Swamiji is forming a society."

Why?

For tax exemption, in case someone gives a big donation, and for other benefits an official religious society might receive.

But these purposes hardly seem urgent or even relevant to the present situation. Who's going to make donations? Except maybe for Mr. Goldsmith, who has any money?

But Prabhupāda is planning for the future, and he's planning for much more than just tax exemptions. He is trying to serve his spiritual predecessors and fulfill the scriptural prediction of a spiritual movement that is to flourish for ten thousand years in the midst of the Age of Kali. Within the vast Kali Age (a period which is to last 432,000 years), the 1960s are but an insignificant moment.

The *Vedas* describe that the time of the universe revolves through a cycle of four "seasons," or *yugas*, and Kali-yuga is the worst of times, in which all spiritual qualities of men diminish until humanity is finally reduced to a bestial civilization, devoid of human decency. However, the Vedic literature foretells a golden age of spiritual life, beginning after the advent of Lord Caitanya and lasting for ten thousand years—an eddy that runs against the current of Kali-yuga. With a vision that soars off to the end of the millennium and beyond, yet with his two feet solidly on the ground of Second Avenue, Prabhupāda has begun an International Society for Krishna Consciousness. He has many practical responsibilities: paying the rent, incorporating his society, and paving the way for a thriving worldwide congregation of devotees. Yet he doesn't see his humble beginning as limiting the greater scope of his divine mission. He knows that everything depends on Kṛṣṇa, so whether he succeeds or fails is up to the Supreme. He has only to try.

The purposes stated within ISKCON's articles of incorporation reveal Prabhupāda's thinking. They were seven points, similar to those given in the Prospectus for the League of Devotees he formed in Jhansi, India, in 1953. That attempt had been unsuccessful, yet his purposes remained unchanged.

Seven Purposes of the International Society for Krishna Consciousness:

(a) To systematically propagate spiritual knowledge to society at large and to educate all peoples in the techniques of spiritual life in order to check the imbalance of values in life and to achieve real unity and peace in the world.

(b) To propagate a consciousness of Krishna, as it is revealed in the *Bhagavad Gita* and *Srimad Bhagwatam.*

(c) To bring the members of the Society together with each other and nearer to Krishna, the prime entity, thus to develop the idea within the members, and humanity at large, that each soul is part and parcel of the quality of Godhead (Krishna).

(d) To teach and encourage the sankirtan movement, congregational chanting of the holy name of God as revealed in the teachings of Lord Sri Chaitanya Mahaprabhu.

(e) To erect for the members and for society at large, a holy place of transcendental pastimes, dedicated to the Personality of Krishna.

(f) To bring the members closer together for the purpose of teaching a simpler and more natural way of life.

(g) With a view towards achieving the aforementioned Purposes, to publish and distribute periodicals, magazines, books and other writings.

Regardless of what ISKCON's charter members thought of the society's purposes, Prabhupāda saw them as imminent realities. As Mr. Ruben, the subway conductor who had met Prabhupāda on a Manhattan park bench in 1965, had noted: "He seemed to know that he would have temples filled up with devotees. 'There are temples and books,' he said. 'They are existing, they are there, but the time is separating us from them.' "

The first purpose mentioned in the charter was propagation. "Preaching" was the word Prabhupāda most often used. For him, preaching had a much broader significance than mere sermonizing. Preaching meant glorious, selfless adventures on behalf of the Supreme Lord. Lord Caitanya had preached by walking all over southern India and causing thousands of people to chant and dance with Him in ecstasy. Lord Kṛṣṇa had preached the *Bhagavad-gītā* while standing with Arjuna in his chariot on the battlefield of Kurukṣetra. Lord Buddha had preached, Lord Jesus had preached, and all pure devotees preach.

ISKCON's preaching would achieve what the League of Nations and the United Nations had failed to achieve—"real unity and peace in the world." ISKCON workers would bring peace to a world deeply afflicted by materialism and strife. They would "systematically propagate spiritual knowledge," knowledge of the nonsectarian science of God. It was not that a new religion was being born in July of 1966; rather, the eternal preaching of Godhead, known as *saṅkīrtana*, was being transplanted from East to West.

The society's members would join together, and by hearing the teachings of *Bhagavad-gītā* and *Śrīmad-Bhāgavatam* and by chanting the Hare Kṛṣṇa *mantra*, they would come to realize that each was a spirit soul, eternally related to Kṛṣṇa, the Supreme Personality of Godhead. They would then preach this to "humanity at large," especially through *saṅkīrtana*, the chanting of the holy name of God.

ISKCON would also erect "a holy place of transcendental pastimes dedicated to the Personality of Krishna." Was this something beyond the storefront? Yes, certainly. He never thought small: "He seemed to know that he would have temples filled up with devotees."

He wanted ISKCON to demonstrate "a simple, more natural way of life." Such a life (Prabhupāda thought of the villages of India, where people lived just as Kṛṣṇa had lived) was most conducive to developing Kṛṣṇa consciousness.

And all six of these purposes would be achieved by the seventh: ISKCON would publish and distribute literature. This was the special instruction Śrīla Bhaktisiddhānta Sarasvatī Ṭhākura had given to Śrīla Prabhupāda. He had specifically told him one day in 1932 at Rādhā-kuṇḍa in Vṛndāvana, "If you ever get any money, publish books."

Certainly none of the signers saw any immediate shape to the Swami's dream, yet these seven purposes were not simply theistic rhetoric invented to convince a few New York State government officials. Prabhupāda meant to enact every item in the charter.

Of course, he was now working in extremely limited circumstances. "The principal place of worship, located at 26 Second Avenue, in the city, county, and state of New York," was the sole headquarters for the International Society for Krishna Consciousness. Yet Prabhupāda insisted that he was not living at 26 Second Avenue, New York City. His vision was transcendental. His Guru Mahārāja had gone out from the traditional holy places of spiritual meditation to preach in cities like Calcutta, Bombay, and Delhi. And yet Prabhupāda would say that his spiritual master had not really been living in any of those cities, but was always in

Vaikuṇṭha, the spiritual world, because of his absorption in devotional service.

Similarly, the place of worship, 26 Second Avenue, was not a New York storefront, a former curiosity shop. The storefront and the apartment had been spiritualized and were now a transcendental haven. "Society at large" could come here, the whole world could take shelter here, regardless of race or religion. Plain, small, and impoverished as it was, Prabhupāda regarded the storefront as "a holy place of transcendental pastimes, dedicated to the Personality of Krishna." It was a world headquarters, a publishing house, a sacred place of pilgrimage, and a center from which an army of devotees could issue forth and chant the holy names of God in all the streets in the world. The entire universe could receive Kṛṣṇa consciousness from the International Society for Krishna Consciousness, which was beginning here.

* * *

In Keith, Prabhupāda had a serious follower. Within a week of their meeting, Keith had moved out of the Mott Street apartment and was living with Prabhupāda. He still dressed in his ragged denim shorts and T-shirt, but he began to do all the Swami's shopping and cooking. While in India, Keith had learned some of the etiquette of reverence toward a holy man and the principles of discipleship. His friends watched him curiously as he dedicated himself to the Swami.

Keith: *I saw that he was cooking, so I asked him if I could help. And he was very happy at the suggestion. The first couple of times, he took me shopping, and after that I mostly did it. He showed me how to make* capātīs *without a rolling pin by pressing out the dough with your fingers. Every day we would make* capātīs, *rice,* dāl, *and curries.*

So Keith became the dependable cook and housekeeper in Prabhupāda's apartment. Meanwhile, at the Mott Street apartment, the roommates' favorite topic for discussion was their relationship with the Swami. Everyone thought it was a serious relationship. They knew Swamiji was *guru.* And when they heard that he would be giving daily classes at 6 A.M., up in his apartment, they were eager to attend.

Keith: *I used to walk along the Bowery and look for flowers for him.*

When there were no flowers, I would take a straw or some grass. I loved going over there in the morning.

Howard: *I would walk very briskly over to Swamiji's, chanting Hare Kṛṣṇa, feeling better than ever before. Miraculously, the Lower East Side no longer looked drab. The sidewalks and buildings seemed to sparkle, and in the early morning before the smog set in, the sky was red and golden.*

Chuck: *I brought a few grapes and came to the door of the Swami. This was all new. Previously I would always walk toward McDougall Street, toward Bohemia, aesthetic New York—and now I was walking to the Lower East Side toward the business district, where there were no freaks, artists, or musicians, but simply straight buildings. And somehow, outside the carnival atmosphere, there was the richest attraction for the senses and the heart.*

Howard: *I would sing all the way to the foyer, then ring the buzzer marked "A. C. Bhaktivedanta Swami." And the door would buzz and open and I would walk through the hallway into the small patio and up to his small second-floor apartment, tiptoeing quietly so as not to wake up the neighbors.*

Chuck: *I came into the hall of his building, and there were many, many names printed on plaques over the mailboxes. I immediately found the name, "A. C. Bhaktivedanta Swami," handwritten on a slip of torn paper, slipped into one of the slots. I rang the buzzer and waited. After a few moments, the door buzzed loudly, and I entered through the security lock. I walked through the small garden into the rear building and upstairs.*

Prabhupāda held his classes for almost two months in the privacy of his room, the same room where he typed and talked to guests. To Keith it was not simply a class in philosophy but a mystical experience of sweetness.

Keith: *The sound of his voice, the sun coming up . . . we'd chant for a few minutes, softly clapping hands, and Swamiji would speak. The thing that got me most was simply the sound of his voice, especially while he was chanting Sanskrit. It was like music to my ears to hear him speak the raw sound.*

So as not to disturb the neighbors, Prabhupāda would say, "Chant softly," and he asked the boys to clap softly, so softly that their hands barely touched. Then he would chant the prayers to the spiritual master:

saṁsāra-dāvānala-līḍha-loka. "The spiritual master is receiving benediction from the ocean of mercy. Just as a cloud pours water on a forest fire to extinguish it, so the spiritual master extinguishes the blazing fire of material existence." With his eyes closed, he sat singing softly in the dim morning light. The few who attended—Keith, Howard, Chuck, Steve, Wally—sat entranced. Never before had the Swami been so appreciated.

Chuck: *The Swami was sitting there, and in the mornings he would look not shiny and brilliant, but very withdrawn. He looked as if he could sit like a stone maybe forever. His eyes were only two tiny slits of glistening light. He took out his cymbals and played lightly on the edge—one, two,* three*—and he began to sing in a deep voice that was almost atonal in its intervals. It was a melody-monotone that did not express happiness or sadness—a timeless chant that told no story. We chanted along with him as best we could, but several times Swamiji stopped and said, "Softly." After about thirty minutes of chanting, we stopped. Then he opened his eyes wider and said, "We must chant softly, because sometimes the neighbors are complaining."*

After singing, the Swami would give one of the boys a copy of Dr. Radhakrishnan's edition of *Bhagavad-gītā* to read aloud from. He would correct their mispronunciations and then explain each verse. Because there were only a few people present, there was always ample time for everyone to discuss the philosophy. The class would sometimes run an hour and a half and cover three or four verses.

Steve: *Swamiji mentioned that mangoes were the king of all fruits, and he even mentioned that they were not easily available in this country. It occurred to me that I could bring him mangoes. There was a store on First Avenue that always kept a stock of fresh mangoes in the cooler. I began a regular habit. Every day after getting off work, I would purchase one nice mango and bring it to Swamiji.*

Wally: *Some of the boys would say, "I'm doing this for the Swami." So I went to him and said, "Is there something I can do for you?" So he told me I could take notes in his class.*

The boys were sure that their service to Swamiji was spiritual, devotional service. By serving the spiritual master, who was a representative of Kṛṣṇa, you were serving Kṛṣṇa directly.

One morning Prabhupāda told Howard that he needed help in spreading the philosophy of Kṛṣṇa consciousness. Howard wanted to help, so he offered to type the Swami's manuscripts of *Śrīmad-Bhāgavatam.*

Howard: *The first words of the first verse read, "O the King." And naturally I wondered whether "O" was the king's name and "the king" stood in apposition. After some time I figured out that "O king" was intended instead. I didn't make the correction without his permission. "Yes," he said, "change it then." I began to point out a few changes and inform him that if he wanted I could make corrections, that I had a master's in English and taught last year at Ohio State. "Oh, yes," Swamiji said. "Do it. Put it nicely."*

He was giving them the idea of devotional service. "A devotee may not be perfect at first," he said, "but if he is engaged in service, once that service has begun he can be purified. Service is always there, in the material world or the spiritual." But service in the material world could not bring satisfaction to the self—only *bhakti,* purified service, service rendered to Kṛṣṇa, could do that. And the best way to serve Kṛṣṇa was to serve the representative of Kṛṣṇa.

They picked it up quickly. It was something you could do easily; it was not difficult like meditation—it was activity. You did something, but you did it for Kṛṣṇa. They had seen Swamiji respond to the Bowery bum who had come with a gift of toilet paper. "Just see," Swamiji had said, "he is not in order, but he thought, 'Let me give some service.' " But service had to be done voluntarily, out of love, not by force.

Wally: *Swamiji once asked me, "Do you think you could wear the Vaiṣṇava* tilaka *when you are on the streets?" I said, "Well, I would feel funny doing it, but if you want me to I will." And Swamiji said, "No, I don't ask you to do anything you don't want to do."*

Steve: *One day when I brought my daily mango to him he was in his room surrounded by devotees. I gave him my mango and sat down, and he said, "Very good boy." The way he said it, as if I were just a tiny little boy, made everyone in the room laugh, and I felt foolish. Swamiji, however, then changed their mood by saying, "No. This is actually love. This is Kṛṣṇa consciousness." And then they didn't laugh.*

When Howard first volunteered to do editing, he spent the whole morning working in Swamiji's room. "If there is any more typing," Howard said, "let me know. I could take it back to Mott Street and type there."

"More? There's lots more," Swamiji said. He opened the closet and pulled out two large bundles of manuscripts tied in saffron cloth. There were thousands of pages, single-spaced manuscripts of Prabhupāda's translations of the *Śrīmad-Bhāgavatam*. Howard stood before them, astonished. "It's a lifetime of typing," he said. And Prabhupāda smiled and said, "Oh, yes, many lifetimes."

* * *

Because of Prabhupāda's presence and the words that he spoke there and the *kīrtanas*, everyone was already referring to the storefront as "the temple." But still it was just a bare, squalid storefront. The inspiration to decorate the place came from the Mott Street boys.

Howard, Keith, and Wally devised a scheme to surprise the Swami when he came to the evening *kīrtana*. Wally removed the curtains from their apartment, took them to the laundromat (where they turned the water dark brown from filth), and then dyed them purple. The Mott Street apartment was decorated with posters, paintings, and large decorative silk hangings that Howard and Keith had brought back from India. The boys gathered up all their pictures, tapestries, incense burners, and other paraphernalia and took them, along with the purple curtains, to the storefront, where they began their day of decorating.

At the storefront the boys constructed a wooden platform for Prabhupāda to sit on and covered it with old velvet cloth. Behind the platform, on the rear wall between the two windows to the courtyard, they hung the purple curtains, flanked by a pair of orange ones. Against one orange panel, just above Swamiji's sitting place, they hung a large original painting of Rādhā and Kṛṣṇa on a circular canvas that James Greene had done. Prabhupāda had commissioned James, giving him the dust jacket from his *Śrīmad-Bhāgavatam*, with its crude Indian drawing, as a model. The figures of Rādhā and Kṛṣṇa were somewhat abstract, but the Lower East Side critics who frequented the storefront hailed the work as a wonderful achievement.

Keith and Howard were less confident that Prabhupāda would approve of their paintings and prints from India, so they hung them near the street side of the temple, away from Swamiji's seat. One of these prints, well known in India, was of Hanumān carrying a mountain through the sky to Lord Rāmacandra. The boys had no idea what kind of being Hanumān was. They thought perhaps he was a cat, because of the shape of his upper lip. Then there was the picture of a male person with six arms—two arms, painted greenish, held a bow and arrow; another pair, bluish, held a flute; and the third pair, golden, held a stick and bowl.

By late afternoon they had covered the sitting platform, hung the curtains, tacked up the decorative silks and prints and hung the paintings, and were decorating the dais with flowers and candlesticks. Someone brought a pillow for Swamiji to sit on and a faded cushion from an overstuffed chair for a backrest.

In addition to the Mott Street cache, Robert Nelson took one of his grandfather's Belgian-style Oriental rugs from his garage in the suburbs and brought it by subway to 26 Second Avenue. Even Raphael and Don took part in the decorating.

The secret was well kept, and the boys waited to see Swamiji's response. That night, when he walked in to begin the *kīrtana*, he looked at the newly decorated temple (there was even incense burning), and he raised his eyebrows in satisfaction. "You are advancing," he said as he looked around the room, smiling broadly. "Yes," he added, "this is Kṛṣṇa consciousness." His sudden, happy mood seemed almost like their reward for their earnest labors. He then stepped up onto the platform—while the boys held their breaths, hoping it would be sturdy—and he sat, looking out at the devotees and the decorations.

They had pleased him. But he now assumed a feature of extreme gravity, and though they knew he was certainly the same Swamiji, their titterings stuck in their throats, and their happy glances to each other suddenly abated in uncertainty and nervousness. As they regarded Swamiji's gravity, their joy of a few moments before seemed suddenly childish. As a cloud quickly covers the sun like a dark shade, Prabhupāda changed his mood from jolly to grave—and they spontaneously resolved to become equally grave and sober. He picked up the *karatālas* and again smiled a ray of appreciation, and their hearts beamed back.

The temple was still a tiny storefront, with many hidden and unhidden cockroaches, a tilted floor, and poor lighting. But because many of the decorations were from India, it had an authentic atmosphere, especially with Swamiji present on the dais. Now guests who entered were suddenly in a little Indian temple.

Mike Grant: *I came one evening, and all of a sudden there were carpets on the floor, pictures on the wall, and paintings. Just all of a sudden it had blossomed and was full of people. I was amazed how in just a matter of days people had brought so many wonderful things. When I came that evening and saw how it had been decorated, then I wasn't so much worried that he was going to make it. I thought it was really beginning to take hold now.*

Prabhupāda looked at his group of followers. He was moved by their offering him a seat of honor and their attempts at decorating Kṛṣṇa's storefront. To see a devotee make an offering to Kṛṣṇa was not new for him. But *this* was new. In New York, "this horrible place," the seed of *bhakti* was growing, and naturally, as the gardener of that tender sprout, he was touched by Kṛṣṇa's mercy. Glancing at the pictures on the wall he said, "Tomorrow I will come look at the pictures and tell you which are good."

The next day, Prabhupāda came down to appraise the new artwork on display. One framed watercolor painting was of a man playing a drum while a girl danced. "This one is all right," he said. But another painting of a woman was more mundane, and he said, "No, this painting is not so good." He walked to the back of the temple, followed anxiously by Howard, Keith, and Wally. When he came upon the painting of the six-armed person, he said, "Oh, this is very nice."

"Who is it?" Wally asked.

"This is Lord Caitanya," Prabhupāda replied.

"Why does He have six arms?"

"Because He showed Himself to be both Rāma and Kṛṣṇa. These are the arms of Rāma, and these are the arms of Kṛṣṇa."

"What are the other two arms?" Keith asked.

"Those are the arms of a *sannyāsī.*"

He went to the next picture, "This is also very nice."

"Who is it?" Howard asked.

"This is Hanumān."

"Is he a cat?"

"No," Prabhupāda replied. "He is a monkey."

Hanumān is glorified in the scripture *Rāmāyaṇa* as the valiant, faithful servant of Lord Rāmacandra. Millions of Indians worship the incarnation of Lord Rāma and His servitor Hanumān, whose exploits are perennially exhibited in theater, cinema, art, and temple worship. In not knowing who Hanumān was, the Mott Street boys were no less ignorant than the old ladies uptown who, when Prabhupāda had asked whether any of them had seen a picture of Kṛṣṇa, had all stared blankly. The Lower East Side mystics didn't know Hanumān from a cat, and they had brought back from their hashish version of India a picture of Lord Caitanya Mahāprabhu without even knowing who He was. Yet there was an important difference between these boys and the ladies uptown: the boys were serving Swamiji and chanting Hare Kṛṣṇa. They were through with material life and the middle-class work-reward syndrome. Their hearts had awakened to Swamiji's promise of expanded Kṛṣṇa consciousness, and they sensed in his personal company something exalted. Like the Bowery bum who had donated toilet paper during Prabhupāda's lecture, the Lower East Side boys did not have their minds quite in order, and yet, as Prabhupāda saw it, Kṛṣṇa was guiding them from within their hearts. Prabhupāda knew they would change for the better by chanting and hearing about Kṛṣṇa.

* * *

The summer of 1966 moved into August, and Prabhupāda kept good health. For him these were happy days. New Yorkers complained of the summer heat waves, but this caused no inconvenience to one accustomed to the 100-degree-plus temperatures of Vṛndāvana's blazing summers. "It is like India," he said, as he went without a shirt, seeming relaxed and at home. He had thought that in America he would have to subsist on boiled potatoes (otherwise there would be nothing but meat), but here he was happily eating the same rice, *dāl*, and *capātīs*, and cooking on the same three-stacked cooker as in India. Work on the *Śrīmad-Bhāgavatam* had also gone on regularly since he had moved into the Second Avenue apartment. And now Kṛṣṇa was bringing these sincere young men who were cooking, typing, hearing him regularly, chanting Hare Kṛṣṇa, and asking for more.

Prabhupāda was still a solitary preacher, free to stay or go, writing his books in his own intimate relationship with Kṛṣṇa—quite independent of the boys in the storefront. But now he had taken the International Society for Krishna Consciousness as his spiritual child. The inquiring young men, some of whom had already been chanting steadily for over a month, were like stumbling spiritual infants, and he felt responsible for guiding them. They were beginning to consider him their spiritual master, trusting him to lead them into spiritual life. Although they were unable to immediately follow the multifarious rules that *brāhmaṇas* and Vaiṣṇavas in India followed, he was hopeful. According to Rūpa Gosvāmī the most important principle was that one should "somehow or other" become Kṛṣṇa conscious. People should chant Hare Kṛṣṇa and render devotional service. They should engage whatever they had in the service of Kṛṣṇa. And Prabhupāda was exercising this basic principle of Kṛṣṇa consciousness to the furthest limit the history of Vaiṣṇavism had ever seen.

Although he was engaging the boys in cooking and typing, Prabhupāda was not doing any less himself. Rather, for every sincere soul who came forward to ask for service, a hundred came who wanted not to serve but to challenge. Speaking to them, sometimes shouting and pounding his fists, Prabhupāda defended Kṛṣṇa against the Māyāvāda philosophy. This was also his service to Śrīla Bhaktisiddhānta Sarasvatī Ṭhākura. He had not come to America to retire. So with the passing of each new day came yet another confirmation that his work and his followers and his challengers would only increase.

How much he could do was up to Kṛṣṇa. "I am an old man," he said. "I may go away at any moment." But if he were to "go away" now, certainly Kṛṣṇa consciousness would also go away, because the Kṛṣṇa consciousness society was nothing but him: his figure leading the chanting while his head moved back and forth in small motions of ecstasy, his figure walking in and out of the temple through the courtyard or into the apartment, his person sitting down smilingly to discuss philosophy by the hour—he was the sole bearer and maintainer of the small, fragile, controlled atmosphere of Kṛṣṇa consciousness on New York's Lower East Side.

CHAPTER EIGHT

Planting the Seed

"Does what you told us this morning," Howard asked, "mean we are supposed to accept the spiritual master to be God?"

"That means he is due the same respect as God, being God's representative," Prabhupāda replied calmly.

"Then he is not God?"

"No," Prabhupāda said, "God is God. The spiritual master is His representative. Therefore, he is as good as God because he can deliver God to the sincere disciple. Is that clear?"

—from dialogue with Hayagrīva

August 1966

It was makeshift—a storefront-turned-temple and a two-room apartment transformed into the *guru's* residence and study—but it was complete nonetheless. It was a complete monastery amid the city slums. The temple (the storefront) was quickly becoming known among the hip underground of the Lower East Side; the courtyard was a strangely peaceful place for aspiring monks, with its little garden, bird sanctuary, and trees, squeezed in between the front and rear buildings; the Swami's back room was the inner sanctum of the monastery. Each room had a flavor all its own—or rather, it took on its particular character from the Swami's activities there.

The temple room was his *kīrtana* and lecture hall. The lecture was always serious and formal. Even from the beginning, when there was no dais and he had to sit on a straw mat facing a few guests, it was clear he was here to instruct, not to invite casual give-and-take dialogue. Questions had to wait until he finished speaking. The audience would sit on the floor and listen for forty-five minutes as he delivered the Vedic knowledge intact, always speaking on the basis of Vedic authority—quoting Sanskrit, quoting the previous spiritual masters, delivering perfect knowledge supported with reason and argument. While contending with noises of the street, he lectured with exacting scholarship and deeply committed devotion. It appeared that he had long ago mastered all the references and conclusions of his predecessors and had even come to anticipate all intellectual challenges.

He also held *kīrtanas* in the storefront. Like the lectures, the *kīrtanas* were serious, but they were not so formal; Prabhupāda was lenient during *kīrtana*. Visitors would bring harmoniums, wooden flutes, guitars, and they would follow the melody or create their own improvisations. Someone brought an old string bass and bow, and an inspired guest could always pick up the bow and play along. Some of the boys had found the innards of an upright piano, waiting on the curb with someone's garbage, and they had brought it to the temple and placed it near the entrance. During a *kīrtana*, freewheeling guests would run their hands over the wires, creating strange vibrations. Robert Nelson, several weeks back, had brought a large cymbal that now hung from the ceiling, dangling close by the Swami's dais.

But there was a limit to the extravagance. Sometimes when a newcomer picked up the *karatālas* and played them in a beat other than the standard one-two-*three*, Swamiji would ask one of the boys to correct him, even at the risk of offending the guest. Prabhupāda led the chanting and drummed with one hand on a small bongo. Even on this little bongo drum, he played Bengali *mṛdaṅga* rhythms so interesting that a local conga drummer used to come just to hear: "The Swami gets in some good licks."

The Swami's *kīrtanas* were a new high, and the boys would glance at each other with widening eyes and shaking heads as they responded to his chanting, comparing it to their previous drug experiences and signaling each other favorably: "This is great. It's better than LSD!" "Hey, man, I'm really getting high on this." And Prabhupāda encouraged their newfound intoxication.

26 Second Avenue: *"It had been a curiosity shop, and someone had painted the words Matchless Gifts over the window."*

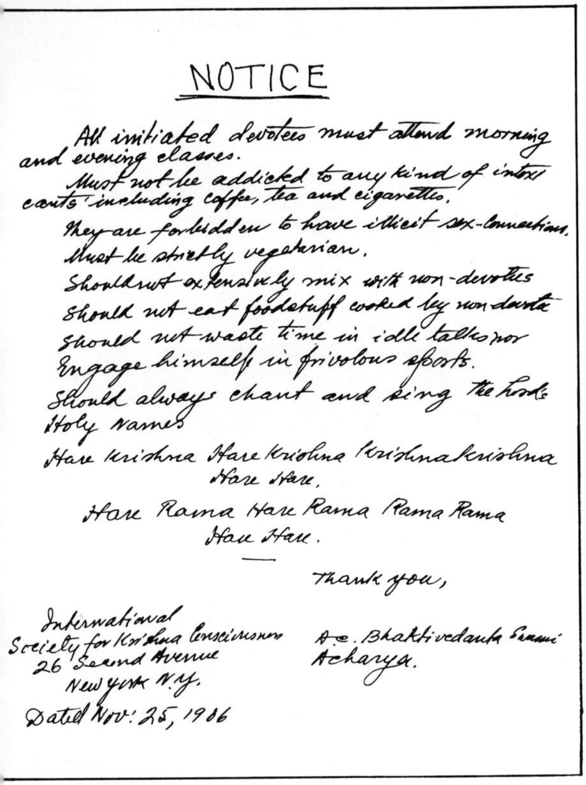

NOTICE

All initiated devotees must attend morning and evening classes.
Must not be addicted to any kind of intoxicants including coffee, tea and cigarettes.
They are forbidden to have illicit sex-connections.
Must be strictly vegetarian.
Should not extensively mix with non-devotees
Should not eat foodstuff cooked by non devotee
Should not waste time in idle talks nor
Engage himself in frivolous sports.
Should always chant and sing the Lord's Holy names
Hare Krishna Hare Krishna Krishna Krishna
Hare Hare.
Hare Rama Hare Rama Rama Rama
Hare Hare.

Thank you,

International
Society for Krishna Consciousness
26 Second Avenue
New York N.Y.
Dated Nov: 25, 1966

A.C. Bhaktivedanta Swami
Acharya.

Śrīla Prabhupāda posted this notice in the storefront.

Śrīla Prabhupāda in the courtyard at 26 Second Avenue.

One of Śrīla Prabhupāda's first expenditures at 26 Second Avenue was the purchase of this sign for announcing his classes.

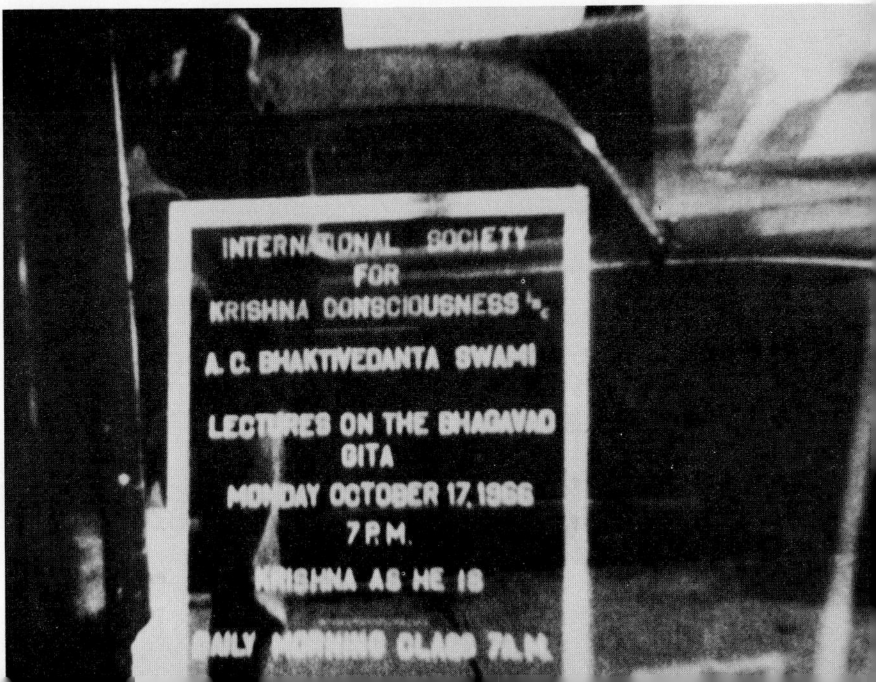

None of the boys knew what he was doing, although he did it every evening. They began to call the ceremony "bells."

Śrīla Prabhupāda and Brahmānanda passing through the courtyard on the way to the evening *kīrtana* in the temple.

Guests coming to the evening *kīrtana.*

In the storefront. From left to right: Dāmodara (with glasses), Jadurāṇī, Gargamuni (playing drum), and Brahmānanda.

Acyutānanda (with turtleneck jersey), Kīrtanānanda, and Hayagrīva. The circular painting of Rādhā-Kṛṣṇa hangs above the Swami's dais.

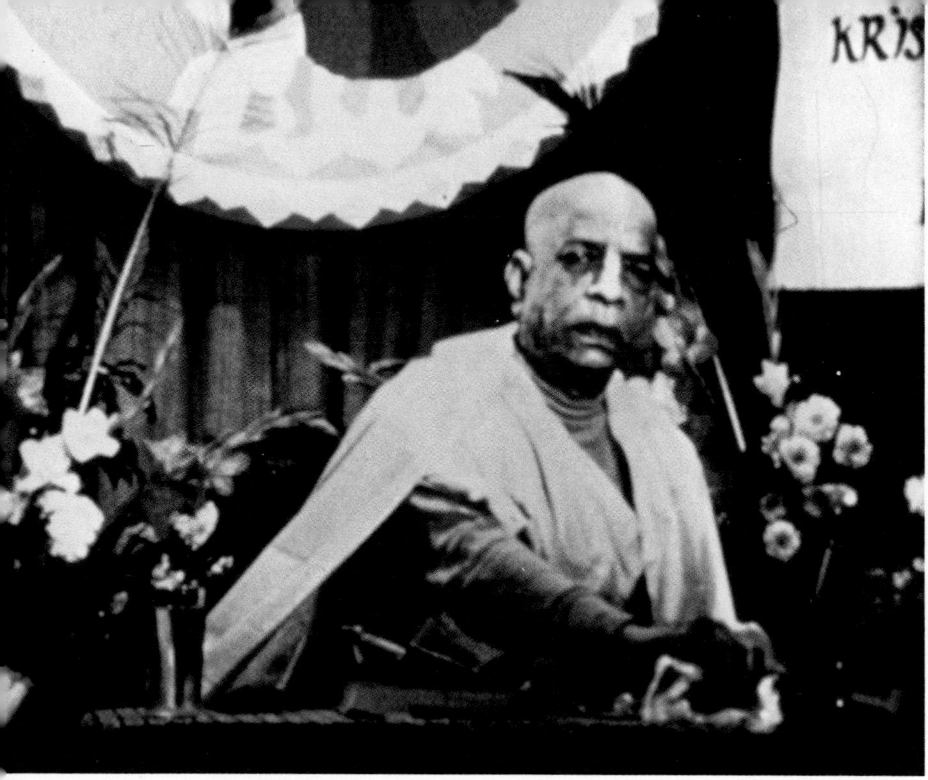

In the storefront, Śrīla Prabhupāda taught the ABC's of Kṛṣṇa consciousness, lecturing from *Bhagavad-gītā* and leading the group chanting of Hare Kṛṣṇa.

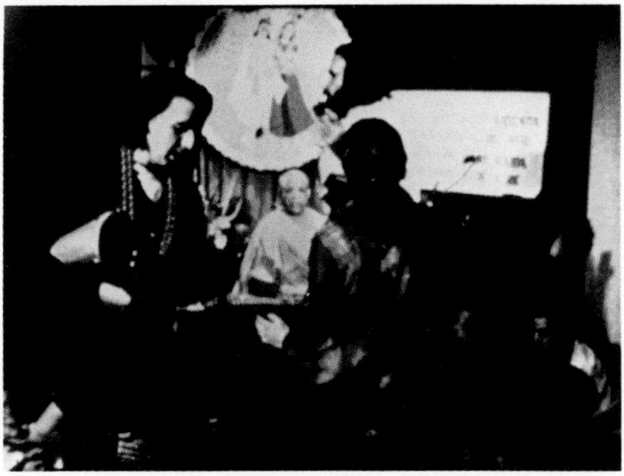

Dancing during *kīrtana.*

Śrīla Prabhupāda would sit back from his typewriter and give his time to talking, listening, answering questions, sometimes arguing, or joking.

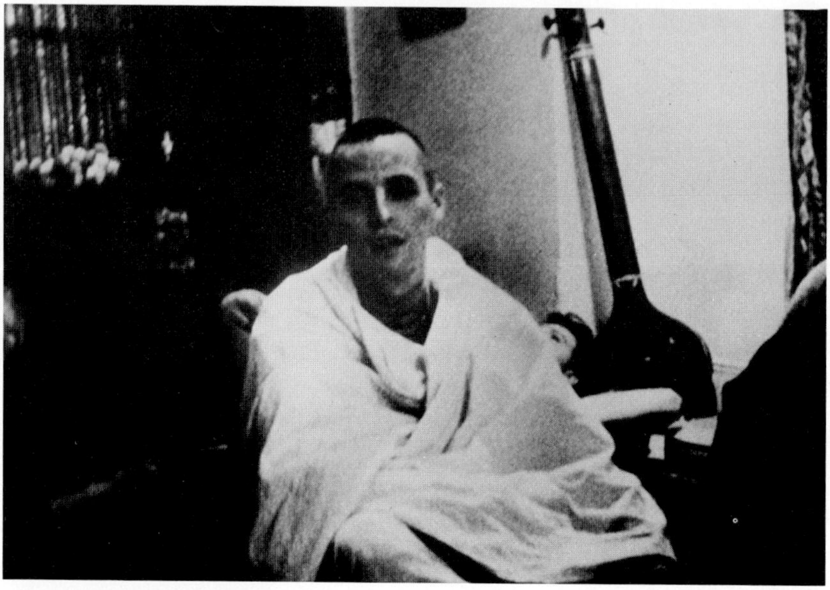

Kīrtanānanda, October 1966.

The photo from *The New York Times*, October 10, 1966: *"Swami's Flock Chants in Park to Find Ecstasy."*

THE east village OTHER

VOL. 1 NO. 22 OCTOBER 15-NOVEMBER 1 20¢ outside nyc 15¢

SAVE EARTH NOW !!

HARE KRISHNA HARE KRISHNA KRISHNA KRISHNA HARE HARE
HARE RAMA HARE RAMA RAMA RAMA HARE HARE ...

The East Village Other's coverage of Śrīla Prabhupāda's first *kīrtana* in Tompkins Square Park.

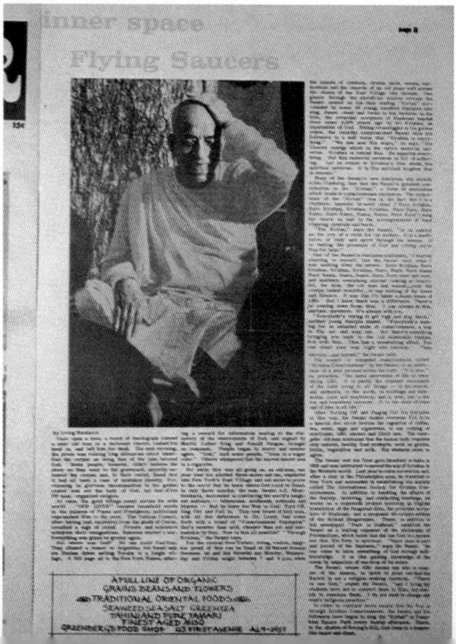

inner space

Flying Saucers

A FULL LINE OF ORGANIC
GRAINS BEANS AND FLOWERS
TRADITIONAL ORIENTAL FOODS
SEAWEED SEA SALT GREEN TEA
TAHINI AND PURE TAMARI
FINEST AGED MISO
GREENBERG'S FOOD SHOP 125 FIRST AVENUE AL4-2557

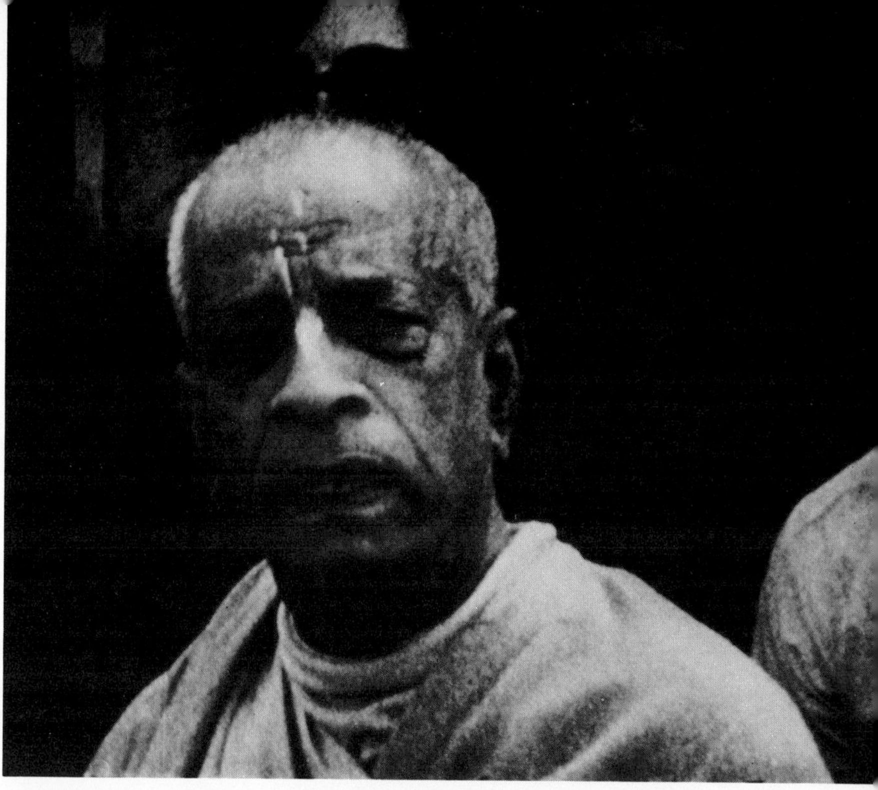

Prabhupāda was striking to see. His brow was furrowed in the effort of singing loud, and his visage was strong. The veins in his temples stood out visibly, and his jaw jutted forward as he sang his "Hare Kṛṣṇa! Hare Kṛṣṇa!" for all to hear. Although his demeanor was pleasant, his chanting was intensive, sometimes straining, and everything about him was concentration. (Page 210)

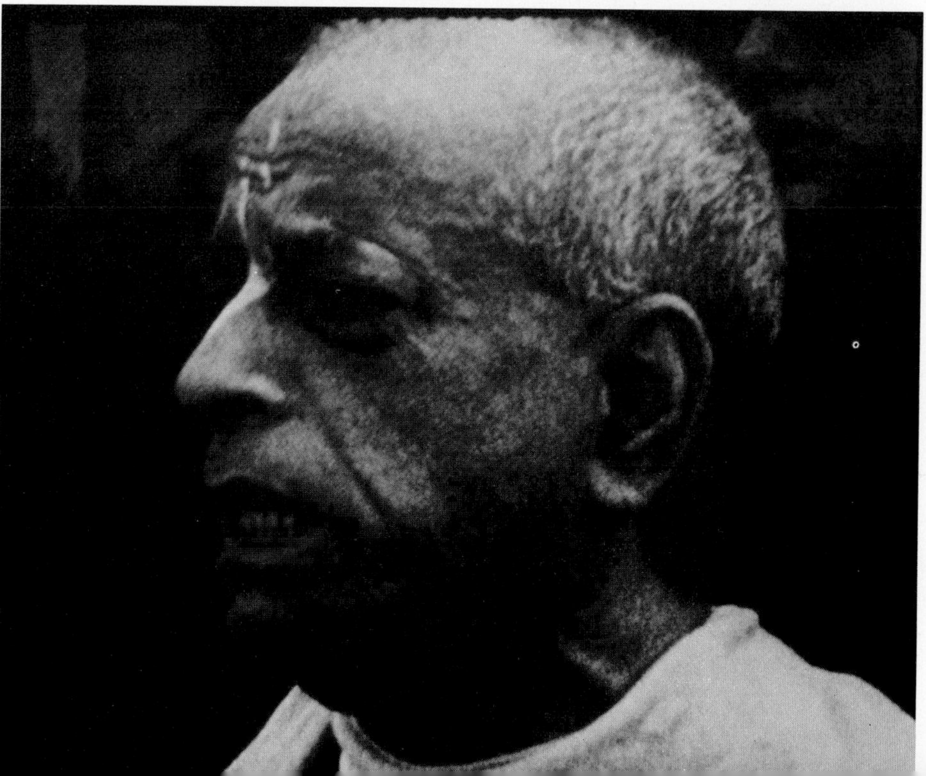

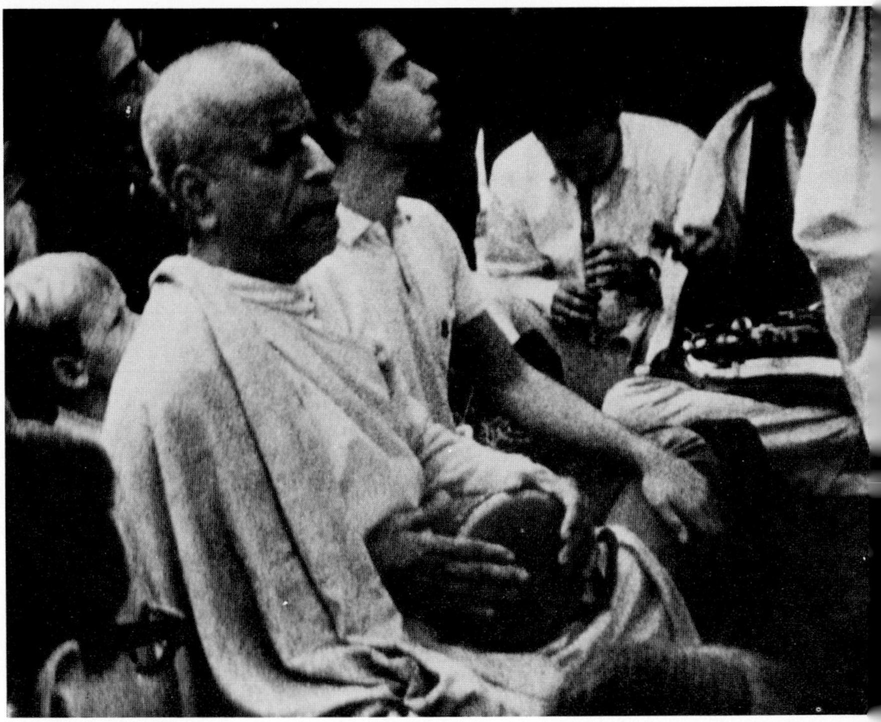

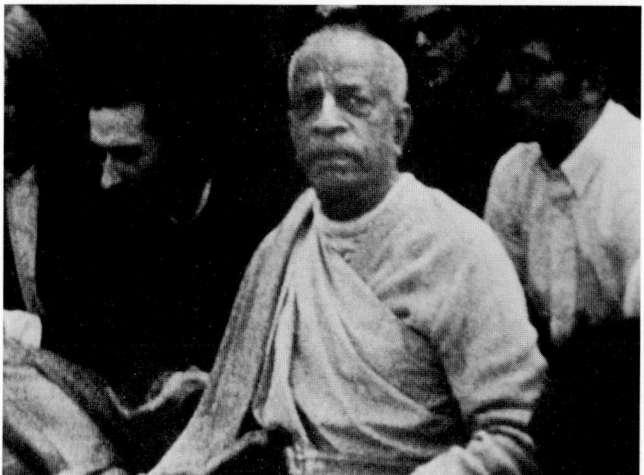

Chanting in Tompkins Square Park, October 1966:
"To choose to attend to the Lower East Side, what kindness and humility and intelligence!"

In the courtyard of 26 Second Avenue. The three windows on the left on the second floor are Śrīla Prabhupāda's rooms.

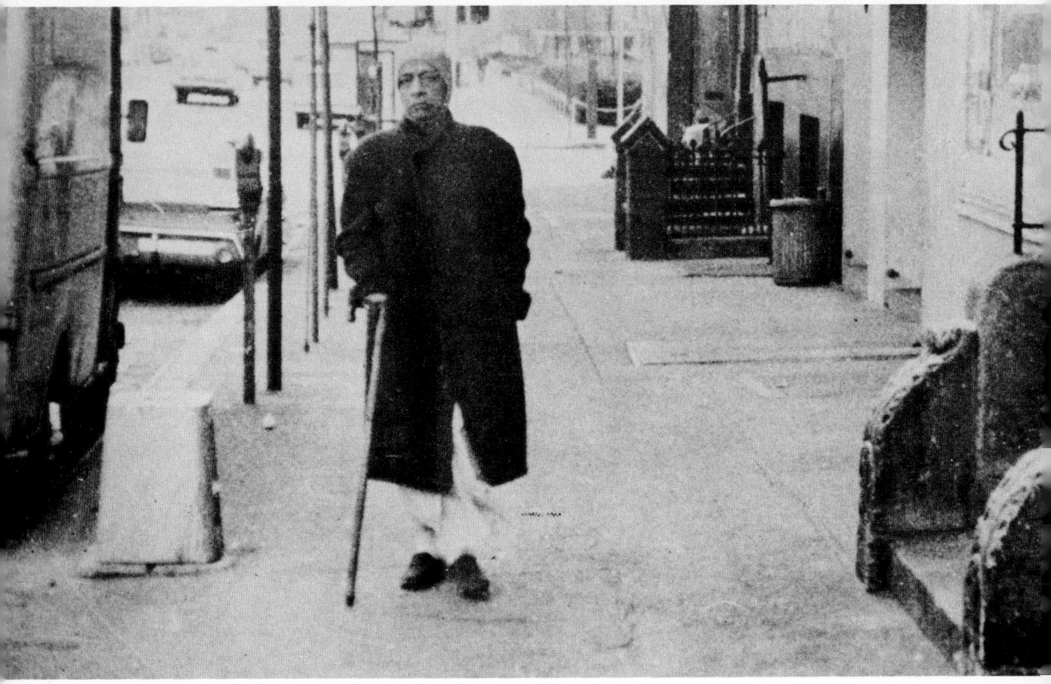

Śrīla Prabhupāda on the Lower East Side, winter 1966.

As maestro of these *kīrtanas*, he was also acting expertly as *guru*. Lord Caitanya had said, "There are no hard-and-fast rules for chanting the holy name," and Prabhupāda brought the chanting to the Lower East Side just that way. "A kindergarten of spiritual life," he once called the temple. Here he taught the ABCs of Kṛṣṇa consciousness, lecturing from *Bhagavad-gītā* and leading the group chanting of Hare Kṛṣṇa. Sometimes, after the final *kīrtana* he would invite those who were interested to join him for further talks in his apartment.

In the back room of his apartment Prabhupāda was usually alone, especially in the early morning hours—two, three, and four A.M.—when almost no one else was awake. In these early hours his room was silent, and he worked alone in the intimacy of his relationship with Kṛṣṇa. He would sit on the floor behind his suitcase-desk, worshiping Kṛṣṇa by typing the translations and purports of his *Śrīmad-Bhāgavatam*.

But this same back room was also used for meetings, and anyone who brought himself to knock on the Swami's door could enter and speak with him at any time, face to face. Prabhupāda would sit back from his typewriter and give his time to talking, listening, answering questions, sometimes arguing or joking. A visitor might sit alone with him for half an hour before someone else would knock and Swamiji would invite the newcomer to join them. New guests would come and others would go, but Swamiji stayed and sat and talked.

Generally, visits were formal—his guests would ask philosophical questions, and he would answer, much the same as after a lecture in the storefront. But occasionally some of the boys who were becoming serious followers would monopolize his time—especially on Tuesday, Thursday, Saturday, and Sunday nights, when there was no evening lecture in the temple. Often they would ask him personal questions: What was it like when he first came to New York? What about India? Did he have followers there? Were his family members devotees of Kṛṣṇa? What was his spiritual master like? And then Prabhupāda would talk in a different way—quieter, more intimate and humorous.

He told how one morning in New York he had first seen snow and thought someone had whitewashed the buildings. He told how he had spoken at several churches in Butler, and when the boys asked what kind of churches they were he smiled and replied, "I don't know," and they laughed with him. He would reminisce freely about the British control of India and about Indian politics. He told them it was not so much Gandhi as Subhas Chandra Bose who had liberated India. Subhas Chandra Bose had gone outside of India and started the Indian National Army; he entered into an agreement with Hitler that Indian soldiers fighting for British India who surrendered to the Germans could be returned to the Indian National Army to fight against the British. And it was this show of force by Bose, more than Gandhi's nonviolence, which led to India's independence.

He talked of his childhood at the turn of the century, when street lamps were gas-lit, and carriages and horse-drawn trams were the only vehicles on Calcutta's dusty streets. These talks charmed the boys even more than the transcendental philosophy of *Bhagavad-gītā* and drew them affectionately to him. He told about his father, Gour Mohan De, a pure Vaiṣṇava. His father had been a cloth merchant, and his family had been intimately related with the aristocratic Mulliks of Calcutta. The Mulliks had a Deity of Kṛṣṇa, and Prabhupāda's father had given him a Deity to worship as a child. He used to imitate the worship of the Govinda Deity in the Mullik's temple. As a boy, he had held his own Ratha-yātrā festivals each year, imitating in miniature the gigantic festival at Jagannātha Purī, and his father's friends used to joke: "Oh, the Ratha-yātrā ceremony is going on at your home, and you do not invite us? What is this?" His father would reply, "This is a child's play, that's all." But the neighbors said, "Oh, child's play? You are avoiding us by saying it's for children?"

Prabhupāda fondly remembered his father, who had never wanted him to be a worldly man, who had given him lessons in *mṛdaṅga*, and who had prayed to visiting *sādhus* that one day the boy would grow up to be a devotee of Rādhārāṇī.

One night he told how he had met his spiritual master. He told how he had begun his own chemical business but had left home and in 1959 had taken *sannyāsa*. The boys were interested, but so ignorant of the things Prabhupāda was talking about that at the mention of a word like *mṛdaṅga* or *sannyāsa* they would have to ask what it meant, and he would go on conversational tangents describing Indian spices, Indian drums, even Indian women. And whatever he spoke about, he would eventually shine upon it the light of the *śāstra*. He did not ration out such talk, but gave it out abundantly by the hour, day after day, as long as there was a real, live inquirer.

At noon the front room became a dining hall and in the evenings a place of intimate worship. Prabhupāda had kept the room, with its twelve-foot-square hardwood parquet floor, clean and bare; the solitary coffee table against the wall between the two courtyard windows was the only furniture. Daily at noon a dozen men were now taking lunch here with him. The meal was cooked by Keith, who spent the whole morning in the kitchen.

At first Keith had cooked only for the Swami. He had mastered the art of cooking *dāl*, rice, and *sabjī* in the Swami's three-tiered boiler, and usually there had been enough for one or two guests as well. But soon more guests had begun to gather, and Prabhupāda had told Keith to increase the quantity (abandoning the small three-tiered cooker) until he was cooking for a dozen hungry men. The boarders, Raphael and Don, though not so interested in the Swami's talk, would arrive punctually each day for *prasādam*, usually with a friend or two who had wandered into the storefront. Steve would drop by from his job at the welfare office. The Mott Street group would come. And there were others.

The kitchen was stocked with standard Indian spices: fresh chilies, fresh ginger root, whole cumin seeds, turmeric, and asafetida. Keith mastered the basic cooking techniques and passed them on to Chuck, who became his assistant. Some of the other boys would stand at the doorway of the narrow kitchenette to watch Keith, as one thick, pancakelike *capātī* after another blew up like an inflated football over the open flame and then took its place in the steaming stack.

While the fine *bhasmatī* rice boiled to a moist, fluffy-white finish and the *sabjī* simmered, the noon cooking would climax with "the *chaunce*." Keith prepared the *chaunce* exactly as Swamiji had shown him. Over the flame he set a small metal cup, half-filled with clarified butter, and then put in cumin seeds. When the seeds turned almost black he added chilies, and as the chilies blackened, a choking smoke began to pour from the cup. Now the *chaunce* was ready. With his cook's tongs, Keith lifted the cup, its boiling, crackling mixture fuming like a sorcerer's kettle, and brought it to the edge of the pot of boiling *dāl.* He opened the tight cover slightly, dumped the boiling *chaunce* into the *dāl* with a flick of his wrist, and immediately replaced the lid. . . . POW! The meeting of the *chaunce* and *dāl* created an explosion, which was then greeted by cheers from the doorway, signifying that the cooking was now complete. This final operation was so volatile that it once blew the top of the pot to the ceiling with a loud smash, causing minor burns to Keith's hand. Some of the neighbors complained of acrid, penetrating fumes. But the devotees loved it.

When lunch was ready, Swamiji would wash his hands and mouth in the bathroom and come out into the front room, his soft, pink-bottomed feet always bare, his saffron *dhotī* reaching down to his ankles. He would stand by the coffee table, which held the picture of Lord Caitanya and His associates, while his own associates stood around him against the walls. Keith would bring in a big tray of *capātīs*, stacked by the dozens, and place it on the floor before the altar table along with pots of rice, *dāl*, and *sabjī.* Swamiji would then recite the Bengali prayer for offering food to the Lord, and all present would follow him by bowing down, knees and head to the floor, and approximating the Bengali prayer one word at a time. While the steam and mixed aromas drifted up like an offering of incense before the picture of Lord Caitanya, the Swami's followers bowed their heads to the wooden floor and mumbled the prayer.

Prabhupāda then sat with his friends, eating the same *prasādam* as they, with the addition of a banana and a metal bowl full of hot milk. He would slice the banana by pushing it downward against the edge of the bowl, letting the slices fall into the hot milk.

Prabhupāda's open decree that everyone should eat as much *prasādam* as possible created a humorous mood and a family feeling. No one was allowed simply to sit, picking at his food, nibbling politely. They ate with a gusto Swamiji almost insisted upon. If he saw someone not eating heartily, he would call the person's name and smilingly protest, "Why are you not eating? Take *prasādam.*" And he would laugh. "When I was coming to your country on the boat," he said, "I thought, 'How will the Americans ever eat this food?' " And as the boys pushed their plates forward for more, Keith would serve seconds—more rice, *dāl, capātīs*, and *sabjī.*

After all, it was spiritual. You were supposed to eat a lot. It would purify you. It would free you from *māyā*. Besides, it was good, delicious, spicy. This was better than American food. It was like chanting. It was far out. You got high from eating this food.

They ate with the right hand, Indian style. Keith and Howard had already learned this and had even tasted similar dishes, but as they told the Swami and a room full of believers, the food in India had never been this good.

One boy, Stanley, was quite young, and Prabhupāda, almost like a doting father, watched over him as he ate. Stanley's mother had personally met Prabhupāda and said that only if he took personal care of her son would she allow him to live in the monastery. Prabhupāda complied. He diligently encouraged the boy until Stanley gradually took on a voracious appetite and began consuming ten *capātīs* at a sitting (and would have taken more had Swamiji not told him to stop). But aside from Swamiji's limiting Stanley to ten *capātīs*, the word was always, "More . . . take more." When Prabhupāda was finished, he would rise and leave the room, Keith would catch a couple of volunteers to help him clean, and the others would leave.

Occasionally, on a Sunday, Prabhupāda himself would cook a feast with special Indian dishes.

Steve: *Swamiji personally cooked the* prasādam *and then served it to us upstairs in his front room. We all sat in rows, and I remember him walking up and down in between the rows of boys, passing before us with his bare feet and serving us with a spoon from different pots. He would ask what did we want—did we want more of* this? *And he would serve us with pleasure. These dishes were not ordinary, but sweets and savories—like sweet rice and* kacaurīs—*with special tastes. Even after we had all taken a full plate, he would come back and ask us to take more.*

Once he came up to me and asked what I would like more of—would I like some more sweet rice? In my early misconception of spiritual life, I thought I should deny myself what I liked best, so I asked for some more plain rice. But even that "plain" rice was fancy yellow rice with fried cheese balls.

On off nights his apartment was quiet. He might remain alone for the whole evening, typing and translating *Śrīmad-Bhāgavatam*, or talking in a relaxed atmosphere to just one or two guests until ten. But on meeting nights—Monday, Wednesday, and Friday—there was activity in every room of his apartment. He wasn't alone any more. His new followers were helping him, and they shared in his spirit of trying to get people to chant Hare Kṛṣṇa and hear of Kṛṣṇa consciousness.

In the back room, he worked on his translation of the *Bhāgavatam* or spoke with guests up until six, when he would go to take his bath. Sometimes he would have to wait until the bathroom was free. He had introduced his young followers to the practice of taking two baths a day, and now he was sometimes inconvenienced by having to share his bathroom.

After his bath he would come into the front room, where his assembled followers would sit around him. He would sit on a mat facing his picture of the Pañca-tattva, and after putting a few drops of water in his left palm from a small metal spoon and bowl, he would rub a lump of Vṛndāvana clay in the water, making a wet paste. He would then apply the clay markings of Vaiṣṇava *tilaka*, dipping into the yellowish paste in his left hand with the ring finger of his right. He would scrape wet clay from his palm, and while looking into a small mirror which he held deftly between the thumb and pinkie of his left hand, he would mark a vertical clay strip up his forehead and then trim the clay into two parallel lines by placing the little finger of his right hand between his eyebrows and running it upward past the hairline, clearing a path in the still-moist clay. Then he marked eleven other places on his body, while the boys sat observing, sometimes asking questions or sometimes speaking their own understandings of Kṛṣṇa consciousness.

Prabhupāda: *My Guru Mahārāja used to put on* tilaka *without a mirror.*

Devotee: *Did it come out neat?*

Prabhupāda: *Neat or not neat, that does not matter. Yes, it was also neat.*

Prabhupāda would then silently recite the Gāyatrī *mantra*. Holding his *brāhmaṇa's* sacred thread and looping it around his right thumb, he would sit erect, silently moving his lips. His bare shoulders and arms were quite thin as was his chest, but he had a round, slightly protruding belly. His complexion was as satiny smooth as a young boy's, except for his face, which bore signs of age. The movements of his hands were methodical, aristocratic, yet delicate.

He picked up two brass bells in his left hand and began ringing them. Then, lighting two sticks of incense from the candle near the picture of Lord Caitanya and His associates, he began waving the incense slowly in small circles before Lord Caitanya, while still ringing the bells. He looked deeply at the picture and continued cutting spirals of fragrant smoke, all the while ringing the bells. None of the boys knew what he was doing, although he did it every evening. But it was a ceremony. It meant something. The boys began to call the ceremony "bells."

After bells Monday, Wednesday, and Friday, it would usually be time for the evening *kīrtana.* Some of the devotees would already be downstairs greeting guests and explaining about the Swami and the chanting. But without the Swami, nothing could begin. No one knew how to sing or drum, and no one dared think of leading the *mantra*-chanting without him. Only when he entered at seven o'clock could they begin.

Freshly showered and dressed in his clean Indian handwoven cloth, his arms and body decorated with the arrowlike Vaiṣṇava markings, Prabhupāda would leave his apartment and go downstairs to face another ecstatic opportunity to glorify Kṛṣṇa. The tiny temple would be crowded with wild, unbrahminical, candid young Americans.

* * *

Don was a test of Swamiji's tolerance. He had lived in the storefront for months, working little and not trying to change his habits. He had a remarkable speech affectation: instead of talking, he *enunciated* his words, as if he were reciting them from a book. And he never used contractions. It wasn't that he was intellectual, just that somehow he had developed a plan to abolish his natural dialect. Don's speech struck people as bizarre, like it might be the result of too many drugs. It gave him the air of being not an ordinary being. And he continuously took marijuana, even after Swamiji had asked those who lived with him not to. Sometimes during the day his girl friend would join him in the storefront, and they would sit together talking intimately and sometimes kissing. But he liked the Swami. He even gave some money once. He liked living in the storefront, and Swamiji didn't complain.

But others did. One day an interested newcomer dropped by the storefront and found Don alone, surrounded by the sharp aroma of marijuana. "You been smoking pot? But the Swami doesn't want anyone smoking here." Don denied it: "I have not been smoking. You are not speaking the truth." The boy then reached in Don's shirt pocket and pulled out a joint, and Don hit him in the face. Several of the boys found out. They weren't sure what was right: What would the Swami do? What do you do if someone smokes pot? Even though a devotee was not supposed to, could it be allowed sometimes? They put the matter before Swamiji.

Prabhupāda took it very seriously, and he was upset, especially about the violence. "He hit you?" he asked the boy. "I will go down myself and kick him in the head." But then Prabhupāda thought about it and said that Don should be asked to leave. But Don had already left.

The next morning during Swamiji's class, Don appeared at the front door. From his dais, Swamiji looked out at Don with great concern. But his first concern was for ISKCON: "Ask him," Prabhupāda requested Roy who sat nearby, "if he has marijuana—then he cannot come in. Our society . . ." Prabhupāda was like an anxious father, afraid for the life of his infant ISKCON. Roy went to the door and told Don he would have to give up his drugs if he entered. And Don walked away.

Raphael was not interested in spiritual discipline. He was a tall young man with long, straight, brown hair who, like Don, tried to stay aloof and casual toward Swamiji. When Prabhupāda introduced *japa* and encouraged the boys to chant during the day, Raphael didn't go for it. He said he liked a good *kīrtana*, but he wouldn't chant on beads.

One time Swamiji was locked out of his apartment, and the boys had to break the lock. Swamiji asked Raphael to replace it. Days went by. Raphael could sit in the storefront reading Rimbaud, he could wander around town, but he couldn't find time to fix the lock. One evening he dropped by the Swami's apartment, opened the lockless door, and made his way to the back room, where some boys were sitting, listening to Swamiji speak informally about Kṛṣṇa consciousness. Suddenly Raphael spoke up, expressing his doubts and revealing his distracted mind. "As for me," he said, "*I* don't know what's happening. I don't know whether a brass band is playing or what the heck is going on." Some of the devotees tensed; he had interrupted their devotional mood. "Raphael is very candid," Swamiji replied smiling, as if to explain his son's behavior to the others.

Raphael finally fixed the lock, but one day after a lecture he approached the Swami, stood beside the dais, and spoke up, exasperated, impatient: "I am not meant to sit in a temple and chant on beads! My father was a boxer. I am meant to run on the beach and breathe in big breaths of air. . . ." Raphael went on, gesticulating and voicing his familiar complaints—things he would rather do than take up Kṛṣṇa consciousness. Suddenly Prabhupāda interrupted him in a loud voice: "Then do it! Do it!" Raphael shrank away, but he stayed.

Bill Epstein took pride in his relationship with the Swami—it was honest. Although he helped the Swami by telling people about him and sending them up to see him in his apartment, he felt the Swami knew he'd never become a serious follower. Nor did Bill ever mislead himself into thinking he would ever be serious. But Prabhupāda wasn't content with Bill's take-it-or-leave-it attitude. When Bill would finally show up at the storefront again after spending some days at a friend's place, only to fall asleep with a blanket wrapped over his head during the lecture, Prabhupāda would just start shouting so loud that Bill couldn't sleep. Sometimes Bill would ask a challenging question, and Prabhupāda would answer and then say, "Are you satisfied?" and Bill would look up dreamily and answer, "No!" Then Prabhupāda would answer it again more fully and say louder, "Are you satisfied?" and again Bill would say no. This would go on until Bill would have to give in: "Yes, yes, I am satisfied."

But Bill was the first person to get up and dance during a *kīrtana* in the storefront. Some of the other boys thought he looked like he was dancing in an egotistical, narcissistic way, even though his arms were outstretched in a facsimile of the pictures of Lord Caitanya. But when Swamiji saw Bill dancing like that, he looked at Bill with wide-open eyes and feelingly expressed appreciation: "Bill is dancing just like Lord Caitanya."

Bill sometimes returned from his wanderings with money, and although it was not very much, he would give it to Swamiji. He liked to sleep at the storefront and spend the day on the street, returning for lunch or *kīrtanas* or a place to sleep. He used to leave in the morning and go looking for cigarettes on the ground. To Bill, the Swami was part of the hip movement and had thus earned a place of respect in his eyes as a genuine person. Bill objected when the boys introduced signs of reverential worship toward the Swami (starting with their giving him an elevated seat in the temple), and as the boys who lived with the Swami gradually began to show enthusiasm, competition, and even rivalry among themselves, Bill turned from it in disgust. He allowed that he would go on just helping the Swami in his own way, and he knew that the Swami appreciated whatever he did. So he wanted to leave it at that.

Carl Yeargens had helped Prabhupāda in times of need. He had helped with the legal work of incorporating ISKCON, signed the ISKCON charter as a trustee, and even opened his home to Swamiji when David had driven him from the Bowery loft. But those days when he and Eva had shared their apartment with him had created a tension that had never left. He liked the Swami, he respected him as a genuine *sannyāsī* from India, but he didn't accept the conclusions of the philosophy. The talk about Kṛṣṇa and the soul was fine, but the idea of giving up drugs and sex was carrying it a little too far. Now Prabhupāda was settled in his new place, and Carl decided that he had done his part to help and was no longer needed. Although he had helped Prabhupāda incorporate his International Society for Krishna Consciousness, he didn't want to join it.

Carl found the Second Avenue *kīrtanas* too public, not like the more intimate atmosphere he had enjoyed with the Swami on the Bowery. Now the audiences were larger, and there was an element of wild letting loose that they had never had on the Bowery. Like some of the other old associates, Carl felt sheepish and reluctant to join in. In comparison to the Seccond Avenue street scene, the old meetings in the fourth-floor Bowery loft had seemed more mystical, like secluded meditations.

Carol Bekar also preferred a more sedate *kīrtana*. She thought people were trying to take out their personal frustrations by the wild singing and dancing. The few times she did attend evening *kīrtanas* on Second Avenue were "tense moments." One time a group of teenagers had come into the storefront mocking and shouting, "Hey! What the hell is this!" She kept thinking that at any moment a rock was going to come crashing through the big window. And anyway, her boyfriend wasn't interested.

James Greene felt embarrassed. He saw that most of the new men were making a serious commitment to the Swami, whereas he could not. He had no bad feeling toward the Swami and his new movement, but he preferred to live alone.

Robert Nelson, Prabhupāda's old uptown friend, never deviated in his good feelings for Prabhupāda, but he always went along in his own natural way and never adopted any serious disciplines. Somehow, almost all of those who had helped Prabhupāda uptown and on the Bowery did not want to go further once he began a spiritual organization, which happened almost immediately after he moved into 26 Second Avenue. New people were coming forward to assist him, and Carl, James, Carol, and others like them felt that they were being replaced and that their obligation toward the Swami was ending. It was a kind of changing of the guard. Although the members of the old guard were still his well-wishers, they began to drift away.

* * *

Bruce Scharf had just graduated from New York University and was applying for a job. One day an exroommate told him about the Swami he had visited down on Second Avenue. "They sing there," his friend said, "and they have this far-out thing where they have some dancing. And Allen Ginsberg was there." The Swami was difficult to understand, his friend explained, and besides that, his followers recorded his talks on a tape recorder. "Why should he have a big tape recorder? That's not very spiritual." But Bruce became interested.

He was already a devotee of Indian culture. Four years ago, when he was barely twenty, Bruce had worked during the summer as a steward aboard an American freighter and gone to India, where he had visited temples, bought pictures of Śiva and Gaṇeśa and books on Gandhi, and felt as if he were part of the culture. When he returned to N.Y.U., he read more about India and wrote a paper on Gandhi for his history course. He would eat in Indian restaurants and attend Indian films and music recitals, and he was reading the *Bhagavad-gītā.* He had even given up eating meat. He had plans of returning to India, taking some advanced college courses, and then coming back to America to teach Eastern religions. But in the meantime he was experimenting with LSD.

Chuck Barnett was eighteen years old. His divorcée mother had recently moved to Greenwich Village, where she was studying psychology at N.Y.U. Chuck had moved out of his mother's apartment to one on Twelfth Street on the Lower East Side, in the neighborhood of Allen Ginsberg and other hip poets and musicians. He was a progressive jazz flutist who worked with several professional groups in the city. He had been practicing *haṭha-yoga* for six years and had recently been experimenting with LSD. He would have visions of lotuses and concentric circles, but after coming down, he would become more involved than ever in sensuality. A close friend of Chuck's had suddenly gone homosexual that summer, leaving Chuck disgusted and cynical. Someone told Chuck that an Indian swami was staying downtown on Second Avenue, and so he came one day in August to the window of the former Matchless Gifts store.

Steve Guarino, the son of a New York fireman, had grown up in the city and graduated from Brooklyn College in 1961. Influenced by his father, he had gone into the Navy, where he had tolerated two years of military routine, always waiting for the day he would be free to join his friends on the Lower East Side. Finally, a few months after the death of President Kennedy, he had been honorably discharged. Without so much as paying a visit to his parents, he had headed straight for the Lower East Side, which by then appeared vividly within his mind to be the most mystical place in the world. He was writing stories and short novels under the literary influence of Franz Kafka and others, and he began to take LSD "to search and experiment with consciousness." *A Love Supreme*, a record by John Coltrane, the jazz musician, encouraged Steve to think that God actually existed. Just to make enough money to live, Steve had taken a job with the welfare office. One afternoon during his lunch hour, while walking down Second Avenue, he saw that the Matchless Gifts store had a small piece of paper in the window, announcing, "Lectures in Bhagavad Gita, A. C. Bhaktivedanta Swami."

Chuck: *I finally found Second Avenue and First Street, and I saw through the window that there was some chanting going on inside and some people were sitting up against the wall. Beside me on the sidewalk some middle-class people were looking in and giggling. I turned to them, and with my palms folded I asked, "Is this where a swami is?" They giggled and said, "Pilgrim, your search has ended." I wasn't surprised by this answer, because I felt it was the truth.*

Bruce and Chuck, unknown to one another, lived only two blocks apart. After the suggestion from his friend, Bruce also made his way to the storefront.

Bruce: *I was looking for Hare Kṛṣṇa. I had left my apartment and had walked over to Avenue B when I decided to walk all the way down to Houston Street. When I came to First Street, I turned right and then, walking along First Street, came to Second Avenue. All along First Street I was seeing these Puerto Rican grocery stores, and then there was one of those churches where everyone was standing up, singing loudly, and playing tambourines. Then, as I walked further along First Street, I had the feeling that I was leaving the world, like when you're going to the airport to catch a plane. I thought, "Now I'm leaving a part of me behind, and I'm going to something new."*

But when I got over to Second Avenue, I couldn't find Hare Kṛṣṇa. There was a gas station, and then I walked past a little storefront, but the only sign was one that said Matchless Gifts. Then I walked back again past the store, and in the window I saw a black-and-white sign announcing a Bhagavad-gītā *lecture. I entered the storefront and saw a pile of shoes there, so I took off my shoes and came in and sat down near the back.*

Steve: *I had a feeling that this was a group that was already established and had been meeting for a while. I came in and sat down on the floor, and a boy who said his name was Roy was very courteous and friendly to me. He seemed to be one who had already experienced the meetings. He asked me my name, and I felt at ease.*

Suddenly the Swami entered, coming through the side door. He was wearing a saffron dhotī *but no shirt, just a piece of cloth like a long sash, tied in a knot across his right shoulder and leaving his arms, his left shoulder, and part of his chest bare. When I saw him I thought of the Buddha.*

Bruce: *There were about fifteen people sitting on the floor. One man with a big beard sat up by the front on the right-hand side, leaning up against the wall. After some time the door on the opposite side opened, and in walked the Swami. When he came in, he turned his head to see who was in his audience. And then he stared right at me. Our eyes met. It was as if he were studying me. In my mind it was like a photograph was being taken of Swamiji looking at me for the first time. There was a pause. Then he very gracefully got up on the dais and sat down and took out a pair of hand cymbals and began a* kīrtana. *The* kīrtana *was the thing that most affected me. It was the best music I'd ever heard. And it had meaning. You could actually concentrate on it, and it gave you some joy to repeat the words "Hare Kṛṣṇa." I immediately accepted it as a spiritual practice.*

Chuck: *I entered the storefront, and sitting on a grass mat on the hard floor was a person who seemed at first to be neither male nor female, but when he looked at me I couldn't even look him straight in the eyes, they were so brilliant and glistening. His skin was golden with rosy cheeks, and he had large ears that framed his face. He had three strands of beads—one which was at his neck, one a little longer, and the other down on his chest. He had a long forehead, which rose above his shining eyes, and there were many furrows in his brow. His arms were slender and long. His mouth was rich and full, and very dark and red and smiling, and his teeth were brighter than his eyes. He sat in a cross-legged position that I had never seen before in any* yoga *book and had never seen any* yogī *perform. It was a sitting posture, but his right foot was crossed over the thigh and brought back beside his left hip, and one knee rested on the other directly in front of him. His every expression and gesture was different from those of any other personality I had ever seen, and I sensed that they had meanings that I did not know, from a culture and a mood that were completely beyond this world. There was a mole on his side and a peculiar callus on his ankle, a round callus similar to what a karate expert develops on his knuckle. He was dressed in unhemmed cloth, dyed saffron. Everything about him was exotic, and his whole effulgence made him seem to be not even sitting in the room but projected from some other place. He was so brilliant in color that it was like a technicolor movie, and yet he was right there. I heard him speaking. He was sitting right there before me, yet it seemed that if I reached out to touch him he wouldn't be there. At the same time, seeing him was not an abstract or subtle experience but a most intense presence.*

After their first visit to the storefront, Chuck, Steve, and Bruce each got an opportunity to see the Swami upstairs in his apartment.

Steve: *I was on my lunch hour and had to be back in the office very soon. I was dressed in a summer business suit. I had planned it so that I had just enough time to go to the storefront and buy some books, then go to lunch and return to work. At the storefront, one of the Swami's followers said that I could go up and see the Swami. I went upstairs to his apartment and found him at his sitting place with a few boys. I must have interrupted what he was saying, but I asked him if I could purchase the three volumes of the* Śrīmad-Bhāgavatam. *One of the devotees produced the books from the closet opposite Prabhupāda's seat. I handled the books—they were a very special color not usually seen in America, a reddish natural earth, like a brick—and I asked him how much they cost. Six dollars each, he said. I took twenty dollars out of my wallet and gave it to him. He seemed the only one to ask about the price of the books or give the money to, because none of the others came forward to represent him. They were just sitting back and listening to him speak.*

"These books are commentaries on the scriptures?" I asked, trying to show that I knew something about books. Swamiji said yes, they were his commentaries. Sitting, smiling, at ease, Swamiji was very attractive. He seemed very strong and healthy. When he smiled, all his teeth were beautiful, and his nostrils flared aristocratically. His face was full and powerful. He was wearing an Indian cloth robe, and as he sat cross-legged, his smooth-skinned legs were partly exposed. He wore no shirt,

but the upper part of his body was wrapped with an Indian cloth shawl. His limbs were quite slender, but he had a protruding belly.

When I saw that Swamiji was having to personally handle the sale of books, I did not want to bother him. I quickly asked him to please keep the change from my twenty dollars. I took the three volumes without any bag or wrapping and was standing, preparing to leave, when Swamiji said, "Sit down," and gestured that I should sit opposite him like the others. He had said "Sit down" in a different tone of voice. It was a heavy tone and indicated that now the sale of the books was completed and I should sit with the others and listen to him speak. He was offering me an important invitation to become like one of the others, who I knew spent many hours with him during the day when I was usually at my job and not able to come. I envied their leisure in being able to learn so much from him and sit and talk intimately with him. By ending the sales transaction and asking me to sit, he assumed that I was in need of listening to him and that I had nothing better in the world to do than to stop everything else and hear him. But I was expected back at the office. I didn't want to argue, but I couldn't possibly stay. "I'm sorry, I have to go," I said definitely. "I'm only on my lunch hour." As I said this, I had already started to move for the door, and Swamiji responded by suddenly breaking into a wide smile and looking very charming and very happy. He seemed to appreciate that I was a working man, a young man on the go. I had not come by simply because I was unemployed and had nowhere to go and nothing to do. Approving of my energetic demeanor, he allowed me to take my leave.

Chuck: *One of the devotees in the storefront invited me upstairs to see the Swami in private. I was led out of the storefront into a hallway and suddenly into a beautiful little garden with a picnic table, a birdbath, a birdhouse, and flower beds. After we passed through the garden, we came to a middle-class apartment building. We walked up the stairs and entered an apartment which was absolutely bare of any furniture—just white walls and a parquet floor. He led me through the front room and into another room, and there was the Swami, sitting in that same majestic spiritual presence on a thin cotton mat, which was covered by a cloth with little elephants printed on it, and leaning back on a pillow which stood against the wall.*

One night Bruce walked home with Wally, and he told Wally about his interest in going to India and becoming a professor of Oriental literature. "Why go to India?" Wally asked. "India has come here. Swamiji is teaching us these authentic things. Why go to India?" Bruce thought Wally made sense, so he resolved to give up his long-cherished idea of going to India, at least as long as he could go on visiting the Swami.

Bruce: *I decided to go and speak personally to Swamiji, so I went to the storefront. I found out that he lived in an apartment in the rear building. A boy told me the number and said I could just go and speak with the Swami. He said, "Yes, just go." So I walked through the storefront, and there was a little courtyard where some plants were growing. Usually in New York there is no courtyard, nothing green, but this was very attractive. And in that courtyard there was a boy typing at a picnic table, and he looked very spiritual and dedicated. I hurried upstairs and rang the bell for apartment number 2C. After a little while the door opened, and it was the Swami. "Yes," he said. And I said, "I would like to speak with you." He opened the door wider and stepped back and said, "Yes, come." We went inside together into his sitting room and sat down facing each other. He sat behind his metal trunk-desk on a very thin mat which was covered with a woolen blanketlike cover that had frazzled ends and elephants decorating it. He asked me my name and I told him it was Bruce. And then he remarked, "Ah. In India, during the British period, there was one Lord Bruce." And he said something about Lord Bruce being a general and engaging in some campaigns.*

I felt that I had to talk to the Swami—to tell him my story—and I actually found him interested to listen. It was very intimate, sitting with him in his apartment, and he was actually wanting to hear about me.

While we were talking, he looked up past me, high up on the wall behind me, and he was talking about Lord Caitanya. The way he looked up, he was obviously looking at some picture or something, but with an expression of deep love in his eyes. I turned around to see what made him look like that. Then I saw the picture in the brown frame: Lord Caitanya dancing in kīrtana.

Inevitably, meeting with Prabhupāda meant a philosophical discussion.

Chuck: *I asked him, "Can you teach me* rāja-yoga*?" "Oh," he said.*

"Here is Bhagavad-gītā.*" He handed me a copy of the* Gītā. *"Turn to the last verse of the Sixth Chapter," he said, "and read." I read the translation out loud. "And of all* yogīs, *he who is worshiping Me with faith and devotion I consider to be the best." I could not comprehend what "faith" and "devotion" meant, so I said, "Sometimes I'm getting some light in my forehead." "That is hallucination!" he said. So abruptly he said it—although he did not strain his person, the words came at me so intensely that it completely shocked me. "*Rāja *means 'king'—king* yoga,*" he said, "but this is* emperor yoga.*"*

I knew that he had attained such a high state not by using chemicals from a laboratory or by any Western speculative process, and this was certainly what I wanted. "Are you giving classes?" I asked. He said, "Yes, if you come at six in the morning I am giving classes in the Gītā. *And bring some flower or fruit for the Deity." I looked into the adjoining room, which was bare with a wooden parquet floor, bare walls, and a tiny table, and on the table was a picture of five humanlike figures with their arms raised above their heads. Somehow, their arms and faces were not like any mortal that I'd ever seen. I knew that the picture was looking at me.*

When I came out on the street in front of the storefront there were a few people standing around, and I said, "I don't think I'm going to take LSD any more." I said it out loud to myself, but some other people heard me.

Steve: *I wanted to show my appreciation for spiritual India, so I presented to Swamiji that I had read the autobiography of Gandhi. "It was glorious," I said. "What is glorious about it?" Swamiji challenged. When he asked this, there were others present in the room. Although I was a guest, he had no qualms about challenging me for having said something foolish. I searched through my remembrances of Gandhi's autobiography to answer his challenging question, "What is glorious?" I began to relate that one time Gandhi, as a child, although raised as a vegetarian, was induced by some of his friends to eat meat, and that night he felt that a lamb was howling in his belly. Swamiji dismissed this at once, saying, "Most of India is vegetarian. That is not glorious." I couldn't think of anything else glorious to say, and Swamiji said, "His autobiography is called* Experiments with Truth. *But that is not the nature of truth. It is not to be found by someone's experimenting. Truth is always truth."*

Although it was a blow to my ego, being exposed and defeated by Swamiji seemed to be a gain for me. I wanted to bring before him many different things for his judgment, just to see what he had to say about them. I showed him the paperback edition of the Bhagavad-gītā *that I was reading and carrying in my back pocket. He perused the back cover. There was a reference to "the eternal faith of the Hindus," and Swamiji began to take the phrase apart. He explained how the word* Hindu *was a misnomer and does not occur anywhere in the Sanskrit literature itself. He also explained that Hinduism and Hindu beliefs were not eternal.*

Bruce: *After I talked about my desire for religious life, I began telling him about a conflict I had had with one of my professors in English literature. He was a Freudian, so he would explain the characters in all the novels and so on in a Freudian context and with Freudian terminology. Everything was sexual—the mother for the son, this one for that one, and so on. But I would always see it in terms of a religious essence. I would see it in terms of a religious impulse, or some desire to understand God. I would write my papers in that context, and he would always say, "The religious can also be interpreted as Freudian." So I didn't do very well in the course. I was mentioning this to the Swami, and he said, "Your professor is correct." I was surprised—I am going to an Indian swami, and he is saying that the professor was correct, that everything is based on sex and not religion! This kind of pulled the rug out from under me when he said that. Then he qualified what he'd said. He explained that in the material world everyone is operating on the basis of sex; everything that everyone is doing is being driven by the sex impulse. "So," he said, "Freud is correct. Everything is on the basis of sex." Then he clarified what material life is and what spiritual life is. In spiritual life, there is a complete absence of sex desire. So this had a profound effect on me.*

He wasn't confirming my old sentimental ideas, but he was giving me new ideas. He was giving me his instructions, and I had to accept them. Talking to the Swami was very nice. I found him completely natural, and I found him to be very artistic. The way he held his head, the way he enunciated his words—very dignified, very gentlemanly.

The boys found Swamiji not only philosophical, but personal also.

Steve: *A few nights later, I went to see the Swami and told him I was reading his book. One thing that had especially caught my attention was a section where the author of* Śrīmad-Bhāgavatam, *Vyāsadeva, was admitting that he was feeling despondent. Then his spiritual master, Nārada, explained that his despondency had come because although he had written so many books, he had neglected to write in such a way as to fully glorify Kṛṣṇa. After hearing this, Vyāsadeva compiled the* Śrīmad-Bhāgavatam.

When I read this, I identified with the fact that Vyāsadeva was a writer, because I considered myself a writer also, and I knew that I was also despondent. "This was very interesting about the author, Vyāsadeva," I said. "He wrote so many books, but still he was not satisfied, because he had not directly praised Kṛṣṇa." Although I had very little understanding of Kṛṣṇa consciousness, Swamiji opened his eyes very wide, surprised that I was speaking on such an elevated subject from the Śrīmad-Bhāgavatam. *He seemed pleased.*

Chuck: *I had come by in the afternoon, and Swamiji had given me a plate of* prasādam. *So I was eating, and a chili burned my mouth. Swamiji said, "Is it too hot?" "Yes," I said. So he brought me a tiny teacup with some milk, and then he took some rice off my plate and took a piece of banana and crushed it all up together with his fingers and said, "Here, eat this. It will kill the action of the chilies."*

Bruce: *There wasn't anything superficial about him, nor was he ever contrived, trying to make some impression. He was just completely himself. In the Swami's room there was no furniture, so we sat on the floor. And I found this to be very attractive and simple. Everything was so authentic about him. Uptown at another swami's place we had sat on big, stuffed living room chairs, and the place had been lavishly furnished. But here was the downtown swami, wearing simple cloth robes. He had no business suit on—he wasn't covering up a business suit with those saffron robes. And he wasn't affected, as the other swami was. So I found myself asking him if I could be his student, and he said yes. I was very happy, because he was so different from the other swami. With the uptown swami I was wanting to become his student because I wanted to get something from him—I wanted to get knowledge. It was selfishly motivated. But here I was actually emotionally involved. I was feeling that I wanted to become the Swami's student. I actually wanted to give myself, because I thought he was great and what he was giving was pure and pristine and wonderful. It was a soothing balm for the horrible city life. Uptown I had felt like a stranger.*

On one occasion, our conversation turned to my previous trip to India in 1962, and I began talking about how much it meant to me, how much it moved me. I even mentioned that I had made a girl friend there. So we got to talking about that, and I told him that I had her picture—I was carrying the girl's picture in my wallet. So Swamiji asked to see. I took out the picture, and Swamiji looked at it and made a sour face and said, "Oh, she is not pretty. Girls in India are more beautiful than that." Hearing that from the Swami just killed any attachment I had for that girl. I felt ashamed that I had an interest in a girl that the Swami did not consider pretty. I don't think I ever looked at the photograph again, and certainly I never gave her another thought.

* * *

Bruce was a newcomer and had only been to one week of meetings at the storefront, so no one had told him that the members of Ananda Ashram, Dr. Mishra's *yoga* retreat, had invited Swamiji and his followers for a day in the upstate countryside. Bruce had just arrived at the storefront one morning when he heard someone announce, "The Swami is leaving!" And Prabhupāda came out of the building and stepped into a car. In a fit of anxiety, Bruce thought that the Swami was leaving them for good—for India! "No," Howard told him, "we're going to a *yoga āśrama* in the country." But the other car had already left, and there was no room in Swamiji's car. Just then Steve showed up. He had expected the boys to come by his apartment to pick him up. They both had missed the ride.

Bruce phoned a friend up in the Bronx and convinced him to drive them up to Ananda Ashram. But when they got to Bruce's friend's apartment, the friend had decided he didn't want to go. Finally he lent Bruce his car, and Swamiji's two new followers set out for Ananda Ashram.

By the time they arrived, Prabhupāda and his group were already taking *prasādam*, sitting around a picnic table beneath the trees. Ananda Ashram was a beautiful place, with sloping hills and lots of trees and sky and green grass and a lake. The two latecomers came walking up to Swamiji, who was seated like the father of a family, at the head of the picnic table. Keith was serving from a big wok onto the individual plates. When Prabhupāda saw his two stragglers, he asked them to sit next to him, and Keith served them. Prabhupāda took Steve's *capātī* and heaped it up with a mound of sugar, and Steve munched on the bread and sugar, while everyone laughed.

Prabhupāda began talking somehow about lion tamers, and he recalled that once at a fair he had seen a man wrestling with a tiger, rolling over and over with it down a hill. The boys, who rarely heard Swamiji speak anything but philosophy, were surprised. They were delighted—city kids, taken to the country by their *guru*, and having a good time.

Steve: *I was walking with Swamiji across a long, gentle slope. I wanted him to see and approve a picture of Rādhā and Kṛṣṇa I had found in a small book,* Nārada-bhakti-sūtra. *I had planned to get a color reproduction of it to give to each of his followers. So as we were walking across the grass I showed him the picture and asked him whether it was a nice picture of Rādhā and Kṛṣṇa for reproducing. He looked at the picture, smiled, nodded, and said yes.*

Bruce: *I walked with Swamiji around the grounds. All the others were doing something else, and Swamiji and myself were walking alone. He was talking about building a temple there.*

Prabhupāda walked across the scenic acreage, looking at the distant mountains and forests, and Keith walked beside him. Prabhupāda spoke of how Dr. Mishra had offered him the island in the middle of the *āśrama's* lake to build a temple on. "What kind of temple were you thinking of?" Keith asked. "How big?" Prabhupāda smiled and gestured across the horizon. "As big as the whole horizon?" Keith laughed. "Yes," Prabhupāda replied.

A few Ananda Ashram men and women came by. One woman was wearing a *sārī.* Prabhupāda turned to the other women and said, "A woman who wears a *sārī* looks very feminine."

It was late afternoon when some of Swamiji's followers gathered by the lake and began talking candidly about Swamiji and speculating about his relation to God and their relation to him.

"Well," said Wally, "Swami never claimed to be God or an incarnation, but he says that he is a *servant* of God, teaching *love* of God."

"But he says that the spiritual master is not different from God," said Howard. They stood at the edge of the mirrory calm lake and concluded that it was not necessary to talk about this. The answers would be revealed later. None of them really had much spiritual knowledge, but they wanted their faith to deepen.

Afterward, Keith, Wally, and Howard wandered into the meditation room. There was a seat with a picture of Dr. Mishra, who was away in Europe. But the most remarkable thing was a blinking strobe light. "I feel like I'm in a head shop on St. Mark's Place," said Wally. "What kind of spiritual meditation is this?" Howard asked. A Mishra follower, wearing a white *kurtā* and white bell-bottoms, replied that their *guru* had said they could sit and meditate on this light. "Swamiji says you should meditate on Kṛṣṇa," said Keith.

After sunset, everyone gathered in the large room of the main building to watch a slide show. It was a loose collection, mostly of assorted slides of India and the Ananda Ashram. A record by a popular Indian sitarist was playing in the background. Some of the slides were of Viṣṇu temples, and when one slide passed by quickly, Prabhupāda asked, "Let me see that. Can you go back and let me see that temple again?" This happened several times when he recognized familiar temples in India. Later in the show, there were several slides of a girl, one of the members of Dr. Mishra's *āśrama*, demonstrating Indian dance poses. As one of her pictures passed, an *āśrama* man joked, "Turn back and let me see *that* temple again." The joke seemed at Swamiji's expense and in poor taste. His followers didn't laugh.

Then came Swamiji's lecture. He sat up cross-legged on the couch in the largest room in the mansion. The room was filled with people—the Swami's followers from the Lower East Side as well as the Ananda Ashram *yogīs*—sitting on the floor or standing along the walls and in the doorway. He began his talk by criticizing democracy. He said that because people are attached to sense gratification, they vote for a leader who will fulfill their own lust and greed—and *that* is their only criterion for picking a leader. He went on for forty-five minutes to explain about the importance of Kṛṣṇa consciousness, his reel-to-reel tape recorder moving silently.

Then he led a *kīrtana* that bridged all differences and brought out the best in everyone that night. Several nights before, in his apartment on Second Avenue, Prabhupāda had taught his followers how to dance. They had formed a line behind him while he demonstrated the simple step. Holding his arms above his head, he would first swing his left foot forward across the right foot, and then bring it back again in a sweeping motion. Then he would swing his right foot over the left and bring it back again. With his arms upraised, Prabhupāda would walk forward, swinging his body from side to side, left foot to right side, right foot to left side, in time with the one-two-three rhythm. He had shown them the step in regular time and in a slow, half-time rhythm. Keith had called it "the Swami step," as if it were a new ballroom dance.

Prabhupāda's followers began dancing, and soon the others joined them, moving around the room in a rhythmic circle of ecstasy, dancing, swaying, sometimes leaping and whirling. It was a joyous hour-long *kīrtana*, the Swami encouraging everyone to the fullest extent. A visitor to the *āśrama* happened to have his stringed bass with him, and he began expertly turning out his own swinging bass improvisations beneath the Swami's melody, while another man played the *tablās*.

The Ananda Ashram members had been divided of late into two tense, standoffish groups. There was the elderly crowd, similar to the old ladies who had attended the Swami's uptown lectures, and there was the young crowd, mostly hip couples. But in the *kīrtana* their rifts were forgotten and, as they discovered later, even healed. Whether they liked it or not, almost all of those present were induced to rise and dance.

Then it was late. The Swami took rest in the guest room, and his boys slept outside in their sleeping bags.

Howard: *I awaken three or four times, and each time I am flat on my back looking up at the stars, which are always in different positions. My sense of time is confused. The sidereal shifts dizzy me. Then, just before morning, I dream. I dream of devotees clustered about a beautiful golden youth. To see him is to be captivated. His transcendental body radiates an absolute beauty unseen in the world. Stunned, I inquire, "Who is he?" "Don't you know?" someone says. "That's the Swami." I look carefully, but see no resemblance. The youth appears around eighteen, straight out of Vaikuṇṭha [the spiritual world]. "If that's Swamiji," I wonder to myself, "why doesn't he come to earth like that?" A voice somewhere inside me answers: "People would follow me for my beauty, not for my teachings." And I awake, startled. The dream is clear in my mind—more like a vision than a dream. I feel strangely refreshed, bathed in some unknown balm. Again I see that the constellations have shifted and that the dimmer stars have faded into the encroaching dawn. I remember Swamiji telling me that although most dreams are simply functions of the mind, dreams of the spiritual master are of spiritual significance.*

Keith also had a dream that night.

Keith: *I saw Kṛṣṇa and Arjuna on the battlefield of Kurukṣetra. Arjuna was inquiring from Kṛṣṇa, and Kṛṣṇa was reciting the* Bhagavad-gītā *to him. Then that picture phased out, and the images changed. And there was Swamiji, and I was kneeling in front of him, and the same dialogue was going on. I had the understanding that now is the time, and Swamiji is presenting the same thing as Kṛṣṇa, and we are all in the position of Arjuna. The dream made it very clear that hearing from Swamiji was as good as hearing from Kṛṣṇa.*

The sun rose over the mountains, streaking the morning sky above the lake with colors. Wally and Keith were walking around the grounds saying to Prabhupāda how beautiful it all was. "We are not so concerned with beautiful scenery," said Prabhupāda. "We are concerned with the beautiful one who has made the beautiful scenery."

Later . . . Prabhupāda sat next to Bruce in the Volkswagen returning to the city. The car went winding around on a ribbon of smooth black mountain road, with lush green forests close in and intermittent vistas of mountains and expansive sky. It was a rare occasion for Bruce to be driving Prabhupāda in a car, because none of the Swami's boys had cars. They would always travel by bus or subway. It seemed fitting for the Swami to have a car to ride in, but this was only a little Volkswagen, and Bruce winced whenever they hit a bump and it jostled Prabhupāda. As they wound their way on through the mountains, Bruce recalled something he had read in a book by Aldous Huxley's wife about the best places for meditation. One opinion had been that the best place to meditate was by a large body of water, because of the negative ions in the air, and the other opinion was that it was better to meditate in the mountains, because you are higher up and closer to God. "Is it better for spiritual realization to meditate in the mountains?" Bruce asked. Prabhupāda replied, "This is nonsense. There is no question of 'better place.' Are you thinking that God is up on some planet or something and you have to go up high? No. You can meditate anywhere. Just chant Hare Kṛṣṇa."

After some time the drive became tiring for Prabhupāda, and he dozed, his head resting forward.

Bruce walked with Swamiji up to his apartment, opening the door for him, adjusting the window as he liked it, and preparing things in his room, as if he were the Swami's personal servant. Prabhupāda settled back into his Second Avenue apartment, feeling pleased with the visit to Ananda Ashram. The *kīrtana* had been successful, and one of Dr. Mishra's foremost students had commented that he was impressed by Prabhupāda's followers: simply by chanting they seemed to be achieving an advanced level of *yoga* discipline, whereas "we have more difficulty with all our postures and breath control."

* * *

The United States' recently increased involvement in Vietnam was creating an increase of opposition to the war. On July 29, American planes had bombed North Vietnam's two major population centers, Hanoi and Haiphong—an escalation which brought expressions of regret from several allied countries, including Canada, France, and Japan. United Nations Secretary General U Thant openly criticized America's policy in Vietnam. Further opposition to the war ranged from the U.S. Senate down to newly formed pacifist groups, and dissenters held peace marches, sit-ins, and rallies in protest of the war and draft.

Religious protest was led by Pope Paul VI. And the World Council of Churches decried America's involvement in Vietnam and called for a halt in the fighting as "the most effective step" toward negotiation. On August 6 (the anniversary of the bombing of Hiroshima) there were demonstrations in many major American cities, including a peace vigil at the United Nations Headquarters in New York.

On August 31, there would be another two-week-long peace vigil before the United Nations General Assembly Building, and Mr. Larry Bogart had invited Prabhupāda and his followers to open the vigil of "praying for peace." Larry Bogart, who worked at the United Nations Headquarters, had become friends with the Swami and had volunteered his help by arranging to print stationery for the International Society for Krishna Consciousness. The letterhead was designed by James Greene with a sketch of Rādhā and Kṛṣṇa, and Mr. Bogart's name also appeared on the stationery at the head of the list of ISKCON trustees.

Prabhupāda accepted Mr. Bogart's invitation to the peace vigil. Prabhupāda saw it as an opportunity to publicly chant Hare Kṛṣṇa, so he was glad to attend. He announced to his congregation that Monday the thirty-first, instead of the usual morning class at 6:30, everyone should meet at the United Nations Headquarters for a special *kīrtana.*

August 31

Some met at the storefront and went by bus, carrying *karatālas*, a tambourine, and the Swami's bongo. Swamiji rode with a few of his followers in a taxi. The typical dress of his followers consisted of well-worn sneakers, black pants or blue jeans, and T-shirts or button-down sport shirts. Traveling uptown in the early morning put the boys in a lighthearted spirit, and when they saw Swamiji at the U.N. in his flowing saffron robes they became inspired. Swamiji began the chanting, but right away the peace vigil organizers stepped in and asked him to stop. This was a "silent vigil," they said, and it should have prayerful, nonviolent silence. The boys were crushed, but Swamiji accepted the restriction and began silently chanting on his beads.

A dignitary stood up before the assembly and made a short speech in which he mentioned Gandhi, and then he turned to Prabhupāda and indicated that he could now speak about peace. Standing erectly, the U.N. skyscraper looming behind him, Swamiji spoke in a soft voice. The world must accept that God is the proprietor of everything and the friend of everyone, he said. Only then can we have real peace. Mr. Bogart had scheduled the Swami for two hours of silent prayer. Prabhupāda had the devotees sit together and softly chant *japa* until their two scheduled hours were up. Then they left.

As Prabhupāda rode back downtown in the heavy morning traffic, he said New York reminded him of Calcutta. Amid the start-and-stop motion and noise of the traffic he explained, "We have nothing to do with peace vigils. We simply want to spread this chanting of Hare Kṛṣṇa, that's all. If people take to this chanting, peace will automatically come. Then they won't have to artificially try for peace."

September 1

The New York Post ran a picture of Swamiji's group at the United Nations Building. Steve brought the clipping in to Prabhupāda: "Swamiji, look. They have referred to you here as 'Sami Krishna'!"

Prabhupāda: " 'Sami Krishna'? That's all right."

In the picture, some of the boys were sitting with their heads resting on their arms. "Where are you?" Prabhupāda asked. Steve pointed. "Oh, you chant like this, with your head down?"

Prabhupāda had participated in the peace vigil to oblige his contact, Mr. Bogart. Now Mr. Bogart was phoning to offer his appreciation and agreeing to visit the storefront. He wanted to help, and he would discuss how the Swami could work with the U.N. and how he could solicit help from important people for his movement of Indian culture and peace.

Prabhupāda regarded Mr. Bogart's imminent visit as very important, and he wanted to cook for him personally and receive him in his apartment with the best hospitality. When the day arrived, Prabhupāda and Keith cooked together in the small kitchen for several hours, making the best Indian delicacies. Prabhupāda posted Stanley downstairs and told him not to allow anyone to come up while he was cooking the feast for Mr. Bogart. Stanley assented, blinking his eyes with his far-off "saintly" look.

Stanley stationed himself downstairs in the storefront. A few of the boys were there, and he told them, "You can't go up to see the Swami—no one can." About twelve noon, Larry Bogart arrived, pale, elderly, and well dressed, by Lower East Side standards. He said he wanted to see

Swami Bhaktivedanta. "Sorry," Stanley informed him, his boyish face trying to impress the stranger with the seriousness of the order, "the Swami is busy now, and he said no one can see him." Mr. Bogart decided he would wait. There was no chair in the storefront, but Stanley brought him a folding chair. It was a hot day. Mr. Bogart looked at his watch several times. A half hour passed. Stanley sat chanting and sometimes staring off blankly. After an hour, Mr. Bogart asked if he could see the Swami now. Stanley assured him that he could not, and Mr. Bogart left in a huff.

Upstairs, Swamiji had become anxious, wondering why Mr. Bogart had not arrived. Finally, he sent Keith downstairs, and Stanley told him about the man whom he had turned away. "What?" Keith exploded. "But that was . . ."

Within moments, Swamiji heard what had happened. He became furious. He came down to the storefront: "You fool! You silly fool!" He turned and angrily rebuked everyone in the room, but mostly Stanley. No one had ever seen the Swami so angry. Then Swamiji walked away in disgust and returned to his apartment.

Stanley had been going off the deep end for some time, and now he became even more abstracted in his behavior. Stanley's mother knew her son had been troubled for years, and she had therefore requested Prabhupāda to keep a very close watch on him. But now the boy deteriorated in his responsibilities and stopped cleaning the kitchen and storefront. He would stand alone looking at something. He was gloomy and sometimes spoke of suicide. And he stopped chanting regularly. The boys didn't know what to do, but they thought perhaps he should be sent home to his mother.

One day, Stanley went up to see the Swami. He came in and sat down.

Prabhupāda: "Yes?"

Stanley: "May I have fifty dollars?"

Prabhupāda: "Why?"

Prabhupāda used to handle all the money himself, so when his boys needed something, even if it were only twenty-five cents for the bus, they had to see Swami. He was never wasteful. He was so frugal that whenever he received a letter, he would carefully tear the envelope apart and use the reverse side as writing paper. So he wanted to know why Stanley wanted fifty dollars. Stanley replied in a small voice, "I want to purchase some gasoline and set myself on fire." Prabhupāda saw Chuck at the doorway and told him to call Bruce at once. Bruce quickly came up and sat with Prabhupāda and Stanley. Prabhupāda told Bruce—whom he had recently appointed to handle petty cash—to give Stanley fifty dollars, and he had Stanley repeat why he wanted the money.

"But Swamiji," Bruce protested, "we don't have that much money."

"There, you see, Stanley," Prabhupāda spoke very calmly. "Bruce says we don't have the money." Then they phoned Stanley's mother. Later Prabhupāda said that because Stanley had asked for fifty dollars for gasoline, which cost only thirty-five cents, he could therefore understand Stanley was crazy.

* * *

Keith was cooking lunch in the kitchen as usual, but today Swamiji was standing by the kitchen stove, watching his pupil. Keith paused and looked up from his cooking: "Swamiji, could I become your disciple?"

"Yes," Prabhupāda replied. "Why not? Your name will be Kṛṣṇa dāsa."

This simple exchange was the first request for discipleship and Prabhupāda's first granting of initiation. But there was more to it than that. Prabhupāda announced that he would soon hold an initiation. "What's initiation, Swamiji?" one of the boys asked, and Prabhupāda replied, "I will tell you later."

First they had to have beads. Keith went to Tandy's Leather Company and bought half-inch wooden beads and cord to string them on. It was much better, Swamiji said, to count on beads while chanting—a strand of 108 beads, to be exact. This employed the sense of touch, and like the Vaiṣṇavas of India one could count how many times one chanted the *mantra.* Some devotees in India had a string of more than a thousand beads, he had said, and they would chant through them again and again. He taught the boys how to tie a double knot between each of the 108 beads. The number 108 had a special significance: there were 108 *Upaniṣads*, as well as 108 principal *gopīs*, the chief devotees of Lord Kṛṣṇa.

The initiates would be taking vows, he said, and one vow would be to chant a prescribed number of rounds on the beads each day. About a dozen of Swamiji's boys were eligible, but there was no strict system for their selection: if they wanted to, they could do it.

Steve: *Although I was already doing whatever Swamiji recommended, I sensed that initiation was a heavy commitment. And with my last strong impulses to remain completely independent, I hesitated to take initiation.*

Prabhupāda's friends saw the initiation in different ways. Some saw it as very serious, and some took it to be like a party or a happening. While stringing their beads in the courtyard, Wally and Howard talked a few days before the ceremony.

Wally: *It's just a formality. You accept Swamiji as your spiritual master.*

Howard: *What does that entail?*

Wally: *Nobody's very sure. In India it's a standard practice. Don't you think you want to take him as a spiritual master?*

Howard: *I don't know. He would seem to be a good spiritual master—whatever that is. I mean, I like him and his teachings a lot, so I guess in a way he's already my spiritual master. I just don't understand how it would change the situation.*

Wally: *Neither do I. I guess it doesn't. It's just a formality.*

* * *

September 8

Janmāṣṭamī day, the appearance day of Lord Kṛṣṇa. One year before, Prabhupāda had observed Kṛṣṇa's birthday at sea aboard the *Jaladuta*, just out of Colombo. Now, exactly one year later, he had a small crew of Hare Kṛṣṇa chanters. He would gather them all together, have them observe a day of chanting, reading scripture, fasting, and feasting—and the next day would be initiation.

At six o'clock, Prabhupāda came down and was about to give his morning class as usual, when one of the boys asked if he would read from his own manuscript. Prabhupāda appeared shy, yet he did not hide his pleasure at having been asked to read his own *Bhagavad-gītā* commentary. Usually he would read a verse from Dr. Radhakrishnan's Oxford edition of the *Gītā*. Although the commentary presented impersonalist philosophy, the translations, Prabhupāda said, were ninety-percent accurate. But this morning he sent Roy up to fetch his manuscript, and for an hour he read from its typewritten pages.

For observing Janmāṣṭamī there were special rules: there should be no eating, and the day was to be spent chanting, reading, and discussing Kṛṣṇa consciousness. If anyone became too weak, he said, there was fruit in the kitchen. But better that they fast until the feast at midnight, just like the devotees in India. He said that in India, millions of people—Hindus, Muslims, or whatever—observed the birthday of Lord Kṛṣṇa. And in every temple there were festivities and celebrations of the pastimes of Kṛṣṇa.

"And now," he said at length, "I will tell you what is meant by initiation. Initiation means that the spiritual master accepts the student and agrees to take charge, and the student accepts the spiritual master and agrees to worship him as God." He paused. No one spoke. "Any questions?" And when there were none, he got up and walked out.

The devotees were stunned. What had they just heard him say? For weeks he had stressed that when anyone claims to be God he should be considered a dog.

"My mind's just been blown," said Wally.

"*Everybody's* mind is blown," said Howard. "Swamiji just dropped a bomb."

They thought of Keith. He was wise. Consult Keith. But Keith was in the hospital. Talking among themselves, they became more and more confused. Swamiji's remark had confounded their judgment. Finally, Wally decided to go to the hospital to see Keith.

Keith listened to the whole story: how Swamiji had told them to fast and how he had read from his manuscript and how he had said he would explain initiation and how everybody had leaned forward, all ears . . . and Swamiji had dropped a bomb: "The student accepts the spiritual master and agrees to worship him as God." "Any questions?" Swamiji had asked softly. And then he had walked out. "I don't know if I want to be initiated now," Wally confessed. "We have to worship him as God."

"Well, you're already doing that by accepting whatever he tells you," Keith replied, and he advised that they talk it over with Swamiji . . . *before* the initiation. So Wally went back to the temple and consulted Howard, and together they went up to Swamiji's apartment. "Does what you told us this morning," Howard asked, "mean we are supposed to accept the spiritual master to be God?"

"That means he is due the same respect as God, being God's representative," Prabhupāda replied, calmly.

"Then he is not God?"

"No," Prabhupāda said, "God is God. The spiritual master is His representative. Therefore, he is as good as God because he can deliver God to the sincere disciple. Is that clear?" It was.

It was a mental and physical strain to go all day without eating. Jan was restless. She complained that she couldn't possibly stay any longer but had to go take care of her cat. Prabhupāda tried to overrule her, but she left anyway.

Most of the prospective initiates spent several hours that day stringing their shiny red wooden beads. Having tied one end of the string to a window bar or a radiator, they would slide one bead at a time up the string and knot it tightly, chanting one *mantra* of Hare Kṛṣṇa for each bead. It was devotional service—chanting and stringing your beads for initiation. Every time they knotted another bead it seemed like a momentous event. Prabhupāda said that devotees in India chanted at least sixty-four rounds of beads a day. Saying the Hare Kṛṣṇa *mantra* once on each of the 108 beads constituted one round. His spiritual master had said that anyone who didn't chant sixty-four rounds a day was fallen. At first some of the boys thought that they would also have to chant sixty-four rounds, and they became perplexed: that would take all day! How could you go to a job if you had to chant sixty-four rounds? How could anyone chant sixty-four rounds? Then someone said Swamiji had told him that thirty-two rounds a day would be a sufficient minimum for the West. Wally said he had heard Swamiji say twenty-five—but even that seemed impossible. Then Prabhupāda offered the rock-bottom minimum: sixteen rounds a day, without fail. Whoever got initiated would have to promise.

The bead-stringing, chanting, reading, and dozing went on until eleven at night, when everyone was invited up to Swamiji's room. As they filed through the courtyard, they sensed an unusual calm in the atmosphere, and Houston Street, just over the wall, was quiet. There was no moon.

As his followers sat on the floor, contentedly eating *prasādam* from paper plates, Swamiji sat among them, telling stories about the birth of Lord Kṛṣṇa. Kṛṣṇa had appeared on this evening five thousand years ago. He was born the son of Vasudeva and Devakī in the prison of King Kaṁsa at midnight, and His father, Vasudeva, immediately took Him to Vṛndāvana, where He was raised as the son of Nanda Mahārāja, a cowherd man.

Prabhupāda also spoke of the necessity of purification for spiritual advancement. "It is not enough merely to chant holy words," he said. "One must be pure inside and out. Chanting in purity brings spiritual advancement. The living entity becomes impure because he wants to enjoy material pleasure. But the impure can become pure by following Kṛṣṇa, by doing all works for Kṛṣṇa. Beginners in Kṛṣṇa consciousness have a tendency to relax their efforts in a short time, but to advance spiritually you must resist this temptation and continually increase your efforts and devotion."

* * *

Michael Grant: *I first heard about the initiation just one day before it was to take place. I had been busy with my music and hadn't been attending. I was walking down Second Avenue with one of the prospective initiates, and he mentioned to me that there was going to be something called an initiation ceremony. I asked what it was about, and he said, "All I know is it means that you accept the spiritual master as God." This was a big surprise to me, and I hardly knew how to take it. But I didn't take it completely seriously, and the way it was mentioned to me in such an offhand way made it seem not very important. He asked me very casually whether I was going to be involved, and I, also being very casual about it, said, "Well, I think I will. Why not? I'll give it a try."*

Jan didn't think she would make an obedient disciple, and initiation sounded frightening. She liked the Swami, especially cooking with him. But it was Mike who convinced her—*he* was going, so she should come along with him.

Carl Yeargens knew something about initiation from his readings, and he, more than the others, knew what a serious commitment it was. He was surprised to hear that Swamiji was offering initiation, and he was cautious about entering into it. He knew that initiation meant no illicit sex, intoxication, or meat-eating, and an initiated disciple would have new responsibilities for spreading the teachings to others. Carl was already feeling less involved since the Swami had moved to Second Avenue, but he decided to attend the initiation anyway.

Bill Epstein had never professed to be a serious disciple. Holding initiation was just another part of the Swami's scene, and you were free to take it seriously or not. He figured it was all right to take initiation, even if you weren't serious. He would try it.

Carol Bekar was surprised to hear that some people would be taking initiation even though they had no intentions of giving up their bad habits. She had stopped coming around regularly ever since the Swami had moved, and she felt no desire to ask for initiation. The Swami probably wouldn't initiate women anyway, she figured.

Robert Nelson hadn't forgotten the Swami and always liked to help whenever he could. But except for an occasional friendly visit, he had stopped coming. He mostly stayed to himself. He still lived uptown and wasn't into the Lower East Side scene.

James Greene thought he wasn't pure enough to be initiated: "Who am I to be initiated?" But the Swami had asked him to bring something over to the storefront. "I came, and it was just understood that I was supposed to be initiated. So, I thought, why not?"

Stanley had been chanting regularly again and had come out of his crazy mood. He was sticking with the Swami and his followers. He asked his mother if he could be initiated, and she said it would be all right.

Steve wanted more time to think about it.

Keith was in the hospital.

Bruce had only been attending for a week or two, and it was too soon.

Chuck was on a week's vacation from the regulated spiritual life at the temple, so he didn't know about the initiation.

No one was asked to shave his head or even cut his hair or change his dress. No one offered Prabhupāda the traditional *guru-dakṣiṇā*, the donation a disciple is supposed to offer as a gesture of his great obligation to his master. Hardly anyone even relieved him of his chores, so Swamiji himself had to do most of the cooking and other preparations for the initiation. He was perfectly aware of the mentality of his boys, and he didn't try to force anything on anyone. Some of the initiates didn't know until after the initiation, when they had inquired, that the four rules—no meat-eating, no illicit sex, no intoxication, and no gambling—were mandatory for all disciples. Prabhupāda's reply then was, "I am very glad that you are finally asking me that."

It was to be a live Vedic sacrifice, with a ceremonial fire right there in the front room of Swamiji's apartment. In the center of the room was the sacrificial arena, a platform of bricks, four inches high and two feet square, covered with a mound of dirt. The dirt was from the courtyard and the bricks were from a nearby gutted building. Around the mound were eleven bananas, clarified butter, sesame seeds, whole barley grains, five colors of powdered dyes, and a supply of kindling. The eleven initiates took up most of the remaining space in the front room as they sat on the floor knee to knee around the sacrificial arena. The guests in the hallway peered curiously through the open door. For everyone except the Swami, this was all new and strange, and every step of the ceremony took place under his direction. When some of the boys had made a mess of trying to apply the Vaiṣṇava *tilaka* to their foreheads, Prabhupāda had patiently guided his finger up their foreheads, making a neat, narrow "V."

He sat before the mound of earth, looking out at his congregation. They appeared not much different from any other group of young hippies from the Lower East Side who might have assembled at any number of happenings—spiritual, cultural, musical, or whatever. Some were just checking out a new scene. Some were deeply devoted to the Swami. But everyone was curious. He had requested them to chant the Hare Kṛṣṇa *mantra* softly throughout the ceremony, and the chanting had now become a continual drone, accompanying his mysterious movements as head priest of the Vedic rite.

He began by lighting a dozen sticks of incense. Then he performed purification with water. Taking a spoon in his left hand, he put three drops of water from a goblet into his right and sipped the water. He repeated the procedure three times. The fourth time he did not sip but flicked the water onto the floor behind him. He then passed the spoon and goblet around for the initiates, who tried to copy what they had seen. When some of them placed the water in the wrong hand or sipped in the wrong way, Swamiji patiently corrected them.

"Now," he said, "repeat after me." And he had them repeat, one word at a time, a Vedic *mantra* of purification:

oṁ apavitraḥ pavitro vā
sarvāvasthāṁ gato 'pi vā
yaḥ smaret puṇḍarīkākṣaṁ
sa bāhyābhyantaraḥ śuciḥ
śrī-viṣṇuḥ śrī-viṣṇuḥ śrī-viṣṇuḥ

The initiates tried falteringly to follow his pronunciation of the words, which they had never heard before. Then he gave the translation: "Unpurified or purified, or even having passed through all situations, one who remembers the lotus-eyed Supreme Personality of Godhead is cleansed within and without." Three times he repeated the sipping of water, the drone of the Hare Kṛṣṇa *mantra* filling the room as the goblet passed from initiate to initiate and back again to him, and three times he led the chanting of the *mantra: oṁ apavitraḥ*... Then he raised a hand, and as the buzzing of the chanting trailed off into silence, he began his lecture.

After the lecture, he asked the devotees one by one to hand him their beads, and he began chanting on them—Hare Kṛṣṇa, Hare Kṛṣṇa, Kṛṣṇa Kṛṣṇa, Hare Hare/ Hare Rāma, Hare Rāma, Rāma Rāma, Hare Hare. The sound of everyone chanting filled the room. After finishing one strand, he would summon the owner of the beads and hold the beads up while demonstrating how to chant. Then he would announce the initiate's spiritual name, and the disciple would take back the beads, bow to the floor, and recite:

nama oṁ viṣṇu-pādāya kṛṣṇa-preṣṭhāya bhū-tale
śrīmate bhaktivedānta-svāmin iti nāmine

"I offer my respectful obeisances unto His Divine Grace A. C. Bhaktivedanta Swami, who is very dear to Lord Kṛṣṇa, having taken shelter at His lotus feet." There were eleven initiates and so eleven sets of beads, and the chanting lasted for over an hour. Prabhupāda gave each boy a strand of neck beads, which he said were like dog collars, identifying the devotee as Kṛṣṇa's dog.

After Wally received his beads and his new name (Umāpati), he returned to his place beside Howard and said, "That was wonderful. Getting your beads is wonderful." In turn, each initiate received his beads and his spiritual name. Howard became Hayagrīva, Wally became Umāpati, Bill became Ravīndra Svarūpa, Carl became Karlāpati, James became Jagannātha, Mike became Mukunda, Jan became Janakī, Roy became Rāya Rāma, and Stanley became Stryadhīśa. Another Stanley, a Brooklyn boy with a job, and Janos, a college student from Montreal, both of whom had rather peripheral relationships with the Swami, appeared that night and took initiation with the rest—receiving the names Satyavrata and Janārdana.

Then Swamiji began the fire sacrifice by sprinkling the colored dyes across the mound of earth before him. With fixed attention his congregation watched each mysterious move, as he picked up the twigs and wooden splinters, dipped them into clarified butter, lit them in a candle flame, and built a small fire in the center of the mound. He mixed sesame seeds, barley, and clarified butter in a bowl and then passed the mixture around. Each new disciple took a handful of the mixture to offer into the fire. He then began to recite Sanskrit prayers, asking everyone please to repeat them, each prayer ending with the responsive chanting of the word "*svāhā*" three times. And with *svāhā* the initiates would toss some of the sesame-barley mixture into the fire. Swamiji kept pouring butter, piling up wood, and chanting more prayers, until the mound was blazing. The prayers kept coming and the butter kept pouring and the fire got larger and the room got hotter.

After fifteen or twenty minutes, he asked each of the initiates to place a banana in the fire. With eleven bananas heaped on the fire, the flames began to die, and the smoke thickened. A few of the initiates got up and ran coughing into the other room, and the guests retreated into the hallway. But Swamiji went on pouring the remaining butter and seeds into the fire. "This kind of smoke does not disturb," he said. "Other smoke disturbs, but this kind of smoke does not." Even though everyone's eyes were watering with irritation, he asked that the windows remain closed. So most of the smoke was contained within the apartment, and no neighbors complained.

Swamiji smiled broadly, rose from his seat before the sacrificial fire, the blazing tongue of Viṣṇu, and began clapping his hands and chanting

Hare Kṛṣṇa. Placing one foot before the other and swaying from side to side, he began to dance before the fire. His disciples joined him in dancing and chanting, and the smoke abated. He had each disciple touch his beads to the feet of Lord Caitanya in the Pañca-tattva picture on the table, and finally he allowed the windows opened. As the ceremony was finished and the air in the apartment was clearing, Swamiji began to laugh: "There was so much smoke I thought they might have to call the fire brigade."

Prabhupāda was happy. He arranged that *prasādam* be distributed to all the devotees and guests. The fire, the prayers, the vows, and everyone chanting Hare Kṛṣṇa had all created an auspicious atmosphere. Things were going forward. Now there were initiated devotees in the Western world. Finally most of the disciples went home to their apartments, leaving their spiritual master to clean up after the initiation ceremony.

*　　　*　　　*

September 10

The morning after the initiation, Prabhupāda sat in his apartment reading from a commentary on the *Śrīmad-Bhāgavatam.* The large Sanskrit volume lay before him on his desk as he read. He wore horn-rimmed glasses, which changed his demeanor, making him look extremely scholarly. He wore eyeglasses only for reading, and this added to the visual impression that he had now gone into a deep professorial meditation. The room was quiet, and brilliant midmorning sunlight shone warmly through the window.

Suddenly someone knocked on the door. "Yes? Come in." He looked up, removing his glasses, as Mike and Jan, now Mukunda and Janakī, opened the door, peering in. He had asked to see them. "Yes, yes, come in." He smiled, and they walked in and closed the door behind them, two vivacious young Americans. From his expressive eyes, he seemed to be amused. They sat down before him, and Prabhupāda playfully addressed them by their new initiated names. "So, you are living together, but now you have taken serious vows of initiation. So what will you do about it?"

"Well"—Mukunda seemed puzzled—"isn't there any love in Kṛṣṇa consciousness?"

Swamiji nodded. "Yes, so I am saying why don't you get married?"

They agreed it was a good idea, and Prabhupāda immediately scheduled a wedding date for two days later.

Swamiji said he would cook a big feast and hold the marriage ceremony in his apartment, and he asked Mukunda and Janakī to invite their relatives. Both Mukunda and Janakī had grown up in Oregon, and their family members found it impossible to travel such a long distance on such short notice. Only Janakī's sister, Joan, agreed to come.

Joan: *Little did I know what kind of wedding it would be. All I knew was that they had met a swami and were taking Sanskrit from him as well as attending his small storefront temple on Second Avenue. When I met the Swami he was sitting beside the window in his front room, bathed in sunlight, surrounded by pots of* prasādam, *which he was distributing to the devotees who were sitting around him against the wall. I was a follower of macrobiotics and not so eager for taking this noonday meal. When I entered the room, the Swami said, "Who is this?" and Mukunda said, "This is Janakī's sister, Joan. She has come from Oregon to attend the wedding." Swamiji said, "Oh? Where is Oregon?" Mukunda said, "It's three thousand miles away, on the other side of the United States." And he asked, "Oh, coming from so far? Very nice. And when will the other members of the family arrive?" Then I said, "I am the only one who is coming for the wedding, Swamiji." He said, "Never mind. It is very nice that you have come. Please sit down and take some* kṛṣṇa-prasādam."

He offered me some dāl, *a rather moist* sabjī, *yogurt, salad, and* capātīs. *But because I was a devotee of macrobiotics, all of this* prasādam *was very unpalatable to me. Practically speaking, it was sticking in my throat the whole time, but I remember looking over at the radiant and beautiful person who was so eager for me to take this* prasādam *that he had prepared. So I took it all, but in my mind I decided this would be the last time I would take this luncheon with the devotees.*

At any rate, somehow I finished the meal, and Swamiji, who had been looking over at me, said, "You want more? You want more?" And I said, "No, thank you. I am so full. It was very nice, but I can't take any more." So finally the prasādam *was finished, and they were all getting up to clean, and Swamiji commented that he wanted to see Mukunda, Janakī, and myself—for making preparations for the wedding the next day.*

So when we were all there sitting in the room with him, the Swami reached over into the corner, where there was a big pot with crystallized sugar syrup sticking to the outside. I thought, "Oh, this is supposed to be the pièce de résistance, but I can't possibly take any more." But he reached his hand into the pot anyway and pulled up a huge, round, dripping gulābjāmun. *I said, "Oh, no. I am so full I couldn't take any." And he said, "Oh, take, take." And he made me hold out my hand and take it. Well, by the time I finished the* gulābjāmun *I was fully convinced that this would be the last time I would ever come there.*

Then he began explaining how in the Vedic tradition the woman's side of the family made lavish arrangements for the wedding. And since I was the only member of the family who had come to assist, I should come the next day and help him make the wedding feast. So the next morning at nine, while Janakī was decorating the room for the fire sacrifice, stringing leaves and flower garlands across the top of the room, I went upstairs to meet Swamiji.

When I arrived, he immediately sent me out shopping with a list—five or six items to purchase. One of those items was not available anywhere in the markets, although I spoke to so many shopkeepers. When I came back he asked me, "You have obtained all the items on the list?" And I said, "Well, everything except for one." He said, "What is that?" I said, "Well, no one knows what tumar is."

He had me wash my hands and sat me down in his front room on the floor with a five-pound bag of flour, a pound of butter, and a pitcher of water. And he looked down at me and said, "Can you make a medium-soft dough?" I replied, "Do you mean a pastry or piecrust or shortcrust dough or pâté brisée *dough? What kind of pastry do you want?" "How old are you?" he said. And I said, "I am twenty-five, Swamiji." "You are twenty-five," he said, "and you can't make a medium-soft dough? It is a custom in India that any young girl from the age of five years is very experienced in making this dough. But never mind, I will show you." So he very deftly emptied the bag of flour and, with his fingertips, cut in the butter until the mixture had a consistency of coarse meal. Then he made a well in the center of the flour, poured in just the right amount of water, and very deftly and expertly kneaded it into a velvety smooth, medium-soft dough. He then brought in a tray of cooked potatoes, mashed them with his fingertips, and began to sprinkle in spices. He showed me how to make and form potato* kacaurīs, *which are fried Indian pastries with spiced potato filling. From eleven until five that afternoon, I sat in this one room, making potato* kacaurīs. *Meanwhile, in the course of the same afternoon, Swamiji brought in fifteen other special vegetarian dishes, each one in a large enough quantity for forty persons. And he had made them singlehandedly in his small, narrow kitchen.*

It was rather hot that afternoon, and I was perspiring. I asked, "Swamiji, may I please have a glass of water?" He peeked his head around the door, and said, "Go wash your hands." I immediately did so, and when I returned Swamiji had a glass of water for me. He explained to me that while preparing this food for offering to the Supreme Lord, one should not think of eating or drinking anything. So after drinking the glass of water, I went in and washed my hands and sat down. About two in the afternoon, I said, "Swamiji, may I have a cigarette?" and he peeked his head around the corner and said, "Go wash your hands." So I did, and when I came back he explained to me the four rules of Kṛṣṇa consciousness. I continued to make the kacaurīs, *and around three-thirty, four o'clock, it was extremely warm in the room, and as Swamiji was bringing in one of his preparations I was wiping my arm and hand across my forehead. He looked down at me and said, "Please go and wash your hands." Again I did so, and upon returning he had a moistened paper towel for me. He explained that cooking for Kṛṣṇa required certain standards of cleanliness and purity that were different than the ones I was accustomed to.*

About thirty people attended. The decorations were similar to the ones for the initiation a few days before, except that they were more festive and the feast was more lavish. Swamiji's front room was decorated with pine boughs, and leaves and flowers were strung overhead from one side of the room to the other. Some of the new initiates came, their large red beads around their necks. They had taken vows now—sixteen rounds a day—and they chanted on their beads just as Swamiji had shown them, and they happily though self-consciously called one another by their new spiritual names.

Janakī: *Swamiji said that I should wear a* sārī *at my wedding, and he said it should be made of silk. I asked him what color, and he said red. So Mukunda bought me an absolutely elegant* sārī *and some very nice jewelry.*

The Swami's friends were used to seeing Janakī, as she always came with Mukunda, but usually she wore no makeup and dressed in very plain clothes. They were astounded and somewhat embarrassed to see her enter wearing jewelry, makeup, and a bright red *sārī*. The bride's hair was up and braided, decorated with an oval silver-filigree hair ornament. She wore heavy silver earrings, which Mukunda had purchased from an expensive Indian import shop on Fifth Avenue, and silver bracelets.

Prabhupāda directed Mukunda and Janakī to sit opposite him on the other side of the sacrificial fire arena. And just as at the initiation, he lit the incense and instructed them in the purification by water, recited the purification *mantra*, and then began to speak. He explained about the relationship between man and wife in Kṛṣṇa consciousness, and how they should serve each other and how they should serve Kṛṣṇa. Prabhupāda then asked Janakī's sister to present her formally to Mukunda as his wife. Mukunda then repeated after Swamiji: "I accept Janakī as my wife, and I shall take charge of her throughout both of our lives. We shall live together peacefully in Kṛṣṇa consciousness, and there will never be any separation." And then Prabhupāda turned to Janakī: "Will you accept Śrīmān Mukunda dāsa brahmacārī as your life's companion? Will you serve him always and help him to execute his Kṛṣṇa conscious activities?" And then Janakī replied, "Yes, I accept Mukunda as my husband throughout my life. There shall never be any separation between us, either in happiness or distress. I shall serve him always, and we shall live together peacefully in Kṛṣṇa consciousness."

No one knew anything of what was going on except Swamiji. He led the chanting, he gave the lines for the bride and groom to exchange, he told them where to sit and what to do—he, in fact, had told them to get married. He had also cooked the elaborate feast that was waiting in the kitchen for the completion of the ceremony.

Prabhupāda asked Mukunda and Janakī to exchange their flower garlands and after that to exchange sitting places. He then asked Mukunda to rub some vermilion down the part in Janakī's hair and then to cover her head with her *sārī*. Next came the fire sacrifice, and finally the feast.

The special feature of the wedding was the big feast. It turned out to be quite a social success. The guests ate enthusiastically, asked for more, and raved about the sensational tastes. Prabhupāda's followers, who were accustomed to the simple daily fare of rice, *dāl*, *sabjī*, and *capātīs*, found the feast intoxicating and ate as much as they could get. Many of

Mukunda's friends were marcobiotic followers, and at first they fastidiously avoided all the sweets. But gradually the enthusiasm of the others wore down their resistance, and they became captivated by the Swami's expert cooking. "God, he's a good cook!" said Janakī. Bruce, who had missed the first initiation, was seeing the Vedic fire sacrifice and tasting the Swami's *kacaurīs* for the first time. He resolved on the spot to dedicate himself to Kṛṣṇa consciousness and become one of the Swamiji's disciples as soon as possible. Almost all the visitors personally approached Swamiji to thank him and congratulate him. He was happy and said it was all Kṛṣṇa's blessings, Kṛṣṇa's grace.

After the ceremony, Mukunda and his wife entertained many of the devotees and guests in their apartment. The evening had put everyone in high spirits, and Hayagrīva was reciting poetry. Then someone turned on the television to catch the scheduled interview with Allen Ginsberg, the poet, and much to everyone's happiness, Allen began playing harmonium and chanting Hare Kṛṣṇa. He even said there was a swami on the Lower East Side who was teaching this *mantra-yoga*. Kṛṣṇa consciousness was new and unheard of, yet now the devotees were seeing a famous celebrity perform *kīrtana* on television. The whole evening seemed auspicious.

Back at his apartment, Prabhupāda, along with a few helpers, cleaned up after the ceremony. He was satisfied. He was introducing some of the major elements of his Kṛṣṇa consciousness mission. He had initiated disciples, he had married them, and he had feasted the public with *kṛṣṇa-prasādam*. "If I had the means," he told his followers, "I could hold a major festival like this every day."

CHAPTER NINE

Stay High Forever

But while this was going on, an old man, one year past his allotted three score and ten, wandered into New York's East Village and set about to prove to the world that he knew where God could be found. In only three months, the man, Swami A. C. Bhaktivedanta, succeeded in convincing the world's toughest audience—Bohemians, acidheads, potheads, and hippies—that he knew the way to God: Turn Off, Sing Out, and Fall In. This new brand of holy man, with all due deference to Dr. Leary, has come forth with a brand of "Consciousness Expansion" that's sweeter than acid, cheaper than pot, and nonbustible by fuzz. How is all this possible? "Through Kṛṣṇa," the Swami says.

—from *The East Village Other*
October 1966

Prabhupāda's health was good that summer and fall, or so it seemed. He worked long and hard, and except for four hours of rest at night, he was always active. He would speak intensively on and on, never tiring, and his voice was strong. His smiles were strong and charming; his singing voice loud and melodious. During *kīrtana* he would thump Bengali *mṛdaṅga* rhythms on his bongo drum, sometimes for an hour. He ate heartily of rice, *dāl*, *capātīs*, and vegetables with ghee. His face was full and his belly protuberant. Sometimes, in a light mood, he would drum with two fingers on his belly and say that the resonance affirmed his good health. His golden color had the radiance of youth and well-being preserved by seventy years of healthy, nondestructive habits. When he smiled, virility and vitality came on so strong as to embarrass a faded, dissolute New Yorker. In many ways, he was not at all like an old man. And his new followers completely accepted his active youthfulness as a part of the wonder of Swamiji, just as they had come to accept the wonder of the chanting and the wonder of Kṛṣṇa. Swamiji wasn't an ordinary man. He was spiritual. He could do anything. None of his followers dared advise him to slow down, nor did it ever really occur to them that he needed such protection—they were busy just trying to keep up with him.

During the two months at 26 Second Avenue, he had achieved what had formerly been only a dream. He now had a temple, a duly registered society, full freedom to preach, and a band of initiated disciples. When a Godbrother had written asking him how he would manage a temple in New York, Prabhupāda had said that he would need men from India but that he might find an American or two who could help. That had been last winter. Now Kṛṣṇa had put him in a different situation: he had received no help from his Godbrothers, no big donations from Indian business magnates, and no assistance from the Indian government, but he was finding success in a different way. These were "happy days," he said. He had struggled alone for a year, but then "Kṛṣṇa sent me men and money."

Yes, these were happy days for Prabhupāda, but his happiness was not like the happiness of an old man's "sunset years," as he fades into the dim comforts of retirement. His was the happiness of youth, a time of blossoming, of new powers, a time when future hopes expand without limit. He was seventy-one years old, but in ambition he was a courageous youth. He was like a young giant just beginning to grow. He was happy because his preaching was taking hold, just as Lord Caitanya had been happy when He had traveled alone to South India, spreading the chanting of Hare Kṛṣṇa. Prabhupāda's happiness was that of a selfless servant of Kṛṣṇa to whom Kṛṣṇa was sending candidates for devotional life. He was happy to place the seed of devotion within their hearts and to train them in chanting Hare Kṛṣṇa, hearing about Kṛṣṇa, and working to spread Kṛṣṇa consciousness.

Prabhupāda continued to accelerate. After the first initiations and the first marriage, he was eager for the next step. He was pleased by what he had, but he wanted to do more. It was the greed of the Vaiṣṇava—not a greed to have sense gratification but to take more and more for Kṛṣṇa. He would "go in like a needle and come out like a plow." That is to say, from a small, seemingly insignificant beginning, he would expand his movement to tremendous proportions. At least, that was his desire. He was not content with his newfound success and security at 26 Second Avenue, but was yearning to increase ISKCON as far as possible. This had always been his vision, and he had written it into the ISKCON charter: "to achieve real unity and peace in the world . . . within the members, and humanity at large."

* * *

Swamiji gathered his group together. He knew that once they tried it they would love it. But it would only happen if he personally went with them. Washington Square Park was only half a mile away, maybe a little more.

Ravīndra Svarūpa: *He never made a secret of what he was doing. He used to say, "I want* everybody *to know what we are doing." Then one day, D-day came. He said, "We are going to chant in Washington Square Park." Everybody was scared. You just don't go into a park and chant. It seemed like a weird thing to do. But he assured us, saying, "You won't be afraid when you start chanting. Kṛṣṇa will help you." And so we trudged down to Washington Square Park, but we were very upset about it. Up until that time, we weren't exposing ourselves. I was upset about it, and I know that several other people were, to be making a public figure of yourself.*

With Prabhupāda leading they set out on that fair Sunday morning, walking the city blocks from Second Avenue to Washington Square in the heart of Greenwich Village. And the way he looked—just by walking he created a sensation. None of the boys had shaved heads or robes, but because of Swamiji—with his saffron robes, his white, pointy shoes, and his shaved head held high—people were astonished. It wasn't like when he would go out alone. That brought nothing more than an occasional second glance. But today, with a group of young men hurrying to keep up with him as he headed through the city streets, obviously about to do *something*, he caused a stir. Tough guys and kids called out names, and others laughed and made sounds. A year ago, in Butler, the Agarwals had been sure that Prabhupāda had not come to America for followers. "He didn't want to make any waves," Sally had thought. But now he was making waves, walking through the New York City streets, headed for the first public chanting in America, followed by his first disciples.

In the park there were hundreds of people milling about—stylish, decadent Greenwich Villagers, visitors from other boroughs, tourists from other states and other lands—an amalgam of faces, nationalities, ages, and interests. As usual, someone was playing his guitar by the fountain, boys and girls were sitting together and kissing, some were throwing Frisbees, some were playing drums or flutes or other instruments, and some were walking their dogs, talking, watching everything, wandering around. It was a typical day in the Village.

Prabhupāda went to a patch of lawn where, despite a small sign that read Keep Off the Grass, many people were lounging. He sat down, and one by one his followers sat beside him. He took out his brass handcymbals and sang the *mahā-mantra*, and his disciples responded, awkwardly at first, then stronger. It wasn't as bad as they had thought it would be.

Jagannātha: *It was a marvelous thing, a marvelous experience that Swamiji brought upon me. Because it opened me up a great deal, and I overcame a certain shyness—the first time to chant out in the middle of everything.*

A curious crowd gathered to watch, though no one joined in. Within a few minutes, two policemen moved in through the crowd. "Who's in charge here?" an officer asked roughly. The boys looked toward Prabhupāda. "Didn't you see the sign?" an officer asked. Swamiji furrowed his brow and turned his eyes toward the sign. He got up and walked to the uncomfortably warm pavement and sat down again, and his followers straggled after to sit around him. Prabhupāda continued the chanting for half an hour, and the crowd stood listening. A *guru* in America had never gone onto the streets before and sung the names of God.

After *kīrtana*, he asked for a copy of the *Śrīmad-Bhāgavatam* and had Hayagrīva read aloud from the preface. With clear articulation, Hayagrīva read: "Disparity in the human society is due to the basic principle of a godless civilization. There is God, the Almighty One, from whom everything emanates, by whom everything is maintained, and in whom everything is merged to rest. . . ." The crowd was still. Afterward, the Swami and his followers walked back to the storefront, feeling elated and victorious. They had broken the American silence.

* * *

Allen Ginsberg lived nearby on East Tenth Street. One day he received a peculiar invitation in the mail:

Practice the transcendental sound vibration,
Hare Krishna, Hare Krishna, Krishna Krishna, Hare Hare
Hare Rama, Hare Rama, Rama Rama, Hare Hare.
This chanting will cleanse the dust from the mirror
of the mind.

International Society for Krishna Consciousness
Meetings at 7 A.M. daily
Mondays, Wednesdays, and Fridays at 7:00 P.M.
You are cordially invited to come and
bring your friends.

Swamiji had asked the boys to distribute it around the neighborhood.

One evening, soon after he received the invitation, Allen Ginsberg and his roommate, Peter Orlovsky, arrived at the storefront in a Volkswagen minibus. Allen had been captivated by the Hare Kṛṣṇa *mantra* several years before, when he had first encountered it at the Kumbha-melā festival in Allahabad, India, and he had been chanting it often ever since. The devotees were impressed to see the world-famous author of *Howl* and leading figure of the beat generation enter their humble storefront. His advocation of free sex, marijuana, and LSD, his claims of drug-induced visions of spirituality in everyday sights, his political ideas, his exploration of insanity, revolt, and nakedness, and his attempts to create a harmony of likeminded souls—all were influential on the minds of American young people, especially those living on the Lower East Side. Although by middle-class standards he was scandalous and disheveled, he was, in his own right, a figure of worldly repute, more so than anyone who had ever come to the storefront before.

Allen Ginsberg: *Bhaktivedanta seemed to have no friends in America, but was alone, totally alone, and gone somewhat like a lone hippie to the nearest refuge, the place where it was cheap enough to rent.*

There were a few people sitting cross-legged on the floor. I think most of them were Lower East Side hippies who had just wandered in off the street, with beards and a curiosity and inquisitiveness and a respect for spiritual presentation of some kind. Some of them were sitting there with glazed eyes, but most of them were just like gentle folk—bearded, hip, and curious. They were refugees from the middle class in the Lower East Side, looking exactly like the street sādhus *in India. It was very similar, that phase in American underground history. And I liked immediately the idea that Swami Bhaktivedanta had chosen the Lower East Side of New York for his practice. He'd gone to the lower depths. He'd gone to a spot more like the side streets of Calcutta than any other place.*

Allen and Peter had come for the *kīrtana,* but it wasn't quite time—Prabhupāda hadn't come down. They presented a new harmonium to the devotees. "It's for the *kīrtanas,*" said Allen. "A little donation." Allen stood at the entrance to the storefront, talking with Hayagrīva, telling him how he had been chanting Hare Kṛṣṇa around the world—at peace marches, poetry readings, a procession in Prague, a writers' union in Moscow. "Secular *kīrtana,*" said Allen, "but Hare Kṛṣṇa nonetheless." Then Prabhupāda entered. Allen and Peter sat with the congregation and joined in the *kīrtana.* Allen played harmonium.

Allen: *I was astounded that he'd come with the chanting, because it seemed like a reinforcement from India. I had been running around singing Hare Kṛṣṇa but had never understood exactly why or what it meant. But I was surprised to see that he had a different melody, because I thought the melody I knew was* the *melody, the universal melody. I had gotten so used to my melody that actually the biggest difference I had with him was over the tune—because I'd solidified it in my mind for years, and to hear another tune actually blew my mind.*

After the lecture, Allen came forward to meet Prabhupāda, who was still sitting on his dais. Allen offered his respects with folded palms and touched Prabhupāda's feet, and Prabhupāda reciprocated by nodding his head and folding his palms. They talked together briefly, and then Prabhupāda returned to his apartment. Allen mentioned to Hayagrīva that he would like to come by again and talk more with Prabhupāda, so

Hayagrīva invited him to come the next day and stay for lunch *prasādam.*

"Don't you think Swamiji is a little too esoteric for New York?" Allen asked. Hayagrīva thought. "Maybe," he replied.

Hayagrīva then asked Allen to help the Swami, since his visa would soon expire. He had entered the country with a visa for a two-month stay, and he had been extending his visa for two more months again and again. This had gone on for one year, but the last time he had applied for an extension, he had been refused. "We need an immigration lawyer," said Hayagrīva. "I'll donate to that," Allen assured him.

The next morning, Allen Ginsberg came by with a check and another harmonium. Up in Prabhupāda's apartment, he demonstrated *his* melody for chanting Hare Kṛṣṇa, and then he and Prabhupāda talked.

Allen: *I was a little shy with him because I didn't know where he was coming from. I had that harmonium I wanted to donate, and I had a little money. I thought it was great now that he was here to expound on the Hare Kṛṣṇa* mantra*—that would sort of justify my singing. I knew what I was doing, but I didn't have any theological background to satisfy further inquiries, and here was someone who did. So I thought that was absolutely great. Now I could go around singing Hare Kṛṣṇa, and if anybody wanted to know what it was, I could just send them to Swami Bhaktivedanta to find out. If anyone wanted to know the technical intricacies and the ultimate history, I could send them to him.*

He explained to me about his own teacher and about Caitanya and the lineage going back. His head was filled with so many things and what he was doing. He was already working on his translations. He always seemed to be sitting there just day after day and night after night. And I think he had one or two people helping him.

Prabhupāda was very cordial with Allen. Quoting a passage from *Bhagavad-gītā* where Kṛṣṇa says that whatever a great man does, others will follow, he requested Allen to continue chanting Hare Kṛṣṇa at every opportunity, so that others would follow his example. He told about Lord Caitanya's organizing the first civil disobedience movement in India, leading a *saṅkīrtana* protest march against the Muslim ruler. Allen was fascinated. He enjoyed talking with the Swami.

But they had their differences. When Allen expressed his admiration for a well-known Bengali holy man, Prabhupāda said that the holy man was bogus. Allen was shocked. He'd never before heard a swami severely criticize another's practice. Prabhupāda explained, on the basis of Vedic evidence, the reasoning behind his criticism, and Allen admitted that he had naively thought that all holy men were one-hundred-percent holy. But now he decided that he should not simply accept a *sādhu,* including Prabhupāda, on blind faith. He decided to see Prabhupāda in a more severe, critical light.

Allen: *I had a very superstitious attitude of respect, which probably was an idiot sense of mentality, and so Swami Bhaktivedanta's teaching was very good to make me question that. It also made me question* him *and not take him for granted.*

Allen described a divine vision he'd had in which William Blake had appeared to him in sound, and in which he had understood the oneness of all things. A *sādhu* in Vṛndāvana had told Allen that this meant that William Blake was his *guru.* But to Prabhupāda this made no sense.

Allen: *The main thing, above and beyond all our differences, was an aroma of sweetness that he had, a personal, selfless sweetness like total devotion. And that was what always conquered me, whatever intellectual questions or doubts I had, or even cynical views of ego. In his presence there was a kind of personal charm, coming from dedication, that conquered all our conflicts. Even though I didn't agree with him, I always liked to be with him.*

Allen agreed, at Prabhupāda's request, to chant more and to try to give up smoking.

"Do you really intend to make these American boys into Vaiṣṇavas?" Allen asked.

"Yes," Prabhupāda replied happily, "and I will make them all *brāhmaṇas.*"

Allen left a $200 check to help cover the legal expenses for extending the Swami's visa and wished him good luck. "*Brāhmaṇas!*" Allen didn't see how such a transformation could be possible.

* * *

September 23

It was Rādhāṣṭamī, the appearance day of Śrīmatī Rādhārāṇī, Lord Kṛṣṇa's eternal consort. Prabhupāda held his second initiation. Keith became Kīrtanānanda, Steve became Satsvarūpa, Bruce became Brahmānanda, and Chuck became Acyutānanda. It was another festive day with a fire sacrifice in Prabhupāda's front room and a big feast.

* * *

Prabhupāda lived amid the drug culture, in a neighborhood where the young people were almost desperately attempting to alter their consciousness, whether by drugs or by some other means—whatever was available. Prabhupāda assured them that they could easily achieve the higher consciousness they desired by chanting Hare Kṛṣṇa. It was inevitable that in explaining Kṛṣṇa consciousness he would make allusions to the drug experience, even if only to show that the two were contrary paths. He was familiar already with Indian "*sādhus*" who took *gañjā* and hashish on the plea of aiding their meditations. And even before he had left India, hippie tourists had become a familiar sight on the streets of Delhi.

The hippies liked India because of the cultural mystique and easy access to drugs. They would meet their Indian counterparts, who assured them that taking hashish was spiritual, and then they would return to America and perpetrate their misconceptions of Indian spiritual culture.

It was the way of life. The local head shops carried a full line of paraphernalia. Marijuana, LSD, peyote, cocaine, and hard drugs like heroin and barbituates were easily purchased on the streets and in the parks. Underground newspapers reported important news on the drug scene, featured a cartoon character named Captain High, and ran crossword puzzles that only a seasoned "head" could answer.

Prabhupāda had to teach that Kṛṣṇa consciousness was beyond the revered LSD trip. "Do you think taking LSD can produce ecstasy and higher consciousness?" he once asked his storefront audience. "Then just imagine a roomful of LSD. Kṛṣṇa consciousness is like that." People would regularly come in and ask Swamiji's disciples, "Do you get high from this?" And the devotees would answer, "Oh, yes. You can get high just by chanting. Why don't you try it?"

Greg Scharf (Brahmānanda's brother) hadn't tried LSD; but he wanted higher consciousness, so he decided to try the chanting.

Greg: *I was eighteen. Everyone at the storefront had taken LSD, and I thought maybe I should too, because I wanted to feel like part of the crowd. So I asked Umāpati, "Hey, Umāpati, do you think I should try LSD? Because I don't know what you guys are talking about." He said no, that Swamiji said you didn't need LSD. I never did take it, so I guess it was OK.*

Hayagrīva: *Have you ever heard of LSD? It's a psychedelic drug that comes like a pill, and if you take it you can get religious ecstasies. Do you think this can help my spiritual life?*

Prabhupāda: *You don't need to take anything for your spiritual life. Your spiritual life is already here.*

Had anyone else said such a thing, Hayagrīva would never have agreed with him, But because Swamiji seemed "so absolutely positive," therefore "there was no question of not agreeing."

Satsvarūpa: *I knew Swamiji was in a state of exalted consciousness, and I was hoping that somehow he could teach the process to me. In the privacy of his room, I asked him, "Is there spiritual advancement that you can make from which you won't fall back?" By his answer—"Yes"—I was convinced that my own attempts to be spiritual on LSD, only to fall down later, could be replaced by a total spiritual life such as Swamiji had. I could see he was convinced, and then I was convinced.*

Greg: *LSD was like the spiritual drug of the times, and Swamiji was the only one who dared to speak out against it, saying it was nonsense. I think that was the first battle he had to conquer in trying to promote his movement on the Lower East Side. Even those who came regularly to the storefront thought that LSD was good.*

Probably the most famous experiments with LSD in those days were by Timothy Leary and Richard Alpert, Harvard psychology instructors who studied the effects of the drug, published their findings in professional journals, and advocated the use of LSD for self-realization and fulfillment. After being fired from Harvard, Timothy Leary went on to become a national priest of LSD and for some time ran an LSD commune in Millbrook, New York.

When the members of the Millbrook commune heard about the swami on the Lower East Side who led his followers in a chant that got you high, they began visiting the storefront. One night, a group of about ten hippies from Millbrook came to Swamiji's *kīrtana.* They all chanted (not so much in worship of Kṛṣṇa as to see what kind of high the chanting could produce), and after the lecture a Millbrook leader asked about drugs. Prabhupāda replied that drugs were not necessary for spiritual life, that they could not produce spiritual consciousness, and that all drug-induced religious visions were simply hallucinations. To realize God was not so easy or cheap that one could do it just by taking a pill or smoking. Chanting Hare Kṛṣṇa, he explained, was a purifying process to uncover one's pure consciousness. Taking drugs would increase the covering and bar one from self-realization.

"But have *you* ever taken LSD?" The question now became a challenge.

"No," Prabhupāda replied. "I have never taken any of these things, not even cigarettes or tea."

"If you haven't taken it, then how can you say what it is?" The Millbrookers looked around, smiling. Two or three even burst out with laughter, and they snapped their fingers, thinking the Swami had been checkmated.

"I have not taken," Prabhupāda replied regally from his dais. "But my disciples have taken all these things—marijuana, LSD—many times, and they have given them all up. You can hear from them. Hayagrīva, you can speak." And Hayagrīva sat up a little and spoke out in his stentorian best.

"Well, no matter how high you go on LSD, you eventually reach a peak, and then you have to come back down. Just like traveling into outer space in a rocket ship. [He gave one of Swamiji's familiar examples.] Your spacecraft can travel very far away from the earth for thousands of miles, day after day, but it cannot simply go on traveling and traveling. Eventually it must land. On LSD, we experience going up, but we always have to come down again. That's not spiritual consciousness. When you actually attain spiritual or Kṛṣṇa consciousness, you stay high. Because you go to Kṛṣṇa, you don't have to come down. You can stay high forever."

Prabhupāda was sitting in his back room with Hayagrīva and Umāpati and other disciples. The evening meeting had just ended, and the visitors from Millbrook had gone. "Kṛṣṇa consciousness is so nice, Swamiji," Umāpati spoke up. "You just get higher and higher, and you don't come down."

Prabhupāda smiled. "Yes, that's right."

"No more coming down," Umāpati said, laughing, and the others also began to laugh. Some clapped their hands, repeating, "No more coming down."

The conversation inspired Hayagrīva and Umāpati to produce a new handbill:

STAY HIGH FOREVER!
No More Coming Down

Practice Krishna Consciousness
Expand your consciousness by practicing the

* TRANSCENDENTAL SOUND VIBRATION *

HARE KRISHNA HARE KRISHNA KRISHNA KRISHNA HARE HARE
HARE RAMA HARE RAMA RAMA RAMA HARE HARE

The leaflet went on to extol Kṛṣṇa consciousness over any other high. It included phrases like "end all bringdowns" and "turn on," and it spoke against "employing artificially induced methods of self-realization and expanded consciousness." Someone objected to the flyer's "playing too much off the hippie mentality," but Prabhupāda said it was all right.

Greg: *When these drug people on the Lower East Side came and talked to Swamiji, he was so patient with them. He was speaking on a philosophy which they had never heard before. When someone takes LSD, they're really into themselves, and they don't hear properly when someone talks to them. So Swamiji would make particular points, and they wouldn't understand him. So he would have to make the same point again. He was very patient with these people, but he would not give in to their claim that LSD was a bona fide spiritual aid to self-realization.*

* * *

October 1966

Tompkins Square Park was *the* park on the Lower East Side. On the south, it was bordered by Seventh Street, with its four- and five-storied brownstone tenements. On the north side was Tenth, with more brownstones, but in better condition, and the very old, small building that housed the Tompkins Square branch of the New York Public Library. On Avenue B, the park's east border, stood St. Brigid's Church, built in 1848, when the neighborhood had been entirely Irish. The church, school, and rectory still occupied much of the block. And the west border of the park, Avenue A, was lined with tiny old candy stores selling newspapers, magazines, cigarettes, and egg-creme sodas at the counter. There were also a few bars, several grocery stores, and a couple of Slavic restaurants specializing in inexpensive vegetable broths, which brought Ukranians and hippies side by side for bodily nourishment.

The park's ten acres held many tall trees, but at least half the park was paved. A network of five-foot-high heavy wrought-iron fences weaved through the park, lining the walkways and protecting the grass. The fences and the many walkways and entrances to the park gave it the effect of a maze.

Since the weather was still warm and it was Sunday, the park was crowded with people. Almost all the space on the benches that lined the walkways was occupied. There were old people, mostly Ukranians, dressed in outdated suits and sweaters, even in the warm weather, sitting together in clans, talking. There were many children in the park also, mostly Puerto Ricans and blacks but also fair-haired, hard-faced slum kids racing around on bikes or playing with balls and Frisbees. The basketball and handball courts were mostly taken by the teenagers. And as always, there were plenty of loose, running dogs.

A marble miniature gazebo (four pillars and a roof, with a drinking fountain inside) was a remnant from the old days—1891, according to the inscription. On its four sides were the words *HOPE*, *FAITH*, *CHARITY*, and *TEMPERANCE*. But someone had sprayed the whole structure with black paint, making crude designs and illegible names and initials. Today, a bench had been taken over by several conga and bongo drummers, and the whole park pulsed with their demanding rhythms.

And the hippies were there, different from the others. The bearded

Bohemian men and their long-haired young girl friends dressed in old blue jeans were still an unusual sight. Even in the Lower East Side melting pot, their presence created tension. They were from middle-class families, and so they had not been driven to the slums by dire economic necessity. This created conflicts in their dealings with the underprivileged immigrants. And the hippies' well-known proclivity for psychedelic drugs, their revolt against their families and affluence, and their absorption in the avant-garde sometimes made them the jeered minority among their neighbors. But the hippies just wanted to do their own thing and create their own revolution for "love and peace," so usually they were tolerated, although not appreciated.

There were various groups among the young and hip at Tompkins Square Park. There were friends who had gone to the same school together, who took the same drug together, or who agreed on a particular philosophy of art, literature, politics, or metaphysics. There were lovers. There were groups hanging out together for reasons undecipherable, except for the common purpose of doing their own thing. And there were others, who lived like hermits—a loner would sit on a park bench, analyzing the effects of cocaine, looking up at the strangely rustling green leaves of the trees and the blue sky above the tenements and then down to the garbage at his feet, as he helplessly followed his mind from fear to illumination, to disgust to hallucination, on and on, until after a few hours the drug began to wear off and he was again a common stranger. Sometimes they would sit up all night, "spaced out" in the park, until at last, in the light of morning, they would stretch out on benches to sleep.

Hippies especially took to the park on Sundays. They at least passed through the park on their way to St. Mark's Place, Greenwich Village, or the Lexington Avenue subway at Astor Place, or the IND subway at Houston and Second, or to catch an uptown bus on First Avenue, a downtown bus on Second, or a crosstown on Ninth. Or they went to the park just to get out of their apartments and sit together in the open air—to get high again, to talk, or to walk through the park's maze of pathways.

But whatever the hippies' diverse interests and drives, the Lower East Side was an essential part of the mystique. It was not just a dirty slum; it was the best place in the world to conduct the experiment in consciousness. For all its filth and threat of violence and the confined life of its brownstone tenements, the Lower East Side was still the forefront of the revolution in mind expansion. Unless you were living there and taking psychedelics or marijuana, or at least intellectually pursuing the quest for free personal religion, you weren't enlightened, and you weren't taking part in the most progressive evolution of human consciousness. And it was this searching—a quest beyond the humdrum existence of the ordinary, materialistic, "straight" American—that brought unity to the otherwise eclectic gathering of hippies on the Lower East Side.

Into this chaotic pageant Swamiji entered with his followers and sat down to hold a *kīrtana.* Three or four devotees who arrived ahead of him selected an open area of the park, put out the Oriental carpet Robert Nelson had donated, sat down on it, and began playing *karatālas* and chanting Hare Kṛṣṇa. Immediately some boys rode up on their bicycles, braked just short of the carpet, and stood astride their bikes, curiously and irreverently staring. Other passersby gathered to listen.

Meanwhile Swamiji, accompanied by half a dozen disciples, was walking the eight blocks from the storefront. Brahmānanda carried the harmonium and the Swami's drum. Kīrtanānanda, who was now shaven-headed at Swamiji's request and dressed in loose-flowing canary yellow robes, created an extra sensation. Drivers pulled their cars over to have a look, their passengers leaning forward, agape at the outrageous dress and shaved head. As the group passed a store, people inside would poke each other and indicate the spectacle. People came to the windows of their tenements, taking in the Swami and his group as if a parade were passing. The Puerto Rican tough guys, especially, couldn't restrain themselves from exaggerated reactions. "Hey, Buddha!" they taunted. "Hey, you forgot to change your pajamas!" They made shrill screams as if imitating Indian war whoops they had heard in Hollywood westerns.

"Hey, A-rabs!" exclaimed one heckler, who began imitating what he thought was an Eastern dance. No one on the street knew anything about Kṛṣṇa consciousness, nor even of Hindu culture and customs. To them, the Swami's entourage was just a bunch of crazy hippies showing off. But they didn't quite know what to make of the Swami. He was different. Nevertheless, they were suspicious. Some, however, like Irving Halpern, a veteran Lower East Side resident, felt sympathetic toward this stranger, who was "apparently a very dignified person on a peaceful mission."

Irving Halpern: *A lot of people had spectacularized notions of what a swami was. As though they were going to suddenly see people lying on little mattresses made out of nails—and all kinds of other absurd notions. Yet here came just a very graceful, peaceful, gentle, obviously well-meaning being into a lot of hostility.*

"Hippies!"

"What are they, Communists?"

While the young taunted, the middle-aged and elderly shook their heads or stared, cold and uncomprehending. The way to the park was spotted with blasphemies, ribald jokes, and tension, but no violence. After the successful *kīrtana* in Washington Square Park, Prabhupāda had regularly been sending out "parades" of three or four devotees, chanting and playing hand cymbals through the streets and sidewalks of the Lower East Side. On one occasion, they had been bombarded with water balloons and eggs, and they were sometimes faced with bullies looking for a fight. But they were never attacked—just stared at, laughed at, or shouted after.

Today, the ethnic neighbors just assumed that Prabhupāda and his followers had come onto the streets dressed in outlandish costumes as a joke, just to turn everything topsy-turvy and cause stares and howls. They felt that their responses were only natural for any normal, respectable American slum-dweller.

So it was quite an adventure before the group even reached the park. Swamiji, however, remained unaffected. "What are they saying?" he asked once or twice, and Brahmānanda explained. Prabhupāda had a way of holding his head high, his chin up, as he walked forward. It made him look aristocratic and determined. His vision was spiritual—he saw everyone as a spiritual soul and Kṛṣṇa as the controller of everything. Yet aside from that, even from a worldly point of view he was unafraid of the city's pandemonium. After all, he was an experienced "Calcutta man."

The *kīrtana* had been going for about ten minutes when Swamiji arrived. Stepping out of his white rubber slippers, just as if he were home in the temple, he sat down on the rug with his followers, who had now stopped their singing and were watching him. He wore a pink sweater, and around his shoulders a *khādī* wrapper. He smiled. Looking at his group, he indicated the rhythm by counting, one . . . two . . . *three.* Then he began clapping his hands heavily as he continued counting, "One . . . two . . . *three.*" The *karatālas* followed, at first with wrong beats, but he kept the rhythm by clapping his hands, and then they got it, clapping hands, clashing cymbals artlessly to a slow, steady beat.

He began singing prayers that no one else knew. *Vande 'haṁ śrī-guroḥ śrī-yuta-pada-kamalaṁ śrī-gurūn vaiṣṇavāṁś ca.* His voice was sweet like the harmonium, rich in the nuances of Bengali melody. Sitting on the rug under a large oak tree, he sang the mysterious Sanskrit prayers. None of his followers knew any *mantra* but Hare Kṛṣṇa, but they knew Swamiji. And they kept the rhythm, listening closely to him while the trucks rumbled on the street and the conga drums pulsed in the distance.

As he sang—*śrī-rūpaṁ sāgrajātam*—the dogs came by, kids stared, a few mockers pointed fingers: "Hey, who is that priest, man?" But his voice was a shelter beyond the clashing dualities. His boys went on ringing cymbals while he sang alone: *śrī-rādhā-kṛṣṇa-pādān.*

Prabhupāda sang prayers in praise of the pure conjugal love for Kṛṣṇa of Śrīmatī Rādhārāṇī, the beloved of the *gopīs.* Each word, passed down for hundreds of years by the intimate associates of Kṛṣṇa, was saturated with deep transcendental meaning that only he understood. *Saha-gaṇa-lalitā-śrī-viśākhānvitāṁś ca.* They waited for him to begin Hare Kṛṣṇa, although hearing him chant was exciting enough.

More people came—which was what Prabhupāda wanted. He wanted them chanting and dancing with him, and now his followers wanted that too. They wanted to be with him. They had tried together at the U.N., Ananda Ashram, and Washington Square. It seemed that this would be the thing they would always do—go with Swamiji and sit and chant. He would always be with them, chanting.

Then he began the *mantra*—Hare Kṛṣṇa, Hare Kṛṣṇa, Kṛṣṇa Kṛṣṇa, Hare Hare/ Hare Rāma, Hare Rāma, Rāma Rāma, Hare Hare. They responded, too low and muddled at first, but he returned it to them again, singing it right and triumphant. Again they responded, gaining heart, ringing *karatālas* and clapping hands—one . . . two . . . *three,* one . . . two . . . *three.* Again he sang it alone, and they stayed, hanging closely on each word, clapping, beating cymbals, and watching him looking back at them from his inner concentration—his old-age wisdom, his *bhakti*—and out of love for Swamiji, they broke loose from their surroundings and joined him as a chanting congregation. Swamiji played his small drum, holding its strap in his left hand, bracing the drum against his body, and with his right hand playing intricate *mṛdaṅga* rhythms.

Hare Kṛṣṇa, Hare Kṛṣṇa, Kṛṣṇa Kṛṣṇa, Hare Hare/ Hare Rāma, Hare Rāma, Rāma Rāma, Hare Hare. He was going strong after half an hour, repeating the *mantra*, carrying them with him as interested onlookers gathered in greater numbers. A few hippies sat down on the edge of the rug, copying the cross-legged sitting posture, listening, clapping, trying the chanting, and the small inner circle of Prabhupāda and his followers grew, as gradually more people joined.

As always, his *kīrtana* attracted musicians.

Irving Halpern: *I make flutes, and I play musical instruments. There are all kinds of different instruments that I make. When the Swami came, I went up and started playing, and he welcomed me. Whenever a new musician would join and play their first note, he would extend his arms. It would be as though he had stepped up to the podium and was going to lead the New York Philharmonic. I mean, there was this gesture that every musician knows. You just know when someone else wants you to play with them and feels good that you are playing with them. And this very basic kind of musician communication was there with him, and I related to it very quickly. And I was happy about it.*

Lone musicians were always loitering in different parts of the park, and when they heard they could play with the Swami's chanting and that they were welcome, then they began to come by, one by one. A saxophone player came just because there was such a strong rhythm section to play with. Others, like Irving Halpern, saw it as something spiritual, with good vibrations. As the musicians joined, more passersby were drawn into the *kīrtana*. Prabhupāda had been singing both lead and chorus, and many who had joined now sang the lead part also, so that there was a constant chorus of chanting. During the afternoon, the crowd grew to more than a hundred, with a dozen musicians trying—with their conga and bongo drums, bamboo flutes, metal flutes, mouth organs, wood and metal "clackers," tambourines, and guitars—to stay with the Swami.

Irving Halpern: *The park resounded. The musicians were very careful in listening to the* mantras. *When the Swami sang Hare Kṛṣṇa, Hare Kṛṣṇa, Kṛṣṇa Kṛṣṇa, Hare Hare/ Hare Rāma, Hare Rāma, Rāma Rāma, Hare Hare, there was sometimes a* Kṛ-ṣa-ṇa, *a tripling of what had been a double syllable. It would be usually on the first stanza, and the musicians really picked up on it. The Swami would pronounce it in a particular way, and the musicians were really meticulous and listened very carefully to the way the Swami would sing. And we began to notice that there were different melodies for the same brief sentence, and we got to count on that one regularity, like one would count on the conductor of an orchestra or the lead singer of a madrigal. It was really pleasant, and people would dig one another in their ribs. They would say, "Hey,* see*!" We would catch and repeat a particular subtle pronunciation of a Sanskrit phrase that the audience, in their enthusiasm, while they would be dancing or playing, had perhaps missed. Or the Swami would add an extra beat, but it meant something, in the way in which the drummer, who at that time was the Swami, the main drummer, would hit the drums.*

I have talked to a couple of musicians about it, and we agreed that in his head this Swami must have had hundreds and hundreds of melodies that had been brought back from the real learning from the other side of the world. So many people came there just to tune in to the musical gift, the transmission of the dharma. *"Hey," they would say, "listen to this holy monk." People were really sure there were going to be unusual feats, grandstanding, flashy levitation, or whatever people* expected *was going to happen. But when the simplicity of what the Swami was really saying, when you began to sense it—whether you were motivated to actually make a lifetime commitment and go this way of life, or whether you merely wanted to appreciate it and place it in a place and give certain due respect to it—it turned you around.*

And that was interesting, too, the different ways in which people regarded the kīrtana. *Some people thought it was a prelude. Some people thought it was a main event. Some people liked the music. Some people liked the poetic sound of it.*

Then Allen Ginsberg and Peter Orlovsky arrived, along with some of their friends. Allen surveyed the scene and found a seat among the chanters. With his black beard, his eyeglasses, his bald spot surrounded by long, black ringlets of hair, Allen Ginsberg, the poet-patriarch come to join the chanting, greatly enhanced the local prestige of the *kīrtana.* Prabhupāda, while continuing his ecstatic chanting and drum-playing, acknowledged Allen and smiled.

A reporter from *The New York Times* dropped by and asked Allen for an interview, but he refused: "A man should not be disturbed while worshiping." The *Times* would have to wait.

Allen: *Tompkins Square Park was a hotbed of spiritual conflict in those days, so it was absolutely great. All of a sudden, in the midst of all the talk and drugs and theory, for some people to put their bodies, their singing, to break through the intellectual ice and come out with total* bhakti*—that was really amazing.*

The blacks and Puerto Ricans were out there with drums too, doing conga. But here was a totally different kind of group, some of them with shaven heads, and it was interesting. It was a repetitious chant, but that was also great. It was an easy chant to get into. It was an open scene. There was no boxed corner there in the actual practice. So, general smiles and approval and encouragement as a beginning of some kind of real communal get-together in the park, with a kind of serious underbase for exchange—instead of just hog-dog on the drums.

Prabhupāda was striking to see. His brow was furrowed in the effort of singing loud, and his visage was strong. The veins in his temples stood out visibly, and his jaw jutted forward as he sang his "Hare Kṛṣṇa! Hare Kṛṣṇa!" for all to hear. Although his demeanor was pleasant, his chanting was intensive, sometimes straining, and everything about him was concentration.

It wasn't someone else's *yoga* retreat or silent peace vigil, but a pure chanting be-in of Prabhupāda's own doing. It was a new wave, something everyone could take part in. The community seemed to be accepting it. It became so popular that the ice cream vendor came over to make sales. Beside Prabhupāda a group of young, blond-haired boys, five or six years old, were just sitting around. A young Polish boy stood staring. Someone began burning frankincense on a glowing coal in a metal strainer, and the sweet fumes billowed among the flutists, drummers, and chanters.

Swamiji motioned to his disciples, and they got up and began dancing. Tall, thin Stryadhīśa, his back pockets stuffed with *Stay High Forever* flyers, raised his hands and began to dance. Beside him, in a black turtleneck, big chanting beads around his neck, danced Acyutānanda, his curly, almost frizzy, hair long and disarrayed. Then Brahmānanda got up. He and Acyutānanda stood facing each other, arms outstretched as in the picture of Lord Caitanya's *kīrtana.* Photographers in the crowd moved forward. The boys danced, shifting their weight from left foot to right foot, striking a series of angelic poses, their large, red chanting beads around their necks. They were doing the Swami step.

Brahmānanda: *Once I got up, I thought I would have to remain standing for as long as Swamiji played the drum. It will be an offense, I thought, if I sit down while he's still playing. So I danced for an hour.*

Prabhupāda gave a gesture of acceptance by a typically Indian movement of his head, and then he raised his arms, inviting more dancers. More of his disciples began dancing, and even a few hippies got up and tried it. Prabhupāda wanted everyone to sing and dance in *saṅkīrtana.* The dance was a sedate swaying and a stepping of bare feet on the rug, and the dancers' arms were raised high, their fingers extended toward the sky above the branches of the autumn trees. Here and there throughout the crowd, chanters were enjoying private ecstasies: a girl with her eyes closed played finger cymbals and shook her head dreamily as she chanted. A Polish lady with a very old, worn face and a babushka around her head stared incredulously at the girl. Little groups of old women in kerchiefs, some of them wearing sunglasses, stood here and there among the crowd, talking animatedly and pointing out the interesting sights in the *kīrtana.* Kīrtanānanda was the only one in a *dhotī,* looking like a young version of Prabhupāda. The autumn afternoon sunlight fell softly on the group, spotlighting them in a golden glow with long, cool shadows.

The harmonium played a constant drone, and a boy wearing a military fatigue jacket improvised atonal creations on a wooden recorder. Yet the total sound of the instruments blended, and Swamiji's voice emerged above the mulling tones of each chord. And so it went for hours. Prabhupāda held his head and shoulders erect, although at the end of each line of the *mantra,* he would sometimes shrug his shoulders before he started the next line. His disciples stayed close by him, sitting on the same rug, religious ecstasy visible in their eyes. Finally, he stopped.

Immediately he stood up, and they knew he was going to speak. It was four o'clock, and the warm autumn sun was still shining on the park.

The atmosphere was peaceful and the audience attentive and mellow from the concentration on the *mantra.* He began to speak to them, thanking everyone for joining in the *kīrtana.* The chanting of Hare Kṛṣṇa, he said, had been introduced five hundred years ago in West Bengal by Caitanya Mahāprabhu. *Hare* means "O energy of the Lord," Kṛṣṇa is the Lord, and Rāma is also a name of the Supreme Lord, meaning "the highest pleasure." His disciples sat at his feet, listening. Rāya Rāma squinted through his shielding hand into the sun to see Swamiji, and Kīrtanānanda's head was cocked to one side, like a bird's who is listening to the ground.

He stood erect by the stout oak, his hands folded loosely before him in a proper speaker's posture, his light saffron robes covering him gracefully. The tree behind him seemed perfectly placed, and the sunshine dappled leafy shadows against the thick trunk. Behind him, through the grove of trees, was the steeple of St. Brigid's. On his right was a dumpy, middle-aged woman wearing a dress and hairdo that had been out of style in the United States for twenty-five years. On his left was a bold-looking hippie girl in tight denims and beside her a young black man in a black sweater, his arms folded across his chest. Next was a young father holding an infant, then a bearded young street *sādhu,* his long hair parted in the middle, and two ordinary, short-haired middle-class men and their young female companions. Many in the crowd, although standing close by, became distracted, looking off here and there.

Prabhupāda explained that there are three platforms—sensual, mental, and intellectual—and above them is the spiritual platform. The chanting of Hare Kṛṣṇa is on the spiritual platform, and it is the best process for reviving our eternal, blissful consciousness. He invited everyone to attend the meetings at 26 Second Avenue and concluded his brief speech by saying, "Thank you very much. Please chant with us." Then he sat down, took the drum, and began the *kīrtana* again.

If it were risky for a seventy-one-year-old man to thump a drum and shout so loud, then he would take that risk for Kṛṣṇa. It was too good to stop. He had come far from Vṛndāvana, survived the non-Kṛṣṇa *yoga* society, waited all winter in obscurity. America had waited hundreds of years with no Kṛṣṇa-chanting. No "Hare Kṛṣṇa" had come from Thoreau's or Emerson's appreciations, though they had pored over

English translations of the *Gītā* and *Purāṇas*. And no *kīrtana* had come from Vivekananda's famous speech on behalf of Hinduism at the World Parliament of Religions in Chicago in 1893. So now that he finally had *kṛṣṇa-bhakti* going, flowing like the Ganges to the sea, it could not stop. In his heart he felt the infinite will of Lord Caitanya to deliver the fallen souls.

He knew this was the desire of Lord Caitanya Mahāprabhu and his own spiritual master, even though caste-conscious *brāhmaṇas* in India would disapprove of his associating with such untouchables as these drug-mad American meat-eaters and their girl friends. But Swamiji explained that he was in full accord with the scriptures. The *Bhāgavatam* had clearly stated that Kṛṣṇa consciousness should be delivered to all races. Everyone was a spiritual soul, and regardless of birth they could be brought to the highest spiritual platform by chanting the holy name. Never mind whatever sinful things they were doing, these people were perfect candidates for Kṛṣṇa consciousness. Tompkins Square Park was Kṛṣṇa's plan; it was also part of the earth, and these people were members of the human race. And the chanting of Hare Kṛṣṇa was the *dharma* of the age.

* * *

Walking back home in the early evening, past the shops and crowded tenements, followed by more than a dozen interested new people from the park, the Swami again sustained occasional shouts and taunts. But those who followed him from the park were still feeling the aura of an ecstasy that easily tolerated a few taunts from the street. Prabhupāda, especially, was undisturbed. As he walked with his head high, not speaking, he was gravely absorbed in his thoughts. And yet his eyes actively noticed people and places and exchanged glances with those whom he passed on his way along Seventh Street, past the churches and funeral homes, across First Avenue to the noisy, heavily trafficked Second Avenue, then down Second past liquor stores, coin laundries, delicatessens, past the Iglesia Alianza Cristiana Missionera, the Koh-I-Noor Intercontinental Restaurant Palace, then past the Church of the Nativity, and finally back home to number twenty-six.

There was a crowd of people from the park standing on the sidewalk outside the storefront—young people waiting for him to arrive and unlock the door to Matchless Gifts. They wanted to know more about the dance and the chant and the elderly swami and his disciples who had created such a beautiful scene in the park. They filled the storefront. Outside on the sidewalk, the timid or uncommitted loitered near the door or window, smoking and waiting or peering in and trying to see the paintings on the wall. Swamiji entered and walked directly to his dais and sat down before the largest gathering that had ever graced his temple. He spoke further of Kṛṣṇa consciousness, the words coming as naturally as breathing as he quoted the Sanskrit authority behind what they had all been experiencing in the park. Just as they had all chanted today, he said, so everyone should chant always.

A long-haired girl sitting close to Swamiji's dais raised her hand and asked, seemingly in trance, "When I am chanting, I feel a great concentration of energy on my forehead, and then a buzzing comes and a reddish light."

"Just keep on chanting," Swamiji replied. "It will clear up."

"Well, what does the chanting produce?" She seemed to be coming out of her trance now.

"Chanting produces chanting," he replied. "Just as when you are calling the name of your beloved. If there is someone you love very much, then you want to repeat his name again and again. It is out of love."

A man spoke up without raising his hand. "But isn't it just a kind of hypnotism on sound? Like if I chanted Coca-Cola over and over, wouldn't it be the same?"

"No," Prabhupāda replied, "you take any word, repeat it for ten minutes, and you will feel disgusted. But we chant twenty-four hours, and we don't feel tired. Oh, we feel new energy." The questions seemed more relevant today. The guests had all been chanting in the park, and now they were probing philosophically into what they had experienced. The Swami's followers marked this as a victory. And they felt some responsibility as hosts and guides for the others. Swamiji had asked Kīrtanānanda to prepare some *prasādam* for the guests, and soon Kīrtanānanda appeared with small paper cups of sweet rice for everyone.

"The chanting process is just to cleanse the mind," said Prabhupāda. "We have so many misunderstandings about ourself, about this world, about God, and about the relationships between these things. We have so many misgivings. This chanting will help to cleanse the mind. Then you will understand that this chanting is not different from Kṛṣṇa."

A boy who was accompanying the long-haired girl spoke out incoherently: "Yes. No. I . . . I . . . I . . ."

Prabhupāda: *Yes. Yes. Yes. In the beginning we have to chant. We may be in whatever position we are. It doesn't matter. If you begin chanting, the first benefit will be* ceto-darpaṇa-mārjanam: *the mind will be clear of all dirty things, and the next stage will be that the sufferings, the miseries of this material world, will subside.*

Boy: *Well, I don't quite understand what the material world is, because . . .*

Prabhupāda: *The material world is full of sufferings and miseries. Don't you understand that? Are you happy?*

Boy: *Sometimes I'm happy, sometimes I'm not.*

Prabhupāda: *No. You are not happy. That "sometimes" is your imagination. Just like a diseased man says, "Oh, yes, I am well." What is that "well"? He is going to die, and he is well?*

Boy: *I don't claim any ultimate happiness.*

Prabhupāda: *No, you do not know what happiness is.*

Boy: *But it's greater or lesser.*

Prabhupāda: *Yes, you do not know what is happiness.*

An older man, standing with his arms folded near the rear of the temple: *Well, of course, that sorrow or that suffering might add the spice to make that suffering that goes in between seem happiness.*

Prabhupāda: *No. The thing is that there are different kinds of miseries. That we all understand. It is only due to our ignorance that we don't care for it. Just like a man who is suffering for a long time. He has forgotten what is real happiness. Similarly, the sufferings are there already. For example* (and he directed himself to the young man with his girl friend), *take for example that you are a young man. Now would you like to become an old man?*

Boy: *I will become an old man in the process of—*

Prabhupāda: *"You will become" means you will be forced to become an old man. But you don't like to become an old man.*

Boy: *I am not going to be* forced *to become an old man.*

Prabhupāda: *Yes. Yes. Forced! You will be forced.*

Boy: *I don't see why.*

Prabhupāda: *If you don't want to become an old man, you will be forced to become an old man.*

Boy: *It's one of the conditions of—*

Prabhupāda: *Yes. That condition is miserable.*

Boy: *I find it* not *miserable.*

Prabhupāda: *Because you're a young man. But ask any old man how he is suffering. You see? A diseased man—do you want to be diseased?*

Boy: *I wouldn't search it out.*

Prabhupāda: *Hmm?*

Boy: *I wouldn't search it out.*

Prabhupāda: *No, no. Just answer me. Do you like to be diseased?*

Boy: *What is disease?*

Prabhupāda: *Just answer.*

Boy: *What is disease?*

Prabhupāda: *Oh? You have never suffered from disease? You have never suffered from disease?* (Prabhupāda looks dramatically incredulous.)

Boy: *I have had... I have had the mumps and the measles and whooping cough, which is what everyone has—and you get over it.* (Some people in the audience laugh.)

Prabhupāda: *Everyone may be suffering, but that does not mean that it is not suffering. We have to admit that we are always in suffering.*

Boy: *If I have never known happiness, I feel sure I have never known suffering either.*

Prabhupāda: *That is due to your ignorance. We are in suffering. We don't want to die, but death is there. We don't want to be diseased, but disease is there. We don't want to become old—old age is there. We don't want so many things, but they are forced upon us, and any sane man will admit that these are sufferings. But if you are accustomed to take these sufferings, then you say it is all right. But any sane man won't like to be diseased. He won't like to be old. And he won't like to die. Why do you have this peace movement? Because if there is war, there will be death. So people are afraid. They are making agitation: "There should be no war." Do you think that death is a very pleasurable thing?*

Boy: *I have never experienced—*

Prabhupāda: *You* have *experienced—and forgotten. Many times you have died. You have experienced, but you have forgotten. Forgetfulness is no excuse. Suppose a child forgot some suffering. That does not mean he did not suffer.*

Boy: *No, I agree. I agree.*

Prabhupāda: *Yes. So suffering is there. You have to take direction from realized souls, from authorities. Just like in the* Bhagavad-gītā *it is said,* duḥkhālayam aśāśvatam: *this world is full of miseries. So one has to realize it. Unless we understand that this place is miserable, there is no question of how to get out of it. A person who doesn't develop this understanding is not fully developed. Just like the animals—they do not understand what misery is. They are satisfied.*

It was late when he finally returned to his apartment. One of the boys brought him a cup of hot milk, and someone remarked they should do the chanting in the park every week. "Every day," he replied. Even while half a dozen people were present, he lay down on his thin mat. He continued to speak for some minutes, and then his voice trailed off, preaching in fragmented words. He appeared to doze. It was ten o'clock. They tiptoed out, softly shutting the door.

* * *

October 10

It was early. Swamiji had not yet come down for class, and the sun had not yet risen. Satsvarūpa and Kīrtanānanda sat on the floor of the storefront, reading a clipping from the morning *Times.*

Satsvarūpa: *Has the Swami seen it?*

Kīrtanānanda: *Yes, just a few minutes ago. He said it's very important. It's historic. He especially liked that it was* The New York Times.

Satsvarūpa (reading aloud): "*SWAMI'S FLOCK CHANTS IN PARK TO FIND ECSTASY.*"

> Fifty Followers Clap and Sway to Hypnotic Music at East Side Ceremony. Sitting under a tree in a Lower East Side park and occasionally dancing, fifty followers of a Hindu swami repeated a sixteen-word chant for two hours yesterday . . .

It was more *than two hours.*

> ...for two hours yesterday afternoon to the accompaniment of cymbals, tambourines, sticks, drums, bells, and a small reed organ. Repetition of the chant, Swami A. C. Bhaktivedanta says, is the best way to achieve self-realization in this age of destruction. While children played on Hoving's Hill, a pile of dirt in the middle of Tompkins Square Park...

Hoving's Hill?

Kīrtanānanda: *I think it's a joke named after the Parks Commissioner.*

Satsvarūpa: *Oh.*

> ...Hoving's Hill, a pile of dirt in the middle of Tompkins Square Park, or bicycled along the sunny walks, many in the crowd of about a hundred persons standing around the chanters found themselves swaying to or clapping hands in time to the hypnotic rhythmic music. "It brings a state of ecstasy," said Allen Ginsberg the poet, who was one of the celebrants. "For one thing," Allen Ginsberg said, "the syllables force yoga breath control. That's one physiological explanation.

Satsvarūpa and Kīrtanānanda (laughing): *That's nonsense.*

> "The ecstasy of the chant or mantra Hare Krishna Hare Krishna Krishna Krishna Hare Hare Hare Rama Hare Rama Rama Rama Hare Hare...

Kīrtanānanda: *The Swami said that's the best part. Because they have printed the* mantra, *it's all-perfect. Whoever reads this can be purified just the same as if they had chanted.*

Satsvarūpa (continuing):

> "...has replaced LSD and other drugs for many of the swami's followers," Mr. Ginsberg said. He explained that Hare Krishna, pronounced Hahray, is the name for Vishnu, a Hindu god, as the "bringer of light." Rama, pronounced Rahmah, is the incarnation of Vishnu as "the prince of responsibility.

What? Where did he get that? It sounds like something out of an encyclopedia.

"The chant, therefore, names different aspects of God," Mr. Ginsberg said.

Why so much from Mr. Ginsberg? Why not Swamiji?

Another celebrant, 26-year-old Howard M. Wheeler, who described himself as a former English instructor at Ohio State University, now devoting his full time to the swami, said, "I myself took fifty doses of LSD and a dozen of peyote in two years, and now nothing."

(Laughter.)

The swami orders his followers to give up "all intoxicants, including coffee, tea, and cigarettes," he said in an interview after the ceremony. "In this sense we are helping your government," he added. However, he indicated the government apparently has not appreciated this help sufficiently, for the Department of Immigration recently told Swami Bhaktivedanta that his one-year visitor's visa had expired and that he must leave, he said. The case is being appealed.

The swami, a swarthy man with short-cropped grayish hair and clad in a salmon-colored robe over a pink sweater, said that when he first met his own teacher, or guru, in 1922, he was told to spread the cult of Krishna to the Western countries through the English language. "Therefore in this old age (71) I have taken so much risk."

It says that we're going to come there and chant every Sunday. "His followers include some social workers." I guess that's me.

Kīrtanānanda: *I think this article will bring a lot of new people.*

The Swami came down for class. The morning was chilly, and he wore a peach-colored turtleneck jersey his disciples had bought for him at a shop on Orchard Street. They had also started wearing such jerseys—a kind of unofficial uniform. Swamiji didn't mention the *Times* article. He began singing the Sanskrit prayers. *Vande 'haṁ śrī-guroḥ:* "I offer my obeisances to my spiritual master . . ." Then he began singing Hare Kṛṣṇa, and the boys joined in. "Sing softly," Prabhupāda cautioned them.

But no sooner had he spoken than water began pouring down through the cracks in the ceiling. The man upstairs didn't like early-morning *kīrtanas*, and he began stomping his feet to show that this flood was no accident.

"What is this?" Prabhupāda looked up, disturbed, but with a touch of amusement. The boys looked around. Water was pouring down in several places. "Get some pots," he said. A boy ran upstairs to Swamiji's apartment to get pots from the kitchen. Soon three pots were catching the water as it dripped in three separate places.

"How does he do it?" asked Umāpati. "Is he pouring water onto the floor?" Prabhupāda asked Brahmānanda to go up and speak to the man, to tell him that the *kīrtana* would be a quiet one. Then he asked everyone to sit back down amid the dripping and the pots and continue chanting. "Softly," he said. "Softly."

That evening, the temple was filled with guests. "It is so much kindness of the Supreme Lord," Prabhupāda said, "that He wants to associate with you. So you should receive Him. Always chant Hare Kṛṣṇa. Now, this language is Sanskrit, and some of you do not know the meaning. Still, it is so attractive that when we chanted Hare Kṛṣṇa in the park—oh, old ladies, gentlemen, boys and girls, all took part. . . . But there are also complaints. Just like we are receiving daily reports that our *saṅkīrtana* movement is disturbing some tenants here."

* * *

Ravīndra Svarūpa was walking down Second Avenue, on his way to the Swami's morning class, when an acquaintance came out of the Gems Spa Candy and News Store and said, "Hey, your Swami is in the newspaper. Did you see?" "Yeah," Ravīndra Svarūpa replied, "*The New York Times.*"

"No," his friend said. "Today." And he held up a copy of the latest edition of *The East Village Other*. The front page was filled with a two-color photo of the Swami, his hands folded decorously at his waist, standing in yellow robes in front of the big tree in Tompkins Square Park. He was speaking to a small crowd that had gathered around, and his disciples were at his feet. The big steeple of St. Brigid's formed a silhouette behind him.

Above the photo was the single headline, "SAVE EARTH NOW!!" and beneath was the *mantra:* "HARE KRISHNA HARE KRISHNA KRISHNA KRISHNA HARE HARE HARE RAMA HARE RAMA RAMA RAMA HARE HARE." Below the *mantra* were the words, "See Centerfold." That was the whole front page.

Ravīndra Svarūpa took the newspaper and opened to the center, where he found a long article and a large photo of Swamiji with his left hand on his head, grinning blissfully in an unusual, casual moment. His friend gave him the paper, and Ravīndra Svarūpa hurried to Swamiji. When he reached the storefront, several boys went along with him to show Swamiji the paper.

"Look!" Ravīndra Svarūpa handed it over. "This is the biggest local newspaper! Everybody reads it." Prabhupāda opened his eyes wide. He read aloud, "Save earth now." And he looked up at the faces of the boys. Umāpati and Hayagrīva wondered aloud what it meant—"Save earth now." Was it an ecological pun? Was it a reference to staving off nuclear disaster? Was it poking fun at Swamiji's evangelism?

"Well," said Umāpati, "after all, this is *The East Village Other.* It could mean anything."

"Swamiji *is* saving the earth," Kīrtanānanda said.

"We are trying to," Prabhupāda replied, "by Kṛṣṇa's grace." Methodically, he put on the eyeglasses he usually reserved for reading the *Bhāgavatam,* and carefully appraised the page from top to bottom. The newspaper looked incongruous in his hands. Then he began turning the pages. He stopped at the centerfold and looked at the picture of himself and laughed, then paused, studying the article. "So," he said, "read it." He handed the paper to Hayagrīva.

"Once upon a time, . . ." Hayagrīva began loudly. It was a fanciful story of a group of theologians who had killed an old man in a church and of the subsequent press report that God was now dead. But, the story went on, some people didn't believe it. They had dug up the body and found it to be "not the body of God, but that of His P.R. man: organized religion. At once the good tidings swept across the wide world. GOD LIVES! . . . But where was God?" Hayagrīva read dramatically to an enthralled group. . . .

> A full-page ad in *The New York Times,* offering a reward for information leading to the discovery of the whereabouts of God, and signed by

> Martin Luther King and Ronald Reagan, brought no response. People began to worry and wonder again. "God," said some people, "lives in a sugar cube." Others whispered that the sacred secret was in a cigarette.
>
> But while all this was going on, an old man, one year past his allotted three score and ten, wandered into New York's East Village and set about to prove to the world that he knew where God could be found. In only three months, the man, Swami A. C. Bhaktivedanta, succeeded in convincing the world's toughest audience—Bohemians, acidheads, potheads, and hippies—that he knew the way to God: Turn Off, Sing Out, and Fall In. This new brand of holy man, with all due deference to Dr. Leary, has come forth with a brand of "Consciousness Expansion" that's sweeter than acid, cheaper than pot, and nonbustible by fuzz. How is all this possible? "Through Krishna," the Swami says.

The boys broke into cheers and applause. Acyutānanda apologized to Swamiji for the language of the article: "It's a hippie newspaper."

"That's all right," said Prabhupāda. "He has written it in his own way. But he has said that we are giving God. They are saying that God is dead. But it is false. We are directly presenting, 'Here is God.' Who can deny it? So many theologians and people may say there is no God, but the Vaiṣṇava hands God over to you freely, as a commodity: 'Here is God.' So he has marked this. It is very good. Save this paper. It is very important."

The article was long. "For the cynical New Yorker," it said, "living, visible, tangible proof can be found at 26 Second Avenue, Monday, Wednesday, and Friday between seven and nine." The article described the evening *kīrtanas*, quoted from Prabhupāda's lecture, and mentioned "a rhythmic, hypnotic sixteen-word chant, Hare Krishna Hare Krishna Krishna Krishna Hare Hare Hare Rama Hare Rama Rama Rama Hare Hare, sung for hours on end to the accompaniment of hand clapping, cymbals, and bells." Swamiji said that simply because the *mantra* was there, the article was perfect.

The article also included testimony from the Swami's disciples:

> I started chanting to myself, like the Swami said, when I was walking down the street—Hare Krishna Hare Krishna Krishna Krishna Hare Hare Hare Rama Hare Rama Rama Rama Hare Hare—over and over, and suddenly everything started looking so beautiful, the kids, the old men and

> women . . . even the creeps looked beautiful . . . to say nothing of the trees and flowers. It was like I had taken a dozen doses of LSD. But I knew there was a difference. There's no coming down from this. I can always do this any time, anywhere. It is always with you.

Without sarcasm, the article referred to the Swami's discipline forbidding coffee, tea, meat, eggs, and cigarettes, "to say nothing of marijuana, LSD, alcohol, and illicit sex." Obviously the author admired Swamiji: "the energetic old man, a leading exponent of the philosophy of Personalism, which holds that the one God is a person but that His form is spiritual." The article ended with a hint that Tompkins Square Park would see similar spiritual happenings each weekend: "There in the shadow of Hoving's Hill, God lives in a trancelike dance and chant."

* * *

October 12

It was to be a "Love-Pageant-Rally," marking California's new law prohibiting the possession of LSD. The rally's promoters urged everyone to come to Tompkins Square Park in elaborate dress. Although the devotees had nothing to do with LSD laws, they took the rally as another opportunity to popularize the chanting of Hare Kṛṣṇa. So they went, with the Swami's blessings, carrying finger cymbals and a homemade tambourine.

The devotees looked plain in their dark jeans and lightweight zippered jackets. All around them, the dress was extravagant—tie-dyed shirts, tie-bleached jeans, period costumes, painted faces. There was even a circus clown. Tuli Kupferberg of the Fugs rock band carried an American flag with the stars rearranged to spell L-O-V-E. But so far the rally had been a dud—just a strange set of drugged young people milling near the large tree where Swamiji had chanted and spoken just a few days before.

Swamiji's boys made their way through the crowd to a central spot and started chanting Hare Kṛṣṇa. A crowd pressed in close around them. Everyone seemed to be in friendly spirits—just unorganized, without any purpose. The idea behind the rally had been to show love and a pageant of LSD vision, but not much had been happening. Someone was walking around with a bucket of burning incense. Some hippies sat back on the park benches, watching everything through colored glasses. But the *kīrtana* was attractive, and soon a crowd gathered around the boys as they chanted.

Kīrtanānanda, his shaved head covered with a knit skullcap, stood beside tall Jagannātha, who, with his dark-framed glasses and wavy hair, looked like a great horned owl playing hand cymbals. Umāpati, also playing hand cymbals, looked thoughtful. Brahmānanda sat on the ground in front of them, his eyes closed and his mouth widely open, chanting Hare Kṛṣṇa. Beside him and looking moody sat Raphael, and next to him, ascetically thin-faced Ravīndra Svarūpa. Close by, a policeman stood watching.

The hippies began to pick up the chanting. They had come together, but there had been no center, no lecture, no amplified music. But now they began clapping and swaying, getting into the chanting as if it were their single purpose. The chanting grew stronger, and after an hour the group broke into a spontaneous dance. Joining hands and singing out, "Hare Kṛṣṇa, Hare Kṛṣṇa, Kṛṣṇa Kṛṣṇa, Hare Hare/ Hare Rāma, Hare Rāma, Rāma Rāma, Hare Hare," they skipped and danced together, circling the tree and Swamiji's disciples. To the hippies, it was in fact a Love-Pageant-Rally, and they had found the love and peace they were searching for—it was in this *mantra.* Hare Kṛṣṇa had become their anthem, their reason for coming together, the life of the Love-Pageant-Rally. They didn't know exactly what the *mantra* was, but they accepted it as something deep within the soul, a metaphysical vibration—they tuned in to it. Even the clown began chanting and dancing. Only the policeman remained aloof and sober, though he also could see that the new demonstration would be a peaceful one. The dance continued, and only the impending dusk brought the Love-Pageant-Rally to a close.

The devotees hurried back to Swamiji to tell him all that had happened. He had been sitting at his desk, translating the *Śrīmad-Bhāgavatam.* Although he had not been physically present at the *kīrtana,* his disciples had acted on his instruction. So even without leaving his room, he was spreading the chanting of Hare Kṛṣṇa. Now he sat waiting for the report.

They burst into his room with shining eyes, flushed faces, and hoarse voices, relating the good news. Not only had they dutifully chanted, but hundreds of people had joined them and sung and danced in a big circle, in a spirit of unity. "Swamiji, you should have seen," Brahmānanda exclaimed, his voice now exhausted from chanting. "It was fantastic, fantastic!" Prabhupāda looked from one face to another, and he also became like them, elated and hopeful that the chanting could go on like this. They had proved that their chanting of Hare Kṛṣṇa could lead the love and peace movement. It could grow, and hundreds could take part. "It is up to you to spread this chanting," Swamiji told them. "I am an old man, but you are young, and you can do it."

October 13

The Village Voice ran four large photographs of the Love-Pageant-Rally. The article stated:

> The backbone of the celebration was the mantras, holy chants from the Sanskrit *Bhagavad Gita*, and for three hours it became like a boat on a sea of rhythmic chanting. Led by fifteen disciples of Bhaktivedanta Swami, who operates from a storefront on Second Avenue, the mantras ebbed and flowed with the rhythm of drums, flutes, and soda-cap tambourines.

October 18

It was Sunday. And again they went to Tompkins Square Park. Swamiji played the bongo as before, striking the drumhead deftly as ever, his nimble fingers creating drum rolls, as he sat on the rug in the autumn afternoon. His authentic, melodic voice recited the prayers to the previous spiritual masters: Gaurakiśora, Bhaktivinoda, Bhaktisiddhānta—the centuries-old disciplic succession of which he was the living representative, now in the 1960s, in this remote part of the world. He sang their names in duty, deference, and love, as their servant. He sat surrounded by his American followers under the tall oak tree amid the mazelike fences of the park.

And the same magic occurred. This time the hippies came by with more ease and familiarity. Allen Ginsberg came again, and a hundred others gathered as Prabhupāda loudly sang: Hare Kṛṣṇa, Hare Kṛṣṇa, Kṛṣṇa Kṛṣṇa, Hare Hare/ Hare Rāma, Hare Rāma, Rāma Rāma, Hare Hare. Of the hundreds who came by, some stayed briefly and then left, some decided to listen and chant for a few minutes or even for the entire afternoon. And a few—very few—marked their encounter with the Swami as an unforgettable change in their lives.

Bob Corens was looking for the Swami. He was walking with his stylishly dressed wife and two-year-old son, Eric. Bob was twenty-six years old and worked as a supervisor in the New York City Welfare Department. He had grown up in Washington, D.C., where he had met his wife. He had a full face and broad forehead, a clear voice and steady eyes.

Bob: *After I graduated from George Washington University, I decided to go straight to what I thought was the heart of the material world, New York City, to seek out whatever was the highest truth. I ended up living around the corner from the first East Village head shop.*

Bob didn't think his job as a social worker really helped anyone—his clients over the years seemed to maintain their same outlook and habits. He and his wife frequented West Village coffee houses, had attended lectures by Leary and Alpert on expanded consciousness, and had taken part in a recent peace march. Bob had come to feel that his aspirations for a master's degree and a better apartment were unfulfilling, and he was looking for something more.

Bob: *I heard about the* I Ching, *a book that was supposed to chart a person's course in life. So I got someone to do a reading for me. The direction was, "Push upward through darkness." I took it as a good sign, a spiritual sign. Then I purchased* The East Village Other, *and I saw the article entitled "Save Earth Now!!" There was a picture of the Swami. I had read in a book by a Sikh teacher that there could be no higher knowledge without a spiritual master.*

Every morning on his way to work, Bob used to pass by the Swami's storefront. Curious, he stopped once and peered in the window, only to find an empty room, with some straw mats on the floor and one of Swamiji's boys. "Oh, these people are Buddhists?" he thought. The door had been open, and the boy came over and invited him in. "No thanks," he said, thinking, "I don't want anything to do with Buddhism." And he went on to his job.

In a head shop one day, he had picked up one of the Swami's

Bhāgavatams and looked through it, but he thought it was too advanced, so he put it back down. After he read the article in *The East Village Other*, his interest increased. He thought that today might be the last Sunday of chanting in the park before the cold weather came. And so he went to the park hoping to find the Swami and his chanters. His wife was beside him, pushing Eric in a stroller, when he heard the *ching-ching* of the hand cymbals and a chorus of rhythmic chanting from the south side of the park. Thinking it must be the Swami, he followed the sound, while his wife took Eric to play on the swings. Alone now, Bob drew closer, moving into the crowd until he could see the *kīrtana* party and the Swami sitting under the tree. Bob stood among a crowd of hundreds, unnoticed.

"Everything is happening because of me," thought nineteen-year-old Judy Koslofsky. "Everything I see is my own creation, and I am the Supreme. Everything is mine." As the thought of being God obsessed her, Judy forgot her father and everything else. She was confused: "If I am God, why can't I control everything, and why am I so fearful on LSD?"

Judy was a student at the City College of New York, majoring in art and history. She was taking guitar lessons from the Reverend Garry Davis, the blues singer and Christian preacher, who was teaching her the art of sad soul music. Today, however, under the influence of LSD, she had the overwhelming impression that she was God. She'd had a fight with her father, who seemed cold and distant to her and couldn't understand her, and she had left her parents' home in the Bronx and traveled downtown. She was going to visit a girl friend, and Tompkins Square Park happened to be on the way. When she reached the park the *kīrtana* was going on, but she couldn't see much because of the crowd. She weaved her way in closer until she could see some men—one shaven-headed, several bearded—dancing with upraised hands. And in the center she saw the Swami sitting on the rug, playing his drum.

Dan Clark was twenty-five, thin, intense, horn-rim bespectacled—an avant-garde filmmaker, and his first film was entitled *Rebirth.* He was a conscientious objector to the Vietnam war and was working at a home for children as alternative governmental service. He had been a member of the SDS and the War Resisters League. He had been arrested during a protest demonstration, and he had been suspended one week from his job for wearing a peace button and a black armband. He was into Buddhism, but he had lately been adding "a little psychedelic seasoning." "Everything is nothing, and nothing is everything," was his slogan, and he would go around chanting it like a *mantra.* But he was feeling that, at least psychologically, he needed a devotional tonic; his voidistic meditation was getting stale.

Dan had come to the park today looking for the Swami and the chanting he had read about in *The East Village Other.* He had seen the Swami before, one evening a few months back. He had been waiting for a bus across the street from the Swami's storefront—he was on the way to a rehearsal for a mixed-media show, and his friend had gone into Sam's Luncheonette for a moment—when he noticed that in the storefront an orange-robed Indian man with a shaved head was lecturing to a small group of young people.

Dan: *When I saw him, I imagined myself walking across the street, going into the storefront, sitting down, and renouncing all worldly connections. But I thought to myself, "It's only my imagination. After all, I'm married, and I'm on my way to rehearsal, and I don't know anything about the Swami anyway." So my friend and I got on the bus.*

But Dan lived only a few blocks away from the storefront, and now and then he would pass by. Once, he had stood for several minutes on the sidewalk looking at the cover of the *Śrīmad-Bhāgavatam* taped onto the window.

Dan: *It showed an oval lotus with planets around it, and right then I was introduced to the idea of spiritual sensuality. And when I saw the painting of Lord Caitanya and His associates in the window, that really threw me. I thought, "Yes, this is what I need—juice."*

Dan and his wife walked the paved pathway through the park. He was looking around for the Swami, but he didn't really know what to look for. He expected to see robes and hear Buddhist-style chanting, but he couldn't find anything. He had given up his search and was wandering around to see what musicians were there when he noticed a big crowd gathered around what he figured must have been some musicians. He was attracted by the beat of their music, a chiming one-two-*three*, one-two-*three*, a simple rhythm with a kind of flamboyance—and very magnetic. He saw an occasional upraised arm above the crowd, and he thought there must be flamenco dancing going on inside the circle. He then got wind of a drifting melody—certainly not flamenco—which accompanied the beat, and this attracted him further. He approached closer and closer, making his way through the crowd. Then he saw people chanting and others dancing and waving their arms in what he took to be a blend of American Indian and Asian dancing. It looked like something from a long-forgotten era. Dan decided that this must be the Hare Kṛṣṇa group. But there were no robes, just the regular dress of the Lower East Side. And where was the Swami? Then he saw him, sitting, inconspicuous, playing a little drum. His eyes were closed, and his brow was knit with concentration.

Dan: *The Swami wasn't calling attention to himself, and at first I didn't attribute any importance to an elderly Indian man's sitting off to one side. He didn't seem to have any special function in the chanting. But it gradually dawned on me who he was. He was the same Swami I had read about in the paper and seen in the storefront.*

After a while he spoke, but I couldn't hear him. Still, I was impressed that he was a very modest person, not interested in getting himself up on a pedestal. He didn't go strutting around, but was still with inner peace, strength, and knowledge.

Bob: *All his disciples were there around his feet. They were chanting, and I tried to chant along and learn the* mantra *too. I had heard the chanting of Hare Kṛṣṇa once before, at a peace march, and I had found it very beautiful. Then the Swami spoke. I had the impression that this person was not earthly, and I thought, "Here is the person I'm looking for." He seemed to be different from anyone else, like he came from some other place or universe. I was attracted.*

After a second *kīrtana*, the Swami and his followers rolled up their rug, picked up their instruments, and began to leave.

Bob walked back to the swings on the other side of the park to find his wife and child, but the image of the Swami stayed with him—"He seemed different from anyone else." His accent had been thick, yet Bob resolved to go to the storefront in a few days to hear him speak. "Here is a leader," thought Bob.

Dan and his wife sauntered off into the park, sampling the various groups of musicians. His wife was surprised that Dan, who was usually shy, had danced at the *kīrtana.* He said he might go over to the storefront one day and hear the Swami speak.

Judy just stood there hallucinating. She held a *Stay High Forever* pamphlet in her hand and read it over and over and over. While she was thinking the whole event must have come from another planet, a man walked up and asked, "Would you like to go to where the Swami is?" She nodded.

At the storefront, one of the devotees offered Judy some *prasādam*—a *capātī*—and then invited her up to the Swami's room. Upstairs, she entered the large front room, which was filled with fragrant smoke. There were tall flower vases, and sesame seeds were on the floor. She saw the Swami bow before the little picture of Lord Caitanya and His associates and then stand and leave the room, closing the door behind him. Judy decided that he must have been bowing to the floor itself. Around her, everyone was softly chanting on beads, and although she couldn't make out the words, it seemed peaceful. One of the Swami's disciples told her she could come into the back room, and she followed, curious. The Swami was sitting there on his mat, looking effulgent. There were about ten other people in the room.

Prabhupāda asked her if she liked the chanting in the park, and she replied, "I loved it."

"Do you live near here?" he asked.

Judy flashed on her idea that she was the all-pervading Truth and answered in a way which she thought must have sounded very mystical. "Oh, I live *veeerrry* near."

"Good," said Swamiji, "then you can come for our morning *kīrtana* and class."

Then she realized that she didn't live so near and that it would mean traveling an hour and a half from the Bronx to visit the Swami. But she decided that since he had asked her, she would come. Then she thought, "I am making this up." But Prabhupāda assured her, as if knowing her thoughts, "This process is nothing you have made up. It is very old, very simple, and sublime." He leaned back. "We are eternal," he said, "and everything around us is temporary." Judy was now coming down from the LSD. By the time she left the Swami, it was late. She had wanted to stay overnight, but the boys hadn't allowed her. But she was determined to join.

For Bob, it seemed natural to follow up on what he had seen in the park. He began attending the evening classes, and he started reading the *Bhāgavatam* at home and chanting. He framed the picture from the *Bhāgavatam* dust jacket depicting the spiritual sky and placed it on his small homemade altar. He would offer flowers before the picture and sit before it chanting Hare Kṛṣṇa.

Bob was fascinated by the philosophy and the books and classes, and from the very beginning he was amazed that Swamiji's teachings answered all his questions. He listened carefully and accepted: "It seemed like once I'd decided that he was telling the truth, I just accepted everything he said. Not that part of it was the truth and the rest of it I would have to think about."

October 19

It was Monday evening, after the Sunday *kīrtana* in the park, and Dan arrived at the storefront for *kīrtana.* The *kīrtana* was in full swing, and when he entered, the first thing he noticed was some people playing on the innards of an upright piano leaning against the wall near the door. A boy handed him some wooden sticks, and he sat down and joined in the *kīrtana.* Then came the Swami's lecture, which Dan thought was long and serious, about how sexual desire causes bondage and suffering. The temple was crowded and stuffy, and Dan was shocked by the lecture, but he stayed on because he knew there would be another *kīrtana.* He felt uneasy that the Swami's followers were all celibate, but because he liked the *kīrtanas,* he resolved to keep coming.

The Swami wasn't quite what Dan had expected. He had imagined something of a lighthearted Zen *roshi,* laughing and joking, with sparkling eyes and words filled with paradoxes. But he found the Swami just the opposite—very straightforward and even cutting in his speech and his mouth turned down at the corners, making him look mournful. Dan happily took to the *kīrtanas*, thinking they would aid his impersonal meditation, but the lectures kept stressing that God was a person. Dan resisted. He mentally debated with Prabhupāda. He was partial to Dr. Radhakrishnan's interpretation of the *Gītā*, and yet the Swami often launched ruthless attacks against such impersonal ideas. Gradually, Dan saw his impersonal barrier crumble, and he came to admit that on every count the Swami was right.

Judy began attending both the morning and evening classes. She had to rise by five o'clock to get to the storefront on time, and her mother and father protested. But Judy didn't care. She would ride an hour and a half on the subway, before dawn, downtown to the Swami's meetings, where she would be the only girl present.

When the Swami heard that Judy was an art student, he asked her to paint for Kṛṣṇa. She set up a canvas in the front room of the apartment, and under his guidance she began painting. For her first assignment, he asked her to paint a portrait of his Guru Mahārāja, Śrīla Bhaktisiddhānta Sarasvatī. He gave her a photo and instructed her: There should be a flower garland around Guru Mahārāja's neck, the *tilaka* should be yellowish, not white, and there should be no effulgence or halo around his head.

Bob: *I began chanting and studying the* Śrīmad-Bhāgavatam *at home and attending the* kīrtana *and classes at the storefront. After the last* kīrtana *in the evening, the Swami would take a bowl made of simulated wood and a little paring knife and a couple of apples that had been sitting on the edge of his lectern, and he would cut the apples up in the little bowl and hand the bowl to a disciple. The disciple would then offer him the first piece, and he would pop it into his mouth. The rest of the pieces of apple would be distributed to the crowd. I remember one time when he was chewing on his piece of apple and he spit the seeds out on the floor up against the wall. They bounced off the wall onto the floor next to the dais. And I was thinking, "How wonderful. No one else can do that. No one else would have the nerve to do such a thing."*

With his aesthetic filmmakers's eye, Dan appreciated Swamiji's manner.

Dan: *There was a sink right next to the dais where he sat. It was so close that he could have leaned over and touched it. After cutting up an apple, he would take the scraps and just fling them into the sink. It was very casual. I was very impressed by that.*

And one time Brahmānanda came up and wanted fifty cents for something, and the Swami reached down and picked up his little black purse—the kind that closes by a metal clasp at the top. He snapped it open, looked inside very perspicaciously, and then his hand came up like a bird, like an eagle hovering in flight above its prey. But the hand didn't pounce. It just delicately drifted down, took out a fifty-cent piece, and rose up again as if it were being lifted up on a balloon. It was graceful. It was a dance, a ballet. He just picked up this fifty-cent piece and lifted it into Brahmānanda's hand. I couldn't believe it. Someone asks you for a fifty-cent piece, you just dig in your pockets and throw it at them. But the Swami seemed to treat everything as Kṛṣṇa's property, and this fifty-cent piece was treated with such care.

The weeks went by. Some of the devotees had spoken to Bob about initiation, but he was unsure. He didn't know exactly what initiation was, but it seemed to him that the other devotees were eager to get him initiated because he was working and had a family. To Bob's way of thinking, he represented maturity to them, a middle-class American, and they were eager to land him. Bob's wife wasn't interested, and his friends were downright opposed. He couldn't spend much time with Prabhupāda or the devotees, since he was either at the office or at home with his family.

Bob: *So they were asking me if I was interested in initiation. I said I would think about it. I hadn't stopped smoking. I hadn't made the final decision.*

The first real personal exchange I had with the Swami was when I asked for initiation. The rest of the time I was so much in awe of him that it didn't occur to me to say anything. I always wanted to. I felt puffed up, and I always thought, "Well, I should be able to talk to him. Maybe I should do something." But I was always kind of reluctant to do it. I didn't think it was my place. I guess maybe I was afraid. But I was getting up early and chanting thirty-two rounds a day, many of them on the subway. I was afraid of the material world because I didn't have much association with devotees, and I wanted to insulate myself by chanting more.

Judy was another person who was considering initiation, and I asked her what she was going to do about it, and she said, "I'm thinking about it." And then she told me she had decided she would get initiated and give up all her bad habits. I began to think maybe I could give up these things too, so I asked what to do—how do I approach him? And Kīrtanānanda said, "Well, you go up to his room." I was surprised it was so easy.

I had prepared a little speech in my mind—"My dear Swamiji, would you kindly accept me as your disciple and teach me about Kṛṣṇa consciousness?" I went up to his room, without an appointment, and knocked on the door. I heard him say, "Come in." I entered the room, and he was sitting behind his desk. He was alone. I made obeisances, and he looked at me and said, "Yes?" And I said, "Swamiji, will you make me your disciple?" and that's as far as I got. I was going to say, "and teach me the philosophy of Kṛṣṇa consciousness." But he didn't let me finish my speech. He said, "Yes." It was so simple. I thought, "Well, there's nothing else to say. He has accepted me." So I thanked him and paid my obeisances and left.

"You know you're not supposed to be up here unless you're initiated," Acyutānanda said.

Judy was flustered. She had come upstairs to put some dirty pots in the kitchen. "Oh, yes," she replied, "that's just what I wanted to talk to Swamiji about." And she went into Prabhupāda's room, where he was talking with a few other people.

"Swamiji, could I please get initiated?" she asked.

And he said, "Do you know the four rules?"

"Yes."

"Can you follow them?"

"Yes."

"Then you can be initiated in two weeks."

Dan was also thinking about initiation, but he wanted to wait. He was chanting sixteen rounds and attending all the classes, despite his reluctant wife. He had always had difficulty with authority figures, but he could feel that the Swami was winning him over and wearing down his impersonal barrier.

Two weeks later, Prabhupāda held another initiation ceremony. Bob became Rūpānuga and Judy became Jadurāṇī. Dan needed a little more time.

CHAPTER TEN

Beyond the Lower East Side

But we were shocked that he was going to leave. I never thought that Kṛṣṇa consciousness would go beyond the Lower East Side, what to speak of New York City. I thought that this was it, and it would stay here eternally.

—Brahmānanda

Hare Kṛṣṇa was becoming popular—regular *kīrtanas* in the park, newspaper coverage. Hayagrīva called it "the Hare Kṛṣṇa explosion." The Lower East Side hippies considered the chanting of Hare Kṛṣṇa "one of the grooviest things happening," and that the Swami's disciples didn't take LSD didn't seem to affect their popularity. The devotees were accepted as angelic people, carrying the peaceful chanting to others and offering free food and a free place to stay. You could get the most interesting vegetarian food free at their place (if you went at the right time). And in their storefront, on the shelf by the door, were books from India.

In the clubs, local musicians played the melody that they had picked up from the Swami when he chanted in the park and at the temple. The Lower East Side was a neighborhood of artists and musicians, and now it was also the neighborhood of Hare Kṛṣṇa.

Burton Green: *Musicians were influenced by it—the Kṛṣṇa chant,* Govinda jaya jaya, *and other chants. I used some of those chants when I recorded. A lot of musicians reached out for this in different ways. We would explode in a short time and blow off, but then keep the chant underneath as a basis. A lot of people found that spiritual vibration even in the midst of this heavy music they were doing. They were becoming devotee-musicians.*

Evening *kīrtanas* were always big. Brahmānanda used to stand by the back door every night and watch the room fill up until there was no place left to sit. There was a lot of interest in the group chanting and music-making, but after the *kīrtana,* when the talk was to begin, people would start to leave. It was not uncommon for half the audience to leave before the talk began, and sometimes people would leave in the middle of the lecture.

One evening, Allen Ginsberg brought Ed Sanders and Tuli Kupferberg of the Fugs to the meeting. The Fugs, a local group that had made a name for themselves, specialized in obscene lyrics. Among the popular songs of Ed Sanders were "Slum Goddess of the Lower East Side," "Group Grope," and "I Can't Get High." Ed had wild red hair and an electric-red beard, and he played a guitar during the *kīrtana.* The devotees were happy to see their prestigious guests. The night of the Fugs, however, Prabhupāda chose to speak on the illusion of sexual pleasure. "Sex pleasure binds us to this material world birth after birth," he said, and he quoted, as he often did, a verse of Yāmunācārya: "Since I have become Kṛṣṇa conscious, whenever I think of sex life with a woman my face at once turns from it, and I spit at the thought." The Fugs never returned.

To speak ill of sexual pleasure was certainly not a strategic move for one who wanted to create followers among the Lower East Side hippies. But Prabhupāda never considered changing his message. In fact, when Umāpati had mentioned that Americans didn't like to hear that sex was only for conceiving children, Prabhupāda had replied, "I cannot change the philosophy to please the Americans."

"What about sex?" asked the ISKCON attorney, Steve Goldsmith, one evening, speaking out from the rear of the crowded temple.

"Sex should only be with one's wife," Prabhupāda said, "and that is also restricted. Sex is for the propagation of Kṛṣṇa conscious children. My spiritual master used to say that to beget Kṛṣṇa conscious children he was prepared to have sex a hundred times. Of course, that is most difficult in this age. Therefore, he remained a *brahmacārī.*"

"But sex is a very strong force," Mr. Goldsmith challenged. "What a man feels for a woman is undeniable."

"Therefore in every culture there is the institution of marriage," Prabhupāda replied. "You can get yourself married and live peacefully with one woman, but the wife should not be used as a machine for sense gratification. Sex should be restricted to once a month and only for the propagation of children."

Hayagrīva, who was seated just to Swamiji's left, beside the large, dangling cymbal, spoke out suddenly. "Only once a month?" And with a touch of facetious humor he added loudly, "Better to forget the whole thing!"

"Yes! That's it! Very good boy." Swamiji laughed, and others joined him. "It is best not to think of it. Best just to chant Hare Kṛṣṇa." And he held up his hands as if he were chanting on a strand of beads. "That way we will be saved from so much botheration. Sex is like the itching sensation, that's all. And as when we scratch, it gets worse, so we should tolerate the itching and ask Kṛṣṇa to help us. It is not easy. Sex is the highest pleasure in the material world, and it is also the greatest bondage."

But Steve Goldsmith was shaking his head. Prabhupāda looked at him, smiling: "There is still a problem?"

"It's just that . . . well, it's been proved dangerous to repress the sex drive. There's a theory that we have wars because—"

"People are eating meat," Prabhupāda interrupted. "As long as people eat meat, there will be war. And if a man eats meat, he will be sure to have illicit sex also."

Steve Goldsmith was an influential friend and supporter of ISKCON. But Prabhupāda would not change the philosophy of Kṛṣṇa consciousness "to please the Americans."

* * *

Judson Hall, on West Fifty-seventh Street, cost two hundred dollars to rent for one night. Rāya Rāma thought it was time Swamiji tried reaching some of the more sophisticated New Yorkers, and since Judson Hall was near Carnegie Hall and sometimes had interesting concerts and lectures, he thought it would be a good place to start. Swamiji agreed to the idea, and Rāya Rāma printed an announcement, which he distributed in the midtown bookstores. On the night of the event the devotees paraded through the midtown entertainment areas, beating a bass drum and handing out leaflets. Then they returned to Judson Hall for the program. Only seven people attended.

The devotees felt terrible—they had misled Swamiji and spent the equivalent of a month's rent. "We can cancel the program if you like, Swamiji," Rāya Rāma said. But Prabhupāda replied, "No, let us chant and speak." So the devotees took the stage and chanted with Swamiji and danced, and then sat beside him as he lectured, his voice echoing through the empty hall. Afterward, Swamiji called for questions, and a young man, about fifteen vacant rows back, asked whether he was correct in understanding that the Swami's philosophy was primarily for reforming destitute young people.

"No," Prabhupāda replied. "Everyone in this material world is lost and destitute, even the so-called successful person, because everyone has forgotten Kṛṣṇa."

After the program, Swamiji sat in a chair by the exit as the few members of the audience were leaving. A respectable-looking couple introduced themselves, and Swamiji sat up very straight with folded palms and smiled. Brahmānanda's mother was present, and Swamiji was very cordial toward her. But in general the devotees were depressed at the small turnout. "I'm sorry, Swamiji. We invited you here and almost no one came," Rāya Rāma apologized. But Prabhupāda raised his eyebrows and said, "No one? You did not see Nārada? You did not see Lord Brahmā? When there is chanting of Hare Kṛṣṇa, even the demigods come to participate."

Back at the temple, Prabhupāda chided Rāya Rāma: "I told you we should have charged money. When something is free, people think it is worthless. But just charge three dollars or five dollars, and people will think, 'Oh, you are offering some very valuable thing.' In Bengal there is the story of a man who went house to house offering free mangoes. And no one would take his mangoes, because everyone thought, 'Oh, why is he giving away these mangoes? There must be something wrong with them.' So he charged three rupees, and then they thought, 'These look like good mangoes. The price is only three rupees—all right.' So, when people see that something is free, they think it is worthless. Charge them some money, and they will think it is very nice."

* * *

Burton Green was a musician, fond of the Swami and fond of banging on the innards of the piano in the temple during *kīrtana.*

Burton Green: *We had a really explosive thing to break out of, with this capitalistic, materialistic egg sitting on us. So there was so much ferocity in the music to break out of. But spinning out like that, you could have a nervous breakdown. So it was great to go to the Swami's and chant in his small storefront on Second Avenue. The streets were full of* māyā *and perversion—and his was a place to really mellow out. It was great to chant there, to balance my life. It was great to sit and have* prasādam *with the Swami and get some real authentic Indian cooking and* capātīs *and talk about things, especially when I had very little money in my pocket. It was always nice to go.*

When Burton asked Prabhupāda to attend his piano recital at Town Hall Theater, Prabhupāda agreed.

Brahmānanda: *About seven or eight of us in our sneakers and jeans had ridden on the subway with Swamiji to Town Hall. We went in and took our seats, and the concert began. Burton Green came out, opened the piano top, took a hammer, and began wildly hitting on the strings inside the piano. And it went on for an hour and a half. We were all sitting there with Swamiji, and we all began chanting on our beads. There were only about two dozen people in the whole theater.*

Then the intermission came, and Swamiji wanted to go to the toilet room, and I went along and helped him—turning on the water in the sink, getting a paper towel for him. Doing these little services for Swamiji seemed like the perfection of my life. There was something so great about him that just doing those things was my perfection. And I felt like I was protecting him, like I was his personal bodyguard. Coming up on the subway, I had shown him how the subway worked and answered his questions. It all seemed very intimate.

Anyway, we went back upstairs to our seats, and Burton Green came right up to Swamiji saying, "Swamiji, are you happy? Are you comfortable? Do you like it?" And Swamiji was very polite and said yes. Then Burton said, "Now the second part is coming." I interrupted and tried to say that Swamiji is very tired and he takes rest at ten. It was already after ten, so I said we had to go back. But he pressed Swamiji to stay for the second half, and so we had to stay.

Then the poets came out and recited poetry. We were there until eleven-thirty, and then we had to ride back on the subway. But a few weeks later I learned that Prabhupāda had another reason for going to Town Hall—he was thinking of renting it for a temple, and he wanted to see it.

* * *

The Gate Theater was a small auditorium on Second Avenue about ten blocks north of the storefront.

Satsvarūpa: *We rented the Gate Theater for one night. It was a dark place, painted all black. The theater was almost empty. We had an easel on stage with a painting of the Pañca-tattva. Swamiji spoke, and his talk became very technical. Pointing and referring back to the painting, he described each member of the Pañca-tattva. He first explained that Lord Caitanya is the Supreme Personality of Godhead appearing as a pure devotee. Lord Nityānanda, to the right of Lord Caitanya, is His first expansion, and to the right of Lord Nityānanda is Advaita, who is the incarnation of the Supreme Lord. To the left of Lord Caitanya, he said, is Gadādhara, the internal energy, and Śrīvāsa is the perfect devotee.*

During the talk, I was thinking that this was maybe too elevated for the audience. But I was sitting close beside Swamiji, and like the other devotees I was really enjoying being with him.

After the Gate engagement, Swamiji and his disciples agreed that it was a waste of time trying to rent theaters. It was better to go to Tompkins Square Park. That was the best place for attracting people, and it didn't cost anything.

* * *

It was 11:00 P.M., and only one light was on in Swamiji's apartment—in the kitchenette. Swamiji was staying up, teaching Kīrtanānanda and Brahmānanda how to cook, because the next day (Sunday) they would be holding a feast for the public. Kīrtanānanda had suggested it be advertised as a "Love Feast," and Swamiji had adopted the name, although some thought it sounded strange at first to hear him say "Love Feast." The devotees had put up posters around the neighborhood and had made a sign for the window of the storefront, and Swamiji had said he would cook enough for at least fifty people. He said the Love Feasts should become an important part of ISKCON. As he had explained many times, food offered to Kṛṣṇa becomes spiritual, and whoever eats the *prasādam* receives great spiritual benefit. *Prasādam* meant "mercy."

His two helpers stood respectfully beside him, sometimes stepping back out of his way as he moved and sometimes looking over his shoulder as he mixed spices or set a pan over the flame or called for another ingredient. He was stirring a big pot of sweet rice with a wooden spoon—it had to be stirred constantly—and slowly adding milk. If the sweet rice burned, it would be ruined, he said, and he handed the spoon to Kīrtanānanda. He next showed them how to make ghee by heating butter in a wok and separating the milk solids from the butterfat. And he simultaneously taught them how to make apple chutney.

Prabhupāda was silent as he cooked. But when Brahmānanda asked him how he had learned so much about cooking, Prabhupāda said that he had learned by watching his mother. He laughed and said it had not been like it is in the West, where you take a lump of flesh from your refrigerator, throw it in a pan, boil it, sprinkle it with salt, and then eat like an animal. And in Korea, he said, they eat dogs. But human beings should eat grains, fruits, vegetables, and milk; and the cow, especially, should not be killed.

While Brahmānanda cut the apples for the chutney and put them in a pot for steaming and Kīrtanānanda stirred the sweet rice, Swamiji prepared *masāla*—the basic mixture of spices—which he would soon add to the steaming apples. The familiar smell of red pepper and cumin seeds entered their nostrils sharply as the *masāla* crackled and smoked in the hot ghee in the tiny frying pan. With three separate operations going at once—sweet rice, steaming apples, and *masāla*—Prabhupāda cautioned Kīrtanānanda to stir the sweet rice steadily and scrape the bottom of the pot, and he took the spoon for a moment from Kīrtanānanda's hand and demonstrated how to stir it properly. Sweet rice, chutney, and certain other dishes could be made in advance of the feast, he explained, but many things would have to be done the next morning.

Prabhupāda rose early, despite having kept late hours the night before, and after the morning class he was back in the kitchen. Now, half a dozen disciples sat in his front room making dough for *purīs* and *samosās*. He had shown them how to make the dough, and Umāpati had kneaded for a while by pounding the soft dough with his fists. But Brahmānanda was better at it, socking the weight of his wrestler's body onto the large lump of dough.

As Swamiji entered the room to examine the quality of the *purīs*, his disciples looked up at him respectfully. They were always serious when he was present. He picked up a *purī* and examined it. "It is not to the standard," he said, "but it will have to do." Then, amid crumpled rejects and oddly shaped pieces of dough, he squatted down beside his helpers, who were trying as best they could, though making a mess. He took a small ball of dough, pressed it flat with his fingers, and then deftly rolled it out until it curled around the wooden pin and then fell off—a perfectly round *purī*. He held it up, displaying a translucent, thin (but not too thin) patty of dough. "Make them like this," he said. "But hurry." On discovering that the dough was too stiff, Swamiji added a little ghee and then a little milk and kneaded the dough to a softer texture. "Everything should be just right," he said, and his disciples took to their menial tasks with concentrated earnestness. Who among them had ever heard of these things before—*purīs* and *samosās*? It was all new, and the challenge something very important; it was a part of devotional service.

Swamiji did much of the cooking as he simultaneously supervised his helpers. He was always near, walking barefoot back to the kitchen, then to the front room, then to his own room in the rear. And even when he went to his back room, his disciples could see him through the window in the wall.

Swamiji saw each of the nearly one dozen dishes through its final stages, and his disciples carried them into the front room in pots, one by one, and placed them before the picture of Lord Caitanya. There was *halavā*, *dāl*, two *sabjīs*, fancy rice, *purīs*, *samosās*, sweet rice, apple chutney, and *gulābjāmuns*, or sweetballs—ISKCON bullets. Prabhupāda had personally spent much time slowly deep-frying the sweetballs on a low heat, until they had turned golden brown and full. Then, one by one, he had lifted them out of the ghee with a slotted spoon and put them to soak in sugar syrup. He recognized that these golden, ghee-fried milk balls, soaked with sugar water, were his disciples' favorite *prasādam* treat. He called them "ISKCON bullets" because they were weapons in the war against *māyā*. He even allowed that a jar of ISKCON bullets, floating in their syrup, be always on hand in the front room, where his disciples could take them without asking permission and without observing any regulated hours. They could take as many as they liked.

Kīrtanānanda brought in the *samosā* filling, which he had prepared from spinach and green peas cooked to a paste and which the Swami had heavily spiced. Stuffing the *samosās* was an art, and Swamiji showed them how to do it. He took a semicircle of dough, shaped it into a cone, stuffed it with a spoonful of filling, and then folded the top over and sealed it—a *samosā*, ready for the hot ghee.

Acyutānanda carried the imperfectly shaped *purīs* into the kitchen, where he and Kīrtanānanda deep-fried them two at a time. If the temperature of the ghee, the consistency of the dough, and the size, shape, and thickness of the *purīs* were all just right, the *purīs* would cook in only a few seconds, rising to the surface of the ghee, where they would inflate like little balloons. The cooks then stood them on edge in a cardboard box to drain off the excess ghee.

As they completed the last preparations for the feast, Swamiji's disciples washed the stiff dough from their hands and went down to the storefront, where they set out the straw mats and awaited the guests and the feast. Upstairs, Swamiji and a couple of his cooks offered all the preparations to Lord Caitanya, reciting the *paramparā* prayer.

The first few Love Feasts were not very well attended, but the devotees were so enthusiastic about the feast *prasādam* that they showed no disappointment over the scarcity of guests. They were prapared to eat everything.

Satsvarūpa: *There was something called* "brāhmaṇa *spaghetti,*" *which was rice-flour noodles cooked in ghee and soaked in sugar water. And there was* halavā, puṣpānna *rice with fried cheese balls*, samosās, *split* mūṅg *beans fried into crunchy pellets and mixed with salt and spices,* purīs, gulābjāmuns. *And everything was succulent—that was the word Hayagrīva used. "Yes," he would say, expressing it waggishly, "everything was very* succulent."

Eating the feast was an intense experience. We were supposed to be subduing our senses all week, following strict regulations, controlling the tongue. And the feast was a kind of reward. Swamiji and Kṛṣṇa were giving us a taste of full spiritual ecstasy, even though we were still beginners and still in the material world. Before taking my plateful, I would pray, "Please let me remain in Kṛṣṇa consciousness, because it is so nice and I am so fallen. Let me serve Swamiji, and let me now enjoy this feast in transcendental bliss." And I would begin eating, going from one taste sensation to another—the good rice, the favorite vegetable, the bread, and saving the gulābjāmun *for last, thinking, "I can have seconds, and if I like, thirds." We would keep our eyes on the big pots, confident that there was as much as we wanted. It was a time of rededication. We all enjoyed with completely open relish and sense gratification. Eating was very important.*

Gradually, attendance picked up. The feasts were free, and they were reputed to be delicious. Mostly local hippies came, but occasionally a higher class of experimenting New Yorkers or even the parents of one of the devotees would come. When the small temple was filled, guests would sit in the courtyard. They would take their *prasādam*-laden paper plates and their wooden spoons into the backyard garden and sit beneath the fire escape or at the picnic table or anywhere. And after eating, they would go back into the storefront for more. Devotees were stationed behind the pots of *prasādam*, and the guests would come by for seconds. The other tenants were not very happy about seeing the courtyard full of festive guests, and the devotees tried to pacify them by bringing them plates of *prasādam*. Although Swamiji would not go down to the temple, he would take a plate in his room and hear with pleasure about the success of his new program.

One time the devotees were eating so ravenously that they threatened to eat everything available before the guests had all been served, and Kīrtanānanda had to admonish them for their selfish attitude. Gradually, they were understanding that the Sunday feast was not just for their fun and pleasure but to bring people to Kṛṣṇa consciousness.

* * *

Prabhupāda had begun *Back to Godhead* magazine in India. Although he had been writing articles since the 1930s, it was in 1944, in Calcutta, that he had singlehandedly begun the magazine, in response to his spiritual master's request that he preach Kṛṣṇa consciousness in English. It had been with great difficulty that through his pharmaceutical business he had managed to gather the four hundred rupees a month for printing. And he had singlehandedly written, edited, published, financed, and distributed each issue. In those early years, *Back to Godhead* had been Prabhupāda's major literary work and preaching mission. He had envisioned widespread distribution of the magazine, and he had thought of plans for spreading the message of Lord Caitanya all over the world. He had drawn up a list of major countries and the number of copies of *Back to Godhead* he wanted to send to each. He sought donations to finance this project, but help was scarce. Then, in 1959 he had turned his energies toward writing and publishing the *Śrīmad-Bhāgavatam.* But now he wanted to revive *Back to Godhead,* and this time it would not be done singlehandedly. This time he would give the responsibility to his disciples.

Greg Scharf, now Gargamuni since his recent initiation, found a press. A country club in Queens was trying to sell its small A.B. Dick press. Prabhupāda was interested, and he rode out to Queens in a borrowed van with Gargamuni and Kīrtanānanda to see the machine. It was old, but in good condition. The manager of the country club wanted $250 for it. Prabhupāda looked over the machine carefully and talked with the manager, telling him of his spiritual mission. The manager mentioned a second press he had on hand and explained that neither machine was actually of any use to him. So Prabhupāda said he would pay $250 for both machines; the country club did not really need them, and besides, the manager should help out, since Prabhupāda had an important spiritual message to print for the benefit of all humanity. The man agreed. Prabhupāda had Gargamuni and Kīrtanānanda load both machines into the van, and ISKCON had its printing press.

Śrīla Prabhupāda gave over the editorship of *Back to Godhead* magazine to Hayagrīva and Rāya Rāma. For so many years he had taken *Back to Godhead* as his personal service to his spiritual master, but now he would let young men like Hayagrīva, the college English teacher, and Rāya Rāma, the professional writer, take up *Back to Godhead* magazine as their service to *their* spiritual master. In a short time, Hayagrīva and Rāya Rāma had compiled the first issue and were ready to print.

It was an off night—no public *kīrtana* and lecture—and Swamiji was up in his room working on his translation of *Śrīmad-Bhāgavatam.*

Downstairs, the printing of the first issue had been going on for hours. Rāya Rāma had typed the stencils, and during the printing he had stood nervously over the machine, examining the printing quality of each page, stroking his beard, and murmuring, "Hmmmmm." Now it was time to collate and staple each magazine. The stencils had lasted for one hundred copies, and one hundred copies of each of the twenty-eight pages and the front and back covers were now lined up along two of the unvarnished benches Raphael had made that summer. A few devotees collated and stapled the magazine in an assembly line, walking along the stacks of pages, taking one page under another until they reached the end of the bench and gave the assembled stack of pages to Gargamuni, who stood brushing his long hair out of his eyes, stapling each magazine with the stapler and staples Brahmānanda had brought from his Board of Education office. Even Hayagrīva, who usually didn't volunteer for menial duties, was there, walking down the line, collating.

Suddenly the side door opened, and to their surprise they saw Swamiji looking in at them. Then he opened the door wide and entered the room. He had never come down like this on an off night before. They felt an unexpected flush of emotion and love for him, and they dropped down on their knees, bowing their heads to the floor. "No, no," he said, raising his hand to stop them as some were still bowing and others already rising to their feet. "Continue what you are doing." When they stood up and saw him standing with them, they weren't sure what to do. But obviously he had come down to see them producing his *Back to Godhead* magazine, so they continued working, silently and efficiently. Prabhupāda walked down the row of pages, his hand and wrist extending gracefully from the folds of his shawl as he touched a stack of pages and then a finished magazine. "ISKCON Press," he said.

Jagannātha had designed the cover, using a pen-and-ink drawing of Rādhā and Kṛṣṇa similar to his painting in the temple. It was a simple drawing set within a pattern of concentric circles. The first page opened with the same motto Prabhupāda had used for years on his *Back to Godhead:* "Godhead is light, nescience is darkness. Where there is Godhead there is no nescience." And on the same page, Hayagrīva had not been able to resist giving a quotation from William Blake, approved by Swamiji, which substantiated the philosophy of Kṛṣṇa consciousness:

> God appears, and God is Light
> To those poor souls who dwell in Night,
> But does a Human Form display
> To those who dwell in realms of Day.

Although the editorial spoke of Blake, Whitman, and Jesus Christ, it stressed:

> ... it is to teach this science [of devotion to God] that Swami Bhaktivedanta has come to America. His message is simple: the chanting of the Holy Name of God: "Hare Krishna, Hare Krishna, Krishna Krishna, Hare Hare ..."
>
> Following the orders of his spiritual master, His Divine Grace Sri Srimad Bhakti Siddhanta Saraswati Goswami Prabhupad, Swami Bhaktivedanta began the initial publication of *Back to Godhead* in 1944. This bi-monthly, published from 1944 to 1956 in Vrindaban, India, ... established Swami Bhaktivedanta as the leading Personalist in India. This issue marks the first publication of *Back to Godhead* in the West.

The main article, a summary of a lecture given by Prabhupāda, was based on notes taken by Umāpati.

> It has been said that when we wake up and when we go to sleep, we should beat our mind a thousand times with a shoe. When the mind says things like, "Why sing 'Hare Krishna?' Why not take LSD?" we should beat it with the same shoe. However, if we always think of Krishna, no beating will be necessary. The mind will be our best friend.

And there was an article by Hayagrīva: "Flip Out and Stay." Hayagrīva had quoted liberally from Hart Crane and Walt Whitman.

> No wonder so many young collegiates are trying to flip out permanently on superdrugs.... Perhaps this is their way of saying, "We don't want any part of this hell you've made for yourselves." So they use psychedelics as a springboard to propel themselves into different realms ... But the drug

> "flip" is only temporary. It is temporary because it is artificial. . . . One really begins to wonder where all these "trips" are leading.

Hayagrīva concluded that *kṛṣṇa-kīrtana* is the quickest way to flip out without coming down.

> Your associates will think you mad. That is the first sign of progress. Just let others be mad for *māyā*, the old ephemeral lures of women and gold. . . . But [you] be mad instead for the Reality.

In the back of the magazine was an ad for Swamiji's essays, *Krishna, the Reservoir of Pleasure* and *Who is Crazy?* and a notice:

> Soon to be printed:
> *Geetopanishad,* or *Bhagavad-gita As It Is,*
> Translated and with commentaries by Swami Bhaktivedanta.

Prabhupāda's first and main instruction to his editors had been that they should produce the magazine *regularly—every month.* Even if they didn't know how to sell the copies or even if they only turned out two pages, they had to continue bearing the standard.

He called Hayagrīva to his room and presented him a complete three-volume set of his *Śrīmad-Bhāgavatam.* On the front page of each volume he had written, "To Sriman Hayagriva das Brahmacari with my blessings, A. C. Bhaktivedanta Swami." Hayagrīva was grateful and mentioned that he had not been able to afford them. "That's all right," Prabhupāda said. "Now you compile this *Back to Godhead.* Work sincerely, and make it as big as *Time* magazine."

Prabhupāda wanted all his disciples to take part in it. "Don't be dull," he said. "Write something." He wanted to give his disciples *Back to Godhead* for their own preaching. Brahmānanda and Gargamuni took the first issues out that same night on bicycles, riding to every head shop on the Lower East Side, all the way to Fourteenth Street and as far west as the West Village, until they had distributed all one hundred issues. This was an increase in the preaching. Now all his students could take part in the work—typing, editing, writing, assembling, selling. It was *his* preaching, of course, but he wasn't alone any more.

*　　　*　　　*

"Over a short four months, the society has expanded sufficiently to warrant larger quarters than the small Second Avenue storefront temple," stated the editorial in the second issue of *Back to Godhead.* Prabhupāda had not abandoned his idea for a big building in New York City. Greenwich Village real estate was too expensive, and midtown was out of the question, but Prabhupāda still said he wanted to buy a building. It was difficult for his followers to think of Kṛṣṇa consciousness as anything more than a Lower East Side movement, because who but the people of the Lower East Side would be interested in Kṛṣṇa consciousness? And anyway, who had money to buy a building in Manhattan?

But one day, Ravīndra Svarūpa had happened to meet someone—a wealthy Jewish heir who was sympathetic toward youth movements—who agreed to loan Swamiji five thousand dollars. Ravīndra Svarūpa had arranged the loan, and Swamiji had designated the money as his building fund, to which he had gradually added another five thousand dollars that he had collected through incidental donations. But with suitable buildings starting at one hundred thousand dollars, even this sum seemed petty.

Swamiji went with Brahmānanda to look at a building on Sixth Street that had previously been the Jewish Providential Bank. It had a large lobby with a mezzanine, marble floors, and the atmosphere of a temple. Brahmānanda suggested that the vault area could be remodeled for use as a dormitory, and Swamiji considered the mezzanine for his own apartment. The large lobby, he said, could be used for *kīrtanas* and lectures. On leaving the building, however, Prabhupāda noted that it was located on the corner, by a bus stop. It would not be a good location. The Gaudiya Math branch at Bhag Bazaar in Calcutta, he said, was also located at a bus stop, and the noisy engines of the buses as they started up created a disturbance.

Prabhupāda next looked at the Temple Emanu-El, also on Sixth Street on the Lower East Side. It was even larger than the bank building, and when some of Swamiji's disciples walked through the cavernous, empty rooms, they became bewildered to think how, even if they could get such a place, they would be able to manage or use it.

He visited other places: one so neglected and in such poor repair that it looked as though it had been vandalized, and another, in similar condition, filled with lumber stacked almost to the ceiling. He asked Rūpānuga, who had accompanied him, what he thought, and Rūpānuga said, "Too much time and money to fix it up." So they left. Swamiji returned to his room and went into the bathroom, where he washed his feet in the tub. He said that it was an Indian custom that after walking outside you wash your feet.

Then the devotees met Mr. Price, an elegantly dressed real estate agent. "You have a handful of stars," Mr. Price told Brahmānanda. "You're incorporated as a tax-free religious organization. You have no idea how much money this will save. So many people have to vacate just because they can't pay their taxes. But 'someone up there' is looking after you people, and I have just the place for you and your Swami."

Mr. Price showed Brahmānanda a handsome three-story building near St. Mark's Place. It was a good downtown location, near the young people, yet in an area where the uptown people would feel safe. The floors were polished hardwood, all the doors were ornately hand carved, and it had a large hall, suitable for a temple. The Marquis de Lafayette had stayed here during his visit in 1824, a fact that added to the building's charm and prestige.

One evening, Mr. Price visited Prabhupāda up in his room, Prabhupāda sitting on the floor behind his desk and Mr. Price sitting on a metal folding chair. Mr. Price wore an elegant suit and a white dress shirt with cuff links and starched cuffs. His expensive dress, meticulously tanned face, and blond hair (which some devotees thought was a wig) contrasted strangely with the Swami's simplicity. Mr. Price kept referring to Swamiji as "Your Excellency," and he expressed much appreciation of Swamiji's work. He spoke optimistically about how, through his connections, he hoped to save Prabhupāda a lot of money and trouble and get him just the place he wanted.

Accompanied by a few disciples, Prabhupāda went with Mr. Price to see the building. While Mr. Price, the devotees, and the custodian of the house were all talking together in a group, Prabhupāda wandered off unnoticed to a corner of the room, where there was an old-fashioned sewing machine. He began pressing the treadle and examining the workings of the machine. As Prabhupāda rejoined the group, Mr. Price said, "If you can just get five thousand dollars down, I can get the owners to draw up a contract. Five thousand dollars down, and another five thousand within two months—that shouldn't be so difficult." Prabhupāda liked the building and told Brahmānanda they should purchase it.

Brahmānanda was inclined to turn the money over right away, but Prabhupāda said that first a suitable contract had to be drawn up. Mr. Price talked to the devotees in private, speaking in the Swami's interest and in the interest of the spiritual movement, and he seemed to be promising them something even *more* than a contract. Perhaps he would *give* them the building. It didn't make sense that he could give the building, but he told them something like that. He wanted the devotees to think of him as their friend, and he invited them over to his house one evening.

When the devotees gathered in his house, sitting stiffly on chairs in his living room, which was lined with bookcases filled not with books, but with two-dimensional designs depicting rows of books, he continued to flatter them. He praised Hayagrīva's writings, and Hayagrīva was obviously embarrassed and flattered. He praised everything about the devotees. He also spoke of how his dog had recently died, and said, "The house seems empty without the little fellow." He was an unusual man, effeminate, and full of flattery and praises. Prabhupāda remained reserved after his first meeting with Mr. Price, though he was interested in getting the building if the proper arrangement could be made.

Brahmānanda continued to negotiate with Mr. Price, and soon, according to Mr. Price, the owners of the building would be expecting the devotees to give proof of their ability to meet the payments. On Prabhupāda's direction, the devotees hired a lawyer to go over the contract. "This Mr. Price is causing us so much pain," Prabhupāda said. "What is the difficulty?" He didn't see the necessity for Mr. Price at all. "Why don't we purchase directly from the owners? Why all these agents?"

"It's just the way it's done here," Brahmānanda said.

* * *

Alan Kallman was a record producer. He had read the article in *The East Village Other* about the swami from India and the *mantra* he had brought with him. When he had read the Hare Kṛṣṇa *mantra* on the front page, he had become attracted. The article gave the idea that one could get a tremendous high or ecstasy from chanting. The Swami's Second Avenue address was given in the article, so one night in November,

Alan and his wife visited the storefront.

Alan: *There were about thirty pairs of shoes in the back of the room—people in the front and shoes in the back. We took off our shoes and sat down. Everyone was seated and very quiet. Front and center was a chair, and everyone was staring at this chair. Even then we felt a certain energy in the room. No one was saying anything, and everyone was staring at the chair. The next thing was our first sight of the Swami. He came in and sat down on the chair, and there was a tremendous surge of energy. The Swami began chanting, and it was a very beautiful sound. Swamiji had this little drum he was hitting—very penetrating and exciting. One of the devotees was holding up a sign with the chant written on it so everyone could follow. Then the devotees got up and danced in a circle, a special dance with steps to it. The Swami was looking around the room, and he seemed to smile as he looked at you, as if to encourage you to join.*

The next day, Alan phoned Prabhupāda to propose that he make a record of the chanting. But it was Brahmānanda who answered the phone, and he gave Alan an appointment with the Swami that evening. So again Alan and his wife went down to the East Village, which to them was the neighborhood where things were happening. If you wanted to have some excitement, you went down to the East Village.

When they entered the Swami's room, he was seated at his typewriter, working. As soon as Alan mentioned his idea about making a record, Prabhupāda was interested. "Yes," he said, "we *must* record. If it will help us distribute the chanting of Hare Kṛṣṇa, then it is our duty." They scheduled the recording for two weeks later, in December, at the Adelphi Recording Studio near Times Square. Alan's wife was impressed by how enthusiastically the Swami had gotten to the point of making the record: "He had so much energy and ambition in his plans."

It was the night before the recording date. A boy walked into the storefront for the evening *kīrtana* carrying a large, two-headed Indian drum. This was not unusual, as guests often brought drums, flutes, and other instruments, yet this time Swamiji seemed particularly interested. The boy sat down and was preparing to play when Prabhupāda motioned for the boy to bring him the drum. The boy didn't move—he wanted to play it himself—but Brahmānanda went over and said, "Swamiji wants to play the drum," so the boy gave in.

Brahmānanda: *Swamiji began to play, and his hands were just dancing on the drum. Everyone was stunned that Swamiji knew how to do this. All we had seen was the bongo drum, so I thought it was the proper Indian drum. But when this two-headed drum came out of nowhere and Swamiji started playing it like a master musician, it created an ecstasy a hundred times more than the bongo drum had.*

After the *kīrtana*, Prabhupāda asked the boy if he could borrow the drum for the recording session the next night. The boy at first was reluctant, but the devotees promised to return his drum the next day, so he agreed and said he would bring the drum the next evening. When he left the storefront that night with his drum under his arm, the devotees thought they would never see the boy or his drum again, but the next day, a few hours before Swamiji was to leave for the studio, the boy returned with his drum.

It was a cold December night. The Swami, dressed in his usual saffron *dhotī*, a tweed overcoat, and a pair of gray shoes (which had long since replaced his original white, pointy rubber ones), got into Rūpānuga's VW van with about fifteen of his followers and their instruments and started for the recording studio.

Brahmānanda: *We didn't start recording right away, because there was a group ahead of us. So we went out for a walk in Times Square. We were just standing there with Swamiji, seeing all the flashing lights and all the sense gratification, when a woman came up to Swamiji and said, "Oh, hello. Where do you come from?" in a very loud, matronly way. And Swamiji said, "I am a monk from India." And she said, "Oh, that's wonderful. Glad to meet you." And then she shook Swamiji's hand and left.*

At the studio, everyone accepted the devotees as a regular music group. One of the rock musicians asked them what the name of their group was, and Hayagrīva laughed and replied, "The Hare Kṛṣṇa Chanters." Of course most of the devotees weren't actually musicians, and yet the instruments they brought with them—a tamboura, a large harmonium (loaned by Allen Ginsberg), and rhythm instruments—were ones they had played during *kīrtanas* for months. So as they entered the studio they felt confident that they could produce their own sound. They just followed their Swami. He knew how to play, and they knew how to follow him. They weren't just another music group. It was music, but it was also chanting, meditation, worship.

Prabhupāda sat on a mat in the center of the studio, while the engineers arranged the microphones and assigned each devotee a place to sit according to his particular instrument. They asked for only two pairs of *karatālas* and they approved of the pairs of rhythm sticks, but they wanted several devotees clapping their hands. Rūpānuga's usual instrument was a pair of brass Indian bells with the tongues removed, and when the engineer saw them, he came over and said, "Let me hear that." Rūpānuga played them, and they passed. Since Ravīndra Svarūpa would be playing the drone on the harmonium, he sat apart with his own microphone, and Kīrtanānanda also had a microphone for the tamboura.

When the engineers were satisfied, they cued the devotees, and Swamiji began chanting and playing his drum. The cymbals and sticks and clapping hands joined him, and the chanting went on steadily for about ten minutes, until an engineer came out of the glass studio and stopped them: Brahmānanda was clapping too loudly, creating an imbalance. The engineer went back into his studio, put on his headphones, balanced everyone, and cued them for a second take. This time it was better.

The first sound was the tamboura, with its plucked, reverberating twang. An instant later Swamiji began beating the drum and singing, *Vande 'haṁ śrī-guroḥ* . . . Then the whole ensemble put out to sea—the tamboura, the harmonium, the clackers, the cymbals, Rūpānuga's bells, Swamiji's solo singing—pushing off from their moorings, out into a fair-weather sea of chanting. . . . *lalitā-śrī-viśākhānvitāṁs ca*. . . .

Swamiji's voice in the studio was very sweet. His boys were feeling love, not just making a record. There was a feeling of success and union, a crowning evening to all their months together.

. . . *Śrī-kṛṣṇa-caitanya, prabhu-nityānanda* . . .

After a few minutes of singing prayers alone, Swamiji paused briefly while the instruments continued pulsing, and then began the *mantra:* Hare Kṛṣṇa, Hare Kṛṣṇa, Kṛṣṇa Kṛṣṇa, Hare Hare. It was pure Bhaktivedanta Swami—expert, just like his cooking in the kitchen, like his lectures. The engineers liked what they heard—it would be a good take if nothing went wrong. The instruments were all right, the drum, the singing. The harmony was rough. But this was a special record—a happening. The Hare Kṛṣṇa Chanters were doing their thing, and they were doing it all right. Alan Kallman was excited. Here was an authentic sound. Maybe it would sell.

After a few rounds of the *mantra*, the devotees began to feel relaxed, as though they were back in the temple, and they were able to forget about making mistakes on the record. They just chanted, and the beat steadied into a slightly faster pace. The word *hare* would come sometimes with a little shout in it, but there were no emotional theatrics in the chorus, just the straight response to the Swami's melody. Ten minutes went by. The chanting went faster, louder and faster—Swamiji doing more fancy things on the drum, until suddenly . . . everything stopped, with the droning note of the harmonium lingering.

Alan came out of the studio: "It was great, Swami. Great. Would you like to just go right ahead and read the address now? Or are you too tired?" With polite concern, pale, befreckled Alan Kallman peered through his thick glasses at the Swami. Swamiji appeared tired, but he replied, "No, I am not tired." Then the devotees sat back in the studio to watch and listen as Prabhupāda read his prepared statement.

"As explained on the cover of the record album . . ." The sympathetic devotees thought that Swamiji, despite his accent, sounded perfectly clear, reading from his script like an elocutionist. ". . . this transcendental vibration by chanting of Hare Kṛṣṇa, Hare Kṛṣṇa, Kṛṣṇa Kṛṣṇa, Hare Hare/ Hare Rāma, Hare Rāma, Rāma Rāma, Hare Hare is the sublime method for reviving our Kṛṣṇa consciousness." The language was philosophic, and the kind of people who usually walked out of the temple as soon as the *kīrtana* ended, before the Swami could even speak a word, would also not appreciate this speech on their record album. "As living spiritual souls," Swamiji preached, "we are all originally Kṛṣṇa conscious entities. But due to our association with matter from time immemorial, our consciousness is now polluted by material atmosphere." The devotees listened submissively to the words of their spiritual master, while at the same time trying to comprehend the effect this would have on the audience. Certainly some people would turn it off at the very mention of a spiritual nature. Swamiji continued reading, explaining that the chanting would deliver one from the sensual, the mental, and the intellectual planes and bring one to the spiritual realm.

"We have seen it practically," he continued. "Even a child can take part in the chanting, or even a dog can take part in it. . . . The chanting should be heard, however, from the lips of a pure devotee of the Lord." And he continued reading on to the end. ". . . No other means, therefore, of spiritual realization is as effective in this age as chanting the *mahā-mantra:* Hare Kṛṣṇa, Hare Kṛṣṇa, Kṛṣṇa Kṛṣṇa, Hare Hare/ Hare Rāma, Hare Rāma, Rāma Rāma, Hare Hare."

Alan again came rushing out of the studio. It was fine, he said. He explained that they had recorded a little echo into the speech, to make it special for the listener. "Now," he pushed back his glasses with his finger. "We've got about ten minutes left on the side with the speech. Would you like to chant again? Or is it too late, Swamiji?" Prabhupāda smiled. No, it was not too late. He would chant the prayers to his spiritual master.

While his disciples lounged around the studio, watching their spiritual master and the technical activity of the engineers behind the glass, Prabhupāda began singing. Again the harmonium's drone began, then the tamboura and drum, but with a much smaller rhythm group than before. He sang through, without any retakes, and then ended the song (and the evening) with a fortissimo drumming as the hand-pumped organ notes faded.

Again, Alan came out and thanked the Swami for being so patient and such a good studio musician. Prabhupāda was still sitting. "Now we are tired," he admitted.

Suddenly, over the studio sound system came a playback of the Hare Kṛṣṇa chanting, complete with echo. When Prabhupāda heard the successful recording of his chanting, he became happy and stood and began dancing, swaying back and forth, dipping slightly from the waist, his arms upraised in the style of Lord Caitanya, dancing in ecstasy. The scheduled performance was over, but now Swamiji was making the best performance of the evening from his spontaneous feelings. As he danced, his half-asleep disciples became startled and also rose to their feet and joined him, dancing in the same style. And in the recording booth behind the glass, the engineers also raised their hands and began dancing and chanting.

"Now you have made your best record," Swamiji told Mr. Kallman as he left the studio for the freezing Manhattan evening. Swamiji got into the front seat of the Volkswagen bus while "The Hare Kṛṣṇa Chanters" climbed into the back with their instruments, and Rūpānuga drove them back home, back to the Lower East Side.

The next morning Prabhupāda didn't get up. He was exhausted. Kīrtanānanda, who was personally serving him, became alarmed when the Swami said something about his heart skipping and about not being able to move. For the first time, it became apparent that he was overexerting himself. Kīrtanānanda thought back through the fall and summer, when the Swami had led them all on hours-long *kīrtanas* in the park or on late-evening ventures—they had come to take it for granted. But now Kīrtanānanda saw that there was cause to be worried for Swamiji's health. Swamiji had no appetite for lunch, although by afternoon he regained his appetite and usual activity.

That same day, a letter arrived from Mukunda in San Francisco. Not long after their wedding, Mukunda and Janakī had left for the West Coast. Mukunda had told Swamiji that he wanted to go on to India to study Indian music, but after a few weeks in southern Oregon he had ended up in San Francisco. Now he had a better idea. He wanted to rent a place and invite Swamiji to come and start his Hare Kṛṣṇa movement in the Haight-Ashbury district, just as he was doing on the Lower East Side. He said that the prospects there for Kṛṣṇa consciousness were very good. On hearing this, Prabhupāda began unfolding his expansive plans. They should open temples not only in San Francisco but, one by one, all over the world, even in Russia and China, and print the *Bhagavad-gītā* in different languages. And he would translate all the volumes of *Śrīmad-Bhāgavatam* into English and take a party of devotees back to India.

The devotees who heard him were amazed. Kīrtanānanda, who had seen the alarming symptoms of Prabhupāda's ill health, began to forget what he had thought earlier that morning. If Kṛṣṇa desired, Kīrtanānanda thought, Swamiji could do anything.

* * *

When Prabhupāda came down to hold his morning class on November 19, he carried a large red book instead of the usual brown one. But no one noticed the difference. He began as always, softly singing prayers to his spiritual master and accompanying himself with a faint rhythm on his bongo (the neighbors were still asleep).

The weather was cold, but the steam radiators kept the storefront warm. There would be no more outdoor chanting now. In Manhattan, the city opens wide in the summer and shuts tight in the winter, which for the evening classes meant no more noisy children outside the door. And although the morning classes had always been quiet, even in the summer, now with winter approaching, the group became a tighter, more committed core of sincere students coming together to hear Swamiji speak.

It was now four months since he had begun ISKCON at 26 Second Avenue. He had held three separate initiations and initiated nineteen devotees. Most of them had become serious, although a few remained casual visitors. Now, in these morning classes, Swamiji wanted to instruct them more about how to become devotees.

He led the chanting of Hare Kṛṣṇa for twenty minutes, cautioning them to respond softly, so that the neighbors would not pour water through the ceiling again—although they hadn't done it lately. Prabhupāda always tried to cooperate with the tenants, but occasionally someone would start a petition—which never amounted to much—against the devotees. Sometimes Prabhupāda would help the landlord, Mr. Chutey, by taking out other tenants' garbage or just giving him a hand.

Mr. Chutey was a husky, beer-bellied Polish refugee who lived alone in an apartment on the first floor. Mr. Chutey respected the Swami for his age and scholarship, and Swamiji was always amiable with him. Whenever Mr. Chutey came to the apartment, he would never take his shoes off, and Prabhupāda would always say, "That's all right, that's all right." And one time, when the plumbing didn't work in Prabhupāda's apartment, Prabhupāda went downstairs and took a shower in Mr. Chutey's apartment.

But Swamiji also considered Mr. Chutey a classic example of a foolish materialist, because although he had spent his life's savings to buy this building, he still had to work so hard. Swamiji said he was a fool for having spent his savings to buy such a run-down building. Because the building was in such poor condition, he had to work like an ass to keep it up. "This is how the materialists work," Swamiji would say.

Mr. Chutey, although respectful to the Swami, didn't like the devotees. Prabhupāda told his disciples, "Treat him as if he were your father." So that's what they did. Any time they would have to deal with Mr. Chutey, they would approach him saying, "We are your sons."

Those disciples who lived at the storefront had risen by six-thirty, bathed, and assembled downstairs by seven, while those who lived outside were arriving separately, taking off their coats and piling them on the shelf of the display window. Although women always attended the evening meetings, Jadurāṇī was usually the only girl who came in the morning. After breakfast, she would begin painting upstairs in the Swami's front room. She used a beginner's technique of dividing the canvas into vertical and horizontal grid lines and transposing bit by bit the corresponding sections of a photograph onto the canvas. The process was painstaking, and sometimes her painting was out of proportion. But Jadurāṇī was sincere, and that pleased Prabhupāda. She had completed several paintings of four-armed Viṣṇu, a new painting of Rādhā-Kṛṣṇa, and a painting of Lord Caitanya and His associates. When the painting of Lord Caitanya was finished, Swamiji had it hung in the temple. "Now," he announced, "there should be no more nonsense here. Lord Caitanya is present."

After the morning *kīrtana* Swami said, as usual, "Now chant one round." They chanted together, following him. They all had a vow to chant sixteen rounds daily, but they chanted their first round in the morning in the Swami's presence, so he could see each of them. As Swamiji chanted, he looked out at Second Avenue, which was mostly deserted, or at the pictures on the wall, or, with concerned glances, at the individual devotees. Sometimes he seemed surprised when he saw them chanting so earnestly, giving evidence of the power of the holy name to deliver even the most fallen. Some of the devotees kept their beads in a bead bag like his, but when they chanted the first round together in the morning, they imitated him by holding their beads out in both hands and chanting along with him: Hare Kṛṣṇa, Hare Kṛṣṇa, Kṛṣṇa Kṛṣṇa, Hare Hare, until they finished one round.

Then he held up the unfamiliar red book. "Because you are a little advanced," he said, "I am going to read today from the *Caitanya-caritāmṛta.*" Caitanya what? No one was able to pick up the pronunciation. They had heard of Caitanya, certainly, but not of this new book. But in his room the night before, Prabhupāda had informed some of the devotees that he would start reading from a new book, *Caitanya-caritāmṛta.* He said that Lord Caitanya had told one of His disciples that understanding Kṛṣṇa wasn't really possible, but that He would give the disciple just a drop of the ocean of Kṛṣṇa consciousness, so that the disciple could then appreciate what the whole ocean must be like. "Be patient as I present this," he had told them. "It is revolutionary, but you should just be patient."

In the storefront Brahmānanda turned on the reel-to-reel tape recorder as Swamiji began reading the Bengali verses, and both Satsvarūpa and Umāpati opened their notebooks and waited, poised for rapid note-taking. It was almost a college classroom atmosphere as Prabhupāda cleared his throat, put on his eyeglasses, and peered over the large open volume, turning to the correct page. Whenever he wore the glasses, he seemed to reveal a new personality of deep Vaiṣṇava scholarship. This feature of Swamiji emphasized his old age—not that it showed him feeble or invalid, but it emphasized his scholarship and wisdom and his contemplation of the scriptures, in contrast to his vigorous drum-playing in Tompkins Square Park or his alert business dealings while looking for a new building.

Swamiji began reading and translating the story of Sanātana (Satsvarūpa wrote "Suta" and Umāpati wrote "Sonotan") and his brother Rūpa, and how they became intimate associates of Lord Caitanya. It was a historical account. Rūpa and Sanātana had been born as *brāhmaṇas* in India, but they had served in the government under the Muslims, who were in power at that time. The two brothers had even adopted Muslim names. But when Lord Caitanya was touring in their part of the country, they had met Him and had become determined to give up their materialistic ways and follow His path of pure love of God. Rūpa, who was so rich that he had enough gold to fill two boats, left his high government post, divided his wealth, became a mendicant, and joined Lord Caitanya. For Sanātana, however, there were more obstacles.

The Nawab Shah, the chief Muslim ruler of the province of Bengal, was dependent on Sanātana's managerial expertise. But Sanātana began staying home and submitting sick reports, while actually he had employed a dozen *brāhmaṇas*, who were teaching him the *Śrīmad-Bhāgavatam.* The Nawab sent his physician to find out the actual state of Sanātana's health, and when the Nawab heard that Sanātana was not actually ill, he himself arrived one day, surprising Sanātana and the *brāhmaṇas.* The Nawab demanded that Sanātana return to his government work and leave him free to do some hunting and to leave Bengal on a military campaign. But Sanātana said that he could not, that he was now determined to study the scriptures, and that the Nawab could do with him whatever he liked. At this challenge, the Nawab imprisoned Sanātana. . . .

Swamiji looked at his watch. Morning classes were shorter than those in the evening—only half an hour—and Rūpānuga, Satsvarūpa, and Brahmānanda had to go to work. He paused in his narration—"So, we will discuss tomorrow." Prabhupāda closed the book, and after a few informal words, he got up and left the storefront, followed by Kīrtanānanda, who carried his book and glasses.

Breakfast was served every morning in the storefront. Either Acyutānanda or Kīrtanānanda would cook an oatmeal cereal for the devotees. Satsvarūpa had read in an English edition of the *Rāmāyaṇa* about some sages preparing a mystical cereal called "Heavenly Porridge." The name had caught on, and the devotees began calling their own cereal Heavenly Porridge. The popular fare would consist of steaming hot Heavenly Porridge (sweetened to taste with sugar syrup from the *gulābjāmun* pot), hot milk, and fruit. And each devotee would get an ISKCON bullet.

At breakfast this morning, the talk was of Rūpa and Sanātana. Umāpati said the *Caitanya-caritāmṛta* was available in an English translation, but maybe the Swami wouldn't want them to read it. "We'll hear it from Swamiji," Kīrtanānanda said. Hayagrīva was amused at the "cliff-hanger" ending of the class. "Tune in tomorrow," he laughed loosely, "and hear what happened to . . . what's his name?" The devotees responded differently: "Santan" . . . "Sonoton" . . . "Sanātana." Hayagrīva: "Yeah, tune in tomorrow and hear. Will Sanāṭana get out of jail?" They were not the most sober group when together, especially after taking the thick, sweet syrup. Acyutānanda spilled some of the syrup on the rug, and Kīrtanānanda admonished him. Jadurāṇī ate silently and hurried to begin a day's painting in Prabhupāda's room. Satsvarūpa adjusted his tie, and he and Rūpānuga and Brahmānanda went to their jobs.

The next morning, the *Caitanya-caritāmṛta* seminar began with

Sanātana in jail, planning how to get free to join Lord Caitanya. His brother Rūpa sent him a note saying that he had left a large sum of gold for Sanātana in the care of a grocer, and Sanātana offered the gold to the jailer as a bribe. He told him, "Sir, I know you are a very learned man, and in your Koran it says that if you aid someone in going to spiritual life, then you will be elevated to the highest post. I am going to Lord Caitanya, and if you will assist me in escaping, it will be spiritual gain for you. Also, I will give you give five hundred gold coins, so it will be material gain as well." The jail keeper said, "All right. But I am afraid of the king." So Sanātana advised him, "Just say that when I was passing stool by the river, I fell in with my chains and was washed away." For seven hundred gold coins, the jailer agreed to help Sanātana and sawed off the shackles. Sanātana, accompanied by his servant, then fled by the back roads until by nighttime he came upon a hotel.

Now this hotel was kept by thieves, and an astrologer at the hotel read Sanātana's palm and judged by the stars that he had money. When Sanātana asked for assistance in passing over the jungle mountains, the hotel keeper said that he would help Sanātana leave, in the dead of the night. They treated Sanātana with great respect, which made him suspicious, since he hadn't eaten in three days and his clothes were unclean. So he asked his servant if he had any money. The servant said yes, he had seven gold coins, and Sanātana immediately took the money to the hotel keeper, who was already planning to kill him during the night and take his money. . . .

Swamiji looked at his watch. Again they had gone overtime. "So we will continue tomorrow," he said, closing the book"—how Sanātana manages to escape the dacoits."

Kīrtanānanda, Brahmānanda, Acyutānanda, Gargamuni, Satsvarūpa, Hayagrīva, Umāpati, Jadurāṇī, Rūpānuga, Dāmodara (Dan Clark)—their lives had all been transformed. Over the months they had transferred the center of their lives to Swamiji, and everything revolved around the routine of classes and *kīrtana* and *prasādam* and coming and going to and from the storefront.

Brahmānanda and Gargamuni had given up their apartment several months ago and moved into the storefront. The ceiling of Acyutānanda's apartment had caved in one day, just minutes after he had left the room, and he had decided to move to the storefront also. Hayagrīva and Umāpati had cleaned up their Mott Street place and were using it only for chanting, sleeping, or reading Swamiji's *Bhāgavatam.* Satsvarūpa had announced one day that the devotees could use his apartment, just around the corner from the temple, for taking showers, and the next day Rāya Rāma had moved in, and the others began using the apartment as a temple annex. Jadurāṇī kept making her early-morning treks from the Bronx. (Swamiji had said that he had no objection to her living in the second room of his apartment, but that people would talk.) Even Rūpānuga and Dāmodara, whose backgrounds and tastes were different, were also positively dependent on the daily morning class and the evening class three nights a week and in knowing that Swamiji was always there in his apartment whenever they needed him.

There were, however, some threats to this security. Prabhupāda would sometimes say that unless he got permanent residency from the government, he would have to leave the country. But he had gone to a lawyer, and after the initial alarm it seemed that Swamiji would stay indefinitely. There was also the threat that he might go to San Francisco. He said he was going, but then sometimes he said he wasn't. If the negotiations through Mr. Price for the building on Tenth Street came through, then, Swamiji said, he would make his headquarters in New York City and not go to San Francisco.

But at least in the morning sessions, as his disciples listened to him speak on *Caitanya-caritāmṛta,* these threats were all put out of mind, and the timeless, intimate teachings took up their full attention. Kṛṣṇa consciousness was a struggle, keeping yourself strictly following Swamiji's code against *māyā*—"No illicit sex, no intoxication, no gambling, no meat-eating." But it was possible as long as they could hear him singing and reading and speaking from *Caitanya-caritāmṛta.* They counted on his presence for their Kṛṣṇa consciousness. He was the center of their newly spiritualized lives, and he was all they knew of Kṛṣṇa consciousness. As long as they could keep coming and seeing him, Kṛṣṇa consciousness was a sure thing—as long as he was there.

Seated on the worn rug, they looked up at him, waiting for him to begin the next installment. Prabhupāda cleared his throat and glanced down at Brahmānanda, who sat beside the silently running tape recorder.

Satsvarūpa entered the date in his notebook. Prabhupāda began reading the Bengali verses and paraphrasing. . . .

Sanātana took the seven gold coins from his servant and gave them to the hotel keeper. "You have *eight* coins," the astrologer said. And Sanātana went back and found that his servant was retaining another gold coin. "Why do you carry this death knell on the road?" Sanātana asked. "You are too attached to money." And he took the gold piece from his servant and told him to return home. Sanātana then brought the gold coin to the hotel keeper. But the hotel keeper, who admitted that he had intended to kill Sanātana for his money, now said, "You are a good man, and you may keep your money." But Sanātana refused. Then the hotel keeper provided Sanātana with four assistants. They helped Sanātana through the jungle and then left him alone.

Free from his nuisance servant and from the dacoits, Sanātana felt liberated as he passed along the road alone. Soon he came upon his brother-in-law, who was traveling along the same road. His brother-in-law was a wealthy man carrying a great deal of money to buy horses. "Please stay with me at least a few days," Sanātana's brother-in-law said. "It's really bad how you look." The brother-in-law knew that Sanātana was going to spiritual life, but he requested that he improve his dress by accepting a valuable blanket from him. Sanātana took the blanket and continued on his way.

At last, Sanātana reached Benares, and he went straight to the home of Candraśekhara, where Lord Caitanya was staying, and waited outside the door. Lord Caitanya knew Sanātana had arrived, and he requested Candraśekhara to go to the door and ask the devotee who was waiting there to come in. Candraśekhara went out but saw only the wretched-looking Sanātana, whom he took to be a half-mad Muhammadan fakir. Candraśekhara returned to Lord Caitanya and explained that there was no devotee outside. "Was there anyone at all?" the Lord asked. "Yes," said Candraśekhara, "some wretched fakir." Then Lord Caitanya went to the door and embraced Sanātana. The Lord cried tears of ecstasy, for He had at last found a devotee whom He knew was worthy to receive His entire teachings. And Sanātana cried tears of joy that his life's ambition was being fulfilled; but because he was dirty from his traveling and not worthy, he asked the Lord not to touch him. The Lord replied, "It is I who benefit from touching you; whoever touches a true devotee is blessed."

Prabhupāda closed the book, ending another morning session.

One of Prabhupāda's main concerns was to finish and publish as soon as possible his translation and commentary of *Bhagavad-gītā,* and one day something happened that enabled him to increase his work on the manuscript. Unexpectedly, a boy named Neal arrived. He was a student from Antioch College on a special work-study program, and he had the school's approval to work one term within the *āśrama* of Swami Bhaktivedanta, which he had heard about through the newspapers. Neal mentioned that he was a good typist, if that could be of any help to the Swami. Prabhupāda considered this to be Kṛṣṇa's blessing. Immediately he rented a dictaphone and began dictating tapes, Hayagrīva donated his electric typewriter, and Neal set up his work area in Swamiji's front room and began typing eight hours a day. This inspired Prabhupāda and obliged him to produce more. He worked quickly, sometimes day and night, on his *Bhagavad-gītā As It Is.* He had founded ISKCON five months ago, yet in his classes he was still reading the *Bhagavad-gītā* translation of Dr. Radhakrishnan. But when *Bhagavad-gītā As It Is* would at last be published, he told his disciples, it would be of major importance for the Kṛṣṇa consciousness movement. At last there would be a bona fide edition of the *Gītā.*

Whatever Swamiji said or did, his disciples wanted to hear about it. Gradually, they had increased their faith and devotion to Swamiji, whom they accepted as God's representative, and they took his actions and words to be absolute. After one of the disciples had been alone with him, the others would gather around to find out every detail of what had happened. It was Kṛṣṇa consciousness. Jadurāṇī was especially guileless in relating what Swamiji had said or done. One day, Prabhupāda had stepped on a tack that Jadurāṇī had dropped on the floor, and although she knew it was a serious offense to her spiritual master, the major importance of the event seemed to be how Prabhupāda had displayed his transcendental consciousness. He silently and emotionlessly reached down and pulled the tack from his foot, without so much as a cry. And once, when she was fixing a painting over his head behind the desk, she had accidentally stepped on his sitting mat. "Is that an offense?" she had asked. And Swamiji had replied, "No. For service you could even stand on my head."

Sometimes Brahmānanda would say that Swamiji had told him something very intimate about Kṛṣṇa consciousness in private. But when he would tell what Swamiji had said, someone else would recall that the same thing was in *Śrīmad-Bhāgavatam.* Prabhupāda had said that the spiritual master is present in his instructions and that he had tried to put everything into those three volumes of the *Bhāgavatam,* and the devotees were finding this to be true.

There were no secrets in Swamiji's family of devotees. Everyone knew that Umāpati had left for a few days, disappointed with the Swami's severe criticism of the Buddhists, but had come back, and in a heavy, sincere exchange with Prabhupāda, he had decided to take to Kṛṣṇa consciousness again. And everyone knew that Satsvarūpa had resigned from his job and that when he went to tell Swamiji about it, Swamiji had told him that he could not quit but should go on earning money for Kṛṣṇa and donating it to the Society and that this would be his best service. And everyone knew that Swamiji wanted Gargamuni to cut his hair—Swamiji called it "Gargamuni's Shakespearean locks"—but that he would not do so.

The year ended, and Prabhupāda was still working on his manuscript of *Bhagavad-gītā,* still lecturing in the mornings from *Caitanya-caritāmṛta* and Monday, Wednesday, and Friday evenings from *Bhagavad-gītā,* and still talking of going to San Francisco. Then New Year's Eve came, and the devotees suggested that since this was a holiday when people go out to celebrate, maybe they should hold a Kṛṣṇa conscious festival.

Rūpānuga: *So we had a big feast, and a lot of people came, although it wasn't as crowded as the Sunday feasts. We were all taking* prasādam, *and Swamiji was sitting up on his dais, and he was also taking* prasādam. *He was demanding that we eat lots of* prasādam. *And then he was saying, "Chant! Chant!" So we were eating, and chanting Hare Kṛṣṇa between bites, and he was insisting on more and more* prasādam. *I was amazed.*

He stayed with us and kept insisting that we eat so much. He stayed until around eleven o'clock, and then he became drowsy. And the party was over.

Morning after morning, the story of Sanātana Gosvāmī unfolded from the pages of Swamiji's big book, which only he could read and explain. Lord Caitanya told Sanātana that he should be very grateful that Kṛṣṇa had been merciful to him, to which Sanātana replied, "You say that Kṛṣṇa is very merciful, but I do not know who Kṛṣṇa is. *You* have saved me."

Lord Caitanya had many devotees in Benares, and He sent Sanātana to the home of one of His friends where he could get something to eat, take a bath, shave, and dress in new clothing. Sanātana, however, refused the new clothing, and he also refused to become dependent on one place for his meals. Now that he had entered the renounced order, he preferred to go begging his meals at a different place each day. When Lord Caitanya saw all this, He was pleased, but Sanātana sensed that his valuable blanket did not please the Lord, so he traded the new blanket for an old one. This pleased Lord Caitanya, who said, "Now you are completely renounced. Your last attachment is gone, by the mercy of Kṛṣṇa."

Sanātana submitted himself at the lotus feet of Lord Caitanya and said, "I have wasted my time in sense gratification. I am lowborn, and I have low association. I have no qualification for spiritual life. I do not even know what is actually beneficial for me. People say that I am learned, but I am fool number one, because although people say I am learned, and although I accept it, still I do not know who I am." Sanātana presented himself as a blank slate, and he inquired from the Lord, "Who am I? Why am I in this material world? Why am I suffering?" Prabhupāda emphasized that this was the perfect way for a disciple to accept a spiritual master.

After narrating the story of Sanātana's joining Lord Caitanya, Prabhupāda began lecturing on the Lord's teachings to Sanātana. Lord Caitanya first explained that the living being is not the material body but an eternal living soul within the body. Then, for two months, Lord Caitanya instructed Sanātana, revealing to him the deepest and most sublime philosophical truths of Vedic wisdom. He enlightened Sanātana regarding the soul and its relationship with Kṛṣṇa, the nature of the material and spiritual worlds, the characteristics of a fully realized soul, and the transcendental nature of Lord Kṛṣṇa and His unlimited forms, expansions, incarnations, and divine pastimes. He explained the superiority of the path of *bhakti-yoga* over the paths of philosophical speculation and yogic mysticism. And He revealed to Sanātana the esoteric knowledge of spiritual ecstasy experienced by those souls who have achieved pure love for Kṛṣṇa. These teachings of the Lord were like an ocean that overflooded the mind of Sanātana Gosvāmī with its sweetness and grandeur. When Lord Caitanya had finished instructing Sanātana, He gave Sanātana the benediction that all those sublime teachings would be fully manifested within his heart, thus enabling him to compose transcendental literature.

For two months Lord Caitanya had instructed Sanātana Gosvāmī, and for two months, starting in mid-November of 1966, Śrīla Prabhupāda narrated in over fifty lectures the *Caitanya-caritāmṛta's* account of those teachings. Although each of his talks covered the subject matter of the verses, his lectures were never limited to his subject, nor were they prepared talks.

* * *

Sometimes, during the evening gatherings in his room, Swamiji would ask whether Mukunda was ready on the West Coast. For months, Prabhupāda's going to the West Coast had been one of a number of alternatives. But then, during the first week of the New Year, a letter arrived from Mukunda: he had rented a storefront in the heart of the Haight-Ashbury district, on Frederick Street. "We are busy converting it into a temple now," he wrote. And Prabhupāda announced: "I shall go immediately."

Mukunda had told of a "Gathering of the Tribes" in San Francisco's Haight-Ashbury. Thousands of hippies were migrating from all over the country to the very neighborhood where Mukunda had rented the storefront. It was a youth renaissance much bigger than what was going on in New York City. In a scheme to raise funds for the new temple, Mukunda was planning a "Mantra Rock Dance," and famous rock bands were going to appear. And Swami Bhaktivedanta and the chanting of Hare Kṛṣṇa were to be the center of attraction!

Although in his letter Mukunda had enclosed a plane ticket, some of Swamiji's followers refused to accept that Swamiji would use it. Those who knew they could not leave New York began to criticize the idea of Swamiji's going to San Francisco. They didn't think that people out on the West Coast could take care of Swamiji properly. Swamiji appearing with rock musicians? Those people out there didn't seem to have the proper respect. Anyway, there was no suitable temple there. There was no printing press, no *Back to Godhead* magazine. Why should Swamiji leave New York to attend a function like *that* with strangers in California? How could he leave them behind in New York? How could their spiritual life continue without him? Timidly, one or two dissenters indirectly expressed some of these feelings to Prabhupāda, as if almost wishing to admonish him for thinking of leaving them, and even hinting that things would not go well, either in San Francisco or New York, if he departed. But they found Prabhupāda quite confident and determined. He did not belong to New York, he belonged to Kṛṣṇa, and he had to go wherever Kṛṣṇa desired him to preach. Prabhupāda showed a spirit of complete detachment, eager to travel and expand the chanting of Hare Kṛṣṇa.

Brahmānanda: *But we were shocked that he was going to leave. I never thought that Kṛṣṇa consciousness would go beyond the Lower East Side, what to speak of New York City. I thought that this was it, and it would stay here eternally.*

In the last days of the second week of January, final plane reservations were made, and the devotees began packing Swamiji's manuscripts away in trunks. Ranchor, a new devotee recruited from Tompkins Square Park, had collected enough money for a plane ticket, and the devotees decided that he should accompany Prabhupāda as his personal assistant. Prabhupāda explained that he would only be gone a few weeks, and that he wanted all the programs to go on in his absence.

He waited in his room while the boys arranged for a car to take him to the airport. The day was gray and cold, and steam hissed in the radiators. He would take only a suitcase—mostly clothes and some books. He checked the closet to see that his manuscripts were in order. Kīrtanānanda would take care of his things in his apartment. He sat down at his desk where, for more than six months, he had sat so many times, working for hours at the typewriter preparing his *Bhagavad-gītā* and *Śrīmad-Bhāgavatam*, and where he had sat talking to so many guests and to his followers. But today he would not be talking with friends or typing a manuscript, but waiting a last few minutes alone before his departure.

This was his second winter in New York. He had launched a movement of Kṛṣṇa consciousness. A few sincere boys and girls had joined. They were already well known on the Lower East Side—many notices in the newspapers. And it was only the beginning.

He had left Vṛndāvana for this. At first he had not been certain whether he would stay in America more than two months. In Butler he had presented his books. But then in New York he had seen how Dr. Mishra had developed things, and the Māyāvādīs had a big building. They were taking money and not even delivering the real message of the *Gītā*. But the American people were looking.

It had been a difficult year. His Godbrothers hadn't been interested in helping, although this is what their Guru Mahārāja, Śrīla Bhaktisiddhānta Sarasvatī Ṭhākura, wanted, and what Lord Caitanya wanted. Because Lord Caitanya wanted it, His blessings would come, and it would happen.

This was a nice place, 26 Second Avenue. He had started here. The boys would keep it up. Some of them were donating their salaries. It was a start.

Prabhupāda looked at his watch. He put on his tweed winter coat and his hat and shoes, put his right hand in his bead bag, and continued chanting. He walked out of the apartment, down the stairs, and through the courtyard, which was now frozen and still, its trees starkly bare without a single leaf remaining. And he left the storefront behind.

He left, even while Brahmānanda, Rūpānuga, and Satsvarūpa were at their office jobs. There was not even a farewell scene or a farewell address.

Appendixes

কৃষ্ণ তব পুণ্য হবে ভাই। (ধ্রু:)
এ পুণ্য করিবে যবে রাধারাণী খুশী হবে
ধ্রুব অতি বলি তোমা তাই॥

শ্রীসিদ্ধান্ত সরস্বতী, শচীসুত প্রিয় অতি,
কৃষ্ণ-সেবায় যাঁর তুল নাই।
সেই সে মহান্ত-গুরু, জগতের মধ্যে উরু
কৃষ্ণভক্তি দেয় ঠাঁই ঠাঁই॥

তাঁর ইচ্ছা বলবান, পাশ্চাত্যেতে ঠাঁন ঠাঁন,
হয় যাতে গৌরাঙ্গের নাম।
পৃথিবীতে নগরাদি, আসমুদ্র নদ নদী
সকলেই লয় কৃষ্ণ নাম॥

তাহলে আনন্দ হয়, তবে হয় দিগ্বিজয়,
চৈতন্যের কৃপা অতিশয়।
মায়া দুষ্ট যত দুঃখী, জগতে সবাই সুখী
বৈষ্ণবের ইচ্ছা পূর্ণ হয়॥

সে কার্য যে করিবারে, আজ্ঞা যদি দিল মোরে
যোগ্য নহি অতি দীন হীন।
তাই সে তোমার কৃপা, মাগিতেছি অনুরূপা,
আজি তুমি সবার প্রবীণ॥

তোমার সে শক্তি পেলে, গুরু-সেবায় বস্তু মিলে
জীবন সার্থক যদি হয়।
সেই সে সেবা পাইলে, তাহলে সুখী হলে,
তব সঙ্গ ভাগ্যতে মিলয়॥

এবং জনং নিপতিতং প্রভবাহিকূপে
কামাভিকামমনু যঃ প্রপতন্ প্রসঙ্গাৎ।
কৃত্বাত্মসাৎ সুরর্ষিণা ভগবন্ গৃহীতঃ
সোঽহং কথং নু বিসৃজে তব ভৃত্যসেবাম্॥
(ভাঃ ৭।৯।২৮)

তুমি মোর চিরসাথী, ভুলিয়া মায়ার লাথি
খাইয়াছি জন্ম-জন্মান্তরে।
আজি পুনঃ এ সুযোগ, যদি হয় যোগাযোগ,
তবে পারি তুঁহে মিলিবারে॥

তোমারে মিলনে ভাই, আবার সে সুখ পাই
গোচারণে ঘুরি দিন ভোর।
কত বনে ছুটাছুটি, বনে খাই লুটাপুটি
সেই দিন কবে হবে মোর॥

আজি সে সুবিধানে, তোমার স্মরণ ভেল
বড় আশা ডাকিলাম তাই।
আমি তোমার নিত্যদাস, তাই করি এত আশ
তুমি বিনা অন্য গতি নাই।
কৃষ্ণ তব পুণ্য হবে ভাই॥

m/v Jaladuta 13/9/65

Prayer to the Lotus Feet of Kṛṣṇa

(refrain)
kṛṣṇa taba puṇya habe bhāi
e-puṇya koribe jabe rādhārāṇī khusī habe
dhruva ati boli tomā tāi

Translation: I emphatically say to you, O brothers, you will obtain your good fortune from the Supreme Lord Kṛṣṇa only when Śrīmatī Rādhārāṇī becomes pleased with you.

śrī-siddhānta saraswatī, śacī-suta priya ati,
kṛṣṇa-sebāya jāra tula nāi
sei se mohānta-guru, jagater madhe uru,
kṛṣṇa-bhakti dey ṭhāi ṭhāi

Translation: Śrī Śrīmad Bhaktisiddhānta Sarasvatī Ṭhākura, who is very dear to Lord Gaurāṅga, the son of mother Śacī, is unparalleled in his service to the Supreme Lord Śrī Kṛṣṇa. He is that great, saintly spiritual master who bestows intense devotion to Kṛṣṇa at different places throughout the world.

tāra icchā balavān, pāścātyete ṭhān ṭhān,
hoy jāte gaurāṅger nām
pṛthivīte nagarādi, āsamudra nada nadī,
sakalei loy kṛṣṇa nām

Translation: By his strong desire, the holy name of Lord Gaurāṅga will spread throughout all the countries of the Western world. In all the cities, towns, and villages on the earth, from all the oceans, seas, rivers, and streams, everyone will chant the holy name of Kṛṣṇa.

tāhale ānanda hoy, tabe hoy dig-vijay,
caitanyer kṛpā atiśay
māyā duṣṭa jata duḥkhī, jagate sabāi sukhī,
vaiṣṇaver icchā pūrṇa hoy

Translation: As the vast mercy of Śrī Caitanya Mahāprabhu conquers all directions, a flood of transcendental ecstasy will certainly cover the land. When all the sinful, miserable living entities become happy, the Vaiṣṇavas' desire is then fulfilled.

se kārja je koribāre, ājñā jadi dilo more,
jogya nahi ati dīna hīna
tāi se tomāra kṛpā, māgitechi anurūpā,
āji tumi sabār pravīṇa

Translation: Although my Guru Mahārāja ordered me to accomplish this mission, I am not worthy or fit to do it. I am very fallen and insignificant. Therefore, O Lord, now I am begging for Your mercy so that I may become worthy, for You are the wisest and most experienced of all.

tomāra se śakti pele, guru-sebāya bastu mile,
jībana sārthak jadi hoy
sei se sevā pāile, tāhale sukhī hale,
taba saṅga bhāgyate miloy

Translation: If You bestow Your power, by serving the spiritual master one attains the Absolute Truth—one's life becomes successful. If that service is obtained, then one becomes happy and gets Your association due to good fortune.

evaṁ janaṁ nipatitaṁ prabhavāhi-kūpe
kāmābhi kāmam anu yaḥ prapatan prasaṅgāt
kṛtvātmasāt surarṣiṇā bhagavan gṛhītaḥ
so 'haṁ kathaṁ nu visṛje tava bhṛtya-sevām

Translation: "My dear Lord, O Supreme Personality of Godhead, because of my association with material desires, one after another, I was gradually falling into a blind well full of snakes, following the general populace. But Your servant Nārada Muni kindly accepted me as his disciple and instructed me how to achieve this transcendental position. Therefore, my first duty is to serve him. How could I leave his service?" [Prahlāda Mahārāja to Lord Nṛsiṁhadeva, *Śrīmad-Bhāgavatam* 7.9.28]

tumi mor cira sāthī, bhuliyā māyār lāthi,
khāiyāchi janma-janmāntare
āji punaḥ e sujoga, jadi hoy jogājoga,
tabe pāri tuhe milibāre

Translation: O Lord Kṛṣṇa, You are my eternal companion. Forgetting You, I have suffered the kicks of *māyā* birth after birth. If today the chance to meet You occurs again, then I will surely be able to rejoin You.

tomāra milane bhāi, ābār se sukha pāi,
gocārane ghuri din bhor
kata bane chuṭāchuṭi, bane khāi luṭāpuṭi,
sei din kabe habe mor

Translation: O dear friend, in Your company I will experience great joy once again. In the early morning I will wander about the cowherd pastures and fields. Running and frolicking in the many forests of Vraja, I will roll on the ground in spiritual ecstasy. Oh, when will that day be mine?

āji se subidhāne, tomāra smaraṇa bhela,
baṙo āśā ḍākilām tāi
āmi tomāra nitya-dāsa, tāi kori eta āśa,
tumi binā anya gati nāi

Translation: Today that remembrance of You came to me in a very nice way. Because I have a great longing I called to You. I am Your eternal servant, and therefore I desire Your association so much. O Lord Kṛṣṇa, except for You there is no other means of success.

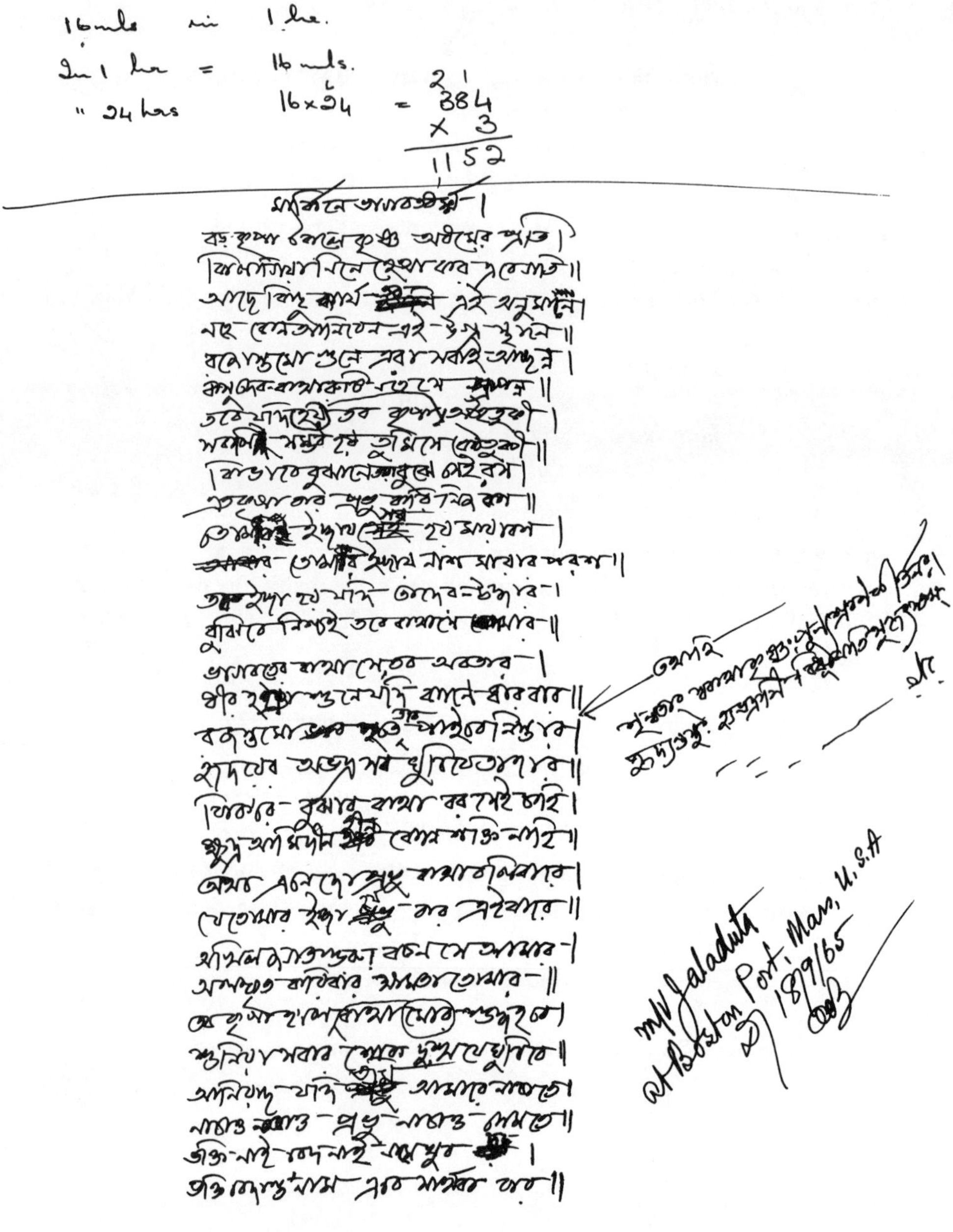

(At the top of the page, it appears that Śrīla Prabhupāda was calculating how far the ship would travel in three days.)

Mārkine Bhāgavata-dharma

baṙo-kṛpā kaile kṛṣṇa adhamer prati
ki lāgiyānile hethā koro ebe gati

Translation: My dear Lord Kṛṣṇa, You are so kind upon this useless soul, but I do not know why You have brought me here. Now You can do whatever You like with me.

āche kichu kārja taba ei anumāne
nahe keno āniben ei ugra-sthāne

Translation: But I guess You have some business here, otherwise why would You bring me to this terrible place?

rajas tamo guṇe erā sabāi āchanna
bāsudeb-kathā ruci nahe se prasanna

Translation: Most of the population here is covered by the material modes of ignorance and passion. Absorbed in material life, they think themselves very happy and satisfied, and therefore they have no taste for the transcendental message of Vāsudeva. I do not know how they will be able to understand it.

tabe jadi taba kṛpā hoy ahaitukī
sakal-i sambhava hoy tumi se kautukī

Translation: But I know Your causeless mercy can make everything possible, because You are the most expert mystic.

ki bhāve bujhāle tārā bujhe sei rasa
eta kṛpā koro prabhu kori nija-baśa

Translation: How will they understand the mellows of devotional service? O Lord, I am simply praying for Your mercy so that I will be able to convince them about Your message.

tomāra icchāya saba hoy māyā-baśa
tomāra icchāya nāśa māyār paraśa

Translation: All living entities have come under the control of the illusory energy by Your will, and therefore, if You like, by Your will they can also be released from the clutches of illusion.

taba icchā hoy jadi tādera uddhār
bujhibe niścai tabe kathā se tomār

Translation: I wish that You may deliver them. Therefore if You so desire their deliverance, then only will they be able to understand Your message.

bhāgavater kathā se taba avatār
dhīra haiyā śune jadi kāne bār bār

Translation: The words of *Śrīmad-Bhāgavatam* are Your incarnation, and if a sober person repeatedly receives it with submissive aural reception, then he will be able to understand Your message.

śṛṇvatāṁ sva-kathāḥ kṛṣṇaḥ
puṇya-śravaṇa-kīrtanaḥ
hṛdy antaḥ-stho hy abhadrāṇi
vidhunoti suhṛt satām

naṣṭa-prāyeṣv abhadreṣu
nityaṁ bhāgavata-sevayā
bhagavaty uttama-śloke
bhaktir bhavati naiṣṭhikī

tadā rajas-tamo-bhāvāḥ
kāma-lobhādayaś ca ye
ceta etair anāviddhaṁ
sthitaṁ sattve prasīdati

evaṁ prasanna-manaso
bhagavad-bhakti-yogataḥ

bhagavat-tattva-vijñānaṁ
mukta-saṅgasya jāyate

bhidyate hṛdaya-granthiś
chidyante sarva-saṁśayāḥ
kṣīyante cāsya karmāṇi
dṛṣṭa evātmanīśvare

Translation: It is said in the *Śrīmad-Bhāgavatam* (1.2.17–21): "Śrī Kṛṣṇa, the Personality of Godhead, who is the Paramātmā [Supersoul] in everyone's heart and the benefactor of the truthful devotee, cleanses desire for material enjoyment from the heart of the devotee who relishes His messages, which are in themselves virtuous when properly heard and chanted. By regularly hearing the *Bhāgavatam* and rendering service unto the pure devotee, all that is troublesome to the heart is practically destroyed, and loving service unto the glorious Lord, who is praised with transcendental songs, is established as an irrevocable fact. At the time loving service is established in the heart, the modes of passion [*rajas*] and ignorance [*tamas*] and lust and desire [*kāma*] disappear from the heart. Then the devotee is established in goodness and he becomes happy. Thus established in the mode of goodness, the man rejuvenated by loving service to the Lord gains liberation from material association [*mukti*] and comes to know scientifically of the Personality of Godhead. Thus the knots of the heart and all misgivings are cut to pieces. The chain of fruitive actions [*karma*] is terminated when one sees the Self as master."

rajas tamo hate tabe pāibe nistār
hṛdayer abhadra sab ghucibe tāhār

Translation: He will become liberated from the influence of the modes of ignorance and passion and thus all inauspicious things accumulated in the core of the heart will disappear.

ki ko're bujhābo kathā baro sei cāhi
khudra āmi dīna hīna kono śakti nāhi

Translation: How will I make them understand this message of Kṛṣṇa consciousness? I am very unfortunate, unqualified, and the most fallen.

Therefore I am seeking Your benediction so that I can convince them, for I am powerless to do so on my own.

athaca enecho prabhu kathā bolibāre
je tomār icchā prabhu koro ei bāre

Translation: Somehow or other, O Lord, You have brought me here to speak about You. Now, my Lord, it is up to You to make me a success or failure, as You like.

akhila jagat-guru! bacana se āmār
alaṅkṛta koribār khamatā tomār

Translation: O spiritual master of all the worlds! I can simply repeat Your message, so if You like You can make my power of speaking suitable for their understanding.

taba kṛpā ha'le mor kathā śuddha habe
śuniyā sabāra śoka duḥkha je ghucibe

Translation: Only by Your causeless mercy will my words become pure. I am sure that when this transcendental message penetrates their hearts, they will certainly feel engladdened and thus become liberated from all unhappy conditions of life.

āniyācho jadi prabhu āmāre nācāte
nācāo nācāo prabhu nācāo se-mate
kāṣṭhera puttali jathā nācāo se-mate

Translation: O Lord, I am just like a puppet in Your hands. So if You have brought me here to dance, then make me dance, make me dance, O Lord, make me dance as You like.

bhakti nāi beda nāi nāme khub daṙo
"bhaktivedānta" nām ebe sārthak koro

Translation: I have no devotion, nor do I have any knowledge, but I have strong faith in the holy name of Kṛṣṇa. I have been designated as Bhaktivedanta, and now, if You like, You can fulfill the real purport of Bhaktivedanta.

BOOKS by His Divine Grace
A.C. Bhaktivedanta Swami Prabhupāda

Bhagavad-gītā As It Is
Śrīmad-Bhāgavatam, cantos 1–10 (29 vols.)
Śrī Caitanya-caritāmṛta (17 vols.)
Teachings of Lord Caitanya
The Nectar of Devotion
The Nectar of Instruction
Śrī Īśopaniṣad
Easy Journey to Other Planets
Kṛṣṇa Consciousness: The Topmost Yoga System
Kṛṣṇa, the Supreme Personality of Godhead (3 vols.)
Perfect Questions, Perfect Answers
Dialectical Spiritualism—A Vedic View of Western Philosophy
Teachings of Lord Kapila, the Son of Devahūti
Transcendental Teachings of Prahlād Mahārāja
Teachings of Queen Kuntī
Kṛṣṇa, the Reservoir of Pleasure
The Science of Self-Realization
The Path of Perfection
Life Comes From Life
The Perfection of Yoga
Beyond Birth and Death
On the Way to Kṛṣṇa
Geetār-gan (Bengali)
Vairāgya-vidyā (Bengali)
Buddhi-yoga (Bengali)
Bhakti-ratna-bolī (Bengali)
Rāja-vidyā: The King of Knowledge
Elevation to Kṛṣṇa Consciousness
Kṛṣṇa Consciousness: The Matchless Gift
Back to Godhead magazine (founder)

A complete catalog is available upon request.

ISKCON Centers

AFRICA: **Durban (Natal), S. Africa**—P.O. Box 212, Cato Ridge, Natal 3680 / Cato Ridge 287; **Johannesburg, S. Africa**—3 Hunter St., Highlands, 2191 / 6140634; **Lagos, Nigeria**—P.O. Box 8793, West Africa; **Mombasa, Kenya, E. Africa**—Madhavani House, Sauti Ya Kenya and Kisumu Rd., P.O. Box 82224 / 312248; **Nairobi, Kenya, E. Africa**—Puran Singh Close, P.O. Box 28946 / 331568; **Mauritius**—Seewoopaul Bldg., Royal Rd., Lallmatie (mail: P.O. Box 718, Port Louis, Mauritius).

ASIA

INDIA: **Ahmedabad, Gujarat**—7, Kailas Society, Ashram Rd., 380 009 / 49935; **Bangalore, Mysore**—40 Hare Krishna Rd., 560 001 / 77664; **Bhadrak, Orissa**—Gour Gopal Mandir, Kuans, P.O. Bhadrak, Dist. Balasore; **Bhubaneswar, Orissa**—National Highway No. 5, Nayapalli (mail: c/o P.O. Box 173, 751 001) / 53125; **Bombay, Maharastra**—Hare Krishna Land, Juhu, 400 054 / 566-860; **Calcutta, W. Bengal**—3 Albert Rd., 700 017 / 44-3757; **Chandigarh, Punjab**—Hare Krishna Land, Dakshin Marg, Sector 36-B, 160 023; **Chhaygharia (Haridaspur), W. Bengal**—Thakur Haridas Sripatbari Sevashram, P.O. Chhaygharia, P.S. Bongaon, Dist. 24 Pargonas; **Derwa, Bihar**—P.O. Derwa, Dist. Rohtas; **Gauhati, Assam**—Post Bag No. 127, 781 001; **Gurura, Bihar**—P.O. Kudra, Dist. Rohtas; **Hyderabad, A.P.**—Hare Krishna Land, Nampally Station Rd., 500 001 / 51018; **Imphal, Manipur**—Paona Bazar, 795 001; **Mayapur, W. Bengal**—Shree Mayapur Chandrodaya Mandir, P.O. Shree Mayapur Dham (District Nadia); **New Delhi, U.P.**—21A Feroze Gandhi Rd., Lajpat Nagar III, 110 024 / 624-590; **Tekari, Bihar**—P.O. Baraílla, Dist. Rohtas; **Vrindavan, U.P.**—Krishna-Balarama Mandir, Bhaktivedanta Swami Marg, Raman Reti, Mathura / 178.

FARMS: **Hyderabad, A.P.**—P.O. Dabilpur Village, Medchal Taluq, Hyderabad District, 501 401; **Mayapur, W. Bengal**—(contact ISKCON Mayapur).

OTHER COUNTRIES: **Bangkok, Thailand**—P.O. Box 12-1108; **Colombo, Sri Lanka**—188, New Chetty St., Colombo 13 / 33325; **Dacca, Bangladesh**—61 Tejkuni Para, Dacca 8 / 317861; **Hong Kong**—5 Homantin St., Flat 23, Kowloon / 3-029113; **Kathmandu, Nepal**—8/6, Battis Putali, Goshalla; **Malaysia**—1, Lintang Melur, Mk 14, Butterworth, P.W. Malaysia; **Mandaue City, Philippines**—231 Pagsabungan Rd., Basak, Cebu / 83254; **Tehran, Iran**—Felistin Ave. (old Kakh), Shemshad St., No. 3 / 644-272; **Tel Aviv, Israel**—147 Hanassi St., Herzliya Pituah / 938-846.

AUSTRALASIA: **Adelaide, Australia**—13-A Frome St. / (08)223-2084; **Auckland, New Zealand**—Hwy. 18, Riverhead (next to Huapai Golfcourse) (mail: c/o R.D. 2, Kumeu) / 412-8075; **Jakarta, Indonesia**—Jalanrawmangun, Muka Timur 80 / 483519; **Lautoka, Fiji**—5 Tavewa Ave. (mail: c/o P.O. Box 125) / 61-633, ext. 48; **Melbourne, Australia**—197 Danks St., Albert Park, Melbourne, Victoria 3206 (mail: c/o P.O. Box 125) / 699-5122; **Sydney, Australia**—112 Darlinghurst Rd., King's Cross, N.S.W. (mail: c/o P.O. Box 159) / (02)357-5162.

FARMS: **Auckland, New Zealand (New Varshana)**—contact ISKCON Auckland; **Colo, Australia (Bhaktivedanta Ashram)**—Upper Colo Rd., N.S.W. (mail: c/o P.O. Box 493, St. Mary's, 2760, N.S.W.) / 04-565-5284; **Murwillumbah, Australia (New Govardhana)**—'Eungella,' Tyalgum Rd. via Murwillumbah, N.S.W., 2484 (mail: c/o P.O. Box 687) / 066-721903.

EUROPE: **Athens, Greece**—133 Solonos; **Amsterdam, Holland**—Herengracht 96 / 020-24 94 10; **Barcelona, Spain**—Pintor Fortuny 11, Barcelona, 1 / 319-69-53; **Catania, Sicily**—Via Empedocle 84, 95100 / 095-552-252; **Dublin, Ireland**—2 Belvedere Place, Dublin 1; **Duedingen, Switzerland**—Im Stillen Tal, CH 3186 Duedingen (FR) / (037) 43.26.97; **Frankfurt a. Main, W. Germany**—Schloss Rettershof uber, 6233 Kelkheim, Ts. / 06174-21357; **Gallarate, Italy**—Via A. Volta 19, Gallarate 20131 (VR) / 0331-783-268; **Lausanne, Switzerland**—11 rue César-Roux, CH-1005 / (021)20.06.21; **London, England (city)**—10 Soho St., London W1 / 01-437-1835; **London, England (country)**—Bhaktivedanta Manor, Letchmore Heath, Watford, Hertfordshire WD2 8EP / Radlett (09276) 7244; **Madrid, Spain**—Calle Arturo Sorio No. 209; **Paris, France**—20 rue Vieille du Temple, Paris 75004 / 500-63-58; **Rome, Italy**—Salita del Poggio Laurentino 7, Rome 00144 / (06)593-075; **Stockholm, Sweden**—Korsnas Gård, 140 32 Grodinge / 0753-29151; **Vienna, Austria**—2103 Langenzersdorf, Haaderstrasse 28 / 02244-29912.

FARMS: **Valencay, France (New Māyāpur)**—Lucay-Le-Male, 36 600 / (54)40-23-26; **London, England**—(contact Bhaktivedanta Manor); **Perignano, Italy**—Via Delle Colline, Localita, La Meridiana, Perignano, Pisa / (0587)-616194.

LATIN AMERICA

BRAZIL: **Belo Horizonte, Minas Gerais**—Rua dos Pampas, 123, Prado / 3371337; **Curitiba, Parana**—Rua Coronel Dulcidio 836, Batel; **Porto Alegre, RS**—Rua Guananas 117, Guaruja 90000; **Recife, Pernambuco**—Ave. 17 de Agosto 257, Parnamirim 50000; **Rio de Janeiro, RJ**—R. Hemenergildo de Barros 21, Gloria 20241; **Salvador, Bahia**—Ave. Otavio Mangabeira 97-A, Itapoa 40000; **São Paulo, SP**—R. Pandia Calogeras 54, Liberdade 01525.

FARMS: **Feira de Santana, Bahia (Chacara Hridayānanda)**—BR 324, Km 99; **Pindamonhangaba, Sao Paulo (New Gokula)**—Ribeirao Grande C.P. 108, 12400.

OTHER COUNTRIES: **Bogotá, Colombia**—Carrera 3A No. 54-A-72 / 255-9842; **Cuzco, Peru**—Avenida Pardo No. 1036 / 2277; **Georgetown, Guyana**—24 Uitvlugt Front, West Coast Demerara; **Guadalajara, Mexico**—Avenida las Americas No. 225, Sector Hidalgo / 163455; **Guatemala City, Guatemala**—Segunda Calle 6-26, Zona 13 / 310833; **La Paz, Bolivia**—Calle Chacaltaya No. 587 / 32-85-67; **Lima, Peru**—Jirón Junín 415, Lima / 47-18-10; **Medellín, Colombia**—Carrera 32, No. 54-42; **Mexico City, Mexico**—Gob. Tiburcio Montiel 45, San Miguel Chapultepec, Mexico D.F. 18 / (905)271-0132; **Panama City, Panama**—43-58 Via España Altos, Al Lado del Cine, Bella Vista; **Quito, Ecuador**—Apdo. 2384, Calle Yasuni No. 404; **St. Augustine, Trinidad and Tobago**—Gordon St. at Santa Margarita Circular Rd. / 662-4605; **San José, Costa Rica**—400 mtrs. Sur Centro Médico de Guadalupe (casa blanca esquinera) Colonia Chapultepec, Guadalupe; **San Salvador, El Salvador**—67 Avenida Sur No. 115, Colonia Escalon / 243 445; **Santiago, Chile**—Eyzaguirre 2404, Puente Alto / 283.

NORTH AMERICA

CANADA: **Edmonton, Alberta**—10132 142nd St., T5N 2N7 / (403)452-5855; **Montreal, Quebec**—1626 Pie IX Boulevard, H1V 2C5 / (514) 527-1101; **Ottawa, Ontario**—212 Somerset St. E., K1N 6V4 / (613)233-3460; **Toronto, Ontario**—243 Avenue Rd. M5R 2J6 / (416)922-5415; **Victoria, B.C.**—4056 Rainbow St., V8X 2A9; **Vancouver, B.C.**—5580 S.E. Marine Dr., Burnaby V5J 3G8 / (604)433-8216.

FARM: **Hemingford, Quebec (New Nandagram)**—315 Backbrush Rd., RR. No. 2, J0L 1H0 / (514)247-3429.

U.S.A.: **Atlanta, Georgia**—1287 Ponce de Leon Ave. NE 30306 / (404)378-9182; **Austin, Texas**—1910 Whitis Ave. 78705 / (512)476-7138; **Baltimore, Maryland**—200 Bloomsbury Ave., Catonsville 21228 / (301)788-3883; **Berkeley, California**—2334 Stuart St. 94705 / (415) 843-7874; **Boston, Massachusetts**—72 Commonwealth Ave. 02116 / (617)536-1695; **Chicago, Illinois**—1014 Emerson St., Evanston 60201 / (312)273-3960; **Cleveland, Ohio**—15720 Euclid Ave., E. Cleveland 44112 / (216)851-9367; **Columbus, Ohio**—99 East 13th Ave. 43201 / (614) 299-5084; **Coral Hills, Maryland**—4715 Marlboro Pike 20028 / (301)568-9194; **Dallas, Texas**—5430 Gurley Ave. 75223 / (214)-827-6330; **Denver, Colorado**—1400 Cherry St. 80220 / (303)333-5461; **Detroit, Michigan**—383 Lenox Ave. 48215 / (313)824-6000; **Gainesville, Florida**—921 S.W. Depot Ave. 32601 / (904)377-1496; **Gurabo, Puerto Rico**—Box 215 B, Route 181, Santarita 00658; **Hartford, Connecticut**—84 Silver Lane 06118 / (203)568-1422; **Honolulu, Hawaii**—51 Coelho Way 96817 / (808)595-3947; **Houston, Texas**—1111 Rosalie St. 77004 / (713)526-9860; **Laguna Beach, California**—644 S. Coast Hwy. 92651 / (714)497-3638; **Las Vegas, Nevada**—6601 Painted Desert Dr. 89108 / (702)-645-4934; **Los Angeles, California**—3764 Watseka Ave. 90034 / (213) 871-0717; **Miami, Florida**—10900 Coral Way 33165 / (305)552-1766; **New Orleans, Louisiana**—2936 Esplanade Ave. 70119 / (504)488-7433; **New York, New York**—340 W. 55th St. 10019 / (212)765-8610; **Philadelphia, Pennsylvania**—41-51 West Allens Lane, 19119 / (215)-247-4600; **Pittsburgh, Pennsylvania**—1112 N. Negley Ave. 15026 / (412)362-0212; **Portland, Oregon**—2805 S.E. Hawthorne St. 97214 / (503)231-5792; **St. Louis, Missouri**—3926 Lindell Blvd. 63108 / (314)535-8085; **Salt Lake City, Utah**—859 Park St. 84102 / (801)355-2626; **San Diego, California**—1030 Grand Ave., Pacific Beach 92109 / (714)483-2500; **San Juan, Puerto Rico**—1016 Ponce de Leon St., Rio Piedras, 00925 / (809)765-4745; **Seattle, Washington**—400 18th Ave. East 98112 / (206)322-3636; **State College, Pennsylvania**—103 E. Hamilton Ave. 16801 / (814)234-1867; **Washington, D.C.**—10310 Oaklyn Rd., Potomac, Maryland 20854 / (301)299-2100.

FARMS: **Carriere, Mississippi (New Tālavan)**—Rt. No. 2, Box 449, 39426 / (601)798-6705; **Gainesville, Florida**—contact ISKCON Gainesville; **Hopland, California (Mount Kailas)**—Route 175, Box 469, 95449 / (707)-744-1100; **Hotchkiss, Colorado (New Barshana)**—P.O. Box 112, 81419 / (303)527-4584; **Lynchburg, Tennessee (Murāri-sevaka)**—Rt. No. 1, Box 146-A, (Mulberry) 37359 / (615)759-7058; **Moundsville, West Virginia (New Vrindaban)**—R.D. No. 1, Box 319, Hare Krishna Ridge 26041 / (304)845-2790; **Port Royal, Pennsylvania (Gita-nāgarī)**—R.D. No. 1, 17082 / (717)527-2493.

Acknowledgments

While our well-wishers have been many, it has been a small staff of workers that has actually produced the finished product. Foremost among my assistants have been Maṇḍaleśvara dāsa and Śeṣa dāsa. Maṇḍaleśvara edited the manuscript with total dedication and good literary intelligence. Śeṣa absorbed himself in supervising the research and solving the sometimes difficult mysteries of chronology and missing facts.

Rādhāballabha dāsa, Bhaktivedanta Book Trust production manager, enthusiastically encouraged me through the progressive stages of the volume, from its beginning to its completion. He also conducted many interviews and was ready to travel at a moment's notice to trace down a witness. Working at the Gīta-nāgarī Farm Community in Pennsylvania, our research staff, Kuṇḍalī dāsa, Baladeva Vidyābhūṣaṇa dāsa, and Kṛṣṇasneha dāsa, kept our files in order and made the constant influx of data available to me in a usable form. Jayādvaita Swami, Śrīla Prabhupāda's own editor, gave a final polishing to the manuscript.

Our faithful typists, Ācārya-devī dāsī, Dāsyarasa-devī dāsī, and Bhakti-mārga-devī dāsī, never balked at typing up another draft or another version throughout the progressive stages of the manuscript. The typists in the BBT office, Mamatā-devī dāsī, Arundhatī-devī dāsī, Duḥkhahantrī-devī dāsī, and Pūrṇacandra-devī dāsī, have been working steadily at the huge task of typing up all of Śrīla Prabhupāda's taped lectures and conversations, which we are consulting and incorporating into the text. The BBT Press production staff of Sureśvara dāsa, Gopīparāṇadhana dāsa, Siṁheśvara dāsa, Bṛhad-mṛdaṅga dāsa, Balāi-devī dāsī, Kṣamā-devī dāsī, and others have done the designing, composing, proofreading, and layout, preparing the volume for press. Vidyānanda dāsa, Ekanātha dāsa, and Parama-rūpa dāsa, who are compiling an archive collection of Śrīla Prabhupāda's tapes and photos, readily supplied materials needed for this volume.

The devotees whose memoirs have contributed most significantly to this volume are Brahmānanda Swami and Hayagrīva dāsa. As this volume has been appearing serially in *Back to Godhead* magazine, BTG readers have given me much advice, which I have considered and tried to incorporate. Some of the names of people appearing in this book have been changed.

Sanskrit Pronunciation Guide

Throughout the centuries, the Sanskrit language has been written in a variety of alphabets. The mode of writing most widely used throughout India, however, is called *devanāgarī*, which means, literally, the writing used in "the cities of the demigods." The *devanāgarī* alphabet consists of forty-eight characters, including thirteen vowels and thirty-five consonants. Ancient Sanskrit grammarians arranged the alphabet according to practical linguistic principles, and this order has been accepted by all Western scholars. The system of transliteration used in this book conforms to a system that scholars in the last fifty years have accepted to indicate the pronunciation of each Sanskrit sound.

The short vowel **a** is pronounced like the **u** in b**u**t, long **ā** like the **a** in f**a**r, and short **i** like the **i** in p**i**n. Long **ī** is pronounced as in p**i**que, short **u** as in p**u**ll, and long **ū** as in r**u**le. The vowel **ṛ** is pronounced like the **ri** in **ri**m. The vowel **e** is pronounced as in th**e**y, **ai** as in **ai**sle, **o** as in g**o**, and **au** as in h**ow**. The *anusvāra* (**ṁ**), which is a pure nasal, is pronounced like the **n** in the French word *bo***n**, and *visarga* (**ḥ**), which is a strong aspirate, is pronounced as a final **h** sound. Thus **aḥ** is pronounced like **aha,** and **iḥ** like **ihi.**

The guttural consonants—**k, kh, g, gh,** and **ṅ**—are pronounced from the throat in much the same manner as in English. **K** is pronounced as in **k**ite, **kh** as in Ec**kh**art, **g** as in **g**ive, **gh** as in di**g h**ard, and **ṅ** as in si**ng.** The palatal consonants—**c, ch, j, jh,** and **ñ**—are pronounced from the palate with the middle of the tongue. **C** is pronounced as in **ch**air, **ch** as in staun**ch-h**eart, **j** as in **j**oy, **jh** as in he**dgeh**og, and **ñ** as in ca**ny**on. The cerebral consonants—**ṭ, ṭh, ḍ, ḍh,** and **ṇ**—are pronounced with the tip of the tongue turned up and drawn back against the dome of the palate. **Ṭ** is pronounced as in **t**ub, **ṭh** as in ligh**t-h**eart, **ḍ** as in **d**ove, **ḍh** as in re**d-h**ot, and **ṇ** as in **n**ut. The dental consonants—**t, th, d, dh,** and **n**—are pronounced in the same manner as the cerebrals, but with the forepart of the tongue against the teeth. The labial consonants—**p, ph, b, bh,** and **m**—are pronounced with the lips. **P** is pronounced as in **p**ine, **ph** as in u**ph**ill, **b** as in **b**ird, **bh** as in ru**b-h**ard, and **m** as in **m**other. The semivowels—**y, r, l,** and **v**—are pronounced as in **y**es, **r**un, **l**ight, and **v**ine respectively. The sibilants **ś, ṣ,** and **s**—are pronounced, respectively, as in the German word **s***prechen* and the English words **sh**ine and **s**un. The letter **h** is pronounced as in **h**ome.

Glossary

A

Ācārya—a teacher in an authorized line of disciplic succession, whose life exemplifies his teachings.

Āśrama—a place of shelter conducive to the practice of spiritual life.

B

Bhagavad-gītā—the paramount scripture of the Vedic tradition, spoken five thousand years ago, embodying the teachings of Lord Kṛṣṇa to His devotee Arjuna and expounding devotion to the Supreme Lord as both the principal means and ultimate end of spiritual perfection.

Bhajanas—devotional music and song performed in worship of God or His pure devotees.

Bhakti-yoga—devotional service to the Supreme Lord.

Brahmacārī—a celibate student and servant of a *guru*.

Brāhmaṇa—a spiritually trained person qualified as a teacher or priest.

C

Caitanya-caritāmṛta—the authorized account of the life and teachings of Lord Caitanya, written in the sixteenth century in Bengali and Sanskrit by Kṛṣṇadāsa Kavirāja.

Cakra—the wheel weapon of Lord Viṣṇu.

Capātī—an unleavened, pancake-sized whole wheat bread.

Chādar—a blanketlike outer garment.

D

Dhotī—a man's lower garment, consisting of a length of wide cloth wrapped around the waist and between the legs.

G

Gauḍīya Math—the mission established in India by Śrīla Bhaktisiddhānta Sarasvatī Ṭhākura for spreading Kṛṣṇa consciousness.

Ghee—butterfat, used in cooking (especially for deep-frying).

H

Haṭha-yoga—the physical practice of postures and breathing exercises as a means toward self-realization.

I

ISKCON—the International Society for Krishna Consciousness.

J

Japa—chanting of the Hare Kṛṣṇa *mantra* softly, for one's personal benefit.

K

Kali-yuga—the current age in history, characterized by quarrel, begun five thousand years ago and continuing for a further 427,000 years.

Karatālas—brass hand cymbals used to accompany *kīrtana*.

Karma-yoga—the process of linking up with the Supreme by selflessly offering the fruits of one's work.

Kīrtana—loud chanting of the Hare Kṛṣṇa *mantra* and other devotional *mantras* and prayers, usually with melody and musical accompaniment.

Kṛṣṇa-bhaktas—devotees of Lord Kṛṣṇa.

Kurtā—an Indian-style shirt.

M

Mahā-mantra—the great chanting for deliverance:

Hare Kṛṣṇa, Hare Kṛṣṇa, Kṛṣṇa Kṛṣṇa, Hare Hare
Hare Rāma, Hare Rāma, Rāma Rāma, Hare Hare

Mantra—a syllable, word, or verse with special spiritual potency.

Mantra-yoga—the process of self-realization by hearing and chanting the holy names of God.

Masāla—a standard mixture of spices, which can be of several varieties, used in Vedic cooking.

Māyā—the illusory energy of the Lord that deludes the living entity into forgetfulness of his real, spiritual nature; the state of forgetfulness of one's relationship with the Lord.

Māyāvādīs—impersonalist philosophers who maintain that there is no difference between God and the living entity.

Mṛdaṅga—a traditional two-headed Indian clay drum used to accompany *kīrtana.*

N

Nārāyaṇa—the Supreme Lord in His majestic feature as Lord of the spiritual world.

P

Pañca-tattva—the Supreme Truth appearing as Lord Caitanya Mahāprabhu together with His four principal associates.

Paramparā—an unbroken disciplic succession of spiritual masters, beginning with Lord Kṛṣṇa. Also, the teachings and traditions of the disciplic succession.

Prasādam—"mercy"; vegetarian foodstuffs and other articles that are sanctified by being first offered to Lord Kṛṣṇa for His enjoyment.

S

Sabjī—any cooked vegetable dish, usually spiced.

Sādhu—a saintly person, especially a pure devotee of the Lord.

Śaṅkarācārya—the influential ninth century teacher of monism, a philosophy which maintains that there is no distinction between God and the living entities.

Saṅkīrtana—congregational *kīrtana;* any public glorification of the Supreme Personality of Godhead and devotional service unto Him.

Sannyāsī—one in the final renounced order of spiritual life.

Sārī—the standard Vedic woman's garment, consisting of several yards of lightweight cloth draped to form both a skirt and a head or shoulder covering.

Śāstra—authoritative Vedic scripture.

Śrīla Bhaktisiddhānta Sarasvatī—the spiritual master of His Divine Grace A. C. Bhaktivedanta Swami Prabhupāda.

Śrīmad-Bhāgavatam—a scripture of eighteen thousand verses in twelve cantos which is one of the eighteen *Purāṇas* (Vedic histories) and advocates and establishes pure devotional service to the Supreme Lord exclusively.

T

Tilaka—auspicious marks of clay worn on the forehead and other places of the body to sanctify it as a temple of the Supreme Lord.

V

Vaiṣṇava—a devotee of the Supreme Lord Viṣṇu (Kṛṣṇa).

Y

Yogī—One who has achieved, or is striving for, union with the Supreme.

Index

References to Śrīla Prabhupāda may be found under the heading Prabhupāda, Śrīla. *Within entries Śrīla Prabhupāda is indicated as* SP.

A

Abortion, 129
Absolute Truth
  nature of, 164
  personal & impersonal features of, 23
  SP presenting, 56, 83–84, 129, 231
  See also: God; Knowledge, transcendental; Philosophy
Ācāryas (saintly authorities), 126
  See also: Authorities, spiritual; Devotees, pure devotees; Spiritual master
A.C. Bhaktivedanta Swami Prabhupāda. *See:* Prabhupāda
Activities
  in Kṛṣṇa's service, 137–38
  at 26 2nd Ave, 145–53
Acyutānanda
  apartment left by, for SP's storefront, 264–265
  before initiation. *See:* Barnett, Chuck
  at breakfast, 263
  dancing in Tompkins Square Park, 210–11
  initiation of, 199
  Judy's encounter with, 234
  purīs cooked by, 245
  quoted on *East Village Other* article, 222
  SP changed life of, 264
Adelphi Recording Studio, 254
Advaita, 61, 242
Advancement, spiritual
  by chanting Hare Kṛṣṇa, 257
  by eating *prasādam* 243
  purification needed for, 180
Agarwals, the
  Brij, 16
  Gopal
    father of, 11
Agarwals
    quoted on SP, 15
    quoted on SP's picture, 11
    SP driven by, from Pittsburgh to Butler, 11–12
    SP seen off by, 20
    as SP's sponsor, 8, 11
  Pamela, 17
  quoted on SP's purpose in America, 14
  Sally
    quoted on herself & her husband, 11
    quoted on SP, 14–17, 20, 194
    quoted on SP's coming, 11
    SP's newspaper interview arranged by, 12–13
  SP as considered by, 194
  SP at home of, 12–17, 20, 52
  SP's arrival perplexed, 11, 12
Age of Kali. *See:* Kali-yuga
A.I.R. lofts, 70, 71
Alan Kallman. *See:* Kallman, Alan
Alan Watts, 113
Aldous Huxley, wife of, cited on places for meditation, 171–72
Allen, David
  background of, 66, 73
  Bill quoted on, 97
  Carl at loft of, 97
  in Carl's loft, 98
  as LSD victim, 73, 94–95, 96, 97, 101
  quoted on SP, 73–74
  SP quoted on, 73, 94
  SP shared Bowery loft with, 68, 73–74, 94–95, 101
  SP's relationship with, 73–74, 94–95, 96, 101
Allen Ginsberg. *See:* Ginsberg, Allen
Allen Larsen, Professor, quoted on SP, 17–18
Alpert, Richard, 200, 226

America
  bhakti in, 64
  consciousness exploration in, 82
  hippies rejected, 109, 110, 111
  materialism in, 10
  in 1960s, *xiii*
  SP interested to know, 16
  SP preaching in, 96, 126–29, 238–39
  SP's arrival in, *xiii*, 5–8, 10
  SP's first public chanting in, 194–95
  SP struggling in, 21–49
  Vietnam war opposition in, 39, 83–84, 109, 129, 172–73, 228
  See also: Western world
American Revolution, Bowery's importance during, 69
Americans
  saṅkīrtana interests, 53
  SP didn't compromise with, 82–84, 238, 239
  SP quoted on, 9, 33, 53, 67–68, 73, 91
  SP to turn, into *brāhmaṇas*, 198
A.M. Hartman, 41
Analogies
  bird in ocean & the author, *xi*
  cars passing & Kṛṣṇa's incarnations, 118
  dog collars & neck beads, 183
  sunshine & Brahman, 23
Ananda Ashram
  meditation room at, 26–27, 169
  SP, Mishra, & students at, 26–28
  SP & followers at, 167–71, 172
Ananta Śeṣa, 107
Animals, ignorant people compared to, 217
A.P. Dharwadkar, 46
Arjuna & Kṛṣṇa in *Gītā*, 53, 56, 80, 82–83, 84, 117, 119, 133, 171
Astrologer, Sanātana's gold known to, 264, 266
Atheism
  SP argued against, 128–29
  See also: Impersonalism; Materialism; Māyāvādīs
Atlantic Ocean, SP crossing, 2, 3, 96
Ātmā defined, 23
  See also: Soul
Author
  acknowledgments by, *x–xi*, 289
  admission by, *xi*
  biographical sketch of, 331
  SP's biography commissioned to, *ix*
Authorities, spiritual, *ix–x*
  See also: Ācāryas; Devotees, pure devotees; Spiritual master

B

Back to Godhead magazine
  Brahmānanda & Gargamuni distributing, 250
  first ISKCON issue of, 248–50
  motto of, 248
  second issue's editorial, 251
  SP founded, 246–47, 249
  SP gave over, to disciples, 247, 250
Bala Krishna, 19, 32, 33, 53
Bala Saraswati, 28–29
Bank, Indian, SP's correspondence with, 91
Barnett, Chuck, 176
  after initiation. *See:* Acyutānanda
  background of, 158
  initiation of, 199
  as Keith's cooking assistant, 149
  quoted
    on finding 2nd Ave temple, 159
    on first seeing SP, 160–61
    on SP & burning chilies, 166
    on SP in 2nd Ave apartment, 137, 162
    on talking with SP in 2nd Ave apartment, 163–64
    on walking to SP's morning class, 136
    on Wally, Keith, & Howard, 113
  at SP's morning class, 137
  on vacation, 181
Bay of Bengal, SP's diary entry at, 1
Beads
  chanting Hare Kṛṣṇa on, 154, 155, 176, 179, 261
  initiates received, 184
  for neck, 7, 183
  SP chanting on, at initiation ceremony, 183
  stringing of, 179

Beauty, SP quoted on, 171
Being. *See:* Consciousness; Life; Living entity; Soul
Bekar, Carol
  background of, 76
  initiation not desired by, 181
  quoted
    on Bowery loft scene, 78
    on Carl & SP, 100
    on Eva & SP, 99
    on SP, 76–77, 79
  SP's 2nd Ave scene disinterested, 156–57
"Bells" ceremony, 153
Benares, Sanātana & Caitanya in, 266, 269
Bengal
  chanting of Hare Kṛṣṇa introduced in, 212
  man with mangoes in, story of, 240
  Nawab Shah in, 262, 263
  SP from, *xiii*
Bengal, Bay of, SP's diary entry at, 1
Bengali
  Caitanya-caritāmṛta in, 262
  prayer offering food to Lord in, 150
  SP's poems aboard ship in, 3, 5n
Bhagavad-gītā
  Arjuna & Kṛṣṇa in, 53, 56, 80, 82–83, 117, 119, 133, 171
  cited on Brahman & Bhagavān, 23
  cited on great man's example, 197
  defined, 78
  English translations of, 212–13
  misinterpretations of, 130–31
  quotations from
    on becoming saintly soon, 120
    on depending on Kṛṣṇa, 97
    on impersonalists, 24
    on material world as miserable, 217
    on seeing Kṛṣṇa everywhere, 49
    on surrender to Kṛṣṇa, 32
    on *yogīs*, best, 164
  Radhakrishnan's edition of, 177, 232, 267
  SP lecturing on, in 72nd St room (307), 52, 53–58, 65
  SP's classes on, at 26 2nd Ave, 111, 114, 117–23, 130–31, 135, 136–37, 164, 177–78
Bhagavad-gītā
  SP's commentary on, 177–78, 250, 267, 272
  SP's knowledge of, 127
  SP's Lower East Side audience aware of, 116
  SP's plans for printing of, 259
Bhagavān, 23
  See also: God; Kṛṣṇa
Bhāgavatam. See: Śrīmad-Bhāgavatam
Bhagavat-prasādam. See: Prasādam
Bhakti
  in America, 64
  defined, 138
  in NYC, 141
  See also: Bhakti-yoga; Devotional service; Kṛṣṇa, love for; Kṛṣṇa consciousness
Bhaktisiddhānta Sarasvatī Ṭhākura, Śrīla (SP's spiritual master)
  as *brahmacārī*, 239
  in disciplic succession, 225
  foreign mission of, 45, 92
  painting of, instructions for, 232
  preaching by, 134–35
  quoted on chanting to the walls, 52
  SP feeling presence of, 38
  SP serving, 143
  SP's first meeting with, 45, 219
  SP's order from, *xiii*, 1, 3, 47–48, 51, 59, 75, 96, 110–11, 134, 219, 246, 249
  in SP's poem, 4
  wanted Kṛṣṇa consciousness preached in West, 4, 29, 31, 96
Bhaktivedanta Book Trust, x
Bhaktivedanta Swami. *See:* Prabhupāda
Bhaktivinoda, 225
Bhakti-yoga
  as highest *yoga*, 27
  immortality offered by, 24
  as superior path, 270
  See also: Bhakti; Devotional service; Kṛṣṇa, love for; Kṛṣṇa consciousness
Bhasmatī rice, 149
Bhava-mahā-dāvāgni
  quoted, 119
Bible, SP quoted on, 128

Bill Epstein. *See:* Epstein, Bill
Biographers, mundane, SP incomprehensible to, *x*
Bird in ocean & the author, analogy of, *xi*
Birth-death cycle
bondage to, 238
freedom from, 82
See also: Death
Blacks, 108, 203, 210
See also: Yeargens, Carl
Blake, William, 114, 198, 249
Bob Corens. *See:* Corens, Bob
Bob Dylan, 128
Body, material
self not, 58, 80
soul in, 269
Bogart, Larry, 173, 174–75
Bohemians. *See:* Hippies
Bon Mahārāja, 42, 43
Bose, Subhas Chandra, 148
Boston, SP in, 5–7, 96
Bowery, the
derelicts of, 69–70, 72, 75, 77, 88, 95, 96, 103
description of, 69–71, 87–88
song about, 69
SP in loft on, 67–95
SP moving from, to 2nd Ave, 103–4
SP quoted on, 67
Brahmā, Lord, 240
Brahmācārī, Mukti, 92, 93
Brahman, Supreme
personal & impersonal views of, 23–25
See also: Absolute Truth; God; Kṛṣṇa
Brahmānanda
appointed Alan Kallman's meeting with SP, 254
by back door at storefront *kīrtanas*, 238
Back to Godhead distributed by, 250
before initiation. *See:* Scharf, Bruce
brother of. *See:* Gargamuni; Scharf, Greg
initiation of, 198–99
kneading *purī* dough, 244
at Love-Pageant-Rally *kīrtana*, 224, 225
mother of, 240
Brahmānanda
& Price, 252–53
quoted
on dancing in Tompkins Square Park, 211
on SP & woman in Times Square, 255
on SP at Burton Green's Town Hall recital, 241–42
on SP leaving NYC, 237, 271
on SP playing Indian drum, 255
SP asked, to speak to angry tenant, 220
SP at Jewish bank building with, 251
SP changed life of, 264
SP got drum from guest via, 254–55
SP handing fifty-cent piece to, 233
SP's "intimate" instructions to, 268
SP's relationship with, 241–42
SP teaching cooking to, 242, 243, 244, 245
SP walking with, to Tompkins Square Park, 205, 206
tape-recording SP's *Caitanya-caritāmṛta* classes, 262, 265
as working man, 248, 263, 272
Brāhmaṇas
caste-conscious, 213
sacred thread worn by, 54
Sanātana learned *Bhāgavatam* from, 262–63
SP to turn Americans into, 198
See also: Sādhus; Sages; Saintly person
"*Brāhmaṇa* spaghetti," 245
Brij Agarwal, 16
British India, 148, 163
Brown, Dr. Norman, 19, 52
Bruce Scharf. *See:* Scharf, Bruce
Bruce, Lord, 163
Buddha
as preacher, 133
SP quoted on, 128
SP resembling, 115, 121, 160
Buddhists
Bob mistook SP's followers for, 226
& Wally (Umāpati), 113, 114, 268
Building, SP seeking, for temple, 31–33, 39, 41–42, 44, 48, 52, 62–63, 88, 242, 251–53, 265

Bums. *See:* Derelicts
Burton Green. *See:* Green, Burton
Butler, Pennsylvania
description of, 12
SP in, 12–20, 147–48, 194
Butler Eagle newspaper
headlines in, 12
SP story in, 13, 17

C

Caitanya-caritāmṛta
Kṛṣṇadāsa Kavirāja attempting to write, *ix*
SP reading to devotees from, 261–63, 263–64, 265–67, 269–70
as SP's solace at sea, 1, 2–3, 5, 48
Caitanya Mahāprabhu (Gaurāṅga)
Bill dancing like, 155
biography of. *See: Caitanya-caritāmṛta*
chanting Hare Kṛṣṇa introduced by, 212
cited on hearing about Kṛṣṇa, 85
civil disobedience movement of, 197
disciples of, 92n, 119, 262
paintings & pictures of, 63, 71, 107, 111, 112, 119, 121, 141, 150, 163, 185, 228, 230, 244, 245, 261
preaching order of, 121–22
quoted
on becoming spiritual master, 121
on chanting the holy name, 147
on four assets, 61
on Māyāvāda philosophy, 24
Rūpa joined, 262
Sanātana instructed by, 269–70
Sanātana joining, history of, 262–63, 264, 266, 269
saṅkīrtana movement of, 40, 104, 133, 197
Sanskrit school of, 75–76
in South India, 133, 192
spiritual era after advent of, 132
SP bowing to, 230
Caitanya Mahāprabhu
SP carrying out will of, 1, 3, 213, 272
SP dancing like, 258
SP explaining, 61, 242
SP offering ceremony to, 153
SP offering food to, 150, 245
SP's love for, 163
in SP's poem, 4
SP spreading word of, 75, 96, 247
Calcutta
Gaudiya Math branch in, 251
Howard & Keith in, 113, 117
NYC compared to, 174
SP began *Back to Godhead* in, 246
SP leaving, for NYC, 1
in SP's childhood, 148
Camus, 127–28
Candraśekhara, 266
Capātīs, 15, 63, 28, 76, 135, 142, 149, 150, 151, 168, 186, 189, 230
Captain Arun Pandia, 1, 2, 5, 8
wife of, 1, 3
Carl Yeargens. *See:* Yeargens, Carl
Carol Bekar. *See:* Bekar, Carol
Cars passing & Kṛṣṇa's incarnations, analogy of, 118
Catholics, Roman, 76, 77
Ceremony
"bells," 153
for initiation, 182–85, 198–99, 235
for Mukunda's marriage, 188–90
Ceto-darpaṇa-mārjanam
quoted, 215
Ceylon, SP stopped at, 2
Chaitanya. *See:* Caitanya Mahāprabhu
Chanting of Hare Kṛṣṇa
album address on, 257–58
by Allen Ginsberg, 190, 196, 197, 198
Allen Ginsberg quoted on, 218–19
on beads, 154, 155, 176, 179, 261
Bruce quoted on, 160
Caitanya introduced, 212
Caitanya quoted on, 147
consciousness raised by, 199, 202, 212

Chanting of Hare Kṛṣṇa (*continued*)
demigods come for, 240
as greeting, 10
by hippies, 115–17, 224, 237
at initiation ceremony, 182, 183, 184–85
japa, 7, 154, 174
LSD surpassed by, 222–23
meaning of, 212
as meditation, 172
mind cleared by, 119, 214–15
musicians influenced by, 78–79, 209–10, 237–38
peace by, 174
in purity, 180
quoted, 115, 119, 183, 195, 202, 207, 209, 218, 221, 222, 224, 225, 256, 257, 258
result of, 214
saṅkīrtana as, 133, 134
sex trouble avoided by, 239
sixteen rounds daily, *x*, 179
spiritual elevation by, 213, 257
by SP
in Agarwals' home, 14
in Bowery loft, 77–79, 81
Mishra enchanted by, 26
in NYC blackout, 30
at Slippery Rock State College, 18
at Tagore Society, 35
at 26 2nd Ave, 115–17, 123, 125, 146–47, 153, 254, 272
by SP & disciples
at Judson Hall, 240
at recording studio, 256–57
at 2nd Ave storefront, 219–20, 259–60, 261
in Tompkins Square Park, 205, 206–11, 212, 217–19, 225–26, 227, 229
at UN peace vigil, 173–74
in Washington Square Park, 194
SP hopeful of spreading, 192, 225
SP quoted on, 214–15, 220
by SP's disciples
at Love-Pageant-Rally, 223–25

Chanting of Hare Kṛṣṇa
by SP's disciples
on Lower East Side, 206
at New Year's Eve feast, 268
yoga by, 172
See also: ISKCON; *Kīrtanas;* Kṛṣṇa consciousness; *Saṅkīrtana* movement
Charles M. Hoyte's Bowery song, 69
Chaunce, 149–50
Children
on 2nd Ave disturbing SP's lecture, 117–18
sex for begetting, 238, 239
in Tompkins Square Park, 203
China
vs India, 12
SP's plans for, 259
Chinatown, 76, 87–88
Ching, I, 226
Christ, Jesus, 15, 128, 133, 249
Christians, 29, 128
Chuck Barnett. *See:* Barnett, Chuck
Churches, World Council of, cited on America's Vietnam policy, 172
Chutey, Mr, 260–61
City life, 7, 72
See also: New York City; *other cities*
Civilization, human
godlessness in, 194–95
in Kali-yuga, 132
See also: Human beings; Kali-yuga; Sixties
Clark, Dan
after initiation. *See:* Dāmodara
background of, 227–28
initiation considered by, 234–35
quoted on SP, 228, 229, 233
quoted on SP's *Bhāgavatam* cover, 228
SP's influence on, 231–32, 234–35, 264
at SP's Tompkins Square Park *kīrtana*, 228–29, 230
wife of, 228, 230, 234–35
Cochin, 2
Cohen, Harvey
as artist, 68, 71
Caitanya painting by, 111, 112

Cohen, Harvey
 at Paradox restaurant, 64, 65
 quoted on SP, 26, 27, 40, 64
 SP sublet Bowery loft from, 68
Colombo, Sri Lanka, 2, 177
Coltrane, John, 159
Commonwealth Pier, 5, 6, 18
Communism
 checking spread of, 29
 spiritual type of, 129
Conditioned souls
 defects of, *x*
 in material world, 128
 See also: Human beings; Living entity
Consciousness
 chanting Hare Kṛṣṇa raises, 199, 202, 212
 as dovetailed with the Supreme, 82–86
 drug-expanded, 110, 115–16, 204–5
 Kṛṣṇa consciousness expands, 191, 222
 matter pollutes, 257
 platforms of, 212
 See also: Knowledge, transcendental; Kṛṣṇa consciousness; Life; Soul
Corens, Bob
 after initiation. *See:* Rūpānuga
 background of, 226
 chanting & studying *Bhāgavatam*, 231, 232, 233–34
 initiation of, 235
 quoted
  on considering initiation, 233–34
  on spiritual search, 226
  on SP at Tompkins Square Park, 229–30
  on SP's apple distribution, 232
  on SP's teachings, 231
 at SP's Tompkins Square Park *kīrtana*, 227, 229
 wife of, 226, 227, 229, 233
Corens, Eric, 226, 227
Cow, 107, 243
Crane, Hart, 249
Creation, material, sound in, 78–79
Culture. *See:* Civilization, human; Vedic culture

D

Dāl, 15, 87, 135, 142, 149, 150, 186, 189, 244
Dāmodara
 before initiation. *See:* Clark, Dan
 SP changed life of, 264, 265
Dance recital, 28–29
Dancing
 of Bill like Caitanya, 155
 of devotees at 26 2nd Ave, 254
 at initiation ceremony, 185
 at Love-Pageant-Rally *kīrtana*, 224
 of SP, disciples, & engineers at recording studio, 258
 at SP's Ananda Ashram *kīrtana*, 170
 at SP's Tompkins Square Park *kīrtana*, 210–11, 227, 229, 230
 SP taught step in, 170
Dan Clark. *See:* Clark, Dan
Daoud Haroon, quoted on SP, 34–36
David Allen. *See:* Allen, David
Davis, Reverend Garry, 227
De, Gour Mohan, 148
Death, 86, 216–17
 See also: Birth-death cycle
Defects, four, *x*
Deity worship
 by SP in childhood, 148
 SP wanting to introduce, in America, 43, 94
 See also: specific Deities
Delhi
 hippies in, 199
 road from, to Vṛndāvana, 10
Demigods
 come to chant Hare Kṛṣṇa, 240
 See also: specific demigods
Democracy, SP cited on, 169
Derelicts
 on Bowery, 69–70
 & SP, 72, 75, 77, 88, 95, 96, 103, 119, 120–21, 138
Devakī, 180
Devotees of Kṛṣṇa
 accepted as angelic, 237

Devotees of Kṛṣṇa (*continued*)
author's acknowledgments to, *x–xi*, 289
Back to Godhead put together by, 248
chanting on beads with SP, 261
chanting on Lower East Side, 206
dancing in 2nd Ave storefront, 254
devotional service purifies, 138
Heavenly Porridge of, 263
in India chanting on beads, 176, 179
in India observing Janmāṣṭamī, 178
Kṛṣṇa's assurance to, 49
League of, 132
at Love-Pageant-Rally, 223–25
at New Year's Eve feast, 268–69
pleased SP by decorating storefront temple, 140, 141
& Price, 252–53
pure devotees, *ix–x*, *xiv*, 49
recording Hare Kṛṣṇa album, 255–58
SP reading *Caitanya-caritāmṛta* to, 261–63
at SP's Gate Theater talk, 242
at SP's Judson Hall lecture, 240
SP's relationship with, 267–68
at Sunday Love Feasts, 245–46
tenants vs, 219–20, 246, 260
See also: Prabhupāda, followers of; *Sādhus;* Saintly person; Vaiṣṇava
Devotional service to Kṛṣṇa
cooking in, 244
devotee purified by, 138
SP engaging boys in, at 26 2nd Ave, 137–39, 143
See also: Bhakti; Bhakti-yoga; Kṛṣṇa, love for; Kṛṣṇa consciousness
Dharwadkar, A.P., 46
Disciples
of Caitanya, 92n, 119, 262
donation from, to spiritual master, 181
spiritual master as accepted by, 178–79, 269
of SP. *See:* Devotees; Prabhupāda, followers of
Disciplic succession
as authority, *x*
Disciplic succession
SP in, 81, 86, 225
See also: Ācāryas; Spiritual master
Disease, 215, 216
Dog, false God as, 178
Dog barking, SP's storefront lecture disturbed by, 118, 121
Dog can "chant," 257–58
Dog collars, neck beads likened to, 183
Don
decorated 2nd Ave temple, 140
as ISKCON trustee-to-be, 131
prasādam eaten by, 149
as 2nd Ave storefront boarder, 124–25
SP's relationship with, 153–54
Don Nathanson, quoted on SP's audience at Carl's loft, 98
Dreams
by David about Kṛṣṇa consciousness, 73–74
by Howard about SP, 170–71
by Keith about Kṛṣṇa & SP, 171
by SP about Kṛṣṇa, 2
by SP about *saṅkīrtana*, 37
Drugs
Back to Godhead article discrediting, 249–50
at Carl's loft, 99
consciousness-expanding, 110, 115–16, 204–5
Don wouldn't give up, 153–54
& Lower East Side hippies, 110, 115–16
spiritual life doesn't require, 200, 201
SP discredited, 199–202
& SP's Bowery audience, 82
See also: Intoxication; LSD
Drum
bongo, 146, 173, 191, 225, 260
Indian, 254–55
Drunks. *See:* Derelicts
Dubois, Roy
after initiation. *See:* Rāya Rāma
background of, 114

Dubois, Roy
initiation of, 184
as ISKCON trustee-to-be, 131
SP's asides to, during 2nd Ave classes, 118, 123, 154
Steve meeting, 160
Duḥkhālayam aśāśvatam
quoted, 217
Dutch West India Company, 69
Dvārakā, 42
Dwarkadish, Lord, 42
Dylan, Bob, 128

E

East Village, 109, 254
East Village Other article on SP, 191, 221–23, 226, 253
Ed Sanders, 238
Elijah, SP likened to, 38
Emerson, Ralph Waldo, 114, 212–13
Empire State Building, 7, 87
Enjoyment. *See:* Happiness; Pleasure
Epstein, Bill, 114
after initiation. *See:* Ravīndra Svarūpa
description of, 64
initiation as considered by, 181
initiation of, 184
as ISKCON trustee-to-be, 131
quoted on David's breakdown, 97
quoted on SP, 64, 65
SP advised by, to move downtown, 66, 68, 107–8
SP's relationship with, 155–56
Eric Corens, 226, 227
Eva Yeargens, 97, 98–100, 101

F

Fasting on Janmāṣṭamī day, 177, 178, 179
Feast. *See: Prasādam*
Ferber, Mrs, quoted on SP, 39–40
Fighting. *See:* War
Fire sacrifice at initiation ceremony, 182, 184–85, 199
Foerster, Joseph, 8, 68
Food
for humans, 243
offered to Kṛṣṇa. *See: Prasādam*
Forest-living, 72
Franz Kafka, 27, 128, 158
Freedom
from birth-death cycle, 82
Lower East Side hippies sought, 110
in spiritual life, 81
See also: Liberation
Freud, 165
Fugs rock band, 22, 238

G

Gadādhara, 242
Gambling, 10, 99, 182, 265
Gandhi, Mahatma, 173
autobiography of, 164
Bruce's interest in, 158
nonviolence of, 148
Gandhi, Prime Minister Indira, 46–47, 48
Gaṇeśa, 158
Gardiner, Paul, 102–3, 131
Gargamuni
Back to Godhead distributed by, 250
Back to Godhead stapled by, 248
before initiation. *See:* Scharf, Greg
brother of. *See:* Brahmānanda; Scharf, Bruce
press for sale found by, 247
SP changed life of, 264
SP disapproved of hair of, 268
Garry Davis, Reverend, 227
Gate Theater, 242
Gaudiya Math
Calcutta branch of, 251
SP appealing to, for help, 29, 30, 31
Gaurakiśora, 225
Gaurāṅga, Lord. *See:* Caitanya Mahāprabhu

Gāyatrī *mantra*, 54, 152
GBC (Governing Body Commission), *ix*
Georges Ohsawa, 63
German immigrants, 69, 108
Gha, L.K., 47
Ghee, 243, 244, 245
Ginsberg, Allen
  gave harmoniums to devotees, 196, 197, 255
  on Lower East Side, 158, 195
  quoted on chanting Hare Kṛṣṇa, 218–19
  quoted on SP, 105, 196–98
  reputation of, 195
  at 2nd Ave storefront, 157, 195–97, 238
  at SP's Tompkins Square Park *kīrtanas*, 209–10, 225
  on TV chanting Hare Kṛṣṇa, 190
Girl
  long-haired, quoted on chanting, 214
  See also: Woman
God
  chanting about. *See:* Chanting of Hare Kṛṣṇa; *Kīrtanas; Saṅkīrtana* movement
  as creator, maintainer, destroyer, 195
  in *East Village Other* story, 221–22
  hippie claiming to be, 126
  Judy thought she was, 227
  Kṛṣṇa as, 7, 129–30
  love for, *xiv*
  peace based on, 173
  perfection by satisfying, 85
  personal & impersonal views of, 23–25
  pure devotee important as, *xiv*
  spiritual master nondifferent from, 169, 178
  spiritual master represents, 145, 179
  SP never claimed to be, 168, 178–79
  SP's knowledge of, 191, 222, 223
  SP spoke to prove, 128–29
  transcendental sound from, 78–79
  Vaiṣṇava presents, 222
  See also: Absolute Truth; Kṛṣṇa
God consciousness
  SP quoted on, 128
  SP's Tagore Society lecture on, 34, 35
  See also: Kṛṣṇa consciousness
Gold
  Rūpa divided, 262
  & Sanātana's escape, 264, 266
  See also: Money
Goldsmith, Stephen
  as ISKCON's incorporation lawyer, 130–32
  SP explaining sex restrictions to, 238–39
Goodness, forest in, 72
Gopal Agarwal. *See:* Agarwals, Gopal
Gopinath, Lord, 1, 3
Gopīs, 176, 207
Gour Mohan De, 148
Governing Body Commission, *ix*
Govinda, Lord, 1, 3
Govinda Deity, 148
Govinda jaya jaya chant, 238
Grant, Michael
  after initiation. *See:* Mukunda
  background of, 79
  as Carl's friend, 74
  at Carl's loft, 98
  girl friend of. *See:* Jan
  initiation as considered by, 180
  initiation of, 184
  as ISKCON trustee, 131
  quoted on hearing about initiation, 180
  quoted on 2nd Ave storefront, decoration of, 141
  quoted on SP, 79–80, 86–87, 101
  SP helped by, in getting 2nd Ave storefront, 101–3
Green, Burton
  quoted on Kṛṣṇa consciousness influencing musicians, 238
  quoted on SP's 2nd Ave storefront, 241
  SP attended piano recital of, 241–42
Greene, James, 114
  after initiation. *See:* Jagannātha
  at Carl's loft, 98
  initiation of, 184
  ISKCON's letterhead designed by, 173
  as ISKCON trustee, 131

Greene, James
quoted on initiation, 181
quoted on SP, 65
Rādhā-Kṛṣṇa painting by, 139
& SP's 2nd Ave movement, 157
Greenwich Village, 63, 108, 158, 193, 194, 204, 251
Greg Scharf. *See:* Scharf, Greg
Guarino, Stephen
after initiation. *See:* Satsvarūpa
at Ananda Ashram, 167–68
background of, 114, 158–59
initiation as considered by, 177, 181
initiation of, 198
quoted
on bringing mangoes to SP, 137, 138
on buying *Bhāgavatams* from SP, 161–62
on initiation from SP, 177
on meeting Roy & seeing SP, 159–60
on reading *Bhāgavatam* & pleasing SP, 165–66
on SP & him at Ananda Ashram, 168
on SP challenging him, 164–65
on SP serving Sunday feast, 151
saw SP's sign for *Gītā* lectures, 114, 159
SP seeing, in news photo, 174
at SP's morning class, 137
at 26 2nd Ave lunch, 149
Gulābjāmuns, 187, 244–45, 246, 263
Gunther, quoted on SP, 77–78
Guru. See: Spiritual master
Guru-dakṣiṇā defined, 181
Guru Mahārāja. *See:* Bhaktisiddhānta Sarasvatī Ṭhākura

H

Haight-Ashbury, 259, 270
Halavā, 244, 245
Hallucinogens. *See:* Drugs; LSD; Marijuana
Halpern, Irving, quoted on SP & Tompkins Square Park *kīrtana*, 205–6, 208–9
Hanumān, 139–40, 141–42
Happiness
ignorance about, 215, 216
by Kṛṣṇa consciousness, 10, 11
See also: Pleasure
Hare
defined, 212
devotees' chanting of, in recording studio, 257
"Hare Kṛṣṇa Chanters," 255, 257, 258
"Hare Kṛṣṇa explosion," 237
Hare Kṛṣṇa *mantra. See:* Chanting of Hare Kṛṣṇa
Hare Kṛṣṇa movement. *See:* ISKCON
Haridāsa Ṭhākura, 119
Haroon, Daoud, quoted on SP, 34–36
Hart Crane, 249
Hartman, A.M., 41
Harvey Cohen. *See:* Cohen, Harvey
Haṭha-yoga, 27, 79, 158
Hayagrīva
Allen Ginsberg speaking with, at 26 2nd Ave, 196–97
background of, 247
Back to Godhead collated by, 248
as *Back to Godhead's* coeditor, 247, 248–50
before initiation. *See:* Wheeler, Howard
Bhāgavatam preface read in public by, 194–95
East Village Other article read aloud by, 221–23
& "Hare Kṛṣṇa Chanters," 255
Hare Kṛṣṇa handbill produced by, 202
initiation of, 184
at Mukunda's wedding reception, 190
Price flattered, 253
quoted
on feast *prasādam* 245
on "Hare Kṛṣṇa explosion," 237
on LSD vs Kṛṣṇa consciousness, 201
on Sanātana story, 263
on sex once a month, 239
SP asked by, about drugs & spiritual life, 200
SP changed life of, 264, 265
SP gave *Bhāgavatams* to, 250

Hayagrīva (*continued*)
typewriter donated by, to SP's *Gītā* production, 267
"Heavenly Porridge," 263
Hermann Hesse, 113
Hinduism, 165, 213
Hindus, 165, 178
Hindu society
woman's position known in, 55, 56
See also: India; Vedic culture
Hippies, 60
chanting Hare Kṛṣṇa, 115–17, 224, 237
in Haight-Ashbury, 270
in India, 199
at Love-Pageant-Rally, 223–24
on Lower East Side, 108–11, 116, 196, 203–5, 237
of Millbrook commune, 200–201
SP challenged by, 126
in SP's Bowery loft, 82, 89–90
SP's initiates resembled, 182
at SP's uptown lectures, 65–66
at Sunday Love Feast, 246
at Tompkins Square Park, 203–5
at Tompkins Square Park *kīrtana*, 211, 225–26
Hiroshima-bombing anniversary, 172–73
Hitler, 148
Holy place(s)
dedicated to Kṛṣṇa's pastimes, 133, 134, 135
in India, 113
See also: Sacred place; Temple (of Kṛṣṇa); Vṛndāvana
Homosexuals, 129, 158
Hotel keeper & Sanātana Gosvāmī, 264, 266
Hoving's Hill, 218, 223
Howard Smith, quoted on SP, 89–91
Howard Wheeler. *See:* Wheeler, Howard
Hoyte, Charles M., Bowery song by, 69
Human beings
food for, 243
See also: Civilization, human; Conditioned soul; Living entity
Hurta Lurch, quoted on SP, 28
Huxley, Aldous, wife of, cited on places for meditation, 171–72
Hymns, Vedic. *See: Mantras*

I

I Ching, 226
Identity. *See:* Consciousness; Self; Soul
Ignorance
degraded place in, 72
material happiness as, 215, 216
See also: Māyā
Illusion
cited in Mishra-SP debate, 24
of material life, 86
of sexual pleasure, 238, 239
See also: Māyā
Immigrants
on Bowery, 69
on Lower East Side, 108, 109
Immortality, 24
Impersonalism
personalism vs, 23–25
of Śaṅkara, 23, 24, 113
SP opposed, 128–29, 232
See also: Māyāvādīs
India
"*brāhmaṇas*" in, 213
British period in, 148, 163
Bruce's interest in, 157–58, 167
Caitanya in southern part of, 133, 192
devotees in, chanting on beads, 176, 179
devotees in, observing Janmāṣṭamī, 178
hippies in, 199
Howard & Keith in, 113
independence won by, 148
Kṛṣṇa as worshiped in, 58
life in villages of, 134
philosophy of, Westerner's view of, 113
Rāma & Hanumān as worshiped in, 141–42
"*sādhus*" in, 199
2nd Ave temple's decorations from, 139, 140
slides of temples in, SP watching, 169

India
SP comparing NYC summer to, 142
SP got no help from, 46–48, 91–93, 192
vegetarian, 164
See also: Hindu society; Vedic culture
Indian National Army, 148
Initiation, spiritual
chanting requirement for, 176, 179
first request to SP for, 176
four rules for, 180–81, 182
SP conducted, 181–85, 198–99, 235, 260
SP explaining, 176, 178, 179
SP's followers considering, 177, 178–79, 180–81, 233–35
stringing beads for, 179
International Society for Krishna Consciousness. *See:* ISKCON
Intoxication
of Lower East Side hippies, 110
"meditation" by, 113
SP condemns, 10, 99, 180–81, 182, 219, 223, 265
SP's *kīrtanas* "better than," 146
See also: Drugs; LSD
Irish immigrants, 108, 203
Irving Halpern, quoted on SP & Tompkins Square Park *kīrtana*, 205–6, 208–9
ISKCON (International Society for Krishna Consciousness)
author's acknowledgments to, *x–xi*
charter of, 132–34, 193
incorporation of, 129–34, 156
Love Feasts by, 243
name of, 129–30
preaching by, 133–34
printing presses obtained by, 247
purposes of, seven listed, 132–34
SP desiring to expand, 193
SP founded, 89, 93, 102–4, 129–35, 142–43, 260, 267
SP protected, 154
SP's biography commissioned by, *ix*
stationery for, 173
trustees of, 102–3, 131, 173
26 2nd Ave as beginning of, 134, 135, 260
ISKCON
See also: Chanting of Hare Kṛṣṇa; Kṛṣṇa consciousness; *Saṅkīrtana* movement
"ISKCON bullets," 244–45, 263
Italy, Little, 88
Iyer, Easwara, 48

J

Jadurāṇī
before initiation. *See:* Koslofsky, Judy
at breakfast in storefront, 263
initiation of, 235
paintings by, 261
SP changed life of, 264, 265
SP's incidents with, 267–68
Jagāi and Mādhāi, 93
Jagannātha
Back to Godhead's cover designed by, 248
before initiation. *See:* Greene, James
initiation of, 184
at Love-Pageant-Rally *kīrtana*, 224
quoted on chanting in public with SP, 194
Jagannātha Purī, 148
Jail keeper, Sanātana bribed, 264
Jaipur, 94
Jaladuta steamship, SP aboard, 1–8, 48
James Greene. *See:* Greene, James
Jan
after initiation. *See:* Janakī
initiation of, 184
as ISKCON trustee, 131
Mike convinced, to take initiation, 180
quoted on SP, 88
restless during Janmāṣṭamī fast, 179
Janakī
before initiation. *See:* Jan
initiation of, 184
marriage of, 185–90
& Mukunda on West Coast, 259
quoted on SP's cooking, 190
quoted on wedding *sārī*, 188
sister of, 186–88, 189

Janārdana, 184
Janitor stole from SP, 67, 68
Janmāṣṭamī festival
  SP & followers observing, 177–78
  SP observing, aboard *Jaladuta*, 2, 177
Janos, 184
Japa, chanting, 7, 154, 174
"Jaya Rādhe!" greeting, 10
Jeep, US Army, 12
"Jesus, Swami," 17
Jesus Christ, 15, 128, 133, 249
Jewish immigrants, 69, 108
Jewish Providential Bank building, 251
Jhansi, India, 132
Joan (Janakī's sister), 186–88, 189
Joan Suval. *See:* Suval, Joan
John Coltrane, 159
Joseph Foerster, 8, 68
Judson Hall, 239–40
Judy Koslofsky. *See:* Koslofsky, Judy

K

Kacaurīs, 151, 188, 190
Kafka, Franz, 27, 128, 158
Kali-yuga (present Age)
  golden Age in, 44, 132
  hippie revolt in, 111
  symptoms of, 44
  See also: Civilization, godlessness in; Sixties
Kallman, Alan
  & SP at 26 2nd Ave, 253–54
  at SP's recording session, 257, 258
  wife of, quoted on SP, 254
Kaṁsa, King, 180
Kaṇṭhi-mālā (neck beads), 7, 183
Karlāpati
  before initiation. *See:* Yeargens, Carl
  initiation of, 184
Karma-yoga, 81
Kavirāja Gosvāmī, Kṛṣṇadāsa, quoted on *Caitanya-caritāmṛta*, attempting to write, *ix*
Keith
  after initiation. *See:* Kīrtanānanda
  at Ananda Ashram, 168, 169, 171
  apartment shared by, 112, 113
  asking SP about Caitanya painting, 141
  asking SP about temple at Ananda Ashram, 168
  asking SP for initiation, 176
  background of, 113, 114
  beads bought by, 176
  cooking for SP, 135, 149
  cooking lunch at 26 2nd Ave, 149–50, 176
  cooking with SP for Larry Bogart, 174
  eating *prasādam*, 151
  in hospital, 178, 181
  in India, 113
  initiation of, 198
  paintings & prints hung by, in storefront temple, 139
  prasādam served by, at Ananda Ashram, 168
  quoted on accepting initiation from SP, 178
  quoted on dream about Kṛṣṇa & SP, 171
  quoted on SP, 135, 136, 169
  SP's dance named by, 170
  at SP's morning class, 136, 137
  as SP's serious follower, 135
  Stanley's blunder discovered by, 175
Kempis, Thomas à, 114
Kennedy, President John F., 158
Khādī defined, 125
Kicharī, 2, 3
King Kaṁsa, 180
Kīrtanānanda
  before initiation. *See:* Keith
  at breakfast, 263
  devotees admonished by, at Sunday feast, 246
  hearing *New York Times* article, 217–19
  hearing SP speak in Tompkins Square Park, 212
  initiation of, 198
  & ISKCON's first printing presses, 247
  "Love Feast" named by, 242
  at Love-Pageant-Rally *kīrtana*, 224

Kīrtanānanda
  prasādam served by, to storefront guests, 214
  quoted on hearing *Caitanya-caritāmṛta*, 263
  quoted on SP, 221
  robes worn by, 205, 211
  shaven-headed, 205, 224
  SP alarmed & amazed, 259
  SP changed life of, 264
  as SP's apartment caretaker, 271
  as SP's attendant, 259, 263
  SP teaching cooking to, 242, 243, 244, 245
  tamboura played by, at recording studio, 256
Kīrtanas
  by Allen Ginsberg, 190, 196
  by SP & followers
    at Ananda Ashram, 170
    in Bowery loft, 71, 72, 75, 77–81
    in Carl's loft, 98
    in 2nd Ave storefront, 115–17, 123, 146–47, 153, 156–57, 160, 191, 219–20, 222, 231, 232, 238, 254–55
    in Tompkins Square Park, 205, 206–11, 212, 227, 229
    in Washington Square Park, 194
  by SP's disciples at Love-Pageant-Rally, 223–24
  on TV, 190
  See also: Chanting of Hare Kṛṣṇa; *Saṅkīrtana* movement
Knowledge, transcendental, 57, 86, 146, 226
  See also: Absolute Truth; Philosophy
Koran, 35, 264
Korea, dog-eating in, 243
Koslofsky, Judy
  after initiation. *See:* Jadurāṇī
  background of, 227
  initiation of, 235
  painting for SP, 232
  SP agreeing to initiate, 234
  SP meeting, 230–31
  SP's classes attended by, 232
Koslofsky, Judy
  at SP's Tompkins Square Park *kīrtana*, 227, 230
Kṛṣṇa, Lord (Supreme Personality of Godhead)
  activity done for, 137–38
  appearance day of, 2, 177, 178, 180
  & Arjuna in *Gītā*, 53, 56, 80, 82–83, 84, 117, 119, 133, 171
  as authority, *ix*, *x*, 128
  Bhāgavatam glorifies, 166
  cited on great man's example, 197
  consciousness expansion via, 181, 222
  depending on, 97
  devotees of. *See:* Devotees
  devotional service to. *See:* Devotional service
  as God, 7, 129–30
  gopīs devoted to, 176
  in Hare Kṛṣṇa *mantra*, 212
  hearing about, 85
  impersonalists misunderstand, 24
  incarnations of, 118
  India worships, 58
  love for, Caitanya taught, 75–76, 262, 270
  material world forgetful of, 240
  parents of, 180
  pastimes of, place dedicated to, 133, 134, 135
  quoted
    on becoming saintly soon, 120
    on depending on Him, 97
    on devotee never perishing, 49
    on impersonalists, 24
    on seeing Him everywhere, 49
    on surrender to Him, 32
    on Vedānta's goal, 128
  Rādhārāṇī &, 198, 207
  as Rāma, 212
  Śaṅkara accepted, 25
  soul part & parcel of, 133
  spiritual master as representative of, 137
  SP as representative of, 81, 85–86, 100, 137, 171, 267
  SP defended, 143

Kṛṣṇa, Lord (*continued*)
SP interested in, not himself, *xiv*
SP lecturing on, 53, 56, 58
SP moved by will of, 110–11, 271
SP quoted on, 128
SP received men & money from, 192
in SP's calendar picture, 107
SP's dependence on, 47–48, 49, 72, 96–97, 132
in SP's dream, 2
as SP's friend, 4–5, 7
SP's poems to, aboard ship, 3–4, 5–6
SP telling birth of, 180
SP worshiped, in childhood, 148
as Supreme Consciousness, 82, 83
surrender to, 32
temple of. *See:* Temple (of Kṛṣṇa)
transcendental, 25
as Vedānta's goal, 128
writing by permission of, *ix–x*
See also: God; Viṣṇu, Lord
Kṛṣṇa-bhaktas. See: Devotees; Vaiṣṇava
Kṛṣṇa-bhakti. See: Bhakti; Bhakti-yoga
Kṛṣṇa-bhakti-rasa-bhāvita
quoted, 130
Kṛṣṇa consciousness
basic principle of, 143
beginners in, 180
as Bhaktisiddhānta's mission, 31
Blake quotation reflecting, 249
Caitanya giving, to disciple, 262
consciousness expansion by, 191, 222
David's dreams of, 73–74
defined, 130
devotees decorating 2nd Ave temple as, 140
for everyone, 213
Haight-Ashbury ready for, 259, 270
handbill promoting, 202
happiness by, 10, 11
hearing about SP as, 267
as highest consciousness, 199–202
love as, 138
on Lower East Side, 237, 272
LSD inferior to, 199–202
Kṛṣṇa consciousness
man & wife in, 189
miseries cured by, 110
preaching of. *See:* Preaching
saintliness by, 120
SP didn't compromise, 82–84, 238, 239
SP's disciples struggling for, 265
as SP's mission, *xiii*, 5–7, 20, 28, 54, 58, 72, 100, 119, 121–22, 126, 128–29, 190, 192–93, 212–13, 246–47
Sunday feast for bringing people to, 246
See also: Bhakti; Bhakti-yoga; Devotional service; Kṛṣṇa, love for
Kṛṣṇa consciousness movement. *See:* ISKCON; *Saṅkīrtana* movement
"Kṛṣṇa dāsa," 176
Kṛṣṇadāsa Kavirāja Gosvāmī, quoted on *Caitanya-caritāmṛta*, attempting to write, *ix*
Kṛṣṇa-prasādam. See: Prasādam
Kṣipraṁ bhavati dharmātmā
quoted, 120
Kumbha-melā festival, 195
Kupferberg, Tuli, 223, 238
Kurukṣetra war, 83, 133, 171

L

Lafayette, Marquis de, 252
Lalitā-śrī-viśākhānvitāṁś ca
quoted, 256
Lanka, Sri, 2
Larry Bogart, 173, 174–75
Larsen, Professor Allen, quoted on SP, 17–18
Lawyer's interpretation, example of, 131
League of Devotees, 132
League of Nations, 133
Leary, Dr Timothy, 128, 191, 200, 222, 226
Liberation
impersonal, 24
See also: Freedom
Life
illusory, 86
in Indian villages, 134

Life
  spiritual. *See:* Spiritual life
  in three modes, 72
  See also: Consciousness; Living entity; Soul
Lifetime in Preparation, xiii
Lions Club, 17, 52
Literature, transcendental
  ISKCON to print & distribute, 133, 134
  writing of, *ix–x*
  See also: Vedas; Vedic literature; *specific Vedic literatures*
Little Italy, 88
Living entity
  identity of, 269
  as Kṛṣṇa conscious originally, 257
  purification of, 180
  See also: Conditioned souls; Human beings; Life; Soul
Loft-living, 71
Lon Solomon, quoted on SP, 126–27
Lord Bruce, 163
Lord Caitanya. *See:* Caitanya Mahāprabhu
Love
  as Kṛṣṇa consciousness, 138
  See also: Bhakti; God, love for; Kṛṣṇa, love for; Marriage
Love-and-peace movement, 82, 84, 204, 216, 224, 225
"Love Feast," 242–43, 245–46
Love-Pageant-Rally, 223–25
Lower East Side
  Allen Ginsberg in, 158, 195
  Brahmānanda & Gargamuni distributing *Back to Godhead* in, 250
  devotees chanting in, 206
  hippies in, 108–11, 116, 196, 203–5, 237
  history of, 108, 109
  Kṛṣṇa consciousness in, 237, 272
  Paradox restaurant in, 63–66
  poets & musicians in, 158
  SP in, *xiii*, 105, 110–11, 116, 117, 126, 136, 142–43, 145–47, 182, 190, 199–202, 272
  Steve in, 158–59
LSD
  & Allen Ginsberg, 195
  & Bruce, 158
  chanting Hare Kṛṣṇa surpasses, 222–23
  & Chuck, 158, 164
  & David, 73, 94–95, 96, 97, 101
  & Judy, 227, 230, 231
  Kṛṣṇa consciousness surpasses, 199–202
  & Leary & Alpert, 200
  Love-Pageant-Rally celebrated, 223
  & Lower East Side hippies, 110, 115–16, 126
  & Mott St boys, 113, 114
  rise in use of, 39
  SP discredited, 129, 199–202
  SP's disciples abstained from, 237
  SP's *kīrtanas* "better than," 146
  & Steve, 158–59
Lurch, Hurta, quoted on SP, 28

M

Macrobiotics, 63, 64, 186, 190
Madana-mohana temple, *ix*
Madhva, 23
Mahā-mantra. See: Chanting of Hare Kṛṣṇa
Malhotra, Mr, 39
Mangoes
  man with, story of, 240
  in NYC, 37
  Steve brought, to SP, 137, 138
Manhattan. *See:* New York City
"Mantra Rock Dance," 270
Mantras
  Gāyatrī, 54, 152
  Hare Kṛṣṇa. *See:* Chanting of Hare Kṛṣṇa
  of purification, 183
  as transcendental sound, 78
Marijuana
  Don wouldn't give up, 153–54
  spiritual search with, 110
  See also: Drugs; LSD
"Mārkine Bhāgavata-dharma" poem, 5–6

Marquis de Lafayette, 252
Marriage
  in Kṛṣṇa consciousness, 189
  of Mukunda & Janakī, 185–90
  sex in, 238–39
  woman in, sign of, 55, 56
Marx, Karl, 129
Masāla, 243
Matchless Gifts store, 102, 104, 106, 114, 158, 159, 214
  See also: Second Avenue, twenty-six
Materialism
  in America, 10
  hippies rejected, 109, 110
  See also: Atheism; Impersonalism
Materialists, 260
  See also: Māyāvādīs
Material world
  conditioned souls in, 128
  Kṛṣṇa forgotten in, 240
  miseries of, 215–17
  sex in, 165, 238, 239
  See also: Māyā; Universe(s)
Matter
  consciousness polluted by, 257
  See also: Material world
Māyā
  defined, 24
  four rules for fighting, 265
  "ISKCON bullets" vs, 244–45
  lures of, 250
  prasādam dispels, 150–51
  See also: Illusion; Material world; Matter
Māyāvādī kṛṣṇa-aparādhī
  quoted, 24
Mayāvādīs
  philosophy of, 24, 143
  SP wanted to counteract, 32
  See also: Atheism; Impersonalism; Materialists; Scholars
Meat-eating
  at Agarwals', 16
  SP condemned, 10, 99, 100, 181, 182, 265
  war due to, 239
  in Western world, 38, 243
Meditation
  at Ananda Ashram, 26–27, 169
  chanting Hare Kṛṣṇa as, 172
  by intoxication, 113
  places for, 171–72
  in SP's Bowery loft, 77, 78, 79, 89–90
  See also: Consciousness; Mind
Mehra, Paramananda, 21
Mental speculators, 128
  See also: Māyāvādīs; Scholars
Metaphysics. *See:* Absolute Truth; Knowledge, transcendental; Soul
Michael Grant. *See:* Grant, Michael
Millbrook commune members vs SP, 200–201
Mind
  chanting Hare Kṛṣṇa clears, 119, 214–15
  See also: Consciousness; Meditation
Mini Sharma, 18
Minuit, Peter, 69
Miseries
  Kṛṣṇa consciousness cures, 110
  in material world, 215–17
  of NYC snowstorm, 57
Mishra, Dr Ramamurti
  background of, 22
  as Māyāvādī, 24, 25
  quoted on SP, 22, 26
  as Śaṅkara's follower, 21, 22, 23, 24, 27
  SP at Ananda Ashram of, 26–28, 167–71, 172
  SP at apartment of, 21–23
  SP at *yoga* studio of, 23, 25, 30, 40, 51, 52, 60, 64, 65
  SP given coat by, 38
  SP quoted on, 21, 57–58
  SP's philosophical difference with, 21, 23–25, 26, 27
  SP's temple offer from, 168
  SP welcomed by, 21
  student of, impressed by SP's followers, 172
Modern age. *See:* Kali-yuga; Sixties
Modes, life in three, 72
Money
  India wouldn't send, for SP's mission, 46–48

Money
SP in charge of, at 26 2nd Ave, 175–76
of SP on American arrival, 8
See also: Gold
Monism. *See:* Impersonalism
Morarji, Sumati
SP's correspondence with, 9, 19, 28–29, 32–34, 37, 47, 53, 91, 93
SP's ship accommodations arranged by, 1
Mott Street boys. *See:* Keith; Wally; Wheeler, Howard
Mukti Brahmacārī, 92, 93
Mukti defined, 24
See also: Freedom
Mukunda
before initiation. *See:* Grant, Michael
initiation of, 184
marriage of, 185–90
in San Francisco, 259, 270
SP's letters from, 259, 270–71
Mulliks, 148
Mūṅg beans, 245
Musical instruments
at Love-Pageant-Rally *kīrtana*, 225
at Mike's apartment, 102
of SP & devotees at recording studio, 255–56, 257, 258
at SP's Ananda Ashram *kīrtana*, 170
in SP's Bowery loft *kīrtanas*, 77, 78, 79
at SP's Tompkins Square Park *kīrtana*, 208–9
at storefront *kīrtanas*, 146
Musicians
Hare Kṛṣṇa chanting influenced, 237–38
at Mike's apartment, 102
& SP at Carl's loft, 98
at SP's Bowery loft *kīrtanas*, 78–79, 80
at SP's Tompkins Square Park *kīrtana*, 208–9
Muslims, 178, 262

N

Nama oṁ viṣṇu-pādāya kṛṣṇa-preṣṭhāya quoted, 183
Nanda Mahārāja, 180
Nārada, 166, 240
Nārada-bhakti-sutra, 168
Nārāyaṇa, Lord, 25
Nārāyaṇaḥ paro 'vyaktāt quoted, 25
Nathanson, Don, quoted on SP's audience at Carl's loft, 98
Nawab Shah, 262–63
Neal, 267
Nelson, Robert
cymbal donated by, 146
description of, 60, 61, 62
quoted on Mishra & SP, 25
quoted on SP, 60, 61–62, 63
rug donated by, 140, 205
in SP's Bowery loft, 72, 74
SP's relationship with, 61, 62, 157, 181
New Amsterdam, 69
Newspaper items
in *Butler Eagle*, 12, 13
in *East Village Other*, 191, 221–23, 226, 253
in *New York Post*, 174
in *New York Times*, 39, 217–19
underground, 199
in *Village Voice*, 102, 129, 225
New Year's Eve feast, 268–69
New York City
bhakti sprouting in, 141
blackout in, 30
Bowery. *See:* Bowery
Chinatown, 76, 87–88
compared to Calcutta, 174
compared to India, 142
crime in, 67, 68, 70
loft-living in, 71
Lower East Side. *See:* Lower East Side
as New Amsterdam, 69
SP during blackout in, 30
SP during summer in, 117–18, 142, 260
SP during winter in, 37–38, 43–44, 48, 147, 255, 260, 272
SP leaving, for San Francisco, 271–72
SP's consciousness not limited to, 49, 51, 54–55, 59, 72, 134–35, 271

New York City (*continued*)
SP's ship arrival in, 7–8
SP struggling in, 37–39, 43–44, 48
SP walking in, *xiii*, 25–26, 37–38, 43–44, 48, 87–88, 103–4, 251–52, 255
26 2nd Ave. *See:* Second Avenue, twenty-six
New York Post, picture in, of SP & followers at UN, 174
New York Times
Allen Ginsberg refusing interview with, 210
in *East Village Other* story, 221–22
headlines in, 39
Tompkins-Square-chanting article in, 217–19
Nietzsche, 128
Nikhilananda, Swami, 29, 38
Nineteen-sixties. *See:* Sixties
Nityānanda, Lord, 61, 93, 242
Norman Brown, Dr, 19, 52

O

Ohsawa, Georges, 63
Old age, 216–17
Oṁ apavitraḥ pavitro vā
verse quoted, 183
Orlovsky, Peter, 195, 196, 209

P

Padampat Singhania. *See:* Singhania, Sir Padampat
Padyāvalī, quoted on Kṛṣṇa consciousness, 130
Pamela Agarwal, 17
Pañca-tattva, 185, 242
Pandia, Captain Arun, 1, 2, 5, 8
Pandia, Mrs, 1, 3
Paradox restaurant, 63–65, 72, 108, 114
Paramananda Mehra, 21
Passion
city in, 72
for sense gratification, 10
Paul VI, Pope, 172
Peace
by chanting Hare Kṛṣṇa, 174, 225
ISKCON's preaching to bring, 133–34
in SP's war example, 82–84
UN vigil for, 173–74
Peace-and-love movement, 82, 84, 204, 216, 224, 225
Pennsylvania, SP's stay in, 11–20
Perfection, 83, 85
Peter Minuit, 69
Peter Orlovsky, 195, 196, 209
Peter Stuyvesant, 69, 108
Philadelphia, SP in, 19, 20
Philosophy
hodgepodge, 113–14
of Kṛṣṇa consciousness, SP didn't compromise, 82–84, 238, 239
of Lower East Side hippies, 110
Māyāvāda, 24, 143
personal vs impersonal, 23–25
SP talking, at 26 2nd Ave, 127–29, 143, 147, 163–65
See also: Absolute Truth; Knowledge, transcendental
Pittsburgh, SP arriving in, 11
Planets
Kṛṣṇa's incarnations on, 118
See also: Material world; Universe(s)
Planting the Seed, *xiii*
Pleasure
impure, 180
of sex, 238, 239
See also: Happiness
Poems by SP, 3–4, 5–6, 18, 96
Polish people, 108, 109, 210, 211
Pope Paul VI, 172
Port Said, 2

Prabhupāda, Śrīla (A.C. Bhaktivedanta Swami)
Absolute Truth as presented by, 56, 83–84, 129, 231
Acyutānanda's life changed by, 264, 265
Agarwals' consideration of, 194
at Agarwals' home, 12–17, 20
Agarwals perplexed by arrival of, 11, 12
age of, *xiii*, 1, 2, 191, 192, 212, 219
& Alan Kallman, 253–54, 257, 258
Alan Kallman's wife quoted on, 254
Allen Ginsberg quoted on, 105, 196–98
Allen Larsen quoted on, 17–18
in America chanting in public, 194–95
American arrival of, *xiii*, 5–8, 10
in America preaching, 96, 126–29, 238–39
in America struggling, 21–49
America's unhappy youths as seen by, 110
America's ways interested, 16
at Ananda Ashram, 26–28, 167–71, 172
Atlantic Ocean crossing by, 2, 3, 96
as author's spiritual master, *xi*
Back to Godhead founded by, 246–47, 249
Back to Godhead given over to disciples by, 247, 250
at *Back to Godhead's* first ISKCON printing, 248
beads for chanting introduced by, 176, 179
Bhāgavatam classes by, in Bowery loft, 72
Bhāgavatam edition by, 268
Bhāgavatam preaching wanted by, 33
Bhāgavatam read by, 185
Bhāgavatams sold by, 8, 36, 39–40, 46, 60–61, 161–62
Bhāgavatam translated by, 27, 28, 72, 75, 76, 125–26, 147, 151, 152, 247, 259, 272
& Bhaktisiddhānta. *See:* Bhaktisiddhānta Sarasvatī Ṭhākura
Bill advised, to move downtown, 66, 68
Bill quoted on, 64, 65
Bill's relationship with, 155–56
"biographers" would not understand, *x*
birthday of, 2
Bob quoted on, 229–30, 231, 232, 234

Prabhupāda, Śrīla
& Bogart (Larry), 173, 174–75
Bon Mahārāja's correspondence with, 42–43
bookstores solicited by, 39–40
in Boston, 5–7, 96
Bowery left by, for 2nd Ave, 103–4
in Bowery loft, 67–95
Brahmānanda asked by, to speak to angry tenant, 220
Brahmānanda at Jewish bank building with, 251
Brahmānanda got drum from guest for, 254–55
Brahmānanda handed fifty-cent piece by, 233
Brahmānanda learning cooking from, 242, 243, 244, 245
Brahmānanda quoted on, 237, 255, 271
Brahmānanda's "intimate" instructions from, 268
Brahmānanda's life changed by, 264
& Brahmānanda's mother, 240
Brahmānanda's relationship with, 241–42
Brahmānanda walking with, to Tompkins Square Park, 205, 206
at Brown's Sanskrit class, 19, 52
Bruce asked, about meditation, 172
Bruce drove, from Ananda Ashram to 2nd Ave apartment, 171–72
& Bruce during Stanley's suicide request, 176
Bruce quoted on, 160, 163, 165, 166–67, 168
Buddha-like, 115, 121, 160
building sought by, for temple, 31–33, 39, 41–42, 44, 48, 52, 62–63, 88, 242, 251–53, 265
at Burton Green's piano recital, 241–42
on bus to Pittsburgh, 9–11
in Butler, Pa, 12–20, 147–48, 194
Butler Eagle article on, 13, 17
Caitanya-caritāmṛta read to devotees by, 261–63, 263–64, 265–67, 269–70
Caitanya-caritāmṛta solaced, at sea, 1, 2–3, 5, 48

Prabhupāda, Śrīla (*continued*)
Caitanya explained by, 61, 242
Caitanya in poem of, 4
Caitanya loved by, 163
Caitanya's message to be spread by, 247
Caitanya's will done by, 1, 3, 213, 272
Caitanya worshiped by, 230
as "Calcutta man," 206
Carl drifted from, 156, 157
Carl helped, to get 2nd Ave storefront, 101–3
Carl helped, to incorporate ISKCON, 130, 156
Carl quoted on, 74–75, 77, 100
in Carl's loft, 97–100, 101
Carol quoted on, 76–77, 79
Carol uninterested in 2nd Ave scene of, 156–57
chanting
in Agarwals' home, 14
at Ananda Ashram, 26
in Bowery loft, 77–79, 81
at initiation ceremony, 183, 184–85
at Judson Hall, 240
in NYC blackout, 30
at recording studio, 256–57, 258
at Slippery Rock State College, 18
at Tagore Society, 35
in Tompkins Square Park, 205, 206–11, 212, 217–19, 225–26, 227, 229
at 26 2nd Ave, 115–17, 123, 125, 136–37, 146–47, 153, 219–20, 259–60, 261, 272
at UN peace vigil, 173–74
in Washington Square Park, 194
See also: Prabhupāda, *kīrtanas* by
chanting's spreading wanted by, 192, 225
childhood of, 148
childlike, 22–23
Chuck quoted on, 137, 160–61, 162, 163–64, 166
& Chutey, 260–61
cited
on *Bhāgavatam's* preaching potential, 29
on Christian missions, 29

Prabhupāda, Śrīla
cited
on God consciousness, 35
on great man's example, 197
on his spiritual master, 134–35
on lion tamers & tiger-wrestling, 168
on Love Feasts, 243
on Pañca-tattva, 242
on spiritual master, 268
on woman, 99
See also: Prabhupāda, lectures by, preaching, quoted
in Colombo, 2
at Commonwealth Pier, 18
compassion of, 10
cooking
in Agarwals' home, 15, 16
in Bowery loft, 76
in Carl's loft, 98, 100
for initiation ceremony, 181
on *Jaladuta* ship, 2, 3
for Larry Bogart, 174
at Mishra's, 22, 25, 28
for Sunday feast, 151, 242–45
at 26 2nd Ave, 135, 142
for wedding feast, 187–88
daily activities of, 25, 85, 125
Dāmodara's life changed by, 264, 265
at dance recital, 28–29
dance step taught by, 170
dancing at initiation ceremony, 185
dancing at recording studio, 258
Dan influenced by, 231–32, 234–35, 264
Dan quoted on, 228, 229, 233
Daoud Haroon quoted on, 34–36
David quoted on, 66, 73–74
David shared Bowery loft with, 68, 73–74, 94–95, 101
David's relationship with, 73–74, 94–95, 96, 101
democracy criticized by, 169
derelicts &, 72, 75, 77, 88, 95, 96, 103, 119, 120–21, 138
devotional service taught by, at 26 2nd Ave, 137–38, 143
diary entries by, 1–3

Prabhupāda, Śrīla
disappearance of, *ix*
disciples of. *See:* Devotees; Prabhupāda, followers of
in disciplic succession, 81, 86, 225
& Don, 124–25, 153–54
Don Nathanson quoted on, 98
dreaming of Kṛṣṇa, 2
dreaming of *saṅkīrtana*, 37
dress of, *xiii*, 7, 38, 43, 62, 88, 89, 112, 125, 150, 153, 160, 161, 161–62, 193, 206–7, 219, 255, 272
drugs discredited by, 199–202
drumming
in Bowery loft, 79
at recording session, 256, 257, 258
in 2nd Ave temple, 146, 191, 254, 255, 260
in Tompkins Square Park, 208, 209, 210, 211, 212, 225, 227, 229, 262
East Village Other article on, 191, 221–23, 226, 253
eating at Ananda Ashram, 167–68
eating at Mishra's apartment, 22
eating at 26 2nd Ave, 150–51, 191, 246, 268
electrician friend of, 68, 69, 103
Elijah-like, 38
English as spoken by, 53, 55, 63
essays by, 250
& Eva, 98–100, 101
expert, 256
father of, 148
fearless, 206
Ferber quoted on, 39–40
& Foerster, 8, 68
followers of
author's acknowledgments to, *ix*, *x*, *xi*, 289
chanting with him in Tompkins Square Park, 207–8
depended on him, 265
dress of, 173
initiation as considered by, 177, 180–81
at Love-Pageant-Rally, 223–25
Mishra's student impressed by, 172

Prabhupāda, Śrīla
followers of
prayer recited by, 183
relationship with him, 267–68
speculating about him, 168–69
at storefront morning class, 261
See also: Devotees
Forty-second Street building, 62–63
frugal, 175
Gardiner named by, as ISKCON trustee, 102–3
Gargamuni's hair disapproved of by, 268
Gargamuni's life changed by, 264
at Gate Theater, 242
Gāyatrī *mantra* recited by, 152
Gītā commentary by, 177–78, 250, 267, 272
Gītā lectures by, at 26 2nd Ave, 111, 114, 117–23, 127, 135, 136–37, 164, 177–78
Gītā lectures by, in 72nd St room (307), 52, 53–58, 65
glasses worn by, 262
Godbrothers didn't help, 47, 91, 92–93, 192, 272
Godhood claim never made by, 168, 178–79
God known by, 129, 191, 222, 223
as God's representative, 267
Goldsmith hearing sex restrictions from, 238–39
Goldsmith helped, to incorporate ISKCON, 130–32
as good man, 18, 23
Gopal as sponsor of, 8, 11
Gopal drove, from Pittsburgh to Butler, 11–12
Gopal quoted on, 15
Gopal saw off, 20
Greg quoted on, 200, 202
Gunther quoted on, 77–78
happy days for, 142, 191–92
Hartman's letter from, 41
Harvey quoted on, 26, 27, 40, 64
Harvey sublet Bowery loft to, 68
Hayagrīva asking, about drugs & spiritual life, 200

Prabhupāda, Śrīla (*continued*)
Hayagrīva given *Bhāgavatams* by, 250
Hayagrīva's life changed by, 264, 265
health of, 1–3, 19, 142, 191–92, 259
heart disorders suffered by, 2, 5, 7, 259
"Hindu" explained by, 165
hippie challenged, 126
Howard asking, about Hanumān picture, 141
Howard asking, about spiritual master, 145, 178–79
Howard quoted on, 112, 114, 169, 170–71
Howard's dream about, 170–71
Howard's first meeting with, 112, 114–15
Howard typed *Bhāgavatam* manuscripts for, 138–39
Howard Smith quoted on, 89–91
Hurta Lurch quoted on, 28
impersonalism opposed by, 232
India didn't help, 46–48, 91–93, 192
& Indira Gandhi, 46–47
initiation explained by, 176, 178, 179
initiations conducted by, 181–85, 198–99, 260
interested in Kṛṣṇa, not himself, *xiv*
intoxication condemned by, 10, 99, 180–81, 182, 219, 223, 265
Irving Halpern quoted on, 205–6, 208–9
ISKCON founded by, 89, 93, 102–4, 129–35, 142–43, 260, 267
ISKCON protected by, 154
ISKCON's expansion desired by, 193
Iyer's letter to, 48
Jadurāṇī's incidents with, 267–68
Jadurāṇī's life changed by, 264, 265
Jadurāṇī's painting pleased, 261
Jagannātha appreciating chanting in public with, 194
on *Jaladuta* ship, *xiii*, 1–8, 48
James drifted from, 157
James quoted on, 65
Janakī married to Mukunda by, 185–90
janitor stole from, 67, 68
Janmāṣṭamī observed by, aboard *Jaladuta*, 2, 177
Janmāṣṭamī observed by, with followers, 177–78

Prabhupāda, Śrīla
Jan quoted on, 88
japa chanting introduced by, 154
& Joan (Janakī's sister), 186–88, 189
Joan Suval quoted on, 22–23
joke at expense of, followers unamused by, 169
at Judson Hall, 239–40
Judy attended classes of, 232
Judy meeting, 230–31
Judy painting for, 232
Judy requesting initiation from, 234
Keith asking, about Caitanya painting, 141
Keith asking, about temple at Ananda Ashram, 168
Keith asking, for initiation, 176
Keith as serious follower of, 135
Keith cooked for, 135
Keith quoted on, 135, 136, 169
Keith's dream about, 171
Kīrtanānanda alarmed and amazed by, 259
Kīrtanānanda as apartment caretaker for, 271
Kīrtanānanda as attendant of, 259, 263
Kīrtanānanda learning cooking from, 242, 243, 244, 245
Kīrtanānanda quoted on, 221
Kīrtanānanda's life changed by, 264
kīrtanas by
at Ananda Ashram, 26, 170
in Bowery loft, 71, 72, 75, 77–81
at Carl's loft, 98
in 2nd Ave temple, 115–17, 123, 146–47, 153, 156–57, 160, 191, 219–20, 222, 231, 232, 254–55
in Tompkins Square Park, 205, 206–11, 212, 227, 229
in Washington Square Park, 194
See also: Prabhupāda, chanting
Kṛṣṇa conscious mission of, *xiii*, 5–7, 20, 28, 54, 58, 72, 100, 119, 122–22, 126, 128–29, 190, 192–93, 212–13, 246–47
"Kṛṣṇa consciousness" rendered by, 130
Kṛṣṇa defended by, 143
Kṛṣṇa depended upon by, 47–48, 49, 72, 96–97, 132

Prabhupāda, Śrīla
Kṛṣṇa in dream of, 2
Kṛṣṇa's birth told by, 180
Kṛṣṇa sent men & money to, 192
as Kṛṣṇa's friend, 4–5, 7
Kṛṣṇa's picture hung by, 107
as Kṛṣṇa's preacher, 271
as Kṛṣṇa's representative, 81, 85–86, 100, 137, 171
Kṛṣṇa's will moved, 110–11, 271
lectures by
at Ananda Ashram, 169
in *Back to Godhead*, 249
on *Bhagavad-gītā*, 114, 117–22, 130–31, 135, 136–37, 164, 177–78
in Bowery loft, 71, 72, 77, 80–86
on *Caitanya-caritāmṛta*, 261–63, 263–64, 265–67, 269–70
at Gate Theater, 242
at Judson Hall, 240
in Pennsylvania, 17–18
at 2nd Ave temple, 145–46, 147
in 72nd St room (307), 52, 53–59, 65
on sex & suffering, 231
on Supreme Consciousness, dovetailing oneself with, 82–85
at Tagore Society, 34–36
at UN peace vigil, 173
See also: Prabhupāda, cited, philosophy talked by, preaching, quoted
letters of, collection of, *x*
at Lions Club, 17, 52
Lon Solomon quoted on, 126–27
on Lower East Side, 105, 110–11, 116, 117, 126, 136, 142–43, 145–47, 182, 190, 199–202, 272
LSD discredited by, 129, 199–202
madman interrupting, during 2nd Ave class, 122–23
manner of, *xiii*, 232–33
married Mukunda to Janakī, 185–90
maxim against *māyā* by, 265
vs Māyāvādīs, 32
Mike helped, to get 2nd Ave storefront, 101–3
Mike quoted on, 79–80, 86–87, 101

Prabhupāda, Śrīla
Millbrook commune members vs, 200–201
Mishra gave coat to, 38
Mishra quoted on, 22, 26
at Mishra's Ananda Ashram, 26–28, 167–71, 172
at Mishra's apartment, 21–23
Mishra's philosophical difference with, 21, 23–25, 26, 27
Mishra's temple offer to, 168
at Mishra's *yoga* studio, 23, 25, 30, 40, 51, 52, 60, 64, 65
Mishra welcomed, 21
modest, 229
money had by, on American arrival, 8
money managed by, at 26 2nd Ave, 175–76
money not sent from India to, 46–48
Morarji's correspondence with, 9, 19, 28–29, 32–34, 37, 47, 53, 91, 93
Mukti Brahmacārī's correspondence with, 92, 93
Mukunda married to Janakī by, 185–90
Mukunda's letters to, 259, 270–71
name of, full, 1
Neal typing *Gītā* edition by, 267
NYC arrival of, 7–8
in NYC blackout, 30
in NYC consciousness never, 49, 51, 54–55, 59, 72, 134–35, 271
NYC left by, for San Francisco, 271–72
in NYC struggling, 37–39, 43–44, 48
in NYC summer, 117–18, 142, 260
in NYC walking, *xiii*, 25–26, 37–38, 43–44, 48, 87–88, 103–4, 251–52, 255
in NYC winter, 37–38, 43–44, 48, 147, 255, 260, 272
New York Times article on, 217–19
Nikhilananda advised, 29, 38
obeisances offered to, 183
offering ceremony to Lord Caitanya, 153
offering food to Lord Caitanya, 150, 245
& Pandia, 2, 5, 8
& Pandia's wife, 3
in Philadelphia, 19, 20
philosophy talked by, at 26 2nd Ave, 127–29, 143, 147, 163–65

Prabhupāda, Śrīla (*continued*)
physical appearance of, *xiii*, 7, 115, 152–53, 160–61, 161–62, 193–94, 206, 219
plans of, worldwide, 259
poems by, 3–4, 5–6, 18, 96
at Port Said, 2
practical, 90, 91
Prakash Shah's letter to, 93
prasādam distribution by, 2, 33, 123–24, 150–51, 185, 186–87, 232
preachers wanted by, 121–22
preaching
in America, 96, 126–29, 238–39
via *Back to Godhead*, 246–47
in Butler, Pa, 147–48
at recording session, 257–58
in 72nd St room (307), 52, 53–60, 65
in Tompkins Square Park, 211–12, 220
at 26 2nd Ave, 126–29, 214–17
See also: Prabhupāda, cited, lectures by, philosophy talked by, quoted
preaching as envisioned by, 133–34
& Price, 252–53, 265
printing presses bought by, 247
quoted
on Americans, 9, 33, 53, 67–68, 73, 91, 198
on Arjuna, 53, 56
on beauty, 171
on Bible, 128
on Bill's dancing, 155
on Bowery, 67
on Bruce's girl friend, 167
on Buddha, 128
on bum giving service, 121, 138
in *Butler Eagle* interview, 13
on Caitanya painting, 261
on Camus, 127–28
on chanting Hare Kṛṣṇa, 212, 214–15, 220
on charging money & charging nothing, 240–41
on Christians, 128
on David, 73, 94
on Freud, 165

Prabhupāda, Śrīla
quoted
on Gandhi's autobiography, 164
on God consciousness, 13, 128
on his mission, 51, 59
on his passing away, 143
on intoxication, 219
on Jesus Christ, 15
on Kṛṣṇa, 53, 56, 58, 128
on Kṛṣṇa conscious preachers, need for, 121–22
on LSD & Kṛṣṇa consciousness, 199
on materialists, 260
on material world & misery, 215–17
on Marx, 129
on Māyāvādī philosophers, 24
on meditation & chanting Hare Kṛṣṇa, 172
on Mishra, 21, 57–58
on Price, 253
on purification for spiritual advancement, 180
on sacred place, 58–59
on sacrificial smoke, 184, 185
on sex life, 238–39
on spiritual master, 53–57
on summer heat, 142
on tenant pouring water, 220
on washing hands while cooking, 63, 188
on woman wearing *sārī*, 168
on writing transcendental literature, *ix–x*
See also: Prabhupāda, cited, lectures by, philosophy talked by, preaching
& Radhakrishnan, 43, 96
Radhakrishnan's *Gītā* used by, 137, 177, 267
Ranchor to accompany, to San Francisco, 271
& Raphael, 124–25, 154–55
Ravi & Udai Shankar met by, 21
Ravīndra Svarūpa brought *East Village Other* article to, 220–21
Ravīndra Svarūpa got $5,000 loan for, 251

Prabhupāda, Śrīla
Ravīndra Svarūpa quoted on, 193
Rāya Rāma arranged Judson Hall lecture for, 239–40
record company rejecting tape by, 61–62
recording Hare Kṛṣṇa album, 255–58
remembered names, 14
Robert in Bowery loft with, 72, 74
Robert quoted on, 60, 61–62, 63
Robert's relationship with, 61, 62, 157, 181
Roy spoken to by, during 2nd Ave classes, 118, 123, 154
Ruben quoted on, 38, 133
Rūpānuga looking at buildings for temple with, 251–52
Rūpānuga quoted on, 268–69
Rūpānuga's life changed by, 264, 265
at St Fidelis Seminary College, 17
Sally arranged newspaper interview with, 12–13
Sally quoted on, 14–17, 20, 194
San Francisco trip begun by, 270–72
San Francisco trip considered by, 265, 268
saṅkīrtana dream of, 37
as *sannyāsī*, 7, 20, 74–75, 112, 148
Sanskrit introduced by, 56, 75–76
Sanskrit translated by, for *Bhāgavatam* commentary, 125–26
Satsvarūpa quoted on, 200, 242
Satsvarūpa's life changed by, 264, 265
Satsvarūpa told to keep job by, 268
as scholar, 262
at Scindia ticket office, 8, 68
seasick, 1, 2, 5, 19
seeing slides of Viṣṇu temples, 169
in 72nd St room (307), 45–46, 51–61, 64–66, 67, 68, 69
in 72nd St room (501), 40, 51
at Sharma's home, 18
Shastri's death upset plans of, 40–41
Singhania's correspondence with, 41, 42, 45, 47, 48
Sixties (1960s) transcended by, 81, 110–11
at Slippery Rock State College, 17–18
as spiritual master, 142–43, 147

Prabhupāda, Śrīla
spiritual master of. *See:* Bhaktisiddhānta Sarasvatī Ṭhākura
Stanley overseen by, 151
Stanley rebuked by, 175
& Stanley's suicide request, 175–76
Steve brought mangoes to, 137, 138
Steve quoted on, 151, 160, 161–62, 164–65, 165–66, 168
Steve seen by, in news photo, 174
as subject for study, *xiv*
at Tagore Society, 34–36
talking in Agarwals' apartment, 15, 16, 17, 52
talking in 2nd Ave apartment, 147–49, 151–52, 161–67
tape recorder & typewriter stolen from, 67–68
thief story by, 120
threats of his leaving NYC, 265
tilaka worn by, 7, 152
Tīrtha Mahārāja's correspondence with, 29–30, 30–31, 44–45, 47
in Tompkins Square Park, 205–13, 217–19, 225–26, 227, 229, 262
at Town Hall Theater, 241–42
transcendental, 85
Traveler's Aid agent met, 8, 11–12
trying to start temple, 31–33, 38, 41–49, 53, 62–63, 72, 88, 89, 91–92, 94, 168
at 26 2nd Ave. *See:* Second Avenue, twenty-six, *SP entries*
Umāpati came back to, 268
Umāpati's life changed by, 264, 265
Universal Book House's correspondence with, 46
at UN peace vigil, 173–74
Vedic knowledge taught by, 86, 146
Village Voice article on, 89
visa extensions for, 37, 48
visa trouble for, 197, 198, 219, 265
Vṛndāvana left by, 86, 212, 272
Vṛndāvana missed by, 1, 3, 4–5, 51, 59
walking from Bowery loft to 26 2nd Ave, 103–4

Prabhupāda, Śrīla (*continued*)
walking in NYC, *xiii*, 25–26, 37–38, 43–44, 48, 87–88, 251–52, 255
walking to & from Tompkins Square Park *kīrtana*, 205–6, 213
walking to Washington Square Park *kīrtana*, 193–94
Wally asked, about Caitanya painting, 141
Wally asked by, about wearing *tilaka*, 138
Wally assigned duty by, 137
Wally quoted on, 168
washing his clothes, 16, 23
washing his feet, 252
in Washington Square Park, 193–95
Western ways not adopted by, 38
woman talking with, in Times Square, 255
at YMCA, 12, 13, 15, 16, 17, 20
youthful, 192
Prahlāda Mahārāja, quoted on compassion, 10–11
Prakash Shah, 93
Prasādam (food offered to Kṛṣṇa)
breakfast at storefront, 263
as God's remnants, 84–85
on Janmāṣṭamī, 2, 179–80
Judy given, 230
Kīrtanānanda served, 214
lunch at Agarwals', 15
lunch at storefront, 149–51
at Mukunda's wedding, 189–90
on New Year's Eve, 268–69
prayer for offering, 150, 245
purifying power of, 150–51
spiritual advancement by eating, 243
SP & followers taking, at Ananda Ashram, 167–68
SP distributing, 2, 33, 123–24, 150–51, 185, 186–87, 232
at Sunday feasts, 151, 242–43, 245–46
See also: specific prasādam preparations
Prayer(s)
for offering food to Lord, 150, 245
by Satsvarūpa before eating feast, 246
to spiritual master, 136–37
by SP aboard ship, 3–4, 5–6
Preaching of Kṛṣṇa consciousness
by Bhaktisiddhānta, 134–35
by SP. *See:* Prabhupāda, preaching
SP's vision of, 121–22, 133–34
See also: ISKCON; *Saṅkīrtana* movement
Present Age. *See:* Kali-yuga
President John F. Kennedy, 158
Price, Mr, 252–53, 265
Psychedelics. *See:* Drugs; Intoxication; LSD
Puerto Ricans, 108, 109, 111, 116, 203, 205, 210
Purāṇas, 213
Purī, Jagannātha, 148
Purification
by devotional service, 138
by eating *prasādam*, 150–51
mantra of, 183
for spiritual advancement, 180
Purīs, 2, 244, 245
Puṣpānna rice, 245

R

Radha Damodar, 1, 3
Rādhā-Dāmodara temple, 72
Radhakrishnan, Dr
Gītā interpretation by, 232
SP &, 43, 47, 96
SP used *Gītā* translation by, 137, 177, 267
Rādhā-Kṛṣṇa picture
on *Back to Godhead* cover, 248
on ISKCON's stationery, 173
by Jadurāṇī, 261
by James, 139
SP approved Steve's, 168
Rādhā-Kṛṣṇa temple, SP trying to start, 41–42, 43, 46, 47, 48, 49, 53, 94, 97
Rādhā-kuṇḍa, 134
Rādhārāṇī, Śrīmatī
appearance day of, 198–99
& Kṛṣṇa, 198, 207
in SP's father's prayer, 148
in SP's poem, 3
Rādhāṣṭamī festival, 198–99

Raghunātha dāsa Gosvāmī, Śrīla, 92n
Rāja-yoga, 27, 163–64
Rāma(candra), Lord
  Allen Ginsberg quoted on, 218
  Hanumān serving, 139–40, 141
Rāma, Rāya. *See:* Rāya Rāma
Ramakrishna, 43, 64
Rāmānuja, 23
Rāmāyaṇa, 141, 263
Ranchor, 271
Raphael
  benches made by, 248
  decorated 2nd Ave temple, 140
  as ISKCON trustee-to-be, 131
  at Love-Pageant-Rally *kīrtana*, 224
  prasādam eaten by, 149
  as 2nd Ave storefront boarder, 124–25
  SP's relationship with, 154–55
Ratha-yātrā festival, SP held, as child, 148
Ravīndra Svarūpa
  before initiation. *See:* Epstein, Bill
  brought *East Village Other* article to SP, 220–21
  harmonium played by, at recording studio, 256
  initiation of, 184
  at Love-Pageant-Rally *kīrtana*, 224
  quoted on SP & disciples chanting in Washington Square Park, 193
  SP got $5,000 loan via, 251
Ravi Shankar, 21
Rāya Rāma
  as *Back to Godhead's* coeditor, 247
  at *Back to Godhead's* first ISKCON printing, 248
  before initiation. *See:* Dubois, Roy
  initiation of, 184
  in Satsvarūpa's apartment, 265
  seeing SP speak in Tompkins Square Park, 212
  SP's Judson Hall lecture arranged by, 239–40
Record companies
  recording SP & disciples, 255–58
  rejecting SP's tape, 61–62
Red Sea, SP's diary entry at, 2
Reincarnation. *See:* Birth-death cycle
Religion. *See:* Devotional service; God; Purification; Worship
Reverend Garry Davis, 227
Richard, 64
Richard Alpert, 200, 226
Rimbaud, 154
Robert Nelson. *See:* Nelson, Robert
Roy Dubois. *See:* Dubois, Roy
Ruben, quoted on SP, 38, 133
Rūpa Gosvāmī, Śrīla
  Caitanya joined by, 262
  as Caitanya's disciple, 92n
  cited on becoming Kṛṣṇa conscious, 143
  quoted on Kṛṣṇa consciousness, 130
  Sanātana fled jail via, 264
Rūpānuga
  before initiation. *See:* Corens, Bob
  bells played by, at recording studio, 256
  initiation of, 235
  quoted on SP at New Year's Eve feast, 268–69
  SP & followers in van of, 255, 258–59
  SP changed life of, 264, 265
  SP looking at buildings for temple with, 251–52
  as working man, 263, 272
Russia, SP's plans for, 259

S

Sabjī, 149, 150, 186, 189, 244
Śacī, mother, 4
Sacred place, 58–59
  See also: Holy place; Temple (of Kṛṣṇa); Vṛndāvana
Sacred thread, 54, 55, 152
Sacrifice, fire, at initiation ceremony, 182, 184–85, 199
Sādhus, 7
  defined, 81, 86
  false, 199
  Gopal's father liked, 11

Sādhus (*continued*)
See also: Brāhmaṇas; Devotees; Saintly person; Spiritual master
Sages
mystical cereal of, 263
in Vṛndāvana, 118
See also: Ācāryas; Brāhmaṇas; Devotees; *Sādhus;* Spiritual master
Saha-gaṇa-lalitā-śrī-viśākhānvitāṁś ca
quoted, 207
St Brigid's Church, 203, 212, 220
St Fidelis Seminary College, 17
Saintly person
Kṛṣṇa consciousness produces, 120
See also: Ācāryas; Brāhmaṇas; Devotees; *Sādhus;* Spiritual master
St Mark's Place, 109, 169, 204, 252
Sally Agarwal. *See:* Agarwals, Sally
Salvation. *See:* Freedom; Liberation
"Sami Krishna," 174
Samosās, 40, 244, 245
Saṁsāra-dāvānala-līḍha-loka
quoted, 137
Sanātana Gosvāmī
Caitanya's teachings to, 269–70
joining Caitanya, history of, 262–63, 264, 266, 269
Sanders, Ed, 238
San Francisco
Mukunda in, 259, 270
SP leaving for, 270–72
SP talking of going to, 265, 268
Śaṅkara
impersonalism of, 113
Kṛṣṇa accepted by, 25
Mishra followed, 21, 22, 23, 24, 27
Saṅkīrtana movement
Americans interested in, 53
of Caitanya, 40, 104, 133, 197
as chanting God's name, 133, 134
painting of, 40
SP's dream of, 37
tenants disturbed by, 220
See also: Chanting of Hare Kṛṣṇa; ISKCON; Preaching of Kṛṣṇa consciousness
Sannyāsī (renunciant), SP as, 7, 20, 74–75, 112, 148
Sanskrit
SP introducing, 56, 75–76
SP translating, for *Bhāgavatam* commentary, 125–26
Saraswati, Bala, 28–29
Satsvarūpa
apartment of, available to devotees, 265
before initiation. *See:* Guarino, Stephen
"Heavenly Porridge" recalled by, 263
initiation of, 198
New York Times article read aloud by, 217–19
quoted on SP & LSD, 200
quoted on SP's lecture at Gate Theater, 242
quoted on Sunday Love Feasts, 245–46
SP changed life of, 264, 265
SP told, to keep job, 268
taking notes at SP's classes, 262, 266
as working man, 263, 272
Satyavrata, 184
"Save Earth Now" article, 221–23, 226
Scharf, Bruce
after initiation. *See:* Brahmānanda
at Ananda Ashram, 167–68
background of, 157–58
brother of. *See:* Gargamuni; Scharf, Greg
gave up girl friend, 167
initiation of, 198–99
at Mukunda's wedding, 190
as newcomer, 181
quoted
on chanting Hare Kṛṣṇa, 160
on finding 2nd Ave temple, 159
on first seeing SP, 160
on SP at Ananda Ashram, 168
on talking with SP in 2nd Ave apartment, 163, 165, 166–67
SP asked by, about meditation, 172
SP driven by, from Ananda Ashram to 2nd Ave apartment, 171–72
& SP during Stanley's suicide request, 176
Wally talking with, 162–63
Scharf, Greg
after initiation. *See:* Gargamuni

Scharf, Greg
brother of. *See:* Brahmānanda; Scharf, Bruce
press for sale found by, 247
quoted on LSD & SP, 199–200, 202
Scholars
Gītā misinterpreted by, 130–31
See also: Ācāryas; Speculators, mental
Scindia Steam Navigation Company, 1, 47, 96
SP & ticket agent of, 8, 68
SDS, 228
Second Avenue, twenty-six
activities at, 145–53
Alan Kallman at, 253–54
Allen Ginsberg at, 195–98, 238
apartment in back of, 102, 103, 104, 107, 145, 162
breakfast at, 263
Burton Green quoted on, 241
courtyard at, 145, 162, 163, 246, 272
decoration of, 139–41
description of, 102, 104, 105–7, 145–49
ISKCON begun at, 134, 135, 260
kīrtanas at, 238, 254–55
lunch at, 149–51
SP & followers chanting at, 115–17, 123, 136–37, 219–20, 254, 259–60, 261
SP in apartment at, 107, 124–26, 135–37, 145, 147–53, 161–67, 172, 179–80, 182–90, 217, 230–31, 242–45, 246, 252, 254, 271–72
SP left, 272
SP pleased by decoration of, 140, 141
SP preaching at, 147, 214–17
SP's arrival at, 102–4, 107, 111
SP's *Caitanya-caritāmṛta* classes at, 261–63, 263–64, 265–67, 269–70
SP's *Gītā* classes at, 11, 114, 117–23
SP's lectures at, 145–46
SP's success at, 191–93
SP's vision of, 134–35
Sunday Love Feasts at, 245–46
tenants at, 219–20, 246, 260
transformed into temple, 139–41
transients slept at, 124
Self
body not, 58, 80
personal & impersonal views of, 23–24
See also: Consciousness; Soul
Sense gratification
passion for, 10
See also: Happiness; Pleasure
Service
material vs spiritual, 138
as natural tendency, 121
See also: Devotional service
Seventy-second Street building, West, 31, 41, 45
Seventy-second Street room (307), 45–46, 51–61, 64–66, 67, 68, 69
Seventy-second Street room (501), 40, 51
Sex life
illicit, 10, 99, 127, 180–81, 182, 239, 265
material world based on, 165, 238, 239
Shah, Nawab, 262–63
Shah, Prakash, 93
Shankar, Ravi & Udai, 21
Sharma, Mohan & Mini, 18
Shastri, Prime Minister Lal Bahadur, 40–41
Sikh teacher, cited on spiritual master, 226
Śikhā hair, 7
Singhania, Sir Padampat
SP depending on donation from, 91, 92
SP's correspondence with, 41, 42, 45, 47, 48
Sins, four, 10
Śiṣyas te 'haṁ śādhi māṁ tvāṁ prapannam quoted, 56
Śiva, 158
Sixties (1960s)
America in, *xiii*
disciplic succession alive in, 225
hippies in, 108–11
in Kali-yuga, 132
loft-living in NYC in, 71
SP transcendental to, 81, 110–11
See also: Civilization, godlessness in; Kali-yuga, symptoms of
Skid Row. *See:* Bowery
Slippery Rock State College, 17
Smith, Howard, quoted on SP, 89–91

Society, human. *See:* Civilization, human; Hindu society; Human beings; Vedic culture
Solomon, Lon, quoted on SP, 126–27
Soul
in body, 269
immortal, 128
as Kṛṣṇa conscious originally, 257
as Kṛṣṇa's part & parcel, 133
See also: Consciousness; Self
Souls, conditioned. *See:* Conditioned souls
Sound, transcendental
God as source of, 78–79
See also: Mantras
Speculators, mental, 128
See also: Māyāvādīs; Scholars
Spirit. *See:* Consciousness; Soul
Spiritual life
American youth sought, on Lower East Side, 111
drugs not needed for, 200, 201
freedom in, 81
sex desire absent in, 165
See also: Devotional service; Kṛṣṇa consciousness; Purification
Spiritual master
acceptance of, 177, 178–79, 269
Caitanya quoted on, 121
disciple's donation to, 181
dreams about, 171
God nondifferent from, 169, 178
in his instructions, 268
knowledge via, 226
as Kṛṣṇa's representative, 137
SP as, 142–43, 147
SP chanting prayers to, 136–37
SP quoted on, 54–57, 145, 179
transcendental knowledge via, 57
writing by permission of, *ix–x*
See also: Ācāryas; Authorities, spiritual; Devotees, pure devotees; Disciplic succession
Spiritual world, 72, 135, 171
Śrī-kṛṣṇa-caitanya, prabhu-nityānanda quoted, 256
Sri Lanka, 2
Śrīla Prabhupāda. *See:* Prabhupāda
Śrīla Prabhupāda-līlāmṛta
as authorized literature, *x*
commissioning of, *ix*
research for, *x–xi*
Śrīmad-Bhāgavatam
Bhaktivedanta purports to, 24, 126
Bob studying, 231, 232
Butler Eagle quoted on, 13
cited on Kṛṣṇa consciousness for everyone, 213
cover of (SP's edition), 228, 231
Hayagrīva given, by SP, 250
Hayagrīva reading, in public, 194–95
Howard typed SP's manuscripts of, 138–39
quoted on spiritual master, 57
of SP loaded on ship, 2
SP reading, 185
SP's classes on, in Bowery loft, 72
SP's edition of, 268
SP selling, 8, 36, 39–40, 46, 60–61, 161–62
SP translating, 27, 28, 72, 75, 76, 125–26, 147, 151, 152, 247, 259, 272
SP wanting to preach, 29, 33
Vyāsadeva compiled, 166
Śrīmate bhaktivedānta-svāmin iti nāmine quoted, 183
Śrī-rādhā-kṛṣṇa-pādān quoted, 207
Śrī-rūpaṁ sāgrajātam quoted, 207
Śrīvāsa, 242
Śrī-viṣṇuḥ śrī-viṣṇuḥ śrī-viṣṇuḥ quoted, 183
Stanley
after initiation. *See:* Stryadhīśa
initiation of, 181, 184
Larry Bogart-SP meeting spoiled by, 174–75
SP & suicide request of, 175–76
SP oversaw, 151
Stanley (from Brooklyn), 184
Statue of Liberty, 7, 109
Stay High Forever flyer, 202, 210, 230
Stephen Goldsmith. *See:* Goldsmith, Stephen

Stephen Guarino. *See:* Guarino, Stephen
Stryadhīśa
before initiation. *See:* Stanley
dancing in Tompkins Square Park, 210
initiation of, 184
Stuyvesant, Peter, 69, 108
Subhas Chandra Bose, 148
Suez Canal, SP at port on, 2
Suffering. *See:* Miseries
Sumati Morarji. *See:* Morarji, Sumati
Sunshine & Brahman, analogy of, 23
Supreme Brahman
personal & impersonal views of, 23–25
See also: Absolute Truth; God; Kṛṣṇa
Supreme Consciousness, dovetailing oneself with, 82–85
Supreme Lord. *See:* God; Kṛṣṇa
Suval, Joan
Mishra & SP in car of, 26
quoted on SP, 22–23
Svāhā chanting, 184
Svarūpa, Ravīndra. *See:* Ravīndra Svarūpa
"Swami, uptown," 22, 166
"Swami Jesus," 17
Swamiji. *See:* Prabhupāda
Swami Nikhilananda, 29, 38
"Swami step," 170, 211
Sweet rice, 151, 214, 243, 244

T

Tad-vijñānārthaṁ sa gurum evābhigacchet quoted, 57
Tagore Society, 34
Tandy's Leather Company, 176
Tasmād guruṁ prapadyeta quoted, 57
Teacher, spiritual. *See:* Spiritual master
Temple (of Kṛṣṇa)
in Haight-Ashbury, 270
2nd Ave storefront became, 139–41
SP envisioning, at Ananda Ashram, 168
SP seeing slides of, 169
Temple (of Kṛṣṇa)
SP trying to start, 31–33, 38, 41–49, 53, 62–63, 72, 88, 89, 91–92, 94
Temple Emanu-El building, 251
Ṭhākura Haridāsa, 119
Thant, U, cited on America's Vietnam policy, 172
Thief story, 120
Thomas à Kempis, 114
Thoreau, Henry David, 114, 212–13
Thread, sacred, 54, 55, 152
Tilaka marks
for Bhaktisiddhānta painting, 232
of initiates fixed by SP, 182
SP wearing, 7, 152
Time cycle, 132
Times Square, SP & woman talking in, 255
Timothy Leary, Dr, 128, 191, 200, 222, 226
Tīrtha Mahārāja, SP's correspondence with, 29–30, 30–31, 31, 44–45, 47
Tompkins Square Park
people, places, & things in, 203–5
SP & disciples chanting in, 205, 206–11, 212, 217–19, 225–26, 227, 229, 262
SP's disciples at Love-Pageant-Rally in, 223–25
SP speaking in, 211–12
as swamp formerly, 108
Town Hall Theater, 241
Transcendence. *See:* Freedom; Kṛṣṇa consciousness; Liberation; Spiritual life
Traveler's Aid representative, SP met by, on New York arrival, 8, 11–12
Tree(s)
SP cited on, at Slippery Rock campus, 18
by SP in Tompkins Square Park, 212, 220, 223, 225, 227
Truth. *See:* Absolute Truth
Tuli Kupferberg, 223, 238
Twenty-six Second Avenue. *See:* Second Avenue, twenty-six

U

Udai Shankar, 21

Ukranians, 108, 109, 203
Ulta Danga, 45
Umāpati
before initiation. *See:* Wally
cited on Americans, sex, & SP's preaching, 238
cited on *Caitanya-caritāmṛta* translation, 263
cited on SP discrediting LSD, 200
Hare Kṛṣṇa handbill produced by, 202
initiation of, 184
kneading *purī* dough, 244
at Love-Pageant-Rally *kīrtana*, 224
notes taken by, at SP's lectures, 249, 262
quoted on *East Village Other* headline, 221
quoted on Kṛṣṇa consciousness, 202
quoted on tenant pouring water, 220
SP changed life of, 264, 265
SP took back, to Kṛṣṇa consciousness, 268
Underground newspapers, 199
United Nations
failure of, 133
Secretary General of, cited on America's Vietnam policy, 172
SP & followers in peace vigil at, 173–74
United States. *See:* America
Universal Book House, 46
Universe(s)
ISKCON's beginning in, 135
Kṛṣṇa's incarnations in, 118
time cycle of, 132
See also: Material world
Upaniṣads, 116, 176
"Uptown swami," 22, 166
U Thant, cited on America's Vietnam policy, 172

V

Vaikuṇṭha, 72, 135, 171
Vaiṣṇava
attempting to write, *ix–x*
desire of, 4
God presented by, 222
Vaiṣṇava
"greed" of, 193
See also: Devotees
Vande 'haṁ śrī-guroḥ
quoted, 207, 256
Vasudeva, 180
Vāsudeva. *See:* Kṛṣṇa
Vedaiś ca sarvair aham eva vedyaḥ
quoted, 128
Vedānta, 128
Vedānta center, 80
Vedas
Kali-yuga described in, 132
sound described in, 78–79
See also: Vedic literature; *specific Vedic literatures*
Vedic culture
spiritual master in, 54
SP planted, in America, *xiii*
See also: Hindu society; India
Vedic hymns. *See: Mantras*
Vedic knowledge. *See:* Absolute Truth; Knowledge, transcendental
Vedic literature
spiritual era foretold in, 132
SP taught & translated, *xiii*
See also: Literature, transcendental; *Vedas; specific Vedic literatures*
Vietnam war, 39, 44, 83–84, 109, 129, 172–73, 228
Village Voice
ISKCON's full name in, 89, 129
Love-Pageant-Rally article in, 225
2nd Ave storefront ad in, 102
SP interview in, 89
Viṣṇu, Lord, 107, 169, 184, 218, 261
Vivekananda, 213
Vṛndāvana (Vraja), 72, 95
Back to Godhead formerly published in, 249
Kṛṣṇadāsa Kavirāja in, *ix*
Kṛṣṇa taken to, at birth, 180
road from Delhi to, 10
as rural town, 42
SP & Bhaktisiddhānta in, 134

Vṛndāvana
SP left, 86, 118, 212, 272
SP missing, 1, 3, 4–5, 51, 59
Vyāsadeva, 166

W

Wally
after initiation. *See:* Umāpati
at Ananda Ashram, 168–69, 171
apartment shared by, 112, 113
background of, 113, 114
Bruce talking with, 162–63
cited on SP's chanting requirement, 179
curtains washed by, for storefront temple, 139
initiation of, 184
quoted
on accepting initiation from SP, 177, 178, 184
on SP as God's servant, 168
on SP asking him about wearing *tilaka*, 138
on SP assigning him duty, 137
SP asked by, about Caitanya painting, 141
at SP's morning class, 137
Walt Whitman, 114, 249
War
Kurukṣetra, 83, 133, 171
& meat-eating, 239
SP's example of, in teaching Absolute Truth, 82–84
Vietnam, 39, 44, 83–84, 109, 129, 172–73, 228
War Resisters League, 228
Washington Square Park, SP & disciples chanting in, 193–94
Water
Ferber fetched, for SP, 40
sipping, at initiation ceremony, 182, 183
storefront ceiling dripping, 219–20
Watts, Alan, 113
Wealth. *See:* Gold; Money
West Coast
Mukunda on, 259, 270
NY disciples criticizing SP's going to, 271
Western world
Back to Godhead's first printing in, 249
Bhaktisiddhānta's desire concerning, 31, 96
Indian philosophy as known in, 113
initiated devotees in, 179, 185
ISKCON to tell, about God, 129–30
meat-eating in, 38, 243
SP didn't adopt ways of, 38
SP introducing Kṛṣṇa consciousness in, 28, 58
See also: America
West Seventy-second Street building, 31, 41, 45
Wheeler, Howard
after initiation. *See:* Hayagrīva
at Ananda Ashram, 169, 170–71
apartment of, 112, 113
background of, 112, 113–14, 219
drugs renounced by, 219
eating *prasādam*, 151
in India, 113
initiation of, 184
paintings & prints hung by, in storefront temple, 139
quoted
on dream about SP, 170–71
on going to Ananda Ashram, 167
on intoxication & meditation, 113
on spiritual master, acceptance of, 177, 178–79
on SP, 112, 114, 169
on typing SP's *Bhāgavatam* manuscripts, 138–39
on walking to SP's morning class, 136
in 2nd Ave storefront, 115
SP explaining Hanumān to, 141
SP explaining spiritual master to, 142, 178–79
SP's first meeting with, 112, 114–15
at SP's morning class, 137
Whitman, Walt, 114, 249

Wife. *See:* Marriage
William Blake, 114, 198, 249
Wisdom. *See:* Absolute Truth; Knowledge, transcendental; Philosophy
Wise men. *See: Ācāryas;* Authorities, spiritual; *Brāhmaṇas;* Devotees; *Sādhus;* Sages; Saintly person; Spiritual master
Woman
  in Hindu society, 55, 56
  SP cited on, 99
  at SP's storefront classes, 261
  in Times Square talking with SP, 255
  wearing *sārī,* 168
  See also: Girl; *specific women*
World. *See:* Material world
World, Western. *See:* Western world
World Council of Churches, cited on America's Vietnam policy, 172
World Parliament of Religions (1893), 213
Worship
  of Deity forms, 43, 94, 148
  of Kṛṣṇa in India, 58
  of Rāma & Hanumān in India, 141–42
  of spiritual master by disciple, 178–79
  See also: Devotional service
Writing transcendental literature, *ix–x*

Y

Yaḥ smaret puṇḍarīkākṣaṁ
  verse quoted, 183
Yāmunācārya, quoted on sex pleasure, 238
Yamunā River, 118
Yeargens, Carl
  background of, 74
  Carol quoted on, 100
  at David's loft, 97
  initiation considered by, 180–81
  initiation of, 184
  as ISKCON trustee-to-be, 131
  quoted on David, 95
  quoted on SP, 74–75, 77, 100
  SP helped by, to get 2nd Ave storefront, 101–3
  SP helped by, to incorporate ISKCON, 130, 156
  SP in loft of, 97–100, 101
  SP's mission disinterested, 114, 156, 157
  wife of, 97, 98–100, 101
YMCA, SP stayed at, 12, 13, 15, 16, 17, 20
Yoga
  "ashrams" of, 28
  by chanting Hare Kṛṣṇa, 172
  See also: Meditation
Yogīs
  best kind of, 164
  See also: Devotees; Sages

Z

Zen *roshi,* 231

The Author

Satsvarūpa dāsa Goswami was born on December 6, 1939, in New York City. He attended public schools and received a B.A. from Brooklyn College in 1961. Then followed two years as a journalist in the U.S. Navy and three years as a social worker in New York City.

In July 1966, he met His Divine Grace A. C. Bhaktivedanta Swami Prabhupāda and became his initiated disciple in September of that year. Satsvarūpa dāsa Goswami began contributing articles to *Back to Godhead*, the magazine of the Hare Kṛṣṇa movement, and later became its editor in chief. In August 1967 he went to Boston to establish the first ISKCON center there. Satsvarūpa dāsa Goswami was one of the original members selected by Śrīla Prabhupāda to form the Governing Body Commission of ISKCON in 1970. He remained as president of Boston ISKCON until 1971, when he moved to Dallas and became headmaster of Gurukula, the first ISKCON school for children.

In May 1972, on the appearance day of Lord Nṛsiṁhadeva, he was awarded the *sannyāsa* (renounced) order by His Divine Grace Śrīla Prabhupāda and began traveling across the United States, lecturing in colleges and universities. In January 1974 he was called by Śrīla Prabhupāda to become his personal secretary and to travel with him through India and Europe. In 1976 he published *Readings in Vedic Literature*, a concise account of the Vedic tradition. The volume is now being studied at various American universities. In 1977 Śrīla Prabhupāda ordered him to accept the duties of initiating *guru*, along with ten other senior disciples. He is presently working on a long-term literary project, preparing further volumes of the biography of His Divine Grace A. C. Bhaktivedanta Swami Prabhupāda.

ONE WAY